FLORENCE

FLORENCE

CITY · OF · THE · LILY

Christopher Stace

Illustrated by Philip O'Reilly

J. M. DENT & SONS

London

First published 1989

Text © Christopher Stace 1989

All rights reserved. No part of this publication may be reproduced,
stored in a retrieval system, or transmitted, in any form
or by any means, electronic, mechanical, photocopying, recording or
otherwise, without the prior permission of J.M.Dent & Sons Ltd

This book is set in Galliard
Printed in Great Britain at The Bath Press, Avon
for J.M.Dent & Sons Ltd
91 Clapham High Street, London SW4 7TA

Designed by Gaye Allen

British Library Cataloguing in Publication Data
Stace, Christopher
  Florence: city of the lily.
  1. Italy. Florence, – Visitors' guides
  I. Title
  914.5'51

ISBN 0-460-04778-7

CONTENTS

CONTENTS

CONTENTS

For Wesley, Melanie and Emma,
tomorrow's Florentines

I am but a link in the chain of individual heretics and failures, a woodwind solo in the interminable symphony, drowned at once by the brass and percussion, but necessary to the composer's score.

Cyril Connolly, *The Unquiet Grave*

PREFACE

'Writing yet another book on Florence', I remarked to Sir Harold Acton, when by chance we found ourselves lunching together at the Savile Club recently, 'seems almost an act of presumption.'

A smile flashed across his face, deprecating. 'So much has been written,' he said, 'so much.' Then he leaned across the table and whispered conspiratorially: 'And much of it bad!' Somehow his careful enunciation lent extra force to the adjective. 'Very *bad*!' His eyes had a dangerous twinkle.

But when I revealed my plan to add to the torrent of verbiage, his reaction was characteristically generous.

'Bravo!' he cried, with an inclination of the head. 'Bravo! When you next come you must look me up.'

'So many things have been said. So many writers. . . .'

I see Sir Harold's smile now, I hear the strange lilt of his precious articulation. 'Oh endless,' he said. '*Endless.*'

And so it is. And so I wrote my own book.

ACKNOWLEDGMENTS

My thanks are due to the following: for botanical advice to Professor Clive A. Stace of Leicester University; for help on matters hagiographical to Fr Denis Mulliner of Bradfield College and Fr Graeme Rowlands of St Silas', Kentish Town; for encouragement and expert advice to Dr Edward Chaney of Lincoln College, Oxford; for unlocking doors to Giovanna Baquis and the ladies of the Azienda Autonoma di Turismo, Florence; for the generous gift of Ginori Lisci's comprehensive reference work *The Palazzi of Florence* to the Cassa di Risparmio di Firenze; for patient proof-reading to Freda Crockford and for friendly editorial direction to Bill Neill-Hall, initially, and subsequently to Malcolm Gerratt of Dent-Weidenfeld.

INTRODUCTION

I look at the face in the small square photograph: a dark-haired boy, the shadow of a secure smile on him. The face is unfamiliar. I don't know this young man: to me he is alien. Who *was* he when he looked as he did then?

Of course, the name is still mine. But everything else, twenty-plus years on, has altered so drastically, so utterly, that I am, quite simply, another human being. I cannot recognise the face, yet I shave it every morning. Did the Browning who wrote *Asolando*, white-bearded and world-weary, recognise his *alter ego* of 50 years earlier – the profile seen in Cook's 1835 engraving, a burning, sensitive youth with bushy side-whiskers? It is hard, setting these two pictures side by side, not to feel a pang of sadness at the gross physical alteration. 'By the age of 40,' say the French, 'we have the face we deserve.'

The photograph was taken for a passport, and the passport was for a holiday in Florence, in 1966. I couldn't know that this was to be the year of the cataclysm, the great flood. One almost accords it a capital letter. The Flood. I couldn't know that after it nothing would be the same again. Within as little as seven years my life had changed irrevocably.

Every man, they say, has a city. Every man has one home. How can one explain otherwise that feeling of ease and comfort in a place apparently quite new? A place where one can be oneself, where one feels safe. (After his *débâcle* in Greece, Herodotus tells us, the retreating Persian King Xerxes could not 'undo his belt' until he had reached the far north.) How can we explain the feeling of unease, the strange inimical ambience of other places, perhaps of the country of one's birth? Florence was to be my city.

I took my wife and baby of ten months in an old Austin A40 and drove there. It was a fine August, past the crown of the year but still brilliant with promise. The journey would be about 1,000 miles, door to door. The boat was late; the baby was teething and fractious from St Quentin to Besançon; the Simplon Pass was hair-raising, jammed with traffic held up by strings of '*Lavori in Corso*'; the slopes were so steep at times the car seemed to be upside down; we lost our way twice in Milan; and on top of all this I had been warned by the mechanic at home not to exceed 40 m.p.h. on the motorways.

I was a nervous and inexperienced driver. Neck-aché and apprehension destroyed my appetite from Calais onwards. The north of France flashed by, low and flat and hypnotically depressing; Switzerland in a bright blur of blue skies, tinkling bells, and varnished chalets. But once in Domodossola – a village undistinguished in itself, but the first to greet one on the Italian side – eupepsia blissfully returned. It returned with a rush of happiness and relief. There was a warm welcome, and good roast veal garnished with rosemary, served in fat, spicy slices with my first carafe of purple Chianti. After the evening meal I beat the bounds of Domodossola. It was late and the streets were deserted. Not a breath of wind, not the slightest sound. How did I know I had come home? But I knew it as soon as I breathed good Italian air. Nothing could cloud my optimism. The road sped south for ever, a succession of loops from mountain top to mountain top, over valleys with snaking streams in rocky river beds, past vineyards and farmhouses, each hill and crest crowned with palaces and monasteries in a streaming, mystical Renaissance backcloth. I had never seen such beauty, such harmony, such perfect juxtapositions of colours. The pines – black-green spikes, umbrellas, mushrooms – so perfectly blending with the sun-blanched terracotta and peach stucco, the fish-scale tiles, the soaring campanili! I wanted to stop every minute, and would have, if each new vista had not been even more arresting than the last.

They say the eel leaps at the first thunder in March. My heart leapt up, it would not settle. And finally, thousands of toll barriers later, four long days and a world away from Sussex, I had my first sight of the City of Flowers. Does one ever forget the first time? She was outstretched in welcome, like a glittering mistress: the shell of the Duomo caught the sun's evening gold, San Lorenzo glowed a burnt sienna. The warm canvas of colour touched some aesthetic nerve in me which has never recovered. Since that day I have measured my solvency by the simplest of yardsticks: can I go back this year?

Things have become expensive. The coach no longer ferries passengers from Pisa to Florence between gorgeous avenues of oleanders, past those endless nurseries with their tortured saplings and variegated shrubs; the traffic regulations are insane; the Piazza del Duomo, at Easter and in summer, can be almost impassable; after dark the Ponte Vecchio has become a rendezvous of the *demi-monde*, the flotsam and jetsam of a dozen countries. But there is a timeless virginity about Florence, as one walks the medieval alleys and peers through gateways into brightly lit court-yards. One finds the same unchanging pulse in Rome, certainly – perhaps in many ancient cities. But my city is small: its limits can be paced in a morning. Forget the sprawling suburbs. Somehow the city itself remains unviolated by what goes on beyond it. There is a loveliness enhanced by contrasts. For all that time has done, the depredations of war and vandals and the Arno, Florence remains synonymous with beauty and good taste. A thousand times I have tramped the streets and shaded cobbled paths from the grand Corsi, the stately Lungarni, to passageways so narrow house-wives can pass pots to each other above one's head, and each time they are the same, and each time different. There is a beauty that is more than skin deep: there is more depth than I had thought possible. Each time there is something new to surprise and ravish the senses.

When I first arrived, before the flood, to live in that splendid apartment in Piazza d'Azeglio with its three balconies, Persian carpeted, marble floored, and furnished with rich antiques, I could hardly have guessed what had begun. It was nothing I had planned. I had come down from University with a degree and not much else: to me the visual arts were not much more than pretty artefacts; about sculpture I knew less than nothing. I enjoyed painting in water colours, but had had no formal education in the Fine Arts. I suppose I had learned to question things, to chase references, to read round a subject and immerse myself in back-ground. That was something. But my response to things of beauty must have been childlike. I must have been an unpromising pupil when I first set foot in Florence.

But there must have been a spark in me that was receptive, something latent in me reaching out to grasp at beauty, because, since that year, since August 1966, Florence has been a major part of my life.

Can anyone explain love? Do any two people see another with exactly the same eyes? My Florence will not be the one that others see. But it is the one I have grown up with, the one who has been mistress of my aesthetic education, shaped my response to beauty, and regulated my development to adulthood. A Ruskin will describe its stones better, a Berenson its pictures. The *Blue Guide* will tell you 'everything you need to know' – but not, in the final analysis, perhaps, very much. Why does one weep at Michelangelo's *Brutus*, say, or Donatello's *David*? To what end do the long crocodiles queue in the heat outside the Accademia, the Palazzo Pitti, the Uffizi? What is it about this place that draws such waves of visitors? Why have generations of artists discovered Florence and chosen to make their home there?

'The contemplation of beauty and truth' (note how Hazlitt, like Plato, links these two abstracts) 'is the proper object of our creation'. Once nurtured in beauty, the spirit longs for the beautiful. Flesh seeks flesh on a wheel of its own turning: spirit yearns upwards. The one craves a satisfaction that is momentary, the other longs infinitely – something Robert Browning expressed beautifully in 'Two in the Campagna', where he writes of 'Infinite passion, and the pain / Of finite hearts that yearn'. Where there is beauty, the sensitive soul will not be content with less; and in Tuscany the impulse to create beauty is everywhere in evidence. It thrusts itself upon one, not only in the bell towers of the country churches, the marbled façade of great cathedrals, but on the rooftop ter- races of humble apartment blocks, where geraniums and wistarias provide gorgeous and fragrant surroundings for the family's evening meal; or on the million tiny balconies, where vines and creepers soften the rigid lines of glass and concrete, and lend such indomitable individualism to an other- wise drab and dispiriting uniformity.

Whether high on Giotto's slender tower, or walking the cool pavement of Santa Croce, whether wandering in the vast Boboli Gardens or discover- ing the tiny SS. Apostoli, one finds an aspiration towards beauty and a refinement of taste that is profound, constant and deeply affecting. This can no doubt be felt elsewhere; but in Florence, I soon discovered, in one square mile, there is more than one can ever properly appreciate.

I went for a month's holiday, and began the search of a lifetime.

CHAPTER

I

The Protestant Cemetery · Robert and Elizabeth Barrett Browning, Landor and Clough · S. Ambrogio · the Cappella del Miracolo · Mino and Cosimo Rosselli · Lisa and Lapo · Donald Shannon · Villa Mirabello, Fiesole · Greve · Lapo's villa · Conte Sanminiatelli and Vignamaggio · Chianti

When one returns home after a long absence there are always errands to run. In Florence two pilgrimages await me.

The English (properly 'Protestant') Cemetery is a small, crowded affair in Piazzale Donatello – an oval island in a sea of traffic, an oasis surrounded by vast deserts of swirling heat and exhaust-fumes.

This year I am staying within a few hundred yards of my first home here, high up in Piazza d'Azeglio, a stately square with fine, soaring planes and a noisy central playground. From my bedroom, with its charming frescoed ceiling (a chandelier erupts tactlessly from the thighs of a languid nymph) I can see the heights of Fiesole, the green cap of the Synagogue, the pinnacles of Santa Croce. Directly ahead, as I sit at my desk, is a forest of greenery which reflects every slightest turn in the city's moods. Piazza d'Azeglio is out of the centre, but within easy reach, and the elegant *graffiti* that cover the façade of no. 20 mean that, even after an extended supper, one is never entirely lost.

In only a matter of minutes I am waiting to find a gap in the solid stream of cars winding its way along the Viale. One can grow old waiting: one must learn the rhythm of the traffic, anticipate its movements – and *coraggio*!

1

Slowly, slowly the old girl appears. Her teeth are fewer now; her Italian is often unrecognisable. These days she supports herself on a stick. A key is found, the gate opens. Already she is pointing gratuitously to the tomb they all come to see. Half way up the tumulus on the left there is a casket which stands on six little pillars.

'*Grazie tante.*'

The heat makes the white stones shimmer. It is morning, but the heat is already knife-like on nose and brow. Behind me she stands watching; I feel her eyes on my back. Then she calls something I cannot hear, and points to the well known spot before vanishing into the cool of the lodge. I nod and thank her again, and am suddenly on my own among the familiar names. Graves and lizards and stately cypresses in a line. I have never been anything but on my own among the tombstones.

There are places that draw and places that repel. Here I have always felt at home. The graves are tolerably well kept: the dead achieve, I suppose, a measure of peace in this teeming city; and, as he picks his way for an hour between the slabs and monuments, so may the tourist. But there is a sadness when one considers the passing fashions, the faded reputations, the names, once celebrated, that are now forgotten.

Sometimes the mortal remains are all that remain. In this small plot lie Elizabeth Barrett Browning (1806–61), Walter Savage Landor (1775–1864) and Arthur Hugh Clough (1819–61), all influential and admired in their day, but now, it seems, largely anthology-fodder. Perhaps Landor's *Imaginary Conversations* linger on the library shelves? I wonder. Clough's *Say not the Struggle Naught Availeth* is part of my literary furniture, not only because I was so often set the poem for turning into Latin verse, but because, presumably, my teachers thought its courageous optimism ('But westward, look, the land is bright!') morally edifying.

Elizabeth Barrett Browning's tomb was designed by her husband, we are told, and executed by no other than Lord Leighton. In her day Elizabeth was much more highly esteemed than her husband Robert (who always thought her more talented than himself): she was the name on everyone's lips in 1850, when Wordsworth died, as next Poet Laureate. *Dis aliter visum.* Robert has finally found his proper place in the poetic pantheon. The story of his correspondence with the young poetess ('I love your book, dear Miss Barrett, and I love you too'), their secret marriage and elopement to Italy in 1846, and subsequent fifteen years of happiness together in Casa Guidi (where Robert tended this frail semi-invalid until she expired finally in his arms) – all this is more memorable today than Elizabeth's poetic *oeuvre*.

Despite the fact that Elizabeth kept her beloved 'Pen' (the Brownings'

Elizabeth Barrett Browning's tomb, Protestant cemetery

only child, a son) in girl's clothes throughout his adolescence; let her passionate interest in the cause of Italian independence vitiate her poetry (at times she became the merest propagandist); and became unhealthily obsessed with spiritualism (*Mr Sludge the Medium* is testimony to her husband's views on the subject), her love for Robert, her sympathetic nature and lively intelligence, impressed a very wide circle of friends and acquaintances, among whom were some of the most famous writers of the day. Also, she soon recognised that Robert's genius was superior to her own. The Brownings were celebrated lovers: Abelard and Eloise; Tristan and Isolde; Romeo and Juliet; Robert and Elizabeth.

But Elizabeth's poetry has not fared well. Modern critics either damn her with faint praise or frankly dismiss her. She lives on in her *Sonnets* ('How do I love thee? Let me count the ways') and, for those who love Elgar's setting, in *A Sabbath Morning at Sea* – neither, arguably, the crowning summit of her achievement. To my mind there is something ineffably sad about Elizabeth, despite her evident self-fulfilment with Robert. Even her funeral was unimpressive. The service was blundered through by a fat English parson in a brutally careless way, 'and she was consigned by him to the earth', wrote a friend, 'as if her clay were no better than any other clay.'

Robert and Elizabeth wrote much of their most famous poetry in Casa Guidi, not far from Palazzo Pitti. 'It contains', says one famous guide book, 'a few mementoes of the Brownings.' For twenty years I never set foot in the place. Something always defeated me.

Immediately to the left of Elizabeth's casket is the burial place of Fanny, wife of Holman Hunt, the great pre-Raphaelite painter. Fanny died on 20 December 1866, in the first year of her marriage. And only a few yards downhill lies Walter Savage Landor. 'I strove with none, for none was worth my strife. / Nature I loved, and next to Nature, Art: / I warm'd both hands before the fire of life: / It sinks, and I am ready to depart.' The poet's most celebrated quatrain (entitled 'Finis') is a strangely inappropriate epitaph. Resigned he never was: it would be nearer the mark to describe him as a lifelong quarreller, a turbulent eccentric whose days ended in ignominious poverty. His simple slab is in a poor state, much of its lettering blurred by encrustations of dirt and lichen.

Landor was prolific and versatile, and in his day admired by Browning (who latterly rescued him from the gutter), Southey and Wordsworth, but today he is a name only, if even that, to students of literature. Despite his delicate lyrics ('Rose Aylmer' and 'To Ianthe' at least have stood the test of time), the prose *Pericles and Aspasia* (1836) and *Imaginary Conversations* (1853), Landor's particular qualities are not the sort to captivate a modern critic. Perhaps the lyrics are too fragile, too slight, his prose just too florid for modern taste.

In the autumn of 1829 Landor moved from Florence to the Villa Gherardesca half way up the hill to Fiesole behind San Domenico, a position commanding superlative views of the city. From the dining room on the first floor of this impressive pile the irascible poet is said to have bodily ejected his cook after an indifferent meal. Recently, I found my way to this villa for the first time. Once a Catholic home for foundlings, it seemed, by 1986, to have become a music conservatory owned by the Comune di Fiesole. Illegally (there is no admittance) I drove past the gate-house and stopped long enough in front of the fourteenth-century loggia to take a snapshot. The situation is lovely, and made more lovely by association: for here, in the grounds of the villa, is the 'Valley of the Ladies' so enchantingly described by Boccaccio in his *Decameron*.

Landor loathed Italians, and almost all things Italian. (He also had a perverse taste in art, preferring Giambologna to Michelangelo, and Fra Bartolommeo to Rafaello!) 'Italy is a fine climate,' he wrote, 'but Swansea better.' He would drink only hock or claret, being profoundly suspicious of the local vintage; but he had high praise for the water, air and oil of Tuscany. And he adored his villa. In one year alone he planted 200 cypresses there, 400 roses, 200 arbutuses, 70 bays and 60 fruit trees. But he was always restless, argumentative, intractable. His relations with his wife can never have been smooth. When the rupture came in 1835, besotted with the young Jane Swifte (his 'Ianthe'), he left her and his children and soon after travelled to England. His was a sad end. He returned to Italy and, when he died in 1864, only two mourners followed him to the spot where he now lies – the little cemetery where, only seven years before, his son Arnold had been buried.

The young Swinburne had visited Landor in his decline, paid him homage, and declared his hero 'alert, brilliant and altogether delicious'. And it is not the words of Landor, of 'Finis', that are cut on his tombstone, but four couplets of Swinburne, which are more distinguished, I think, than the usual sepulchral bromide:

> And thou his Florence to thy trust
>   receive and keep
> keep safe his dedicated dust
>   his sacred sleep
> So shall thy lovers come from far
>   mix with thy name
> As morning star with evening star
>   his faultless fame.

The irony in these verses is poignant. There should surely be oleanders here – some colour, some shade, some care shown to the sadly neglected slab. But upon it there are only scurrying lizards, and behind, a pitiful false *lauro*. Is Landor's only lasting memorial, perhaps, his caricature as Boythorn in *Bleak House*?

Arthur Hugh Clough's tombstone is better situated. His memorial, on the central pathway, is shaded by glossy green shrubbery which forms a pleasant archway above. Clough was at Rugby and Balliol with Matthew Arnold, and, when he died, in the same year as Elizabeth Barrett Browning, he was only 42 years old. (Arnold's wistful, elegiac *Thyrsis*, first published in 1866, is an atmospheric tribute to his friend.) Gosse wrote of Clough that his was 'the sympathetic, modern spirit', and indeed his modernity, his satirical vein and cynical outlook, his questing self-doubt ought to have won him more admirers. But there is, at last, some evidence of a revival of scholarly interest in his writings; 125 years, one supposes, is a short time *sub specie aeternitatis* to wait for recognition.

Frances Trollope (1780–1863), mother of the more famous Anthony, lies not far away. This remarkable woman was author of 115 novels and travel books, an indefatigable scribbler who, turning to writing only when she was past 50, rescued her family from financial ruin. (This, after she had failed at farming in Harrow, and at setting up an Oriental Bazaar in Cincinnati.) 'Fanny' settled in Florence in 1843, and was friend of the Brownings, George Eliot, Lord Lytton, Garibaldi, Dickens and Landor. Her endless series of stories were popular among her contemporaries, and they made her a very wealthy woman, but today her books are consigned to oblivion. She is in good company here.

There are few Shakespeares, Dantes, Virgils; and if the world is made up of lesser mortals, we must be grateful for the perspective they lend; for the way they frame the others' greatness, for all those nameless angels in the mighty Durbah of Heaven who support the archangel at the tip of the golden triangle.

A character in *Edwin Drood* remarks: 'Stranger, pause and ask thyself the question, canst thou do likewise? If not, with a blush, retire.'

So I retire. The old girl is waiting impatiently. The heat is like a scourge. She is holding a plastic bottle of *acqua minerale*, beaded with ice-droplets from her refrigerator. I seize the bottle, smiling and nodding my gratitude, only to discover, as she waves arthritic fingers at me and gargles unintelligible Italian, that she is not offering me hospitality: she merely wants my younger, stronger wrists to break the plastic seal.

'Prego, Signora.'

She snatches the bottle and the note in my hand. The gate swings ajar, and with a final Thankyou I am outside again, in the snarl of the Piazzale. The traffic now seems unaccountably dimmer; as I cross a magically deserted slice of the Viale, cars part before me. The world is quieter. I have left my thoughts for a moment in the little cemetery.

When one considers the names of the dead, and adds, for example, Shelley and Ouida at Viareggio, the caustic 'Smelfungus' Smollett near Livorno, it seems almost as if a wave of artists, men and women, lemming-like, have come to Tuscany to die. Certainly, the English have always had a special affection for the area. Each year, Florence heaves and groans with the tribes of English tourists. During the flood of 1966, at least, the Florentines had reason to be grateful for our attachment.

Some came to find fame and fortune; some to escape embarrassment at home; or they came because the cost of living was lower; or to take advantage of the warmer climate, to convalesce; or, increasingly after Ruskin's championing of Renaissance art, to study the culture.

Everyone had good reasons for leaving the dampness and dullness of the north and heading south; but it was probably the middle classes who took the people of Italy most eagerly to their hearts. This came about partly as a result of the Industrial Revolution; partly, too, because, after the defeat of Napolean, Europe was gradually opened up for travel. The British poured in: amateur botanists, water colourists, ornithologists, retired majors, aspiring poets and sculptors, architects, essayists, pamphleteers. In 1910, by which time the railway had come to Italy, there were no less than 35,000 British residents in Florence. Although the last war scared some away, the Tuscan countryside is still so costive with British immigrants that it has acquired the nickname of 'Chiantishire'.

I visit the Protestant Cemetery each year not merely to contemplate my own mortality. In the Cradle of the Renaissance where the things of the soul have played a role so crucial, the skeleton is easily discernible beneath the skin. All Florence, in one sense, is a tomb, a *camposanto*, a memorial to the lives and achievements of great men; constantly one feels diminished, humbled by their genius. Nor do I go merely to pay tribute: I go to rediscover and cherish my roots. I am, after all, a link in the great chain that binds Britain and Tuscany. The Brownings, the Cloughs, the Landors found their homes here, as I have: they are at rest in Florence, as I am. From them I derive hope and inspiration. The ancient Greeks had their heroes, famous mortals, men and women, each worshipped within their sacred precinct; in return for this the heroes protected their worshippers, championed them. The English writers dead in Piazzale Donatello have all played their parts in the history of letters. They have lent the passing moment words and wings. They are, if you like, my heroes.

As I drift back to Piazza d'Azeglio and the decorated facade of no. 20, it strikes me that the old *graffito* artists were incomparably superior to the modern. Tasteful curlicues and arabesques, tendrils, lyres and swooning nymphs somehow lend so much more *style* to a wall than today's monosyllables. And each time I pass the Accademia in Via Ricasoli the four-letter obscenity daubed within one foot of the della Robbia lunette screams out as a potent symbol of the twentieth-century sickness. Could there be a more violent contrast? On the one hand balance, restraint, refinement and delicacy, a demonstration of the city's devotion to the Madonna (it is to her that the Angel presents the emblem of Florence at the Annunciation): on the other, the outward manifestation of an ugly cancer at the heart of our society. Today the lovely churches of Florence are empty in the City of the Lily, the cult of *merda* thrives.

It is not easy to lose oneself in the mile or so of central Florence. However high the buildings, however narrow the street, the Duomo soars above everything as the heart and vital centre of things. Sooner or later, you catch sight of the octagonal, ribbed cupola, or a section of the polychrome marble facings. The roads radiate like arteries from the Duomo; they are constructed more or less in a grid-system. It takes no time at all to learn the main routes. Then the side streets begin to yield up their treasures. Often it pays to take the first unfamiliar turning and simply to follow your nose.

This was how, many years ago, I first came upon S. Ambrogio. It stands in an area with an atmosphere all its own. Not a smart quarter, this – far from it: the nexus north of S. Croce, before the 1966 flood the most thickly populated area of the city, was once notorious for its low life. Via de' Macci, a favourite haunt of mine, used to be called *Malborghetto*, the 'Street of Shame'; in neighbouring streets one can find old inscriptions banning prostitution. Borgo Allegri (*borgo* means a street outside the city walls) was an artists' quarter: here Cimabue, Ghiberti, and Antonio Rossellino had their *botteghe* (workshops). And a certain louche excitement can be experienced even today around Vasari's stylish Loggia del Pesce in Piazza dei Ciompi. This lovely arcade was originally designed to stand in the Piazza del Pesce near Ponte Vecchio; but it was in fact erected in the Old Market, and reconstructed here only in the last century, when the Old Market was destroyed to make way for the Piazza della Repubblica. Today Vasari's Loggia bears the usual *graffiti*; it abuts a flower kiosk and shades a book-stall. Behind it is the Mercatino, or 'flea-market', where good antiques, junk, bric-à-brac and *bibelots* of every kind can be found. The narrow streets are dotted with excellent *trattorie*; housewives, leaning from sixth-floor windows, haul up on long, knotted ropes their baskets full of provisions from the pavement below; carpenters, framers and restorers sit in shop windows or outside on wooden boxes, unselfconsciously working away at their crafts. The area of S. Ambrogio oozes unpretentious, bustling Florentine life. It makes not the slightest concession to the tourist.

The church of S. Ambrogio stands on the north-eastern corner of the Piazza which bears its name. Benedictine, and originally a fifth-century foundation, it is one of the most ancient churches of Florence, but it has been twice rebuilt (in the thirteenth and eighteenth centuries) and was badly damaged in the flood. The nineteenth-century façade is uninviting: the church itself looks to be that rarest of things in Florence – 'ordinary'. So it may seem until one climbs the steps and enters.

The interior is dark. There is a single aisle, the roof is of open timber, the choir is slightly raised. One is struck immediately by the fresco of the *Virgin and Child Enthroned with Saints* in the second chapel on the south side. This is attributed to the School of Orcagna (*fl*. 1344–68). Mary appears as a pleasant, full-faced lady with a very adult *bambino* at her breast, which he sucks contentedly through a convenient vent in her gorgeous scarlet robe.

But the real treasures are at the east end. The atmosphere here is still and numinous: there is a mystery about it. Incense often hangs motionless in aromatic swathes along the aisle, as if Mass had just taken place.

To the left of the high altar is the Cappella del Miracolo, whose centre-piece is a wonderful tabernacle by Mino da Fiesole (1429–84), the genius of *basso rilievo* who worked at no. 7 Via Pietrapiana, only a few hundred yards away. (An all-important light can be located on the right. The fact that it is not coin-operated means that you will not be disturbed: S. Ambrogio is not on the tourist routes.) Mino himself is buried here, as are also the sculptor Verrocchio (*c*. 1435–88), teacher of Leonardo da Vinci; the architect Cronaca (1454–1508), who designed the great Council Chamber of the Palazzo Vecchio; and Granacci (*c*. 1470–1543), painter-friend of Michelangelo, and, like him, a pupil of Domenico Ghirlandaio. It is also said that Lorenzo di Credi (1458–1537) lies here, Leonardo's fellow pupil under Verrocchio, and Albertinelli (1474–1515), collaborator with Fra Bartolommeo in the San Marco workshop. Albertinelli is something of a curiosity of art history: he gave up art for innkeeping, and remarked, rather winningly, that he was 'sick of this everlasting talk of perspective'! The church is a veritable necropolis of famous artists. It is, in more than one sense, holy ground.

The tabernacle is one of the 'unknown' sights of Florence. It houses a miraculous chalice. A thirteenth-century priest had negligently left communion-wine in the cup, and subsequently found it smeared with the blood of Christ. Beneath there is an exquisite relief of a priest pouring into a chalice held by a kneeling woman; and above the altar stands one of those happy, serene, and altogether delicious *putti* which can be found scattered about Florence. One itches to reach out and touch. The Bambino in this neglected tabernacle is high up. Out of reach, he gives a smiling benediction. On either side of the altarpiece kneels a lovely angel candelabrum by Andrea della Robbia. The result is perfection.

Covering the left wall is a magnificent fresco by Cosimo Rosselli (1439–1507) which depicts a procession reaching the piazza outside S. Ambrogio. A crowd is gathered to adore the miraculous chalice. Rosselli ran an important *bottega* and taught, among others, Piero di Cosimo and Fra Bartolommeo. He was also commissioned, along with Botticelli, Ghirlandaio and others, to assist with the 1481 fresco cycle in the Sistine Chapel. But nowadays he is generally dismissed as 'uninspired' and 'pedestrian'. Vasari (1511–74, painter and author of the important *Lives of the Artists*) wrote him off as 'not a very rare or excellent painter', but includes among his 'meritorious' works an unspecified picture here in S. Ambrogio ('on the right as one enters'). Presumably, this is the *Virgin in Glory with SS. Francis and Ambrose*, currently at the third altar on the left. His fresco, the *Miracle of the Sacrament*, Vasari grudgingly considers 'quite a good work'; apparently it was thought his best in Florence.

Among the throng of citizens accompanying the bishop (who carries the Tabernacle of the Miracle), all dressed colourfully in the costumes of the day, is Pico della Mirandola (d. 1494), the companion of Lorenzo the Magnificent, and friend of Poliziano and Ficino, scholars and members of the Academy of neo-Platonists. Pico was a brilliant, aristocratic and handsome philosopher-poet who was said to know twenty-three languages. Vasari informs us that his portrait is 'so excellent that he seems alive'. Rosselli is also there himself, on the left.

However much fashions have changed, people's faces are much the same. (That swarthy man with the prominent, proud nose was surely selling tripe in the market this morning!) There is an air of something happening here, an air of occasion; here are real Florentines of the *quattrocento* come to life, friends and enemies of the characters who inhabit Ghirlandaio's frescoes in the Sassetti Chapel at S. Trìnita (where Lorenzo, his sons, Luigi Pulci and Poliziano their tutors, and the donor Sassetti and his sons are featured). They chatter busily to each other; a small child looks down on the crowd from the upstairs window of a building abutting the church. Who *are* they all?

Also well worth seeing are the wooden statuette of S. Sebastian by Leonardo del Tasso (*c.* 1500) in its fine tabernacle between the third and second altars on the north side, with the small monochrome *Annuniciation* by Filippino Lippi; and the fragmentary frescoes of *Scenes from the Life of S. Onophrius*, attributed to the Maestro di Figline (Figline is on the road from Florence to Arezzo in the Valdarno), a distinguished follower of Giotto.

The S. Onofrio fresco was discovered as recently as 1965, when a *Madonna and Child* by a different painter was removed from the wall. The head of this hermit-saint is immediately striking: it has all the gravity and imposing weight of an Old Testament prophet – long-haired, with flowing beard and shaggy knotted brows. There is great power and emotional strength in these lines. The surface is pitted all over (these were anchors for the upper layer of smooth plaster for the new fresco), and the method of its design (partly drawing, partly colour applied to dry plaster) is exceedingly rare. Once discovered, this fresco was itself detached, fastened to a support of polyester and fibreglass, and so preserved for posterity. However little is left, we must be grateful for it. And the saint's head is undeniably haunting: perhaps, as one critic has claimed, there is nothing quite so powerful in the whole of *quattrocento* Florence.

How many dozens of times have I come here? I push open the door again, it takes a while for my eyes to grow accustomed to the darkness. Then I take in an amazing scene.

In the sanctuary sits a fat sacristan: next to him, an overweight boy (his son, surely, or grandson) slumps in a grand episcopal throne with arms as padded as his own. There is an air of secret privilege as fat sacristan and fat boy preside over their little, dark demesne. It appears that some sort of clandestine service is in progress. An older youth, with a waste-paper basket perched on his tight black curls, stands at the lectern and apes a reading of the Scriptures. The voice he is affecting has a strange, piping crackle; there is a wonderful mock reverence to his rendering. Whoever he is, he knows the lilt and cadences of the liturgy. His straight face, his knowing, homiletic tones make the fat boy laugh out loud; he claps his chubby thighs and smacks the padded arms of his chair! The youth wearing the waste-paper basket hat reads on, his apparent seriousness provoking the fat boy to further outbursts of laughter, sudden and helpless and prolonged. The laughter echoes through the church, it beats at the frescoes, the wooden rafters.

11

Suddenly a shaft of light pierces the gloom. Enter a priest in his soutane. He is a tall, thin, brown-faced man with crispate hair, once raven, now flecked with white. I stand transfixed, awaiting the explosion. None comes. All four engage in an animated but amicable conversation that echoes down the aisle. I cannot follow what they say, but as soon as the priest opens his mouth I realise the youth is an accomplished mimic. Later, I was to come upon the same priest in mid-Mass, his arms akimbo, like some giant bat, voice cracking, in a mist of incense at the foot of the sanctuary; the fat boy, robed as a server, was passing amongst the scattered congregation with a long-handled butterfly net. He paused every now and then to engage an acquaintance in conversation, kneeling, at the elevation, to jog a praying woman with his elbow.

As I turn to leave, the youth is swiftly at my side pressing a poor reproduction of the head of Jesus in my hand. It is a detail from the famous Leonardo *Last Supper*. For a moment I am taken aback.

'What,' I ask him, 'is this?'

'*Come?*' (affected incredulity)

'This.' I wave the little slip of paper. 'What is it?'

He rolls his eyes to heaven. 'Is Gesù Cristo!'

Then he begs for money. '*Per mangiare*,' he whines, and illustrates his meaning with a grotesque hand-to-mouth movement. He looks about as hungry as the fat sacristan and the fat boy server, but I drop some coins into his hand and observe his modified gratitude. Soon afterwards I watch him head for the Bar S. Ambrogio, where he is greeted familiarly by the owner, a short, stocky, broken-nosed Florentine who has detached himself from the Rosselli fresco especially to pour the beggar's third *grappa*.

But the sun is high and the day is flying. S. Ambrogio has been a typical digression: there is still my second pilgrimage. I must find the green Fiat in the garage in Borgo S. Jacopo and go south. Lisa has assured me there is petrol in the tank.

I first met Lisa in Rome in the cold Easter of 1976. She was muffled in a fur coat collecting teapots in the flea-market at Porta Portese. Her hair was longer then, in smartly lacquered waves. Now it is frizzy and modern. She is of medium height, slim, wiry, very determined. Lisa is my pass-key to the strangest places. Through her, I have seen parts of Florence most visitors never learn the existence of. 'Exit' signs, 'No Entry' signs mean nothing to her. Opening-times and closing-times she negotiates; she flirts with custodians, argues with policemen, and rides roughshod over security guards; officialdom she laughs at; she shouts at beggars, cajoles shopkeepers, terrifies sacristans, thumbs her nose at anyone attempting to thwart her. And all the time I am treated to a running commentary which reveals better than anything else the unique flavour of her complex and formidable character. 'Just *look* at him! How *ugly* he is!' (She will stop the car to point out the unfortunate man.) '*Che bellezza!*' (A view she admires; a beautiful girl.) '*Idiota!*' (Someone disagrees with her.) '*Comunista!*' (She disagrees with someone.) Or there is the ubiquitous and explosive '*Ma!*', a word capable of so many shades of meaning it is untranslatable.

Lisa is married to Lapo. Their lovely riverside apartment is a stone's throw from the Ponte Vecchio. Lapo is an eye-surgeon in a hospital near Pisa; Lisa works for a firm that exports shoes, and her English (American, rather) is idiomatic and fluent. In the hottest months, Lisa and Lapo like to set off for Elba or Corsica. This year the holiday is scheduled, the ferry has been booked, but out of the blue I bump into Lisa in the flea-market in Piazza dei Ciompi. She wants a few days on her own, she tells me; she will join Lapo and the children at the end of the week. In Florence I have learned to question nothing.

'Where shall we go?' she asks on impulse.

'Greve?'

'*Perchè no?*'

In holiday mood, we set off between the glove and tie shops of Por S. Maria towards the Old Bridge, the romantic, shop-lined thoroughfare almost synonymous with Florence, with its row of glittering window displays – rainbows of coral, jade, pearl, lapis, ivory, agate and every kind of silver and gold. Borgo S. Jacopo, a pretty, narrow street crammed with jewellers, antique shops and good restaurants, leads west off the southern end. The car lives in an expensive underground hotel half way along. When we retrieve it, it has no petrol.

'*Calmati.*' Lisa jabs a finger at the dial. 'The red light is on. We have 25 kilometres left.'

We thunder up the dark spiralling exit into a brilliant afternoon. The road outside is jammed and snarling. No one gives way. Somehow Lisa squeezes her bumper between a taxi and a motor-cycle.

'*Imbecille!*' I observe the eloquent gestures, their tired, expressive economy – a sort of artistic shorthand, a distillation.

Eventually, after a series of expert, illegal manoeuvres, we are running east along the Lungarno. The climb up Viale Michelangelo is always sublime, winding, pine-shaded, offering at every turn views familiar from chocolate box and place-mat, but always fresh, always arresting. In the Piazzale Michelangelo the false David is being photographed by shoals of orientals, but we flash past it and up the hill so quickly that I scarcely glimpse the city spread out beyond, the celebrated vista of dome and tower and pinnacle; onwards and upwards we rush into the grand Viale Galileo, to Poggio Imperiale, past Galileo's famous Observatory. And already the traffic is thinning and Florence begins to fade behind us.

The petrol gauge is now showing well below zero. As the countryside becomes more interesting, I seem to sense the indicator falling. We are entering the Colli di Chianti, the densest wine-producing area on earth: mile after mile of heaving hills of vine and olive, olive and vine. Here is that most perfect harmony of 'what Nature did and man made'. Originally the Tuscan *contado* was run by brigand barons, each levying a toll and dispensing his own rough justice; on every hilltop sat another menacing fortress. But gradually these feudal lords were overthrown, their fortresses dismantled, and the country was replanted. There is still a certain barrenness; here and there a ruined castle catches the eye, dilapidated walls, memories of grim days long ago; but the general effect is of sweetness and tranquillity. The Tuscans have made of their land what it is: it thrives on its orderliness, its fruitfulness, its sudden, violent contrasts. They have bent Nature to their will and by the sweat of their brow achieved a beauty that beggars description.

The road to Greve passes through arguably the most glorious landscape in all Tuscany. Seen through glossy vine-leaves, framed by grape-clusters, over acres of soldier-straight fruit trees, one glimpses the ochres and terra-cottas of the farmhouses (*case coloniche*) that are the soul of old Tuscany: the pigeon-lofts; the ramshackle sun-baked rooftiles; the stark, archaic windows, shuttered and grilled; the parasol pines contrasting delightfully with the spiky black cypresses that march uphill to the grand villa or the bell-towered church. On every slope sits ordered beauty; every farmhouse framed to perfection, every shadow exactly the right length; the light green of terraced vines against the grey clumps of pruned and pollarded olives; the sudden spears of cypresses striding so purposefully up to the *casa*; and in the distance a sweeping backcloth of forested hills fading into blueness; carpet upon carpet of variegated greens against the dusty earth; lushness beside dryness; patchwork upon patchwork intersecting into far-off mountains that loom and melt palely into the sky. Majestic, awe-inspiring, almost impossibly lovely. This winter the olives have been hard hit: they are black now, stumps merely, with baby shoots fuzzing their lopped extremities. Five years will pass before they produce good oil again. But still they survive (an olive is productive from its 30th to its 300th year), torn and gnarled and dry, leaning in every direction down the long slope of the hill. It is the sudden lift and lurch of the terrain that plucks at the heart. Some parts of Tuscany can be moonlike and grim (the approach to Volterra, that forbidden outpost of the Maremma, is black and intimidating), but here there is fertility, a deep peace. Nowhere I know is remotely like it.

We still have to find a petrol station. But when we finally arrive in the Piazzetta of Greve, we are somehow no longer looking for one. My head is still reeling with the breathtaking undulations of vineyards and olive groves, thoughts of vast luminous watercolours. And I am thinking of Donald Shannon, because he first brought me to Greve.

Donald ran a thriving prep school in Berkshire and I met him through friends who had a child at his school. He was a bachelor: intelligent, creative, and, after a lifetime of being coerced into explicitness by squeaking minors, a man of decided and very individual opinions. He adored Florence, Mozart and cricket. Our association seemed predestined. For twenty-five years he returned to the same cottage in Melazzano, a tiny cluster of old houses in the countryside near Greve. Donald treated Melazzano as his second home, and he travelled to and fro as often as work permitted.

Of all the men I have known, Donald was the supreme giver. His parties were frequent, spontaneous, and memorable. Here was no typical school beak: there was nothing petty or pedantic about him. He had vision. Donald could read a bright pair of eyes and feed an enquiring mind: he knew how to inspire. And he was unsparing of himself. Each year tireder and tireder, his eyes failing, he would take colleagues and friends with him to his Tuscan retreat. Before me is his 1972 Christmas card, an artist's impression of the cottage, high up, overlooking a million hectares of olive and vine, a few firs hedging it in, a scattering of other buildings by its side; nothing else but row upon row of vine and olive, the slope of the land hypnotic. The archetypal Tuscan landscape. You could only find Melazzano if you were lost.

In 1978 a friend offered me the family villa in Fiesole for the summer. 'It's nothing really,' I recall her saying defensively. 'It hasn't got a pool.' Gratefully, I accepted; even if it were a tiny bungalow it would be a good base.

Shall I ever forget threading my way through the sleeping city in Lisa's old Fiat, round the Viale, and finally past San Domenico and up the cliff-face of Via Vecchia? This narrow 'road', in places dizzily steep and veering off into hairpin bends, was the old way up the hill to Fiesole – the one the Medicis took, Pico della Mirandola, Poliziano, Marsilio Ficino, and San Bernardino himself. They must have been men of grit and stamina. In daylight one can appreciate its lovely old villas, sequestered behind high walls, and between cypresses there are superb views over the Mugnone Valley and away past the old Badia, with its pale, austere geometry of coloured marble, towards Via Bolognese. At night the hill is best avoided by those of a nervous disposition.

15

But Villa Mirabello was worth the climb. I finally stopped counting the rooms when I reached the charming little chapel. In the gardens there were peaches, apricots, plums, figs, and a plantation of bamboos that touched the sky, soaring canes with stems as thick as my wrist. There were shaded arbours with stone seats, and dripping, leaded wells; there were terraced vines, and the smell of wild thyme and rosemary floating on balmy air; potted geraniums blazed scarlet against the lemon trees on the terrace, against the glazed terracottas of the Virgin. Lizards, bright emerald maybugs (and at night, miraculous squadrons of fireflies) flitting clumsily around in the heat. There were a hundred shuttered and bolted windows, balcony on balcony, balusters threaded with thick-stemmed creepers trailing their fragrant mauve blooms like grape clusters. Inside, I found a library with enough reading to last a lifetime, and, climbing high up, a soaring tower which afforded the most memorable views I have ever known – a thousand villas of ochre and white and peach and terracotta, all spiked with cypresses of dark viridian; and the square, battle-mented walls of palaces – all fading into a pink and ochre and dun carpet from which rose the warm peach-coloured cupola of the Duomo, Giotto's campanile, San Lorenzo, Palazzo Vecchio, the Bargello... On a clear day one could make out Piazzale Michelangelo beyond the city, the dazzling white marble of San Miniato above it.

No pool, indeed!

And there, by the hospital at the very summit of Via Vecchia, on 21 August 1978, at 11.00 a.m. I saw Donald Shannon. I see him now just as he was then: myopic and frail; wisps of white hair falling over that fine, broad forehead; eyes unnaturally enlarged by the thick lenses; carelessly dressed in baggy gabardine trousers held up by an old striped belt; a check shirt open at the neck, sleeves rolled; and the ubiquitous sandals – an other-worldly figure, his mind on other things. In fact, Donald was a Tertiary Franciscan. I asked him one day what being a Tertiary meant: he was secretive, but I gathered that it involved taking vows of poverty (no hardship for a schoolmaster, he joked), chastity, and obedience. St Francis was a saint for whom Donald had a special reverence; both he and I found ourselves at home in S. Croce, the great Franciscan church of Florence. It seems to me that Franciscan establishments exude their own particular ambience, one quite different from that of other orders.

I was returning from shopping when I saw him. I gave a shout. Sightlessly he looked round. At first he didn't know me, but then the craggy features betrayed genuine surprise and pleasure. I took his arm and steered him down the steep slope to Mirabello. There followed a very long, happy, impromptu lunch of salami and cheese (*pecorino, parmigiano*), peaches, nectarines, grapes and Chianti. We were very content in our shaded arbour; he had been lonely, I think; I had missed him. It was decided that I would drive him back to Melazzano. Donald was anxious to show off his little cottage, and, once I had found my way there, he suggested, I could drop in whenever I wanted. We would take the old Siena road, and he would navigate. The route was a little tricky.

As we sped along the N22 Donald chattered away uninhibitedly. He knew by instinct when the turning was near; from time to time he peered through the window verifying his intuitions as we came upon a lonely signpost.

Then all at once we knew we were lost. There were no landmarks: as far as the eye could see there were only olives and vines. Three times we passed the same spot: three times I stopped *contadini* on bicycles and got different directions. It had taken us 25 minutes to turn off the *autostrada*: we had been in the vine-maze for a further 45, I estimated; then Donald announced suddenly that he thought he recognised the next junction. Ten minutes later we pulled up triumphantly outside his cottage. (We had bypassed Greve completely, though he assured me it was 'a couple of minutes' down the hill.) Inside, his guest, a pale fleshy young man with strangely flushed cheeks, was in truculent mood. After a brief tour, I made my excuses and left.

When I next made the journey south, in April of 1982, Donald was dead. He had driven into the back of a lorry. Death had been instantaneous. I went to the memorial service at his school. A Franciscan monk of my acquaintance gave the address. It was no gushing encomium. Donald had had his faults, and Brother Anselm knew him through and through. But Donald had touched and transformed the lives of many people, young and old, who had come into contact with him. He had that gift.

Ritually, I bought salami, *parmigiano,* and a bottle of the local Vignamaggio in the store (Vignamaggio, along with Lilliano, were Donald's favourite Chiantis), went to the village church at the end of the Piazzetta and lit a candle in the gloom. In the loft behind me as I knelt, some young organist was practising, and the sound was eerie and lugubrious. Aimlessly I took the first hill out of Greve. The Fiat nosed up and up, through pines, round scarifying bends, over ruts, over holes, until the air at last began to thin, the landscape opened out, and I felt the engine pleading for a rest.

On my left there was a most miraculous view. I was transfixed. In the approved Tuscan manner, I rolled the car against a tree to prevent it from careering downhill, spread a rug on the edge of a precipitous cliff-

edge, and drank in a scene that was pure Renaissance. How many *Virgins,
Crucifixions, Nativities, Depositions, Assumptions, Transfigurations* had been
painted against hills and towers and trees like these? I sat and gazed in
wonder and adoration.

The salt in the parmesan stung the roof of my mouth, the salami was
moist and piquant. I had no corkscrew, but in fifteen minutes had nibbled
away with a small fruit knife sufficiently to coax a trickle of the liquid
through the cork. I drank from the bottle greedily. And until I die, I
shall remember that solitary picnic as the most precious: dizzied by the
landscape, my eye swooped from castle to farmhouse to church; with
a light head I absorbed the serenity of a perfect Tuscan day. I slept, woke
gently, then drove on up the hill. I had no idea where I was going,
how far I had driven: there were no signposts, only a hundred fire warnings
and No Hunting notices. On my left, a tiny chapel appeared and I experienced a sudden shiver. A priest was opening the door. There was something about the place, the lie of the land! I *did* know it! My mind raced
back four years. *Surely!* I drove to the crest of the hill. *Melazzano!* The
cottage there – it was Donald's! By chance I had driven straight to him!
Incredulously, I walked into the driveway. From inside the cottage a babble
of German reached me: at the side of the building I noticed two squat
Volkswagens. Feeling I was intruding, I got back into the car and rolled
down the hill.

'*Abbia pazienza, padre.*'

'*Prego!*'

He was opening up the chapel for Easter, he told me. There would
be a midnight vigil on the 10th.

'Tell me, Father,' I said, 'do you remember an Englishman, Signor
Shannon? He lived in the villa up on the hill. Every year he came.' I
described him in shorthand. He had white hair, I told him; his eyesight
was poor.

'*Sì, sì!*' he cried. '*Come no?*' He smiled to himself. '*L'inglese, sì!*' A
good man, he nodded, yes, a good man. '*Sempre pregava, sempre pregava.*'
He was always praying.

When I explained that he was dead, he shook his head sadly. 'I will
pray for him. He was a good man.'

'He was killed – in a car crash.'

He nodded. 'And his wife? She is alive?'

'No, no. He was *celibe*. He had no wife.'

'*Ma!*' A moment's confusion: his brow furrowed. 'She was here always,
always. An *americana*.' He smiled uncomprehendingly.

'A guest, perhaps? He had many guests.'

'*No!*' He spread his hands and shrugged. '*No.*' Then he threw the thought away. 'You would like to see the chapel? The Englishman always came here. He was a *professore,* no?'

Deep in thought I drove back along the Via Cassia, seeing nothing until I came to under the planes of Piazza d'Azeglio. I could not get it out of my head. A mistaken identity, of course.

And once again I am shopping in the pretty, elongated Piazza at Greve. It is August 1986, and Lisa is with me. The market is already breaking up. It is past 12.45. I have already left the traditional candle burning in the village church. Curiously, some young organist was wrestling with Handel's *Largo*. It strikes me now, too, that we have parked the Fiat in exactly the same side street where I parked before. And all my other visits are summarised in this one: they have coloured and shaped it, given it meaning and resonance. This little village in Chianti has become for me inextricably associated with Donald Shannon, with Mozart and St Francis; and now it is also bound up with the lazy picnic on the hillside in 1982, and the country priest opening the tiny chapel for Easter high up among the vines.

I pause at the ironmonger's stall. Here many years ago I bought some poultry-dividers. (Where are they now?) A vast array of goods is on sale, from pinking-shears to grandfather scythes, a jumble of shining cutlery and tools; knives, saws, planes and bill-hooks. I usually buy something here, and the urge to maintain an innocent tradition is always strong. I seize a reasonably priced knife-sharpener which Lisa snatches from me and tosses back among a hundred others.

'It's no good,' she hisses. 'It *eats* the knives.'

Instead I buy a tin-opener to which Lisa does not object, and we move on across the Piazza past 'jewellery' and bags to the lively little shops behind the arcades at the far end. The British have always loved Greve: in the local bookshop there is a whole shelf of books in English on things Tuscan. There are also the latest thrillers by Dick Francis and Jeffrey Archer. Somehow I resist them.

While I am in the general store next door selecting a decent Vignamaggio, and Lisa is arguing with the proprietor about the freshness of his *panini*, a portly, moustachioed gentleman enters. Immediately Lisa tunes in to his rich, crackly tones as he exchanges greetings. She listens with a Florentine's eager acuteness and gives me a running translation as the greetings end and a conversation ensues.

'He is complaining,' she tells me. 'He says the wine is priced too high!'

But I can tell that the tone is anything but acrimonious: it is genial, bantering almost. The shopkeeper and the portly stranger are old friends. 'He is the owner of a vineyard.' She listens a moment longer, then points to the bottle in my hand. 'Of Vignamaggio!'

I pay for our provisions and, screwing up all my courage, waylay the gentleman as he leaves the store. I address him in Italian. In impeccable English, he introduces himself as Ranieri Sanminiatelli, presents me with an impressive visiting card, and invites me to call on him. (His accent is quite extraordinary: it is impossible to decide whether he is English or Italian.) He will be sailing off Corsica for the next fortnight or so, but would I care to 'phone him . . . around the 25th?

'Come and have tea,' he calls to me jovially over his shoulder as he makes for his car, 'and we will talk about Chianti.' Then, with his bulging plastic bags, he vanishes.

Suddenly Lisa and I abandon thoughts of rolls and buy a *porchetta* in the square. Lisa tells the old man with the skin like a crocodile handbag and deepset, ancient eyes that I am a famous English writer gathering material for a book on Tuscan food. He must do his best for me – for Tuscany, for Italy! He has a moral duty to *far figura*, to impress his distinguished English guest, to make the most succulent and flavourful *porchetta* of all time! But why have we come so late, the old man asks? The herbs, there were so many, now there are only a few! Deftly the mottled parchment fingers fly about their familiar task; with a knife that must have done service in the Hannibalic Wars he slices into the hot, glistening pork; the whole scene is timeless, antique. I watch his stubby fingers and notice that one, at least, lacks its final joint. The chopping-block has been used so long it has the contours of the Alps. Behind him a fat, jolly wife crams pork fat into her wet mouth.

'*Ecco!*' he cries at last with a flourish, scooping the remains of the fennel and rosemary (and no doubt wood-shavings from his chopping block) onto the steaming meat, making a sandwich so fat that even Italian honour is finally satisfied, and he can hardly pick it up. '*Ecco, Signore! Buon appetito!*' Proudly he beams at his masterpiece, the work of his own hands, and, as we take our leave and walk away over the shimmering square, the whole village seems to breathe up the fragrance of spicy, roast meat. Greve, indeed, does have a special aura. I wonder often these days if Donald was not right to prefer the country. In the hills there is peace and solitude. (I would choose somewhere just south of Greve near Panzano, where the roadside is crowded with fennel and tansy and yellow thistles and figs and peaches and poppies and vetch and wild sweet pea; where a thousand acres of indescribable dusty dryness are touched into brilliance by outcrops of chrome-yellow broom.) No wonder that centuries of holy men lost themselves and found their God in its beatific wilderness – hermits, priests, reformers and visionaries. Perhaps I shall come to it later.

We return to the car and hurriedly open the windows. Lisa catches me nervously eyeing the petrol gauge and points to the red light: 'We still have 25 kilometres!' We have already come more than 25 kilometres, but argument is useless. Then, round the next corner, like some divine paraclete, an Agip petrol station beckons. 'We could have got back,' Lisa insists. *'Easily.'* I bite my tongue and pour just short of 40,000 lire-worth of petrol into the car. Lisa calls her Fiat BOBO, and I swear I hear BOBO croak Thankyou.

'Have you seen Lapo's villa?'

Lisa is teasing, surely. I am tired and her humour can be oblique at times.

But no: it is on our way back home, high in the hills south of Florence, in sight of the Certosa.

'It is small, it is nothing now,' Lisa complains, 'not as it used to be when Lapo's father was alive.'

At a speed which is both reckless and uncomfortable, we bump up a narrow track traversed by roots, pitted with boulders, shoot suddenly 90 degrees left, then swing right through vines and apple trees. For some reason the car does not turn over, but everything in the front levitates and flies into the back. 'Leave it!' Lisa threatens, and urges her gallant Fiat on: *'Vai, BOBO!'*

Finally we emerge in a courtyard shaded by a noble fig tree, its fruit just ripening. Behind us I see a huge garden, wonderfully overgrown. I have always adored old gardens, their unidentifiable varieties of fruit, their unexpected hidden treasures. We are greeted by two surprised but friendly *contadini*.

The villa itself is large and dilapidated, but heavenly in its situation: there is total seclusion and a fine, commanding view of the city. But all is decay.

Here, from May to October, Lapo's entire family would translate itself and pass the summer months in sequestered rusticity, away from the heat and bustle of Florence. Then, for practical reasons, the villa was rented to a long-term tenant. When Lapo's father died, his mother decided to sell. The tenant refused to move (the old, familiar plot): Lapo had to find 15 million lire to 'buy him out'.

The tenant, who felt himself hard done-by, left the villa in terrible disrepair. There is damp, dry-rot, the stucco is cracked and patchy, the roof rickety, and balusters are missing on the verandah. Lisa estimated (typically bleakly) that it might cost as much as 150 million to put the house in decent order.

The *contadina*, an agreeable, confiding woman who has shown us with proprietorial air over the whole site, clucking at every broken catch, ruined casement, and warped cupboard, forces a jar of bottled tomatoes and a couple of warm eggs upon Lisa. (Lisa and Lapo are entitled to 50 per cent of the produce of the estate, but they take nothing. This is the first time Lisa has been to the villa for two years.) Is there anything much sadder than the sadness of decay? Why is ruined lovelinesss so poignant? The villa could be a treasure: how it called to me with its terracotta tondo of S. Cristoforo, its heavy flower pots so prettily moulded; the secret terrace, south-facing; its faded grandeur, its neglected, overgrown fruit trees!

'Lapo hates the country,' Lisa tells me as we bump back down the hill. 'He *always* hated the country!'

'And you?'

'Me?' She holds my eye for a moment. 'I want to die in such a place.'

It had been a sad little visitation. Lapo's villa, Lisa's dream. Both in ruins.

Now, high above the Ponte Vecchio on the balcony of Lisa and Lapo's apartment, I listen to the tireless buzz and hum of Florence, and drink a glass of Orvieto. In the arcades below Vasari's Corridor some louts are rivalling even the traffic's screech and roar with their amplified pop music. If, momentarily, that ceases, there is an eerie pipe-music floating up from the Old Bridge, where hippies are selling, in a haze of marijuana, their gallimaufrey of rubbish to tired trippers: masks and flutes and belts and puppets. On the balcony next door, mercifully screened from my gaze, Italians shout with uninhibited good nature at some American guest. On Lisa's record player the St Anthony Chorale is playing. The family below warms to its first fight of the evening, and from the riverside restaurant there rises the ambrosial incense of garlic. Quite often, after the quiet bliss of the country, I wonder how much more of this I can take. But here I am in Florence, a Juvenal after his Third Satire, a Johnson after his *London*.

Finally, I run Signor Sanminiatelli to ground. It has taken several phone-calls, and I have had some hilarious misunderstandings with someone I take to be his aged mother. (I examine the visiting card again: it bears a most impressive emblem – a coronet pierced by a sword.) The crackly smoker's voice is reassuring. The sailing has been good. Would 4.00 p.m. on the 30th be convenient? Good.

So I will learn about Chianti from the horse's mouth. I buy a film for my camera and petrol for the car. On the 30th the sun is brilliant. Something is telling me that I am unlikely to pass this way again. My intuitions are unreliable. Yet only yesterday, as I was crossing the Piazza della Signoria something told me that I was about to meet someone I knew. I darted into a dark, narrow alley only to bump straight into an ex-pupil. Whatever you fear most gets you in the end. My intuition had been right, my instinct wrong.

Greve is still and asleep when I arrive; the Piazza deserted. The road to Vignamaggio lies south. My sense of direction is not highly developed, but in Italy I somehow know where I am going. I turn left out of the village, and begin to zigzag the steep hill. Some of the patchworks of cultivation below me are too ravishing to pass, and I stop frequently (once on a sharp bend, where I learn new colloquialisms from an angry Alfa Romeo). Above, to my right, is an imposing villa, and below it an eternity of vines in razor-straight rows, the earth seared almost white between them. Beyond, an *oliveto*, vines trailing languidly along the stubby branches, stretches to the edge of the villa's garden. There are parasol pines to the right of the villa, soft and close like a cloud-carpet; cypresses line either side of the hill and meet around the villa, a cluster of giant black needles. The villa itself, turreted and creeper-clad, has roofs that overhang so far they look like the brim of a large sun-hat. I try to count the windows and give up. There is grace and strength here, an elaborate beauty: once again man has improved on Nature's generosity.

But I am not there yet. I am beginning to wonder how much further up the hill I must go when a small, unpretentious sign tells me I have arrived. *Vignamaggio – Vendita Diretta*. Now it has always been the Tuscan tradition that its noble families have made and sold their own wine on their own premises: I draw up at the side of the large house and ring the bell. While I am waiting, I see through a barred window a large display of bottles bearing the familiar label. From the first floor the head of a *contadino* pops suddenly, as if on a string.

'*Scusi. Ho un appuntamento col Signor Sanminiatelli,*' I mumble. '*Signor Ranieri –* '

'*Fin su,*' says the toothless head, nodding. Up there. The villa is further up. He gestures.

So up I go; and there at last I find the villa, its magnificent rose-pink façade beckoning between the stately cypresses. I gaze at the heavily grilled windows, the delicate tendrils of crimson creeper spreading in every direc-

23

tion. The formal Italianate garden, its immaculately topiaried hedges –
pyramids, arches, walls of box and bay – and shining statuary are so imposing that I find myself quite unable to make a frontal assault. I crawl down
a green, shady path to the side, the tradesmen's entrance, park the car
in an inconspicuous corner, and find an elderly, bucolic retainer staring.

'*Abbia pazienza,*' I begin.

'*Signore,*' he bobs deferentially.

'I have an appointment with Signor Sanminiatelli.'

'*Venga, Signore.*' He leads me by a side entrance into the coolness of
the villa; we cross an enchanting, small *cortile*, with virginia creeper and
a dripping well, and reach the heart of the building through tall French
windows. I stand by a long refectory table piled with magazines and news-
papers and look through a windowed recess over terraced lawns and parterres. A black-and-tan dachshund eyes me doubtfully from where he
lies panting in the shade of a statue. The walls are lined with breastplates,
halberds, helmets, pikes, spears, and crossbows, all arranged in symmetrical
patterns.

A younger, liveried manservant approaches, and the old man has words
with him. I understand two of them: '*Il Conte.*' The Count. His tones
are hushed, reverential. I realise now the significance of the coronet on
the visiting card.

The liveried servant smiles charmingly. 'The Count will be here in a
moment.'

I am left fidgeting. But not for long, because the Count suddenly appears,
in jeans and red v-necked sweater, plumply benevolent, cigarette in hand.
He ushers me into an intimate, book-lined library and rings for tea. I
notice a piece of Gothic stone-carving which serves as a door-stop.

The villa, he tells me, is fifteenth-century and was owned by the Gherardini family. Mona Lisa, herself a Gherardini, was born here. The Count
was brought up here. His grandfather had been a small-time vintner near
Pisa; his father, a gifted, versatile man, was author of many books, and
an artist of distinction (in the *Studio* I saw some excellent nudes). For
many years he had written on the arts for *Corriere della Sera*. It was he
who in 1925 bought the villa from a wily old rogue who dealt in antiques,
and who sold the property cheaply rather than leave it to his relatives.

When the Count took over Vignamaggio, the name was already known,
but it had never been exploited commercially. The estate is of average
size: 165 hectares, of which the majority is woodland; the remaining
land (64 hectares) is divided equally between vines and olives. He pauses
to unwrap a fresh packet of cigarettes, removes a gift token, stores it
carefully away, then lights another cigarette.

Above all, he stresses, one needs a first-class oenologist these days to manage the technical side of things. His is the key role of balancing the grapes from the different areas of the vineyard; the alcohol yield of grapes varies from slope to slope, because alcohol depends on sugar content, and too much alcohol kills bouquet. So it is all a question of skilful balance. It is the technician's job, too, to decide on the exact time to harvest the grapes. The microclimate of the valley here is exceptionally good, on the warm side. The Count has a good technician, and a good micro-climate: the rest is patience, experience and luck. At the beginning of September the weather usually settles (the second half of August is tradi-tionally unsettled); then the leaves are pruned away to expose the grapes to the sun. Harvesting usually takes place around 20 September. 'But,' he looks anxiously out of the window, 'everything depends on the weather.' Gone are the days when God did most of the work, and the farmer placed his vines among the olives and walnuts, piled all his vintage with pips and stalks and skins into one barrel and forgot about it. Today the wine-producers are hard-headed businessmen: their approach is com-mercial and scientific. They have ploughed, drained, deforested, levelled, planted and experimented endlessly to get the best out of the land and their vines. They are not in viticulture for fun.

What does the average foreigner know about Chianti? Perhaps no more than that it is nearly always red, and comes in a straw-jacketed *fiasco* (a brilliant marketing gimmick). But the best stuff is sold in bottles with shoulders, like a claret, and there are Chiantis and Chiantis, some cheap and new, others old and rich and heady. They can be table wines for gulping, or distinguished old vintages for sipping and relishing – and the best of these are as good as Burgundy. The term 'Chianti' covers wines as different as Beaujolais Nouveau and a twelve-year-old Rioja.

The lowest form of Chianti, one perfectly acceptable and pleasant to drink, is lively and almost *pétillant*. This is because it is *'governato'* – a process whereby a secondary fermentation is induced by the addition to the must of a second quantity of grapes which have been sun-dried on straw. This gives the wine a quick turn-over (and a deceptive strength). The Count disapproves of such methods. He lights yet another cigarette.

These days 'Chianti' is tightly *'controllato'*, but it still has a poor repu-tation in some parts of the world (the French – who else? – despise it) because formerly it was a generic term for any red wine from Italy. Now there are *consortia*, there are strictly applied standards. Vignamaggio is in the very middle of the 'Chianti Classico': the medallion of the *Gallo Nero*, the Black Cock, is on the neck of every bottle produced that is of sufficient quality. 'Only the *Gallo Nero* can be entirely trusted,' warns the Count.

(Those bottles bearing the emblem of a cherub or a bunch of grapes are from inferior areas.) Yet I bought an excellent Vignamaggio in Greve for the equivalent of £2.00! 'Too dear,' he assures me, shaking his head. 'Too dear!'

Before he became a vintner, the Count was an electromechanical engineer. He has a good head for facts and figures, and, as I sip my tea, he reels them off.

Vines have an average life of about 15 years. At 20 years, they produce excellent wine: at 23 or 24 years the quality is good, but the quantity begins to decline and it becomes uneconomical to continue using them. It costs 30 million lire to instal each hectare of a new vineyard: then nothing is worth having for 5 or more years. The investment is therefore high. The risks, too, are high. So, I can well imagine, despite the Count's careful collection of cigarette tokens, and his insistence on travelling economy-class on short-haul flights, are the profits, if he considers £2.00 excessive for a decent bottle of Chianti Classico.

Labour is the main expense. Amazingly, the Count employs only four men full-time; for the harvesting, which must be done as quickly as possible, and takes around a fortnight, he brings in 25 to 30 labourers. His average yield is 2,000 hectolitres, all of it red except for a small quantity of white produced for domestic consumption. When the work is done, the rest is chance. The 1985 vintage was exceptional, producing 200,000 bottles. (Bottling is done on the spot by a visiting team who arrive in a Mercedes lorry, and manage between 12,000 and 15,000 bottles a day!) Judging from all the signs, 1986 should also be good. If only the weather stays settled! Again he glances out of the window. 1984 was a disaster: a low-grade vintage which resulted in only *vino da tavola* – not a single bottle of Chianti Classico. To produce something drinkable, he admits candidly, he was forced to blend the vintage with Cabernet Sauvignon. Naturally these bottles did not wear the *Gallo Nero*. Unlike some of the larger combines, Vignamaggio does not make a practice of 'buying in'.

'My technician,' he tells me, as we sip more lemony tea, 'is the second best in Chianti.' The leader of viticulture in Chianti, a brilliant man with the best oenologist and a long history of wine-making in his family, is his friend Pino Antinori. All the wine-producing families know each other well. The best stabilised wine is Ruffino, run by the Folonari family. ('It is,' he says with a tinge of envy, 'as consistent as Coca Cola.') Ruffino is a big industry. The family possesses vineyards, but they are tiny in relation to its vast output, so it 'buys in' most of its wine. Also, it buys up large numbers of vineyards from disappointed first-time owners. Many of these owners are foreigners, mostly English. Vines take between four and eight years to produce acceptable wine: just as they are becoming productive, the inexperienced owner loses patience, and another vineyard becomes part of the Ruffino empire.

Currently the biggest foreign market for Vignamaggio is Germany: the Germans were the first to discover its quality, and for them it is cheaper and better value than French wine. Last year around 50,000 bottles went north to Germany alone. 'In England', the Count agrees, 'it is much too expensive. What you get is neither good nor representative.' The competition from subsidised claret and hock is too keen.

'But there are so many misconceptions about wine,' he goes on. 'People will still tell you Chianti does not age well, it needs to be drunk young! It's not true,' he says with a shrug. 'We are now drinking the '83, and at my daughter's wedding in '84 I served my guests the 1957 vintage!' Among those present were members of the Ricasoli, Frescobaldi, Antinori and Folonari families, names synonymous with excellence in Chianti production, and every one of them personally complimented the Count on the rare excellence of his wine. 'Admittedly,' he adds, with that engaging touch of candour, 'I had to taste every single bottle first to be absolutely sure! I rejected . . . about 20 per cent as of less than the highest quality. But the rest – !' he threw his eyes to heaven, *'Well!'*

Today is his daughter's birthday, and she and her husband have driven up from Rome to celebrate. The Count has three daughters: one has just left school in England; the other two are married. One of these has already presented him with a granddaughter; the other is pregnant. Do I detect a gleam of hope in his eye for a grandson?

He shows me to the main door, and after friendly goodbyes leaves me to walk the long paved terrace. It is cool now; the sun is low on the other side of the villa; the evening is deep and golden.

On the far wall of the terrace, facing south, sit a large stone dog and lion, keeping their unblinking watch over the valley beyond. Between them, floating above coils of jasmine-scented *glicine*, is a Tuscan paradise; the sun is gilding the vines and olives, and the long shadows are knife-edged between the rows. My eyes are carried out far over the valley. Impassively, the two custodians of Villa Gheradini scan the hillside opposite, its sprinkling of cottages among the trees, and the sea of pine and cypress beyond, wilderness alternating with cultivation towards a far skyline where the undergrowth has been shaved away and yet another vineyard or olive grove is being installed. They have seen it all before. Here there is the most vivid sense of history, of the timeless moment now and always, of a continuous reciprocity between man and his environment. For centuries the famous names have pressed the grape and sold their wine from palace and villa. Today Vignamaggio carries on the Tuscan tradition with pride.

The Count himself is abstemious: he enjoys a glass of wine with his supper. I myself have no such inhibitions. Burdened with bottles of various vintages, I chink my way back to Florence to drink his health. I shall drink to Elizabeth Barrett Browning, too; to Landor, and Clough, and Rosselli, and my friend Donald Shannon.

I shall not be waiting for supper.

C H A P T E R

I I

S. Maria del Carmine · true fresco · detachment: stacco and strappo · S. Croce and Giotto: the Bardi and Peruzzi Chapels · St Francis and La Verna · Masaccio and the Cappella Brancacci in the Carmine · 'Sabatino' · the S. Maria Novella Trinity

Today I shall be fresco-hunting.

Since 1981 the Cappella Brancacci in S. Maria del Carmine has been closed. Each year one is greeted by scaffolding and plastic sheets and canvas and notices shouting 'BRANCACCI FRESCOES CLOSED'. Olivetti is financing a thorough restoration, and outside the little chapel stands a forlorn video-guide which affords the thwarted tourist tantalising glimpses of what he has missed. While workmen thump about on the walkways overhead, the masterpieces of Masaccio and Masolino and Filippino Lippi have been screened off. Though intrepid aesthetes have torn holes in the plastic sheeting in order to peek at the famous treasures, the chapel is all but hermetically sealed. Only Adam and Eve are visible, on the entrance arch, their faces and attitudes crying horror and shame as they are hounded from Paradise. Postcards, another helpful notice announces, are on sale outside the sacristy, which is superintended (the notice does not add) by a crusty and stone-deaf old Carmelite.

This is the single most important fresco-cycle in Florence: to these celebrated paintings, beloved of and copied by Michelangelo, paintings which influenced the whole course of decorative art in the Renaissance, miraculously preserved after a devastating fire in 1771, one returns again and again.

29

The appreciation of fresco-painting is an important part of the Florentine experience, and it helps to know something of the methods of its execution. For six years now, balked of an opportunity to see again the Masaccio frescoes, I have gone to the Cloisters below and walked round a little exhibition entitled '*Come nasce un Affresco*' ('How a fresco is born'). It is a brave show, so few yards from the chapel, with its mangled English translations, detailed directions to non-existent illustrations (and misleading explanations of existing ones), every label dotted by now with the well-meaning corrections of cultivated polyglot tourists, and an end-result (the 'finished' fresco) one might think twice about hanging in a garden shed – a dismal commentary on twentieth-century craftsmanship. Still, they have tried.

Hopefully I thread the streets of Oltrarno in the direction of the Carmine. Because of the fire, its interior is now largely late Baroque, lofty and cool and dim and somehow massively sober, its curlicues and sunsplashes dwarfed and paling into insignificance. My eyes race down the aisle, I see at once that the Brancacci Chapel is still boarded up. Half the nave seems under wraps today. Next year, perhaps: I settle once again for the exhibition. The old Carmelite cloisters are shaded and quiet, at least: few tourists get further than the little chapel with its famous treasures. Here one can study in peace the series of plaster squares which illustrate the various stages in the making of a fresco.

A true fresco is painted on plaster (*intonaco*) that is still fresh. The artist applies his pigment on damp (*fresco*) plaster (a mixture of lime and sand), and, as it hardens, the colour and plaster become bonded. By a chemical reaction in which calcium carbonate is formed through the combination of carbon dioxide in the air with calcium hydroxide in the wet *intonaco*, the pigments are dried into the surface of the wall.

This resulted in brilliant colours and a rare permanence, but at the same time it demanded a sure hand and great speed of execution. The golden age of 'true' fresco was that from Cimabue to Michelangelo (*c.* 1250–1550); earlier and later than the golden age, frescoes (*affreschi*, paintings *a fresco*) were done *a secco*, i.e. on dry *intonaco*. For this method a glue or some other medium had to be used to bind pigments and make them adhere to the wall (egg-white for tempera, oil or lime for oil paints). Also, a method termed '*mezzo fresco*' emerged in which paint was applied to partly dried plaster. *Secco* painting required a roughened surface for better adhesion. Vasari himself scratched the plaster with the edge of his trowel; other artists preferred a covering of minute grains of sand. Different artists developed their own techniques. Many liked to add finishing touches of gold, or blue, *a secco*. But these did not last. Blues were always a problem. To be durable, colours needed to be soluble, and the only blues known to early painters (*lapis lazuli* – ultramarine, and *Alemagna Blue* – azurite) were not very soluble: they had to be painted onto the surface *a secco*, with glue for adhesion (egg-white, apparently, turned them green), and the result is that they have faded badly. Variations of tone, too, resulted from application on different days: corrections in tempera were applied, but with time these have almost all disappeared and all that is left is the underpainting.

True fresco is the most durable method of all. The reasons why artists abandoned this method is clear: it was chancy (brush-strokes were immediately absorbed and could not be corrected); colours changed as they dried; great speed was required; and the whole process was time-consuming. The art required a long apprenticeship. Commissions had to be met, and increasingly the artist's time was money. Painting *a secco* was surer and less time-consuming.

In the Cloisters of the Carmine, each stage of the process is clearly represented. First, the artist would spread the '*arriccio*', or rough layer of uneven, coarse plaster on the wall: this was usually made of two parts lime to one of sand. On this he laid the smooth plaster, the *intonaco*, trowelled on in creamy sections, which would receive the paint. Only enough for each day's work was applied, so that one can often detect the order of daily work-units (*giornate*); and the painting was always executed from top to bottom, so that splashes would land on unpainted areas. In compositions of great height, where scaffolding (*pontate*) was used, the surface plaster was laid on in horizontal bands. The joins are visible, each day's work slightly overlapping the previous day's. By various ingenious methods, the outline of the compositions was transferred to the *intonaco*; underpainting of *terra verde* (green earth pigment) was applied for flesh tints, then red over that (later yellow over the red), and last the overpainting, and the fresco assumed its finished appearance. Finally there was a touching-up *a secco* after the main coat had dried into the plaster.

Great fresco painting is endlessly fascinating because the result seems as brilliant and spontaneous as the process was long and primitive. First the sketch or cartoon was drawn by the Master in charcoal onto the *arriccio*. As a guide to the centre of the area to be painted, a cord soaked in red paint was pulled taut and beaten or pressed against the wall. (On very large compositions, the process was repeated, resulting in a grid of horizontal and vertical lines.) When this was done, he painted a thin solution of ochre over the charcoal and erased the outlines with a bunch of feathers. Then the faint ochre line had to be redrawn in red: the resulting drawings are called *sinopie*, from the place Sinope on the Black Sea where the red earth was obtained. These drawings, which have been revealed in large numbers since the perfection of fresco-detachment, are of enormous interest. Often displayed in churches or galleries beside the finished coloured mural, they can show important modifications of design. (The Master himself executed them, so his original intentions can be inferred from *sinopie*: the fresco itself, on the other hand, was generally the joint work of master and pupils.) Because it was not usual to draw on paper or parchment, *sinopie* are almost the only drawings that survive from early times. They were never meant to be seen, of course, except perhaps by the patron of the work, and the changes the original design underwent can be instructive.

With the red outline on the *arriccio*, the *intonaco* was spread on in sections varying in size according to the difficulty of the painting, and the *sinopia* was obliterated. The outlines were then retraced on the *intonaco*. The *sinopia* method prevailed until the 1430s, when it was displaced by other techniques, though in the sixteenth and seventeenth centuries in Florence it for some reason again found favour. Another method was that of dusting, or 'pouncing' cartoons: *spolvero*. Drawings were done of the actual size of the fresco; the outlines were pricked with a needle and, section by section, transferred onto the *intonaco* by a dusting of very fine charcoal powder. The little dots left can often be seen quite clearly. Another way of transferring the design was by tracing it onto medium-thick paper and attaching it to the *intonaco*, again in sections, then going over the outlines with a sharp stylus.

True frescoes achieved a high degree of brilliance and permanence, but time, weather, and inexpert renovations have still done them incalculable harm. It is a well concealed fact that for a considerable part of the year Italy can be extremely cold. In summer, I have been drenched to the skin in tropical downpours or cowered in penthouses while electric storms rattle window-panes and lightning flashes sizzle through a sky of lead and cut electricity supplies. Happily, many frescoes are on inside walls; but many, too, are in cloisters, porticoes, tabernacles, and on the façades of buildings, and the study of frescoes is often the study of faded fragments, the history of 'might have been'.

Damp is the greatest enemy, rising from the earth, or sinking from the roof: it attacks surface plaster and diminishes its cohesiveness; if nitrates and other salts come with it (as happened in the flood of November

1966 in the case of many churches, where the surrounding soil is full of nitrates due to the presence of decomposed bodies), the colour is spoilt and the paint actually flakes off. Much was ruined for ever; certainly Florence can never be the same again. But good came with the tragedy. New techniques of restoration were developed, and as a result exciting new discoveries have been made. Our knowledge of art history has been enormously enriched – but at what a price! After the cataclysm, when the *intonaco* began to dry out in spring, and the salts rose to the surface, desperately quick action was needed to save the murals. Some would certainly have been lost for ever had they not been detached. The rescue operation was complex and frenetic, and many acts of heroism and self-sacrifice went unrecorded. To these unnamed restorers the tourist owes an enormous debt of thanks as he walks around Florence and feasts his eyes on the colours. The plain facts are that in 18 months 2,300 square metres of mural were detached. In two cases, large frescoes were removed in single pieces, both of them more than 110 square metres in size; these were the Nardo di Cione *Inferno* in S. Maria Novella, and the Taddeo Gaddi *Crucifixion* in S. Croce.

Now the removal and transfer of frescoes is no new thing. Its history is one of ingenuity, pertinacity, and much frustration, and goes back at least as far as the days of Vasari. (To the Aretine Vasari, as well as the *Lives*, we owe the great *Corridoio* which links the Uffizi with the Palazzo Pitti, a number of paintings – many of them second-rate – in Palazzo Vecchio, and the vandalising of many of the great Gothic churches of Florence.) In the sixteenth century, frescoes might be detached because they were being attacked by the atmosphere, and a better situation had been found; or else they were rescued from buildings due to be demolished. Originally, detachment meant merely the transfer of whole sections of wall from one place to another: the masonry was simply sawn through and bound with chains before being transferred. The two famous Ognissanti frescoes of St Jerome and St Augustine by Ghirlandaio and Botticelli were removed when the monks' old choir was pulled down in 1564. Amazingly, this operation, which involved their bodily translation to the middle of the church, was quite successful.

The techniques of detachment seem incredibly finicky and dangerous, and so, to begin with, they were; but by the nineteenth century the operation was well mastered, though the removed paintings could often be ruined by subsequent treatment.

There are two methods: one (*stacco*) detaches the *intonaco* and painting together; the other (*strappo*), the painting alone. Both require great skill and painstaking finesse. When the fresco is well preserved, and colour and *intonaco* still adhere, *stacco* is used: *strappo* is used when the colour is detaching itself from the *intonaco*, as is generally the case with cloister frescoes, and those open to the effects of the atmosphere.

In both techniques the first step is a careful cleaning. Then canvas, usually of double thickness, is attached to the paint-surface (different 'glues' are used for the different techniques) to stop it cracking when the tense moment of separation arrives. In *stacco*, the *intonaco* is now slowly, gently detached from the *arriccio* by a knife, and pounded by a wooden or rubber hammer to ease the process of separation. The whole thing is now laid flat, canvas-down, and the *intonaco* is removed from the paint. The result is cleaned, glued to a support of masonite or resin, and mounted. Lastly the canvas is removed from the front of the fresco.

The *strappo* method is equally hair-raising. Here the adhesive used between canvas and colour must be stronger than that between colour and *intonaco*. When the adhesive has thoroughly dried, the canvas is gently but firmly pulled from the wall. Any bits of *intonaco* that still cling to it are now cleaned off. The result is glued to a support, mounted, and the canvas removed.

Experiments in *stacco* were made as early as the fourteenth century, and increasingly afterwards, with greater or lesser success. A *strappo* was carried out successfully in about 1725 by a Ferrarese painter called Antonio Contri, and in the eighteenth century many frescoes in Italy were successfully detached. But some of these were mounted on canvas, which sagged, causing the colour to flake. Also, when the *intonaco* with its residual damp was not entirely removed from the back, the painting simply continued to deteriorate. But to the perfection of these techniques the world owes the survival of a wealth of precious mural painting.

Hopefully I try the door to Allori's *Last Supper*, but it is tightly locked, and I climb the steps to the dim church. Mass is in progress. I have always loved the feel of the Carmine – the area, the church itself. The frescoes in the Brancacci Chapel portray acts of the Apostles, reminding us of the work of the Carmelites in the Third World today, and of the sick and crippled who seem to spring from the stones of the tiny streets in the poor quarter around the Carmine. Filippo Lippi (father of Filippino who finished the Brancacci cycle) was himself a Carmelite friar ('Fra Lippo Lippi'), and was born just nearby: Masaccio worked almost exclusively for the Order. Despite the great fire, despite the generally undistinguished Baroquery, there is still here, indelibly, something of the old Oltrarno, of the real Florence, which is daily becoming harder and harder to find.

But to begin at the beginning one has to visit S. Croce and see Giotto

Santa Croce

– or what is left of him – in the Bardi and Peruzzi Chapels. There is much to distract: S. Croce is the mausoleum of great Florentines. Here Galileo, Michelangelo, Ghiberti, Machiavelli and the great humanists Leonardo Bruni and Carlo Marsuppini lie. Until 1560 when Vasari removed the Gothic choir and rood screen, S. Croce must have been one of the most magnificent Franciscan churches in existence, quite covered in frescoes, as tantalising fragments along the nave walls indicate. Tedious national monuments have now obtruded themselves, and the glory is obscured for ever. The church is still fine – its vast interior, its open, painted timber roof, and wonderful sanctuary windows, three brilliant lancets (fourteenth century), the central one whitish, the right yellow-gold, the left radiant blue-green and pink. It is T-shaped, in the typical Gothic pattern of churches made for Friars Preacher and Friars Minor. But Arnolfo di Cambio (probably the architect who rebuilt the church at the end of the thirteenth century) intended it to be covered with great paintings, and what we see today is the tiniest fraction of what there was.

The 'church', comments one guide book, 'is much visited by tourist groups' – an understatement of epic proportions. It positively heaves with rival groups shouting in a Babel of languages, with young people in bikini bottoms and tee-shirts, shorts and bikini tops, with lovers and loonies, pick-pockets and aesthetes. Amid all this the brown habits float with saintly tolerance. They are sorely tried.

One suffers the ugly nineteenth-century monument to Dante outside, which throws off balance the whole fussy, white façade (also nineteenth-century, and paid for by the Englishman Francis Sloan, who now has a chapel decorated with appropriately tasteless modernity named after him in the north transept); one ignores the monuments of bad taste right and left (Vasari's tomb of Michelangelo stands in vile contrast with the superlative Bruni tomb by Bernardo Rossellino, and opposite it the exquisite Marsuppini tomb by Desiderio da Settignano), and proceeds towards the chapel immediately next to the high altar on the right. With luck the majority of the hordes are still munching their breakfast, but a few intrepid souls will be there already. However early one rises, one never quite avoids the Miss Lavishes and the Lucy Honeychurches.

Today I pass a French youth who sits carelessly caressing his sweetheart's thigh; a small German boy runs down the nave singing a martial song (his parents hush him proudly). In the organ loft (a fine instrument this, claimed to be the best in Italy: its reeds need tuning) I hear a workman's electric drill. But in the sanctuary there is brilliant colour, faded, antique, grandly affecting. I join a small group of intense American art students in the Bardi Chapel: *Scenes from the life of St Francis*. The cycle runs in tiers, and it tells a story. (Most church-goers of the day were illiterate, and these narrative frescoes would have been a vivid way of familiarising them with the life and works of the great saint.) I stand and gaze. Franciscan churches are friendly places: in their pictures Christ is the suffering God Incarnate rather than the grim judge we see so often elsewhere. St Francis had been, above all, a humanising influence on the Church.

Giotto di Bondone (c. 1267–1337) is most famous today for the *campanile* ('Giotto's Tower') of the Duomo, and his dramatic frescoes in Padua, Assisi, and the two chapels here in S. Croce. He worked elsewhere in Italy: in Naples between 1329 and 1333, for example, and elsewhere in Florence (his Ognissanti *Madonna* of c. 1310 is now in the Uffizi; S. Maria Novella has an early crucifix of his; and fragments of his painting were discovered in 1958 in the Badia). Dante wrote of his reputation as the leading Florentine artist of the day, and Ghiberti endorsed this verdict. Vasari goes so far as to call him 'the true restorer of the art of painting'.

A charming tradition is preserved in Vasari's *Lives* that he was 'discovered' by Cimabue while, as a shepherd boy tending his father's flocks, he sketched a sheep with a pointed stone on the surface of a smooth rock. Under Cimabue in Florence the boy made swift progress: as he developed he broke away from the rather stiff Byzantine style towards a new realism (compare the *Madonnas* by Giotto and his Master which hang side by side in the Uffizi). Giotto's paintings are instinct with religious feeling: the attitudes and expressions of the monks around St Francis's deathbed on the left wall of the Bardi Chapel speak volumes; his figures are rounded, fleshly, solid, human. He was immensely influential: his humanism and emergence as an all-round artist (painter, sculptor, architect) prefigures the spirit of the High Renaissance.

The Bardi frescoes (c. 1315–20?), once partly hidden by wall-tombs and covered by whitewash (hence the lacunae in the lower scenes), have been extensively restored, and are in poor condition. Almost certainly Giotto designed the whole, but assigned some of the tiers to pupils, as was the normal practice. Two of his closest followers were Taddeo Gaddi and his son Agnolo, both of whom worked in S. Croce. The usual appellation is 'Giotto and his workshop'; I prefer to leave 'shop', with its vulgar connotations of early closing, inflated prices and nonchalant incivility, in Italian: *bottega*. The *bottega* was not a 'shop'; it was where the Master and his pupils worked.

The most easily viewed of the frescoes is the celebrated *Death of St Francis* on the left wall. How compelling are the faces and attitudes of the anxious watchers around the saint's deathbed; their strange, distinctive slit eyes, the rapt gaze and parted lips of the tonsured monk who peers through the curtains; the slant eyes all trained on the one focal point; the sadness of the black-hatted dignitary who watches behind the man in a skull-cap (his right arm raised as if in blessing); the variety of tonsures and costumes! The tension, the intensity of grief, the capturing of a precise psychological moment, the achievement of a magnetic focal-point by skilful grouping! The unbelieving judge who touches the wound in the saint's side! The simple friar at the saint's head who gazes at his soul as it rises heavenwards! These are the details which convince. The impact comes surely from the artist's effort to make one *believe*. The details of the faces may be lost, but the general design seems secure, the drama is almost undiminished. No wonder this became a classic; no wonder so many other versions were subsequently based on it.

The other scenes go from left top to right top, left middle to right middle, and so on. Outstanding is also the *Ordeal before the Sultan* (right middle, and still relatively easy to see), a fine illustration of Giotto's synthesis of dramatic realism and classicism, in lovely olives and whites and ambers and browns.

Who was he, this saint who won such an affectionate, spontaneous following, whose image one sees the length and breadth of Italy, and the world over? The saint who called the birds and beasts his 'little brethren and little sisters'?

'Francesco' (baptised Giovanni) Bernardone was born around 1181 at Assisi in Umbria. After a riotous youth he was disowned by his wealthy father, and became the 'bridegroom of poverty', tended lepers, and gave to the poor. In 1210 Pope Innocent III authorised Francis and eleven followers to be itinerant preachers: these were the 'Friars Minor', whose centre of operations was near Assisi. The fraternity grew quickly, and another was founded at Bologna. They practised humility and chastity, shunned all worldly preferment, and lived in simplicity and lowliness. By 1217 the movement had become so large it was all but a religious order: various groups of the friars were sent to proselytise abroad – Francis himself went on an unsuccessful mission to Egypt and the Holy Land. (The *Trial by Fire* illustrates his meeting with Sultan Malek al-Kamel around the year 1220. The Sultan appears singularly unimpressed by the intrepid Umbrian – or is he rather shamed by the cowardice of his own retinue? In any case, the saint got nowhere with the Saracens.) Others went to England. The rule was revised and finally received papal approval in 1224.

It was in the same year that the approval of God set the indelible mark on this saintly man. Francis had retired to a rocky fastness called La Verna, north of Arezzo, and east of Vallombrosa, not far from Poppi and Bibbiena in the wilds of the Casentino. It is south south-east of Camaldoli, the lower eminence where St Romuald had founded his isolated order for hermits around the year 1012.

I had tried many times to get Lisa to go to La Verna.

'It is very far.'

'We've been to Arezzo. That wasn't so far.'

'It is very far. Further than Arezzo.'

'No, really.' I brandish the map, but she has mislaid her reading spectacles.

'Much further. And very high.'

Argument is futile. But the seed has been planted, and one day in 1987 we are sitting in the *Piazza Grande* of Arezzo in the midday heat and Lisa suddenly has an idea.

'We could go to La Verna!'

Little BOBO noses north, and soon we are in dramatic, hilly country. I have filled the car with petrol: the fuel gauge shows zero, but a sharp rap jerks the needle beyond the half-way mark. Lisa drives like an inspired maniac, and my vocabulary grows with every hairpin bend. In the heat, Lisa wears gloves, as if, in the event of an accident, she wishes to leave no fingerprints. Bends are for swinging around, and one swings round them most spectacularly if one first swerves over onto the wrong side of the road – a manoeuvre fraught with complications if a motorist of similar intentions is coming fast from the opposite direction.

''*Becil'!*'

'*Contadino!*'

Occasionally, a silent gesture wins: temporarily outfaced, Lisa mutters to herself darkly. We go up and up until the air seems to lie lighter on the lungs at every corner. It is almost fizzy, like champagne.

La Verna lies on the roof of the world (1129 m) surrounded by cool, fragrant pine forests, an eagle's eyrie, with its famous spring water. The locality is enchanting and much frequented by picnickers: it is mountainous, yet lush, with broom, mallow, thrift, and a hundred different whites and blues at the roadside. Large orange fritillaries hop aimlessly about; one sees a few Small Blue butterflies; a couple of enormous, unwieldy black ones impale themselves on our radiator-grille. There are beeches and sycamores, and here and there beneath their branches, droves of Italian holidaymakers; their children yell and laugh and cry on the fresh hillside. There is no stillness. The monks are geared for tourism, and tumult, and they offer the St Francis Tour with practised enthusiasm and worldly

39

tolerance. Everything at La Verna is in good repair: lavatories are clearly signposted; there is an unobtrusive gift-shop; a sour-faced nun sells the usual jelly-baby crucifixes and rosaries, as well as learned tracts on the great Founder of the Order.

Surely this was a very holy man. I saw his bed among the rocks, in a cave, where the atmosphere was vaporised ice; the several little chapels, including one where St Anthony of Padua stayed a while; and breathtaking masterpieces by Andrea della Robbia – his most elaborate and perfect works I know – in the Basilica (a vast *Assumption*) and in the *Cappella delle Stimmate* (a vast *Crucifixion*). These alone are eminently worth the long climb.

In this last chapel one day (history records it was on 14 September 1224, on the festival of the Exaltation of the Holy Cross) St Francis was praying: he prayed to be allowed to share our Lord's suffering. In a vision a Seraph appeared, and Francis was wounded five times with the wounds of the Passion: once in each foot and hand, where the nails had been driven, and once – a wound three fingers wide – in his breast, where the spear had been thrust. Illustrations show these stigmata as caused by bright, piercing rays like laser beams. The flesh around them was charred, and blackened, as if discoloured by the iron nails. These wounds gave Francis intense physical pain (after 1224 he was no longer able to walk) and he carried them for the rest of his life, the two years between 1224 and 1226 which he spent here at La Verna. His wounds were witnessed by a select few; otherwise Francis said nothing. He returned to Assisi finally and welcomed 'Sister Death' on 3 October 1226; two years later he was canonised.

I am in the little Chapel of the Stigmata wondering about this strange tale (sudden conversions from profligacy to a life of self-denial are always intriguing), and admiring the elaborately inlaid stalls, when a forty-three monk procession, carrying crosses, singing plainsong and saying prayers bars my retreat. I fight my way out of the choir and join a reverent throng at the back of the chapel. The atmosphere is suddenly Lourdes-like: a large crowd, fingering beads and wailing responses, has followed the procession. I cannot get out, so I study the monks in choir. They are men of all nations, and the régime here must be liberal: one wears a digital watch, one a bangle, and another has a bright blue shirt beneath his habit. The Abbot speaks into a microphone which relays his very audible borborygm to the assembled worshippers, and I find myself wondering what St Francis himself would have made of it all: the telephones and ice cream shops, the snack bar and flash guns and gimcrack frippery. Back in the Basilica a priest absolves a very fat lady, arms akimbo, head lowered. In the body of the church a hundred scouts and guides, with alpenstocks and guitars and saucepans banging on their buttocks, traipse up and down behind a monk with a megaphone. Later when the aisle is clearer, a Brother is received in his coffin. The organ contributes a few bright silvery chords in his honour. Afterwards, the monks shamble off in every direction, and some, I notice, are incredibly young. How, in the face of such persistent invasions, do they manage to live the religious life? The sour breath of the whole world is on them: here is no longer a simple, isolated mountain retreat where monks can live a life of deprivation and solitude. Tourists must surely be the ultimate test of the true vocation.

Yet somehow, tenuously but certainly, the spirit of the saint is over this place. The chapels and other sites are still full of mystery. The overhanging, rocky crag where St Francis is said to have hidden from the devil is dizzily ravishing, it floats in the sky (below, I saw half a dozen spotlights aimed at the area and wished I could be there at night). And it is impossible not to be moved by the site of his chilly bed. In these lonely woods he conversed with the birds and animals and found God. The surrounding hillsides seem instinct with sanctity: the picnickers cannot drive out the *genius loci*, any more than the camera flashes can dull the della Robbias.

'100 days indulgence' here; '200 days' there. 'One Ave, two Paternosters' over there. Legends have been invented about almost every rock. (That one looks vaguely like a man's head. 'Here the Devil, etc. . . .')

There is no sign of Franciscan fervour abating. When the last tourist has gone let us imagine the monks shutting their cell doors tight and practising their vocation in devoted silence. Let us resist the probably more accurate picture of coffee machines, TV rooms, amateur dramatics and Space Invaders.

La Verna is a 'going concern', but does St Francis smile at all the goings-on? Whatever else he is doing, currently he must be busy interceding for Greenpeace and similar organisations, because in 1979 Pope John Paul II made him the Patron Saint of Ecologists. I think he *must* be smiling.

Lisa has now had enough. She buys a lollipop, smokes a cigarette, curls up in the back seat of the car and wakes up in Florence. Vigorously she denies having been asleep and complains that I have driven far too fast. Too fast. *Very* fast.

'Why do you drive so fast?' she complains.

We have in fact taken a long time to get back. The route through the picturesque Casentino is slow and winding. I have approached each corner painstakingly, carefully, so as not to wake my passenger. I have driven deliberately at snail's pace in order to enjoy the scenery. There have been many hold-ups, too, including the usual mess at Pontassieve.

'Sorry.'

I am soon forgiven. Lisa prepares *rognoncini trifolati* for supper, and happily I eat them on the verandah as I watch the busy traffic at Ponte Vecchio, wonder what La Verna is like in the grip of winter, and pray earnestly never to be blessed with stigmata. And who *says* prayer doesn't work?

The Peruzzi Chapel frescoes, next to the Bardi, are maturer Giotto (1320–6?), and in better shape. (The nineteenth-century 'restoration' was removed in 1959 to reveal, quite unexpectedly, that these scenes are painted not in true fresco, but in tempera on dry plaster.) Yet it seems altogether stiffer, inviting one to wonder if the Bardi cycle owes its great modern appeal mostly to modern repainting. Perhaps the themes (on the left wall *Scenes from the Life of the Baptist*, and on the right *Scenes from the Life of St John the Evangelist*) were less congenial to the artist, as they were further removed from him in history. St Francis, after all, died only about forty years before Giotto was born. But the Salome story, whose gruesome theme was popular in the *trecento*, was widely copied. Note the dramatic grouping to the right of Herod's table, the solemnly watching servants, the classical architectural flourishes, and the as yet nascent perspective. This is also a good example of the fresco as a narrative: the soldier brings the head of the Baptist on a trencher to Herod; Salome looks on. At the right extremity, Salome gives her mother the head. The fresco is both eloquent and simple: no redundant extras stand in the wings. The figures are dignified and sculptural. Ruskin enthused madly over the striped curtaining behind Herod's table: I find the muted olive of Salome's gown perfect against the brighter leaf-green of the portico behind her. Again, the blues and faded, bloody maroons delight; and the pale musician, playing his antique viol, stands by the feasters like some pallid wraith. In the *Birth and Naming of the Baptist*, the loss of Elizabeth's head, as she lies in childbirth, is a tragedy. But her husband, the priest Zacharias, as he writes his son's name (the name the angel had given him in the vision illustrated above) looks most appropriately dumbstruck. The grouping in this scene, the colours, the variety of attitudes, the draperies are masterly. How can any one painting stand out in a city so crammed with masterpieces? Genius, I suppose, has a way of shouldering difficulties aside.

The *Assumption of St John* (the Evangelist: bottom right) represents the curious tradition that this St John, traditionally 'the disciple whom Jesus loved', was taken up to heaven body and soul, and his tomb, when the disciples investigated it, was discovered full of manna. Again there are fine groupings, and classical structures; again the story is told unmistaka-bly, economically, *con brio*: the rays of gold from the Almighty, flanked by a company of the Heavenly Host, draw up the haloed disciple with a force one can almost feel. Happily, we are spared a Martyrdom of St John (he was boiled alive in oil): for that we must go (if go we must) to S. Maria Novella for Filippino Lippi's frescoes in the Strozzi Chapel.

I emerge finally from S. Croce with Giotto's glorious images glowing in my head. Outside the sun is blinding, the spacious piazza bakes. Pigeons, beggars, exhausted tourists, card-sellers. A swarthy gigolo chats hopefully to two statuesque Dutch girls who sit splay-legged on the wide sweep of the steps. An Englishman wearing only frayed denim shorts lies placidly scanning *The Times*. The Test Match, he tells me, was a draw (rain): Gooch made nearly 200. His daughter was inside (he jerked his head languidly at the church). She liked that sort of thing, he supposed. No he hadn't bothered, himself. Gooch had hit x fours and y sixes. I pass Michelangelo's 'Gold Market' and Cellini's 'Gold, Silver, Souvenirs' and collapse into the first *trattoria* I can find.

Next morning, doggedly, I return to the Carmine. The great piazza, big enough for a couple of football pitches, is currently a car park. Every space is taken, and the cars sit huddled shoulder to shoulder, nose to nose; at times one can almost hear them blister. Florence cries out for space in which to breathe. 'There is something majestic', E. M. Forster wrote, 'in the bad taste of Italy.'

I sit on the steps and wait. The church seems awfully, determinedly shut. Yet on the dot of 8.30 I hear the bolts shot back suddenly, a thin sliver of blackness appears between the two halves, and a shaven head dutifully peers out.

Will some of the scaffolding be down today? Shall I be able to glimpse, at least, the *Expulsion from Paradise*, see *The Tribute Money* again? The spacious interior, deliciously cool, yawns open. *In restauro*. One of the most important artistic shrines of the Renaissance is *chiuso*. The Masaccio frescoes are 'shut'. Visitors are requested not to poke holes in the polythene covering. Only the uninteresting ceiling of the little chapel is visible from a distant point in the north transept. Even the Corsini chapel is in *restauro*. But when will the wraps be taken off, when will the chapel be reopened? The sacristan gives me a world-weary shrug: *Chi lo sa?*

Through one or two strategically poked holes in the polythene covering there are tantalising blurs of colour, a head, drapery, a hand pointing.

Year after long year there has been disappointment in the Carmine. Originally the restoration, begun in 1981, was to take two years. So far it has lasted eight. According to a typically optimistic statement by the Director of Operations, Umberto Baldini, in a February 1988 edition of *La Nazione*, work should have been finished and the chapel reopened by the beginning of summer 1988. But summer came and went, and officials are now talking of a date at the end of spring 1989. *Magari*.

I must return to the day when I last walked into the church and my eye, racing ahead of me to the small chapel at the end of the right transept, saw it was open, and I stood and looked at the priceless paintings until my eyes and neck and back ached for relief. It is 1980, and I am 38, married, alone.

I try to see the chapel as it was in the *quattrocento*, with a long lancet window (not the wide window of today behind the intrusive baroque altar), covered in frescoes of bright fresh colours, untarnished and perfect. I erase the marble picture-railing and the eighteenth-century nonsense in the vault and lunettes: originally these formed part of the fresco-cycle, and in the vault I can picture the four Evangelists, in the side-lunettes more scenes from the life of St Peter. Vasari tells us of at least one further scene on one side of the top of the window: *St Peter Weeping*, and if he is right, of course, another would have balanced it on the other side. In 1933 two further bits of fresco were uncovered: a small area below the trabeation of the altar revealed a head in the top left of *St Peter Baptising*; and another in the top right of Masolino's *St Peter Preaching*. More recently a male head has been discovered in the decoration on the right-hand splay of the original window, and a female head on the left-hand splay. Also, clusters of foliage have come to light in the window splay, and the fragment of another scene, probably of *The Martyrdom of St Peter*. The chapel today is a sad ghost of what it was.

The importance of this cycle is hard to exaggerate. The frescoes are by three artists, two working in the first quarter of the fifteenth century, and the third, much more easily distinguishable, some 60 years later. Sometimes I believe I could spend an entire lifetime on these few square metres of wall, reading and writing, guessing and arguing. Here came all the great artists of the time: Fra Angelico, Lippi, Andrea del Castagno, Botticelli, Perugino, Leonardo, Michelangelo, Raphael, and countless others. For more than a century this chapel was the Mecca of Florentine art. It was on this spot, according to Cellini, that Torrigiani (the artist who sculpted the tombs of Henry VII and Elizabeth of York in Westminster Abbey) gave Michelangelo his distinctive broken nose for sneering at his efforts to copy Masaccio's figures. All the famous names came to see the masterpiece of Tommaso di Ser Giovanni, the genius who, in a cruelly short life (he died aged 27 or 28), managed to change the whole direction of painting. He is better known as 'Masaccio', a comic nickname hard to render in English, the suffix *-accio* implying dislike or feigned disapproval.

The chapel is named after a distinguished aristocrat, Felice Brancacci, and was commissioned by him on his return from a diplomatic mission to Egypt in 1423. It is therefore a patrician chapel in a poor working-class area.

The two earlier painters involved were Masolino da Panicale (1383– *c*. 1440) and Masaccio (1401–28/9), and for centuries it was supposed (perhaps for no better reason than that he was twenty years older) that Masolino was Masaccio's master. Not only has this been proved impossible (Masolino could not take pupils until 1423, when he registered with the Guild of Painters: Masaccio had registered in 1422), but a close examin-ation of the frescoes suggests that the exact opposite was true. If Masolino was not Masaccio's pupil in the strictest sense, then it seems at least that, as each worked on the Brancacci frescoes, Masolino felt Masaccio's influence, and, perhaps unconsciously, perhaps consciously, began to imi-tate him. Recent scholars have come to the conclusion that it was Masolino who was originally commissioned and who started the cycle, beginning in the vaults. We know he left Florence at various stages for Rome, and Hungary, and the work was interrupted. Masaccio continued the painting, himself leaving for Rome in 1428, where he died. Parts of the frescoes already begun may have been still incomplete at this date. Then, in 1436, Brancacci was exiled as an enemy of the Medici, and the cycle was not completed until Filippino Lippi came on the scene more than half a century later.

All this makes for interesting detective work. Scholars argue over details, but what can safely be regarded as authentic Masaccio? I stand at the entrance and face the High Altar. On the left of the entrance arch, familiar as the *Primavera* or *David* or *St George*, are Masaccio's Adam and Eve in the moving *Expulsion from Paradise* (only a few paces away from Masoli-no's own account of the Expulsion, but in depth of feeling and drama a light year distant). On the upper left wall *The Tribute Money*; on the lower left side of the altar wall *St Peter Healing with his Shadow*; and on the lower right side *The Distribution of Communal Goods and the Death of Ananias*.

St Peter Baptising on the upper right half of the altar wall is held by some to be Masolino, by others Masaccio. Masaccio also probably painted the *St Peter Enthroned* part of the lower left wall. Just conceivably he was also responsible for the two Apostles in Masolino's *The Raising of Tabitha*

45

on the upper right wall, but where two hands are detected in a single scene, the extent of each artist's contribution is hotly debated.

Masolino's contributions are: *St Peter Preaching* (upper left half of the altar wall), part of the upper right wall (*St Peter Raising Tabitha*), and the *Expulsion* on the upper part of the right entrance pier.

The rest, all in the lower halves of the walls, is the work of Filippino. So, leaving aside the disputed *St Peter Baptising*, this makes Masaccio's contribution the largest, Filippino's the second largest, and Masolino's the smallest.

It was to see the Masaccio frescoes that all the artists of the *quattrocento* came, and so have I. Filippino I ignore, delightful though some of his work is, with its fascinating portraits of contemporary Florentines. But Masolino's juxtaposition with Masaccio is instructive. Masolino's style is 'international Gothic', with its rather cluttered details of nature and architecture. Masaccio thought on a much broader scale: he goes for drama, for moral purpose, for the significant moment, and his figures are massive, fleshly, full of dignity. He hardly uses outlines; his figures emerge from darkness into light; they stand firmly on the ground, three-dimensional, palpable. He is above all *serious*. 'Gravity' is a word I associate with these extraordinary creatures: gravity in both its denotative and connotative senses.

I look and look and I ask myself what I see. There are so many fresco cycles in this city. Why has so much been made of this one? (There is a click and the chapel is suddenly dark. I fumble for another 100-lire piece. But each time the frescoes are reilluminated their impact is renewed. I hear a sharp intake of breath.) First, the subject: on each of the piers is a scene from Genesis: inside the chapel, a series of episodes each of a known subject, but comprising – what? Some see the theme as one of 'sinners redeemed'; others see a more narrow reference: 'the acts of the Apostles as exemplifying the Carmelite Rule.' At least one recent writer has looked for connections with contemporary events in Florence. The choice of *The Tribute Money* may have been prompted by the tax imposed on Florentines in 1427, called the *Catasto*. Masaccio's own name is recorded in these first income tax returns. Apparently he lived in great poverty, supporting a widowed mother and a young brother.

Second, in accordance with a delightful practice of the day, there are several portraits of contemporary figures in these fresco scenes. Vasari tells us that Masaccio included himself in *The Tribute Money*: he is the young man with a pointed beard at the extreme right of the central group (others claim this is Brancacci). Botticelli, Filippino's teacher, is on the far right of the *Crucifixion of St Peter*, also in profile, next to the youth who holds the viewer's eye. In *St Peter Enthroned*, in the figure on the extreme right, we have a portrait of the great Brunelleschi. Masolino may be the man in a hat immediately to the left of the saint in *St Peter Healing*. There are certainly more portraits. Two were covered by the Baroque altar and therefore left relatively untouched by the fire of 1771. Only in 1933 was the covering stone removed, and two heads discovered, fresh and bright, showing just how overlaid with grime and layers of well-meaning varnish the cycle had become. (There was also a deal of repainting at one time or another, especially of the background scenery. Its extent will only be determined accurately when the current restoration is finished. Then finally we may see something nearer the crisp colours of the original paintings and adjust our appraisal of the total effect of the cycle.) In 1980 it seemed that Masolino's colours were brighter than Masaccio's, that Masaccio's palette was dull and muted; but there has been so much repainting, such a lengthy accretion of grime. In 1980 we saw through a glass darkly: thereafter, only through peepholes in polythene. Already, Umberto Baldini has announced that, ironically, it is Masolino who gains more from the cleaning, that Masaccio clearly acquired his sense of colour from the older painter. In *St Peter Preaching* three faces appear behind the saint which can only be those of contemporary figures. There are probably more portraits than we will ever know. Yet, so far as we can tell, references to contemporary *events* are rare in Florentine frescoes, and of the Brancacci family's political allegiances we know too little to grasp confidently at 'meaning'.

We are faced, anyway, with man's Fall and his Redemption – a fitting theme, I suppose, for any chapel in any church.

The whole place is crowded with figures, like Madame Tussaud's. And one soon notices that all the scenes are lit as if from the altar window. (This had for a century been the normal practice in Florence, but here the illusion of light is more overpoweringly convincing than almost anywhere else I know.) Adam and Eve are shadowed as if light poured on them from the one window. This means, of course, that *St Peter Healing* is lit, and the figures assume their solidity, with light coming from the right; *The Distribution of Communal Goods* from the left. Except possibly where a figure has been repaired, shape is achieved by use of light and dark, and so boldly is this done that Adam and Eve (for example) stand out as if three-dimensional, as if they are free-standing statues. This was a startling innovation in Florentine art.

The groupings, too, are harmonious and full of drama: based on the semi-circle, less important figures are arranged around a central and important figure (Christ in *The Tribute Money*, Peter in the *Healing* and *Distribution* scenes), and one group leads to the next with economy and grace. One is invited *into* these scenes. Masaccio is a master of illusion, making the eye travel into his compositions – but only so far, or uncomfortable 'holes' can open up in the walls. Wall-frescoes above all tell a story and must be decorative. Mountain and trees stop the eye travelling too far back into the fictive distance. Walls are walls: they are there for a purpose.

One feels strongly a new *realism* about these figures crowding the tiny chapel. Giotto's scenes somehow admit they are glimpses of the past. Here are solid figures moving in a believable space, and the setting *contemporary*. In *St Peter Healing* and *The Distribution* the buildings, as unmistakably as the mother and child, the washing-lines and the monkey walking on the window-ledge in Masolino's *Raising of Tabitha*, are those of *quattrocento* Florence. *The Distribution*, in fact, is one of the earliest examples of a painting in which architecture is spatially and proportionally realistic. The buildings are on a scale with the figures: they have doorways a human being could walk through. It is precisely this difference that was to shape the whole direction of later Florentine art. I feel the world of these saints is my world; they stand and move and have their being in the world in which I live. They might step out, or I in. And when I contemplate these figures, ordinary men in an ordinary world (even if they are spiritually superior beings and sport soup-plate glories), men wearing simple everyday robes, I am reminded of Condivi's story of Pope Julian II's attempted intervention in Michelangelo's painting of the ceiling of the Sistine Chapel. The importunate Holy Father, on visiting the chapel, missed the *a secco* touches of ultramarine and gold which were normal in frescoes; he wanted the painting to appear more costly and rich. He wanted *gold*. 'It should be touched with gold,' he insisted. But Michelangelo was adamant. 'I do not see that men wear gold,' he replied. The Pope said again: 'It will seem poor.' And Michelangelo retorted, 'Those who are painted here *were* poor.' Just so.

Where else can one see, in such tight juxtaposition, the old and the new? Masolino's *Temptation of Adam and Eve* is delightful: Eve's high, boyish breasts, the convenient modesty-frond touched in with such delicacy; her endless, tapering legs and lovely delicate face. But the poses are merely elegant. The two figures tiptoe out of the garden; they hover, like insubstantial wisps, they tell me nothing. Masaccio's *Expulsion* is, by contrast, expressively almost horrific: the lovely, but implacable angel hovering in menace above them, and the desolate figures below plodding in humiliation from Paradise, Adam with his head bowed, his hands hiding his eyes in shame, powerful, dejected; Eve, her right hand hiding her breasts and her left hand her groin, like some ancient statue of *Venus*

Pudica, furrowing her brow, tilting back her head and seeming to let out an almost audible wail of anguish. They appear to be moving on, on, away from the enchanted land for ever, and the future looks barren and forbidding. Masaccio's design, composition and use of gesture perfectly match the emotional psychology of the moment. Everything is pared to a minimum, like emotion distilled in poetry. There are no superfluous details.

The subject of *The Tribute Money* is interesting. In Jesus's day the Jews had to pay an annual Temple Tax of a half shekel (equivalent to an Attic didrachma, or two drachmas). In the story recorded in Matthew (XVII 24–27), Peter is asked by the tax collectors: 'Does your master not pay Temple Tax?' He replies: 'He does.' Then, when he goes indoors to put the matter to Jesus, Jesus forestalls him by asking: 'What do you think about this, Simon? From whom do earthly monarchs collect tax or toll? From their own citizens or from aliens?' 'From aliens,' says Peter. 'Why then,' says Jesus, 'the citizens are exempt. But as we do not want to cause difficulty for these people, go and cast a line in the lake; take the first fish that comes to the hook, open his mouth, and you will find a silver coin; take that and pay it in; it will meet the tax for both of us.' The point Jesus makes is apparently this: if kings on earth do not tax their families and subjects, why should God? The Jews, as aliens, must pay taxes to the Lord of the Temple, but the Son of God and his followers are exempt. But, disinclined to cause trouble, he performs a miracle. Surely this smacks of legend, or of some meaning hidden from us.

The episode is a mystery, both in Matthew's account and in Masaccio's use of it here. The *Catasto* explanation, or something similar, is very tempting: a mystery-miracle adduced as illustration of a contemporary issue. But why in Felice Brancacci's Chapel?

The fresco itself, generally reckoned as Masaccio's masterpiece, is the largest of the scenes in this chapel that are wholly his. It is a continuous triptych: three scenes are integrated into one, and in it, unexpectedly, St Peter appears three times. This practice, commonplace in earlier fresco-cycles, but by now rather old-fashioned, is known as 'simultaneous narration'. In one frame, a number of scenes take place involving the same character(s). In the centre, St Peter stands to the left of a tranquil Christ, his brows knit, signifying with an outstretched right arm (which leads the eye to the lakeside) that he understands the Master's instructions. Opposite him, and with his back to the viewer, is the tax collector, his arm suggestive of lively controversy, but also contributing both to the leftward movement, and linking with the third scene on the right of the picture, in which he reappears. On the left, Peter bends to extract the coin from the fish's mouth. He is severely foreshortened, a strange, twisted shape, doubled with effort; he appears at waist level of the central group – those disciples grouped so earnestly about the Master, all in attitudes of such earnest moral engagement. Something important is in the air, one feels an electricity.

Finally (right) St Peter, powerful and purposeful, gives the tax collector his money, the arch of his body emphasised by the arch of the building that frames him; his right arm, thrust forward, completes the lift and fall of arm and body which takes the eyes through this wonderfully poetic composition. *The Tribute Money* is an outstanding example of '*disegno*', that drawing, design and harmony of form of which Masaccio was a master. These figures have an inner grace which cannot be described or taught, only intuited.

Each time I look, I see more. The way the artist makes each pose, each gesture speak; his single-mindedness about this; his interest in figures only in so far as they express the action in which they are engaged; his drapery depending on the form beneath it; his rejection of stiff formality or decorative flourishes for their own sake. In this chapel, in the gloom, one's eyes are dazzled. There are so many golden babes and pink-tipped Virgins in this city, goldfinches and grapes and banner-streaming angels: but here is the real thing – immediate, permanent, a statement of faith for all time.

There is a tradition that Masaccio left Christ's face for Masolino to paint – and indeed it is more 'finished' than the rest. If this was a deliberate change of technique on Masaccio's part, it is remarkable, and, so far as I know, unparalleled. I cannot believe it. Legends about the Master have multiplied. Vasari, who lived only 100 years after the artist, has him die at 41 and makes Masolino his master; whereas Masaccio was younger, and seems to have led the way in the Brancacci 'collaboration'. Here it seems clear that Masolino's international Gothic was influenced during the painting by Masaccio's naturalism. Also, just as interestingly, it may be possible here and there to see Masolino influencing Masaccio.

A few hundred miles away, but under the glare of intense publicity, more celebrated grime is being washed away in an operation which continues to excite the liveliest controversy. Olivetti have financed the Brancacci restoration: NTV (Japanese) have given 3 million dollars to the Vatican for exclusive rights to film the cleaning of the Sistine Chapel frescoes, and to produce photographs. While arguments rage in Rome, the Florentine restorers proceed, benefiting quietly from the diversion – because, of course, the same objections apply here. As conservators talk of the 'darkness fallacy' and the 'sculptural fallacy' of Michelangelo's painting, so here our ideas of Masaccio's palette and technique may have drastically to be revised in the light of the work being carried out.

The little Carmelite Friar is making ostentatious noises at my elbow: he rattles keys hopefully and taps on the floor with his sandalled feet. It is time to leave again. Trembling now with tiredness I burst into the brilliant sunshine of the piazza.

A little way along Borgo S. Frediano is 'Sabatino', a *trattoria* crammed with workaday Florentines lunching in jeans and overalls, unshaven and noisy. A long thin room bustles with the tireless energy of Oltrarno. There is one small table where a single customer sits reading his newspaper. A small female child appears with wine, and I see I am sitting near a vast photographic portrait of Clough (not Arthur Hugh, but Brian). It is framed by stained anoraks and flyswatted wallpaper. Beneath it a little vase of plastic lilies of the valley is attached to the wall like an offering. A wizened crone eyes me as she sits chewing guinea fowl in her toothless, gummy mouth.

My companion is relishing his fish: juice streams down the grey-white stubble on his chin. As he mops up the thick sauce with the end of a stick loaf he catches my eye.

'*Razza*,' he enunciates carefully. '*È molto buono.*'

Razza is skate, and he is right. A thick, generous wing steamed in butter and lemon tastes of heaven with a chilled, dry white wine. I eat slowly and contentedly and feel the tiredness drain from me. A mixed salad of Homeric dimensions turns up: cucumber, crisp yellow tomatoes and lettuce, flavoured with basil and mint and drenched in green olive oil; boiled white beans follow, always a local favourite. With half a bottle of *acqua frizzante* the bill soars finally to 12,600 lire. 'Sabatino' is the nearest I shall ever get to 'Sabatini', I suppose, with its vast and glittering international menu. But I seriously wonder if I could be happier.

A beautiful, wine-inspired lull comes over me as I feed on the fish and the frescoes. I mull over the hours I have spent in the Carmine and find myself worrying about *St Peter Baptising*. Am I wrong to think it is Masaccio after all? And what is the precise meaning of *The Tribute Money*? Who is the figure kneeling, partly masked, behind St Peter in *The Distribution* – the figure wearing a Cardinal's robes? What exactly is the significance of the figures who stare so dramatically out of the paintings into the viewer's eye? Why are Filippino's figures *larger* than Masaccio's? What have I missed? Another day I shall come and see it all new, and then perhaps it will seem clearer.

So I resolved. I could not have known then that, in a short time, the 'Brancacci Frescoes' would be 'closed', and that seven years later they would be only a memory.

51

Outside the Carmine there is only one other fresco of Masaccio's in existence. Like the Carmine frescoes, it is enigmatic, it has suffered from repainting, and it is in Florence. Dated around 1425–7, it is a *Trinity* painted for the very spot it occupies today on the left wall of S. Maria Novella, but covered by an altar until its discovery in 1861. It was detached and moved elsewhere, then cleaned and subsequently returned to its original position, where a skeleton, painted in *trompe l'oeil* perspective, was discovered below. The skeleton lies on a chest, and either side columns support a fictive altar table.

Here is a puzzling composition. God the Father looms above the crucified Christ supporting the cross-piece and standing on a ledge behind it: either side of the foot of the cross, Mary and St John are depicted; Mary gesturing at her son, John rapt and tragic. The kneeling donors have been identified by some as of the Lenzi family, presumably husband and wife. But where is the third member of the Trinity? At first one searches in vain for the Holy Spirit (some of us search for ever). But then it appears, as a white dove descending between the Father's face and the Son's drooping, haloed head; and once seen it never hides again. The dove is so like a handkerchief around the Father's neck that its presence is almost sleight-of-hand. The five holy figures are set in a room: lofty and elongated, with coffered barrel vault, and framed by Tuscan Doric columns; they themselves framed by fluted pilasters crowned with Corinthian capitals. Against these, the outer frame, kneel the donors. The recession is startling and deep. Below, an inscription above the supine skeleton ('I was once what you are, and what I am, you will be too') warns passers-by to remember their own end – an occurrence unique in a *Trinity*. The lighting, too, is remarkable and illogical, seeming to emanate from around the body of Christ. The palette, too, is interesting: muted blues and pinks, with the donors standing out nearest to the viewer's eye, he in bright red, she in blue, balancing the Trinity, Mary and St John, and throwing them by contrast further back. The composition is brilliantly original, the fictive architecture completely convincing, but the subject, its purpose and interpretation, remains a mystery. Its contrast with the Brancacci frescoes begs many questions about relative dating, which for the present remain unanswered.

The National Gallery in London has a large painted panel by Masaccio (no. 3046: a *Virgin and Child with Angel Musicians*) which is generally agreed to be the central part of an altarpiece he was commissioned to paint for the Carmine in Pisa, and which Vasari saw *in situ*. I am immensely attached to this arched panel, with its golden spandrils, solemn, pensive, monumental Virgin, and solid, bonny Child; the two angels kneeling behind the throne, and the two foreshortened angel-musicians fingering lutes below (one of whom, charmingly, is listening critically to his own playing). In the cold north its golden warmth is consoling; the shapes, palpable and massy, recall so vividly the Brancacci figures, as does the simplified, heavy drapery, and the shading of the faces. I rarely go to London without sitting wistfully in front of this lovely work.

The Madonna hands the Child some grapes (symbols of his Passion, blood-shedding, the wine of the Eucharist), and he sucks two of the fingers of his right hand; whether he is teething, listless, or relishing the sticky grape-juice, who can say? But the pose is essentially childlike and realistic – how much more so than the pious, two-finger Benediction of tradition! Mary sits heavily on a strongly foreshortened throne somewhat above the viewer's sightline, ponderous, touchable, not hovering in a brilliant mid-air of gold, but in the world we know. The one-point perspective is masterly, and the single-source lighting lends further conviction to the solidity of the forms. The shadow Mary casts on her throne is notable, too (shadows are rarely shown in paintings of the early fifteenth century). The figures live and breathe, things are direct and near. One has only to compare other contemporary altarpieces (by Lorenzo Monaco, say, or Gentile da Fabriano) to see what the young Masaccio achieved. The change is a shock. Masaccio was doing in painting what Donatello had already begun to do in sculpture, and neither art was ever to recover.

He lived for a few short years only, and in his lifetime his success was really only a *succès d'estime*: much more popular was Gentile da Fabriano's intricate, elegant Gothic style. But in a mere five or six years Masaccio's immortality was ensured. Vasari lists at length the famous artists who flocked to see and copy his frescoes. He was buried (Vasari says) in the church he had made famous: it is a fitting resting-place. *Si monumentum requiris, circumspice.*

CHAPTER

III

St Mark's Church, Via Maggio · S. Simone · S. Giuseppe ·
S. Remigio · S. Maria Novella: Chiostro Verde · Uccello · Sir John
Hawkwood · Settignano · Bernard Berenson and I Tatti · S. Maria
dell'Assunta · S. Martino a Mensola

Early sunshine slants through the shutters on to the turkey carpet. I open wide the windows and outside the planes are motionless, a still sea of molten green-gold. The innocent brightness of a new-born day.

It is Sunday, and today I shall go to S. Maria Novella. The Spanish Chapel will be open: *ingresso libero*. But first, I make my weekly pilgrimage to Via Maggio.

Via Maggio runs south from the Arno at Ponte S. Trìnita. Once, as its name suggests, it was the principal thoroughfare of Oltrarno: today it has a string of wonderful, horrifyingly expensive antique shops. Tall and imposing *palazzi* soar skywards on either side, their overhanging roofs in places seeming almost to touch. Among them, the Palazzo di Bianca Cappello stands out, with its fantastic graffiti: it has been extensively restored, and is currently under a new restoration.

Bianca Cappello was the great love of Francesco I (son of Cosimo I, Duke from 1537 to 1570), a Venetian girl, first his mistress (the Palazzo has a secret underground passage leading to the Palazzo Pitti), then, after the death of his wife Joan of Austria, his Grand Duchess in 1579. The romantic couple eventually died within hours of each other at the Medici Villa at Poggio a Caiano. In 1580 Montaigne visited them there, and recorded his impression of the Duchess: she was 'handsome, according to Italian ideas', and had 'a pleasant and dignified face, big bust, and breasts as they like them.'

No. 16, home of St Mark's, the English Church, is a *palazzo* said to have been owned by Niccolò Machiavelli (1469–1527), that extraordinary Renaissance figure – politician, political theorist, and, though the fact is not commonly known today, a gifted and celebrated writer of comedy. The church is entered through an atrium, and occupies the ground floor; its decorations are revived Gothic. The lowish ceiling is a series of barrel vaults supported by pillars with gilded capitals that give the distinct feeling of an ancient stables. And that, appropriately, is precisely what it was. Above, in literally palatial apartments, high-ceilinged and endless, lives the priest: above him are more apartments belonging to the church.

St Mark's was bought originally by a Rev. C. Tooth, a gentleman of Tractarian sympathies, and opened for worship on the Feast of SS. Simon and Jude in 1877. (In 1910 the neighbouring *palazzo* was given to the chaplaincy by a Thomas Brocklebank.) St Mark's was not the first Anglican Church in Florence: that was Holy Trinity in Via La Marmora (near S. Marco), and it was there in 1820, presumably, that Shelley's fourth child, Percy Florence, was baptised. (In 1966 Holy Trinity was sold to the Waldensians.) Until 1980 St Mark's was in the Diocese of Fulham and Gibraltar, and under the jurisdiction of the Bishop of London; since 1980 it has had full Diocesan status. It is now in the Diocese of Gibraltar in Europe, and in the Province of Canterbury. It is all very complicated and improbable, but these are verifiable facts.

St Mark's is small and intimate, with a nice golden triptych as altarpiece; a show cabinet at the rear displaying rich vestments; a dire, breathy organ; and sanctuary lights that twinkle charmingly between the arches. After Mass the whole congregation is invited upstairs to the *piano nobile* for drinks – a civilised tradition, and a thoughtful gesture when so many of them are at St Mark's for the first time, and perhaps anxious to meet compatriots on a Sunday, that day still set apart from others in England, and somehow instinct with memories of home and family.

We are a motley bunch: holiday-makers in swimming trunks; leggy girls in sailing shoes and teeshirts with daring logos; black-suited, pallid, octogenarian clerics doing the ecclesiastical grand tour; locals with boiled lobster faces and names like Rex and Kitty and Marjory; faded gentle-women wearing sensible brogues; and perspiring blimps in white duck jackets carrying canes and floppy hats, their shuffling feet pointing at twenty to four.

Here one feels part of some strange, esoteric society – which is, I suppose, what one is. Outside, the world grates and roars: there is the constant clip-clop of horses, the squeal of tyres, and Afro-rhythms blaring from open cars. (The acrid smell of horse-droppings seems utterly right beside the stables of Machiavelli.) In high summer most of the congregation are birds of passage: the rest, priests and choir and sidesmen and servers, remain a while and go back home. Only a few stay on. The ambience of continuity seems tenuous. Even the priest-in-charge tends to be on leave, and his place is taken by a series of locums, with whom one takes pot luck.

Each year I look around me: *mutatis mutandis* they are the same people: Rexes and Kitties and Marjories, the Hamiltons and the Hendersons and the Knee-Robinsons. We are not *thoroughly* Italianate ('*inglese italianizzato, diavolo incarnato*'); there are not the constant comings and goings of Roman Catholicism, that curious mixture of the rapt and everyday. But our manners and practice have become, shall we say, a trifle *unEnglish*. The *Pax* is a telling moment. To decent Englishfolk, of course, the mere suggestion of physical contact seems anathema, indecent almost, redolent of emotional revivalist gatherings and symbol of all excess. The massive elder, dressed in a thin, rumpled suit, which hangs about his impressive corporation, extends a damp, limp hand, then grunts 'Morning'. One daring young locum insisted on shaking all of the congregation by the hand, a gesture greeted by one embarrassed young lady with an uncertain 'Thank you'.

Then a trendy ecumenical came who constantly referred mysteriously to the 'gaft of maracles', 'rast eternal' and the 'holy sparat'. He also tended to drop his voice at the end of each phrase, with disconcerting results: 'In the name of the Far, and of the, and of the Holy.'

Another locum was chaplain to a large North Country Polytechnic and *en route* to Rome. Another, a dear old boy from deepest Devon, chanted 'I was glad when they said unto me' in tones of the most abject misery, and managed to turn 'The Lord be with you' into a sort of threat. Yet another delivered a memorable homily on the Sacrament of Confession (he was for it), in which Miss Flyte from *Bleak House*, Cardinal Newman, and the Prodigal Son all contrived to make apparently logical appearances.

These summer priests seem terribly vulnerable in such alien surroundings, so unsure of themselves, with trousers and plimsolls peeping from under borrowed surplices, somehow so very disturbingly human. They are people on holiday merely, away from home, like the rest of us.

Over *vin santo* (what else?) in the Upper Room one meets some interesting individuals. The tall, imposing Old Testament prophet turns out to be a painter whose studio, overlooking Piazza S. Croce, once belonged to Annigoni. Now in his mid-60s, he is converting St Saviour's

Church, Aberdeen Park, Highbury (where, in 'the great red church of ... my parents' Sir John Betjeman was baptised) into a 'Centre for Creative Arts'. The chemistry teacher from Lincolnshire is back again, with his sun-bleached mane, gold teeth and startling broken nose. He knows Florence intimately, has been coming for more than twenty years, and remembers the place when it was quieter and more civilised. Each year he wonders if he has had enough. But he always comes back.

There is the usual dotting of visitors and expatriates. Among them, a quiet gentleman in short sleeves and slacks, rather carelessly shaven, introduces himself as Derek Pattinson. He is Secretary of the General Synod, a position thrust recently into unwonted and tragic prominence. Strange to consider the immense power this rather nondescript personage wields back at home, in his black jacket and pinstriped trousers. Subsequent events have burned that brief encounter on my mind.

People come and people go, and St Mark's plods on. The same bodies are scattered about the place, some kneeling, some standing, everyone perspiring. The same organist improvises (surely) a sub-Mozartian prelude, and then we sing George Herbert's 'Teach me my God and King' at the same funereal tempo. A mountainous American, all beams and burs and shaggy eyebrows, reads an Epistle in which the word 'multood' occurs at least six times. The choir consists of two females, one youngish. The other offers 'Let all mortal flesh keep silence' during the communion – a prayer echoed fervently by the congregation, since she sings a quarter tone sharp throughout.

The organ sighs and wheezes asthmatically, and the organist pumps the swell pedal like a frenzied punkah-wallah. And today a bald, rather clever cleric from Northampton preaches a good sermon on Grumbling (he was against it), but declines to invite us to the traditional *vin santo* afterwards (an omission which goes down badly with some sections of the congregation). The pew in front of me is occupied by a transvestite, complete with insistent transplants and metallic blond wig. I wonder why I come here. But I am in good company. Here is Clough (Arthur Hugh, not Brian) in '*Amours de Voyage*':

Rome is better than London because it is other than London.
It is a blessing, no doubt, to be rid, at least for a time, of
All one's friends and relations, – yourself (forgive me!) included –.
All the *assujettissement* of having been what one has been,
What one thinks one is, or thinks that others suppose one;
Yet, in despite of all, we turn like fools to the English.

Have dactylic hexameters, I wonder, ever been put to more novel use in English?

Florence is thin and strung out. The *botteghe* are shuttered and barred as if they had never existed. The city is a hot morgue.

It is the Lord's Day, *domenica*, a splendid opportunity to breach the ramparts of many a tiny church that remains fortress-tight during the week. It pays to abandon projects and dart inside. Meanly, the *Comune* decided some years back to withdraw the traditional privilege of free entry to museums on Sundays, but churches are still 'free'.

As I cross the graceful Ponte S. Trìnita, I recall it was on just such a day that I first entered the church of S. Simone, near 'Vivoli', the most celebrated *gelateria* in Florence, in Via Isola delle Stinche. It stands forlorn and forgotten now, in a charming little square. Originally a twelfth-century foundation, S. Simone was enlarged first in the thirteenth, then in the seventeenth century, when (commissioned by the Galilei family) Gherardo Silvini altered the east end and added blind arcading to the walls of the nave. So the interior is seventeenth-century, but there are a number of *trecento* works, among them the large, Giottesque *St Peter Enthroned* above the first altar right, and, above the side door of the left nave, a polychrome terracotta tabernacle by the della Robbia, with all the lovely cherubs and garlands one expects. Inside it is a Gothic altar (late fourteenth century) containing a marble bust of the mysterious virgin S. Ursula – a very early attempt at realistic portraiture.

While two almost naked German girls sucked their ice creams on the steps beneath the fine wooden door outside, inside the lone figure of a priest was dressing the altar for Mass. As the hour came and went and nobody arrived, I saw him kneel before the High Altar, immensely solitary, in an attitude of mute entreaty.

Another Sunday morning I wandered down Via delle Conce towards S. Croce. A drugged youth was spiralling up the road, colliding with every other doorway, bloodied and bemused, and precocious young Madonnas, their high breasts swaying under skimpy vests, giggled and joked as they clacked past him on the other side of the road. For once, I found S. Giuseppe open. Mass was in progress: three women and a priest, in the costliest of chasubles, speaking into a microphone. Here was an opportunity too rare to let slip.

The church has been modernised (the façade is a nineteenth-century renovation) but it is basically early sixteenth-century, the work of Baccio d'Agnolo. S. Giuseppe was founded on the site of the *Madonna del Giglio*, a thaumaturgical image which comforted criminals *en route* to their death. (This little church next door, S. Maria della Croce al Tempio, founded in 1428 by the Compagnia dei Neri to help those condemned to death, seems permanently closed. It apparently contains a fifteenth-century crucifix which was carried along the road, called – with bitter Florentine humour – the Via de' Malcontenti, to the place of execution.) This image is displayed over the middle altar on the left side. It worked few wonders for me, but conceivably it has been robbed of its powers by layers of overpainting. Today it looks miraculously commonplace.

The interior of S. Giuseppe is high-vaulted, a rectangular aula with side chapels; the feeling is a mixture of restrained Classical and unrestrained Baroque. This place suffered cruelly in the flood, and many of its treasures are still being restored. An important early Santi di Tito *Nativity* belongs here. There is also a massive painted crucifix by Lorenzo Monaco. Behind the High Altar soars a glorious organ casement of the eighteenth century, perfectly matching the baroquery of the painted ceiling. I remember vividly the lofty, colourful tunnel-vaulting, the gorgeous display of organ pipes, and being shown the unpromising outside again almost immediately as the three women left and the priest carefully locked the huge south door behind him.

S. Remigio, in Via de' Magalotti (which joins Via de' Neri and Borgo de' Greci) nearby, is another ancient church which can easily be overlooked even when it is open. (S. Remigius was not canonised for his oarsmanship, as I had guessed, but was a Bishop of Rheims who baptised the Merovingian Frankish King Clovis in 497. He also baptised Clovis's family and court, numbering some 3,000 persons, in a remarkable job lot. Remigius was reputed to be able to 'touch' for scrofula, and to have transmitted the gift to Clovis, and via him to the French and English royal families, who later 'touched' for the 'King's Evil'.) The church is a rectangular hall-church of the eleventh century, originally a pilgrims' hostel, then a seminary for canons.

One Sunday I found a chink in its door, and in the gloom inside came upon a congregation of one man and one woman. The holy water, when I reached for it, was in a stoup which bore the legend 'PASTICCERIA NANNINI, SIENA', a novel and enterprising form of advertisement. Before I had time to reach for my guide, the woman, a cyphotic witch with crocodile skin and a wen in one eye, had sprung from her pew and was waving skeletonic arms at me. She waved so violently that the tattered mantilla she wore slipped from her head and fell to her neck. 'No camera!' she hissed. 'No camera.' When I explained that I had no camera, she was momentarily blank, but returned to the attack with even more grotesque deaf-and-dumb sign language. I gathered I was neither to read nor write during Holy Mass.

'*Ho capito*,' I nodded finally, with as much sarcasm as I could muster, '*Signora*.'

And that is my memory of old S. Remigio: not of the fresco fragments nor the lovely Cimabuesque *Madonna* nor the sixteenth-century *campanile*. I recall only the black and white banding of the vaulting ribs, the modern east end, the bellicose *nonna*, and wondering who on earth crept from the woodwork to light all those candles and sanctuary lamps.

Scullers glide silently past in twos and threes as I stroll up the fashionable Via Tornabuoni. No time to stop and stare. With the most perfunctory of glances I pass the *Croce al Trebbio*. Its name comes from the Via al Trebbio, derived apparently from Latin *trivium*, the meeting of three ways (as *carfax* means four ways) – though here we have in fact five. It was erected to mark the spot where in 1244 the so-called Patarene Heretics were set upon and slaughtered at the instigation of St Peter Martyr. The Patarenes were a sort of hippy sect of vegetarian pacifists. Among other things they believed the world was ruled by the Devil; they were anti-Church and anti-Pope and plainly had to be eliminated. Bearing in mind the Church's performance in those times, its corruption (simony, trafficking in indulgences, etc.), and the bloody battles fought by the Vicar of Christ with anyone who threatened his temporal power, the Patarene reaction, prefiguring those of Savonarola and Luther, becomes easier to comprehend. Well, St Peter, the Grand Inquisitor Dominican who lived by the sword, was eventually martyred by it, as paintings constantly remind us.

I have no time to admire the spacious Piazza S. Maria Novella, all brilliant white in the sun's stare, and the graceful colonnaded Loggia di S. Paolo to the south; nor, on the north side, the greatest Gothic pile in all Tuscany, those lovely, delicate scrolls that connect the nave roof with the aisle roofs; the gorgeous marble inlays and banding, in greens and pinks and grey-blues; the way the arching inlays of the lower course reproduce the curves of the niches below, themselves repeated in a series of arched '*avelli*' to the right of the church round the old cemetery, a marvel of harmony that ravishes the eye.

The Piazza is a good spot for a picnic; teenagers are bathing in the fountain; tired feet are dipped all round into the cool and brilliant waters. There is lush green grass, a million scruffy pigeons, and a brave stall defies the heat and sells coconut in creamy chunks beneath a jet of water. The two marble obelisks topped with bronze lilies, which stand on tortoises of solid bronze by Giambologna, are seventeenth-century. There are prints showing chariot races in this Piazza, where the two obelisks served as turning markers.

Inside the great Dominican church are jewels: outside are the cheapest postcards in Florence. But I am late. I make straight for the entrance left of the façade and rush past the kiosk, though I am called back by a yawning ticket collector who insists on issuing me with a free ticket before turning back to his comic.

Immediately I am in a cloister – the Chiostro Verde, two sides of which are covered in strange grey-green frescoes. They are by Uccello and other artists of the first half of the fifteenth century, and depict scenes from Genesis; faint now, and recently returned after restoration, they seem eery and ghostly under the vaulting and the portraits of Dominican saints. The arches rest on octagonal pilasters, and a low wall runs round the courtyard: four great cypresses encircle a central well. S. Maria Novella has a labyrinth of cloisters, smaller and greater. The Chiostro Grande, decorated by the best artists of the seventeenth century (Poccetti, Santi di Tito, Cigoli) and the only means of access to the Cappella dei Papi, frescoed by Pontormo, is now a Scuola dei Sottufficiali Carabinieri.

On the north side of the Chiostro Verde is the 'Spanish Chapel', actually the old Chapter House, where Cosimo I's wife, Eleonora of Toledo, worshipped with her retinue. It is frescoed from top to bottom, most gloriously. In the far left corner of the cloister is the *Cenacolo*, with treasures that must wait for another day. Today I have come to look at two frescoes on the east wall. They are both by the extraordinary eccentric nicknamed 'Uccello' ('Bird'), apparently because of his fondness for animals, which he kept in large numbers, alive and stuffed, in his house. His real name was Paolo di Dono; he was born in *c*. 1396/7, and lived until 1475. While Masaccio was working on the Brancacci Chapel, Uccello was away in Venice: his roots and training were in the 'international Gothic' school, but when he returned to Florence he was gripped by the new fever for '*prospettivo*' – perspective. The idea, so familiar to us, was then new, and its practice nothing short of revolutionary.

Perspective is a system for representing three-dimensional objects in ordered spatial recession on a two-dimensional surface. It was first invented and systematised in the early fifteenth century, probably by the architect Brunelleschi. Parallel lines, of course, never meet, but to the eye they appear to do so. The 'vanishing point' of a composition is conceptional, but a concept that today needs neither explanation nor discussion. In early painting, the scene is viewed from one central viewpoint; but a

Chiostro Verde, S. Maria Novella

greater sense of reality is achieved if there are two or more viewpoints on the horizon.

Uccello was obsessed by the idea. He experimented with Measuring Points (a means of drawing objects exactly to scale), and spent (wasted, some might say) years constructing more and more elaborate effects. It became an end in itself. There is a well known story that when his long-suffering wife called him to bed one night, all that could be heard by way of reply was the artist muttering ecstatically to himself: '*Ah! Che bella cosa è questa prospettiva!*' If it is not true, then it ought to be. We know Uccello lived a solitary and melancholy life, and was dreadfully poor. No wonder.

The extraordinary and disturbing composition on the east wall of the Chiostro Verde, called 'The Deluge' ('*Diluvione*'), is probably Uccello's masterpiece. Already in 1436 he had produced in the Duomo his famous 20-foot-high memorial to Sir John Hawkwood ('Joannes Acutus', the English *condottiero* who led Conan Doyle's 'White Company'), with a rather disconcerting double viewpoint – one for the horse and rider, another for the base on which they stand. It is in *chiaroscuro*, coloured with *terra verde*, a painted equestrian monument posing as a real one. (The story goes that the stingy Florentines had promised their hero a real tomb, but in the event got away with a mere painting. Yet the funeral the Council gave him was costly and splendid; rich dowries were voted for each of his three daughters, and a handsome annual pension was allotted to his widow. So a charge of stinginess seems ill-founded.) When Sir John died in 1394, he had commanded the Florentine army for nearly twenty years. He is on the shortish side, but powerful, centaur-like, rooted in his saddle. In his right hand he carries the baton of command, and he looks hardly the sort to be trifled with. The fact that St Catherine of Siena could address him (in a letter) once as '*O carissimo e dolcissimo fratello in Cristo Gesù*' may throw more light on her character than his.

But *The Deluge* (*c.* 1446) is a *tour de force*, unique in *quattrocento* Florence for its technical virtuosity and its nightmarish impact. It is no exaggeration to say that, once seen, it stays in the mind forever, disturbing in its message, impressive for its mastery of spatial illusion, and poignantly relevant, too, for a city troubled throughout its history by the most terrible floods. No doubt its ghastly details were provided from the artist's own experience.

The painting is a lunette done mainly in greenish *grisaille*; there are touches of orange-brown for the wood of Noah's Ark and darker green-black for foliage and stormy sky. All is made dramatic by light and shade, its play on the various planes, the way it rests on draperies and flesh.

The Deluge is another example of 'simultaneous narration'. There are two arks, one either side, framing the figures. On the left, it leans rather dizzily away like the side of a vast yawing ship; on the right it is serenely at rest, and the long-bearded Noah leans out of a window in its side. The two sides of the ark slide sharply away towards the vanishing point, and in between is a confusion of human figures, clothed and naked, as the storm shrieks, shredding the branches of a tree which is struck by lightning. Panic and terror are everywhere. A dead, naked child, miraculously foreshortened, seems to float on his back, his body horribly bloated and arched, arms pressed to his sides. Another corpse, this time clothed and apparently adult, lies at right-angles to the child, as if to demonstrate the artist's mastery of foreshortening. On the right, a crow pecks out the eyes of the corpse of a boy. Opposite, two horsemen fight with club and sword. Mankind, it seems, is damned. Humanity struggles and flounders, each man for himself. One figure heaves himself through the neck of a barrel; in the foreground, a woman desperately grasps the waist of a man as they sit astride a buffalo. Swimmers splutter and flail. In the middle-ground, a naked man fends off an importunate bear. Every kind of struggle for survival seems to be going on, claustrophobic, horrible, the stuff of sick dreams. And against all this, right of centre, towers a splendid figure of calm in an attitude of prayer – rock-like, dignified, and in stern profile. This must be Noah (I can find neither Shem nor Japheth nor Ham) before the flood, before he has embarked, when he was a mere 600 years old. The bearded figure is Noah after the year-long voyage and the two months waiting in the ark, releasing the dove to see how far the waters have subsided. He is now 601, a gaunter, more fragile being (he was to last another 350 years) who had survived a great cataclysm, and had his faith confirmed and rewarded.

Around this shining, ethereal figure are the men and animals that were wiped from the face of the earth. Statue-like, Noah stands fixed in his purpose, impassive amid the catastrophe, deaf to the noise of the storm and the cries of terror. The last great flood of Florence had happened in 1333: the next was to be in 1547. But there were regular floods of a more minor nature. It seems Uccello knew exactly what he was painting, from swollen infant to marauding crow.

Next to *The Deluge* is the *Drunkenness of Noah*, faded now, but once the marvel of all Florence for the famous trellis, or pergola, with its clever, strong foreshortening, and the inverted figure of God the Father, who seems to be whizzing head-first down the surface of the wall. Unfortunately, too much paint has been lost, too little is clear today for a proper assessment. The frescoes around the 'Green Cloister' are generally pale remnants: a *Creation of Man*, a *Creation of Eve*. We are left with the sons of Noah, the faint, wispy *Original Sin*, with a red-tressed serpent coiled about the trunk of the tree looking as pure and innocent as all successful temptresses must, and the two elongated figures of Adam and Eve, sexless and elegantly formal in attitude, their long limbs tapering into nothingness. But these are impressions only, hardly the stuff from which art historians grind out their theses. The freshness and brilliance of the originals has been ruined by time and the Arno, and one can only dream.

Uccello died very poor, in 1475, and was buried in S. Spirito. Donatello for one thought he was wasting his talents on problems of perspective, and told him as much ('These things are no use except for marquetry'), and indeed it does appear that he 'polished one facet of his genius' (Vasari's phrase) at the expense of others. After Masaccio, there is something backward-looking in his work. But *The Deluge* stands as a monument to both his technical brilliance and the visionary power of his creative imagination. (Compared with the drama of this single work, the three vast oil paintings of the Battle of San Romano, say, are like sketches for drapery.) I go regularly to the Chiostro Verde to see it, and each time I simply stand and stare. There is nothing in Florence like it. It haunts the imagination.

It is time to go. My eyes have already gone. The custodian looks grimly determined to have his siesta. I stagger into the brilliant world outside and head east towards the Duomo. ... I must eat, but there are things to *see*. Will S. Maria Maddalena dei Pazzi be open? The Perugino *Crucifixion*? I feel my legs working faster. When the fever takes me, I wear seven-league boots, and seem hardly to notice the heat. Churches are open on Sundays, surely.

But I know without trying the massive door in Borgo Pinti that I am too late. '(S) 9–12, 15–18', states one guide; 'Entrance no. 56. 17–19', says another, more up-to-date. 'Entrance at no. 58. *Ingresso libero*', yet another says: '*offerta*'. The truth is probably quite different. Perugino will have to wait. I note the times listed on the noticeboard outside.

Thwarted, but still eager, I thread Via Colonna towards Piazza San Marco and pick up the first bus to come along. It is a no. 10, so I am bound for ... Settignano. Settignano, home of sculptors and painters and artists of all kinds: on its little eastern hill the air will be cooler, and, if the church is shut, I can eat an ice cream and wait. This little *Seitensprung* was surely meant, because the bus is half empty and there is a seat with my name on it. Gratefully I sink into it and take in the less familiar purlieus of the city: the swimming pool, bursting with ripe brown flesh and flashing teeth, glinting medallions, minuscule bikinis; a zoo; and is that the Stadium, colossal in the distance? The images swirl as we lose the dense streets and climb. On impulse I disembark at Ponte a Mensola, deciding to cover the last few hundred metres of the ascent on foot, up the Old Road.

The day is still sizzling as I turn up the slope towards I Tatti, Berenson country, Boccaccio country, and with a world of other literary and artistic associations: Leigh Hunt, Eleonora Duse, Janet Ross, John Addington Symonds, Mark Twain, Edward Hutton. They all came here. It was home, too, to luminaries like Desiderio, the sculptor brothers Bernardo and Antonio Rossellino, Luca Fancelli, D'Annunzio, Niccolò Tommaseo, and 'the Divine' Michelangelo himself.

I Tatti, Bernard Berenson's secluded villa, stands back off the road and snuggles into the hillside behind needle cypresses that stand in ranks like soldiers. One has to climb the road a little way left, beyond the river, which is now dried to a trickle: this is the Mensola, on its way to join up with the Arno. An insignificant gate at road level belies the grandeur beyond. The villa, ochred and long, with green shutters that melt into the pines and cypresses of the tower-topped hill behind, is well protected from prying eyes. Fiesole and Maiano are north-west. The curious Castle of Vincigliata, built for the Englishman John Temple Leader in the mid-nineteenth century, where Queen Victoria stayed, is further on up the hill. Temple Leader was MP for Westminster (1837–47), and originally lived on a small *podere* at Maiano. The massive Vincigliata was in the eleventh century the castle of the Visdomini family. Temple Leader bought it in ruins and had it entirely rebuilt, decorating it with frescoes and coats of arms he picked up in Florence. Those were the days when good Primitives could be had for around a hundred pounds, and a collector could acquire his own museum of treasures for a comparatively modest outlay. Those happy days.

By the time he died in 1959, Bernard Berenson, the greatest Renaissance art historian and connoisseur of his day, had amassed an enormous collection, now beyond price. In high summer admission to I Tatti is not easy. My first visit was a triumph of sheer nerve. A weary female American voice (the villa belongs to Harvard University) explained firmly that the villa was shut: visits would recommence in the fall. But I persisted shamelessly, and, 'Oh, a *professore dottore*?' Well ... in that case it might just be possible. A German professor of Art and his wife were to be given a private tour the next day. If I were quiet she supposed I might tag along.

So I tagged. The German professor's companion was half his age, with a close crew cut; and he turned out to be a surgeon. Our tour leader was a plump girl, practised and efficient. She showed us paintings by

Giotto and his Bottega, Bernardo Daddi, Domenico Veneziano, Cima da Conegliano, Simone Martini, a Giambono, and a wonderful Foppa *Madonna*.

I glimpsed, too, a portrait of Berenson's terrifying wife, Mary, a New England Quaker turned Catholic who lost her faith, sister of the depressive Logan Pearsall Smith. None of her writings, nor other writers' anecdotes about her, endear this strong-willed, obsessive character to me. Her likeness, displayed in a proprietorial position by the exit, positively made me shudder. The clock tower she added to the fine, austere Tuscan manor house while Berenson was away is tasteless and wrong, and spoils an otherwise authentic and unpretentious façade. On first seeing it, Berenson took to his bed in a dead faint. But it was up, and up it stayed. The truly ghastly fresco with which Rene Piot covered the two lunettes in the Library is also directly attributable to Mary. How well I recall the shock, in such noble surroundings, of seeing those dazzling vulgar blues and lumpy nudes in orange and pink and white! In fact it is my single most vivid memory of the entire visit. It is said 'BB', on returning from a business trip, fainted and was bedstricken for a week; when finally he was able to speak again, he ordered the lunettes to be painted over: Piot threatened legal action, and the frescoes were finally covered over. But they were certainly on view on 26 July 1978. There was no uncovering operation, only horror and gloom. Berenson's magnificent library of art, extensive and beloved, and the wonderful collection of master-paintings, stand as an eloquent testimonial to the Sage of Settignano: the clock tower and frescoes are Mary's memorial.

The sloping italianate garden (too baroque for the period of the villa) is grand still, but the cypresses had been stricken by some disease and were blue after treatment with a copper solution. The topiary is neglected and the borders have that indefinably overrun look. As I made my way down through the greenery to the gateway, listening to the German 'Professor of Art's' rather frivolous jokes to his 'wife', I heard one of the Harvard students playing the grand piano: the windows of his room were wide open, and the music floated down the still garden and seemed to crowd the valley. It was popular music, ham-fisted and amateur, as out of keeping with I Tatti as Piot's ugly mural. I found myself wondering, with a shudder, what 'BB' would have thought: the man who lived for beauty, and ranged the churches of these hills and valleys on his bicycle, his pockets full of candles and matches, to see and draw and list the works of the artists he made his life's study.

Today the villa is shuttered and barred, its serried eyes closed tightly, and the shadows cast by its raking roof are deep and dark and sharp-edged. A solitary pine, naked for three-quarters of its length, then topped by a cone of foliage the size of a large Christmas tree, breaks the line of the hill and makes the whole into a perfect composition. Berenson knew what he was about. The place aches to be painted. A single bright red Fiat parked by the little bridge, and a string of washing from a window above, are the only modern intrusions in a timeless scene. The stillness here is audible.

Behind me, a few paces above, in its little piazza is the ancient S. Martino (Masses Sunday 7.30 and 11.00; weekdays '5.00 *or* 6.00'), its pretty campanile a prominent landmark. I consult my guidebook. 'Visitors ring at the door on the right.' So they do, but they get no response: S. Martino will have to wait.

Here, adjoining the Benedictine church (in a room shared later by Kenneth Clark and his bride Jane) a plaque commemorates the deathplace of 'Andrew the Scot', '*il Beato Andrea di Scozia*', in AD 682. Legend relates that Andrew was the first Abbot of S. Martino, and the original oratory on this side is said to be a ninth-century foundation. But hagiographers describe Andrew as the Irish travelling companion of the Irish Bishop Donatus of Fiesole (died *c.* 876) and call him 'Andrew of Fiesole', because he was archdeacon there. The facts are hardly watertight, but there were many Irish missionaries in Tuscany in the ninth century, and few legends are entirely groundless. A decorated *cassone* in a room of the sanctuary houses the saint's relics, and a stone slab in the pavement marks his resting-place. Andrew's sister, later S. Brigid III, miraculously forewarned of his impending demise, was spirited from Ireland to be at his bedside, and, at his request, stayed nearby after his death in a locality close to Fiesole still called Santa Brigida.

I resolve to try again tomorrow, late afternoon. Buses run every twenty minutes, seven days a week, and the area is heavenly, secret, crowded with enchanting views and pregnant with associations.

(But when I next ring the bell to the right of the church, boldly, repeatedly, the door opens only a few inches, and an antiquated peasant woman stands outlined against the gloom. She has left her teeth in a glass by the bed and her lips seem pleated. No, no, the church is closed. Father is ill. Before I can launch into my impassioned plea, the head is withdrawn into the shadows, the door is shut again, and bolted, and I am alone in unearthly silence. Ponte a Mensola seems a world away from anywhere. I would have to try again, again. Whatever else it is, Tuscany is certainly character-forming.)

I gaze up at the hill of Settignano, its pretty, sloping piazza, and the famous villas that cluster round it. Boccaccio knew this area intimately. His father's house is Villa Corbignano, and there Edward Hutton lived and wrote his travel books, and formed the splendid library which, together with Lina Waterfield's collection, was to become the kernel of the British Institute. The house has been much rebuilt, but one needs only a little imagination to see how things might have been: in some places, somehow the *genius loci* obstinately lingers on. In the loud and jostling streets of the city, saints and miracles have been frightened away by the faces that come and gawp. Only a few numinous spots remain. But in the countryside, far from the babel of guided tours, the same old gods, the same nymphs and fauns can be found in their old haunts. In the country nothing changes.

Only a few hundred yards away (and, I suppose, a few less metres) lived Lina Waterfield's mother, the formidable Janet Ross. Janet Ross was an upper-class Victorian beauty of distinction, and a disguised character in many a novel, including one by Meredith and another by her arch enemy Ouida. Among other things, she wrote on Florentine life and history, and concocted a Vermouth from an ancient Medicean recipe which sold successfully at the Army & Navy Stores in London. Here she presided in her castellated fastness, Villa Poggio Gherardo, where tradition maintains the group of young fugitives from a plague-stricken Florence stayed at the beginning of Boccaccio's *Decameron*. 'A palace,' Boccaccio describes it, 'surrounded by beautiful gardens, delightful meadows and cool springs, and in the midst was a great and beautiful court with galleries, halls and rooms adorned with paintings.' In the evenings, the ladies would walk in the shade of an idyllic valley nearby and dabble in a clear brook that tumbled down the hill into Mensola.

Vernon Lee (Violet Paget), an eccentric pro-German transvestite who wrote prolifically on history, aesthetics and travel, lived not far away in the village of Maiano. And on the southern slope of Settignano is Villa Michelangolo (so reads the sign outside: one sees various orthographies in the artist's own hand: Michalangiolo and Michelagnolo are two other variations. But Shakespeare surely wins). Here the great artist spent part of his childhood. Michelangelo was wet-nursed by the wife of a local stone-cutter, and later in his life told Vasari: 'With my mother's milk I sucked in the hammer and chisels I use for my statues.' The villa stands behind dense fir and laurel hedges, immaculately topiaried, wonderfully impenetrable.

At the Villa Capponcina, D'Annunzio and his mistress, the great actress Eleonora Duse, lived, and in Villa Viviano in 1894 Mark Twain wrote *The Tragedy of Pudd'nhead Wilson*.

South-east of the village off the road to Terenzano is Villa Gamberaia. This was the home of the fifteenth-century sculptor brothers Gamberelli, Antonio and Bernardo Rossellino. In their day no doubt a simple farm-house stood here. *No admission.* ('Try', suggests one guide book hopelessly, 'ringing the bell.') More a palazzo than a villa today, the Gamberaia was badly knocked about in the last war, but has been lovingly restored. It is in private hands, and I have never yet managed to visit the gardens: there are (one reads) various levels in which large open terraces alternate with shady ilex woods. But the *pièce de résistance* is the water garden. This is in the familiar renaissance pattern of four parterres with an open centre occupied by a fountain. The lower end of the water garden is enclosed by a tall, semicircular topiaried hedge in which arched doorways have been cut, at whose foot shallow steps slope down to an *orchestra*, giving the impression of a tiny theatre. The garden layout dates from 1610. The owners wish to preserve the place as it is, and who can blame them for keeping the public out? Still, I now have a telephone number to ring, and next year I shall try it. Georgina Masson, connoisseur of the palaces and gardens of Italy, considers the Gamberaia the 'loveliest and most typically Tuscan' she has seen. What better recommendation could there be?

But this is all enchanted country: the very air seems charged with the greatnesses of the artists who have lived here. The atmosphere of the past hangs rich and heavy about the place, clings to the stones, leaves almost a palpable deposit. Sculpture was the master art of the *quattro-cento*, and Fiesole, Maiano and Settignano produced the great names in such concentration that one feels even fifth-century Athens might lose by comparison. On almost every side the views are paradise: the air is cool and clean; everywhere there is stone to quarry. In less than 150 years these tiny villages, now small working-class communities, saw European Art transformed and Florence the artistic metropolis of the Western World. This was the cradle of one of the greatest schools of sculpture in history, these scattered houses and green slopes and sun-ruined, lizard-infested walls. Where I stand; all around me.

I pause to gather pine kernels outside I Tatti and take a last look at the Abbey Church. What a sight Berenson's funeral must have been in 1959 as the procession passed from I Tatti to S. Martino, with its gaudy colours, the flags of Florence and Fiesole held aloft by standard-bearers in medieval costume, and the torches carried up the little hill between the olives to the church by a line of mourners led by seminarists in pure white vestments: what a brilliant blaze of colour against the yellow ochre and raw sienna and silver-greys! How very *quattrocento*! How *right*!

The temperature is 33C, and the heat sits on my forehead as I plod up the Via Vecchia to Settignano. Today the path is overgrown, exhausting, and steep. Butterflies hop lazily in the bright air: small blues, commas, enormous whites with pitch black wingtips; long, electric-blue dragon-flies hover and dart. A tiny newborn kitten mews pitifully among the loose-strife. There is a riot of tansy, and vetch, blackberries still unripe, wild figs; and in the gardens tomatoes hang orange and glossy red, in long regimented rows. There is a deep, golden quiet over the land. The gorgeous villas sleep behind their thick hedges, and large, forbidding steel gates hide their beauties. Under the high sun the climb is hard work, but the views must not be missed.

S. Maria dell'Assunta, the small village church in Piazza Tommaseo, originally of the early sixteenth century, was reconstructed much later, and from the outside, at least, looks unpromising. A delicious breath of wind stirs on the hillside, but that is all. Not a soul is in view. But the church does not sleep: its doors are open, as all church doors should be, and I enter the coolness and focus immediately on the Michelozzo statue of Santa Lucia. In the second altar on the north side there should be frescoes: they have been detached for an exhibition. On the south side, there are frescoes framing an 'ancient wooden crucifix' (the body of Christ, at least, is old). There is a fine pulpit of the sixteenth century by Buontalenti. Behind the altar is a lovely sixteenth-century organ with loft and pipes superlatively restored, which I itch to play. But the dearest treasures are on a ledge in the sanctuary over and behind the High Altar: a Madonna and Child flanked by two kneeling angels, three exquisite pieces from the della Robbia work-shop, all in purest white glazed terracotta. They are attributed to Andrea.

The trip to Settignano is worthwhile for this group alone. There is little or nothing more *simply* lovely in all the Bargello. The enamelled terracotta gleams in the dim light of the little hill church. The left-hand angel kneels, hands joined in prayer, eyebrows delicately arching, pupils col-oured, hair tumbling about her cheeks and shoulders. The other crosses her arms over her breast in humility, her head bent lower, the drapery of her robe flowing wonderfully. She is less well preserved than her twin, but still a treasure. (The secret of the della Robbia died with them and nothing so lovely has been seen again.) I draw up a chair in the stillness and try to take a photograph. No one is near me: my shutter clicks with an alarming echo. I am quite alone. I reach out and touch the lovely creatures. They are not so large; I could even lift them. And here they stand, unattended, all day long, waiting for the fateful day when they are taken to end up – where? In Osaka, Texas, Bavaria? A small Fiat, anonymous and dusty, drives to a side door: one man stands smoking a cigarette on the steps outside the main doors. It is a hot, lazy day like today, the square is dead. Two men cover the angels with sacking, lift them swiftly from their ledge, and place them on their sides in the boot of the waiting Fiat. Are they superstitious about taking the Madonna? Not a bit of it. Nonchalantly, the lookout stubs out his cigarette, turns into the church, bobs, crosses himself and, using the same chair as his accomplices lifts down the Virgin, and soon she has joined the two angels and the boot is closed. She may be chipped in the process: an angel may lose a nose, a lock of hair, a finger. But it will not affect the price. The Fiat rolls quietly down the hill and S. Maria has lost more than a collection box. And what she has lost, some rich collector, none too scrupulous about provenances, perhaps, is going to gain. Perhaps these three pieces, singly or together, bought in good faith for a figure like a telephone number, will end up in one of our own museums, and perhaps one day some humble parishioner on vacation may exclaim as he recognises it, and we shall read about the legal proceedings in *The Times*.

With a sigh I climb down.

Outside I sit on a seat in the square and write a postcard to someone I love, someone far away. There is a dusty postbox nearby which has surely never been emptied, and my card must travel many thousands of miles! *'Per la Città'*, says one side; *'Per tutte le altre destinazioni'* says the other. The breeze gathers strength and tugs at my shirt as, doubtfully, I drop the frail card into the dirty yellow box. But I am soon ashamed of my little faith when a smart van draws up, a postman unlocks the yellow box, and, holding beneath it a cunning divided container (green for the city, brown for elsewhere) collects 95 per cent of the mail. The rest flutter away into the street as he relocks it; these he casually retrieves and flicks *en bloc* into the 'city' pocket.

A bar is open – not the fashionable and expensive 'Caffè Desiderio' in the square, where D'Annunzio loved to stop, leaving his beloved greyhounds, inseparable companions, in the piazza outside; but one above the square called 'L'Oasi', where the service is lethargic, but there is a fine terrace on which to drink iced tea among begonias and azaleas and hydrangeas, and dream over the hills and gather strength for the descent.

Via Simone Mosca leads down to the panoramic Piazza Desiderio, where I lie on the wall, propped on one elbow, and simply gaze. There is a slight heat-haze, but I can still pick out over sun-bleached towers and tiles the cupolas of the Duomo and S. Lorenzo; the Badia (just), and beyond the obtrusive Synagogue a glimpse of S. Croce. On the right, bearded with green, heaves Monte Cerceri, where Leonardo, that archetypal Renaissance man, once tried to become a second Daedalus. From here the hills look gentle enough, like moss mounds, cypresses alternating with umbrella pines, and the last, like so many puff-ball parasols, create on their own the effect of a cloudy dreamland, a thousand soft parachutes settling among the cypress needles. With a shock I realise I am hungry. Only a handful of pine kernels since last evening, and, as everyone knows, the tourist marches on his stomach.

A couple of days later, escaping from the city, I steal Lisa's car and return in the cool of evening. In the hills the air is intoxicating, the light perfection. The countryside is pure Lippi, and little S. Martino is – open!

It is ten minutes past six and the door is open! The six o'clock Mass, of course, has not yet begun. Inside there follows a rustic rite attended by four peasant women and celebrated by an old priest who has seen much of life and dispensed now with all fripperies.

Taddeo Gaddi's triptych of the Madonna between SS. Maddalena and Lucia smiles from the little altar at the end of the right aisle: opposite is a superlative *Annunciation* by a follower of Fra Angelico. On the first altar of the right aisle, in a splendid Renaissance frame, is a *Madonna and Child enthroned between SS. Andrew and Sebastian*, which some scholars give to Cosimo Rosselli, and above it a fragmentary fresco of the Crucifixion. Opposite, on the corresponding altar of the left aisle, which is beautifully carved, is a fine Neri di Bicci *Madonna with SS. John Baptist, Francis, Mary Magdalen and Clare*, and above, in the lunette, a fifteenth-century fresco of St Francis receiving the stigmata.

But dominating all, on the High Altar, is a sumptuous triptych by a follower of Orcagna of the *Madonna and Child between Saints*, including a portrait of the donor, Amerigo Zati (after whom Berenson's villa is supposed to have been named); the predella is decorated with a *Pietà* and stories of the saints.

For a tiny church in the middle of nowhere, these are remarkable treasures – or so one might think if one had not seen it all a dozen times before. In the half light the rich gilding and gorgeous colours glow against the sombre stonework, reminding me of the long, long history of worship and devotion here: a thousand years of prayer have gone before, and these paintings are a symbol of worship and an outward sign of man's faith. Could the artists who painted them ever have dreamed, I wonder, how much an irreligious and materialistic world would one day pay for their works?

At last I find the little stone marking St Andrew's tomb, and, inside the sacristy, see the legendary *cassone* decorated with stories from the life of the saint. There is also a fine coloured, wooden bust of the saint dating from the fifteenth century. I would love to know exactly how the artists mixed and preserved their colours, so that, five centuries on, they could burn and pierce so keenly, yet with such depth and subtlety. Age lends a mellow distinction, that venerable patina which somehow reassures, while reminding us of our own littleness.

I emerge into the evening and drive towards Fiesole, up past I Tatti, endlessly up a snaking road to the little cluster of houses called Maiano, and suddenly come upon 'Le Cave', a fashionable *trattoria*. (It stands on an unlikely spot, but locals as well as tourists beat a path here most of the year round.) Nearby are the quarries of *pietra serena* for which the locality is famous. Benedetto da Maiano (1442–97) had his home here, a sculptor of genius whose sketches for the superb pulpit in S. Croce can be seen in our own Victoria and Albert Museum.

Then, slipping downhill again, using my nose as guide, I finally reach Villa Il Salviatino, shown on my map, I later find, as a children's hospital. The villa once belonged to the Bardi, a wealthy banking family. Today it stands in boring suburbs, and a sign informs the passing world that it now belongs to Stanford University. I Tatti is Harvard, La Pietra ('Villa Acton') will be left to the University of New York. Back home I peruse the curious document called 'Concierge Information', with its facts and figures and times (these range from massage parlours to Rotary Club meetings), and come across a page devoted to 'American Schools, Colleges and Universities' in the area. I count no less than 21, and resolve firmly to wave the flag and register with the Istituto Britannico next time I pass its offices in Via Tornabùoni. The British Institute – that strange, rather lovable gathering of limp-wristed art historians, Ruskin-devouring spinsters, and language students, with yesterday's daily papers, noisy air conditioning, and splendid roomy w.c. complete with sun-warmed throne.

Why not?

CHAPTER

IV

*Trattoria 'Da Nello' · garden of the Museo Archeologico · Piazza della
Santissima Annunziata · Palazzo Grifoni · Giambologna and Grand
Duke Ferdinand I · Ghirlandaio and the Ospedale degli Innocenti · alarm
in 1966 · Arciconfraternita della Misericordia · the
Annunziata · frescoes in the Chiostrino dei Voti: Andrea del Sarto,
Pontormo, Franciabigio · ristorante 'Paoli'*

 I am in Purgatory. Last year I travelled the famous cricket pitches of the civilised world with Mosey and Boycott. This year, with Bonagiunta and Sordello and Statius and the gluttons and the shameless women of Florence, I am gulping the penal waters. I am lumped with the eleventh-hour penitents, the contumaceous, the lethargic, the headlong, on the terraces where the proud, envious, irascible, slothful, avaricious and lustful are chastened and corrected. *O Fiorenza mia!* O the grim prospect! The Inferno was dreadful enough, but if those who die 'in contumacy of Mother Church' really do stay thirty years on the lowest slopes of Purgatory for every year they have shown disobedience in their earthly lives, what crowds there will be, what a great wailing and gnashing of teeth! In this respect, perhaps, if in no other, English shops and Italian time-keeping are salutary training.

My landlady is short, of mercurial temper, small-boned, with raven hair and aquiline nose. To a gentle Anglo-Saxon Fiammetta can be terrifying. She is separated from her husband, her delightful children have grown up and moved away. I seem to have known her for ever.

Fiammetta sometimes works, sometimes not. Mostly she grumbles and frets and smokes. In 1577, Don Vincenzo Borghini called Florence 'a city with a good eye and an evil tongue', and he knew his Florentines.

But for some reason I am fond of Fiammetta. Her apartment is grand and old, only a few yards from my first home in Piazza d'Azeglio. 'Nothing works,' she tells me, without exaggeration. She takes lodgers, all sorts: opera singers, students, even impecunious schoolmasters. She is not proud. A large useless cat lopes about the place shedding hair and bullying for food. The arrangement suits me quite well. Fiammetta sleeps long and for days our paths do not cross. Occasionally, when she is even more bored than usual, we blossom into conversation.

'I don understand you.'

'Oh?'

'You do *narthing*. Read. You only *read*.'

'Well . . .'

'What do you read?'

'It's Purgatory. Dante's *Purgatorio*.'

Incredulity, contempt.

'I don understand Eenglishmen.'

She leaves and does not return until the small hours: I count six turns of the massive key in the fortress door and hear the imperious click-clack of her heels over the tessellated floor. I annoy her, I know it. She hates my *Eenglishness*.

'Why you don speak Italian?' She speaks English to show her contempt.

'Why *you* don't?'

'Ah!' she throws back her head in furious resignation. '*Ah!*'

Even in the extreme violence of her temper, Fiammetta remembers to show herself off to advantage.

'I'm going to the Annunziata today.'

'Annunziata!' she spits, slightly correcting my pronunciation. '*Tu sei pazzo!*' Now she pouts, and suddenly her waist looks very tiny. 'You are crazy!'

'Fiammetta!' I plead.

And the brow of thunder dissolves and her eyes become doe-like. 'You want to go dancing?' Gratuitously, in a voice full of Florentine promise, she adds 'With me?' She enjoys late nights and later mornings: I go to bed early.

'I'm invited out this evening. Sorry.'

'*Fa niente.*' Already she is gone. This will mean flowers or cigarettes. I can tell from her tone, from the swivelling of her slim legs, from the defiant wag of her behind. Flowers or cigarettes must follow, but they are easier than dinner or dancing. Dancing is loathsome, and dinner with Fiammetta always involves quails' tongues in aspic or strawberries out of season.

As the sun climbs, Purgatory palls. I grab my *borsetto*, turn the long, unwieldy key six times in the front door, and cut through the park in the centre of the square. A couple of tramps lie asleep on benches; children scream their morning happiness; and bold pigeons pick their way about beneath the planes with round, watchful eyes of amber.

It is only a few minutes along Via della Colonna to the Piazza della Santissima Annunziata. But as I pass the crossing with Borgo Pinti, something tugs at me. The corner house, I know, was where Michelangelo built himself a studio in 1503. But it was something else. Ah yes: 'Da Nello', at no. 56, a neat little *trattoria* with interesting pastel portraits hung on the walls. I have always liked this place. I ate my first *dentice all griglia* there (dentex is sea bream, a costly fish like a larger, flatter version of red mullet, and with a delicate, moreish flavour to its white flesh); and Mario, with his distinctive silver thatch, always has time to stop and talk; and Pasquale, the chef and owner, with his equally distinctive droopy, French moustache, will show you your fish, tell you exactly what he is going to do to it, and cook it practically in front of you. Pasquale is a great character and the complete professional; his kitchen smells are ambrosial. Mario brings the fish to your table and, in less than a minute, has filleted it. There is a nice family atmosphere about the place. Mario's pretty wife and young daughter argue and flirt with a nice hint of discretion. A trickle of tourists find their way here (a well-known *pensione* stands almost opposite), but by and large the clientèle is Italian.

I wander on down the Borgo towards no. 58. But the great doors of S. Maria Maddalena dei Pazzi are shut and silent again. Again I note the putative opening-hours and turn back to the long Via della Colonna, its newspaper kiosks and small-fronted shops, the high, gaunt façade, dirty now and graffitoed, of the Liceo Michelangelo. This closes the north-east side of the old monastic complex: the refectory, on the opposite side, in Via dei Pilastri, is in the steely hands of the Carabinieri: the chapter house is home of the famous Perugino *Crucifixion*. Such proximity is a torture. Everywhere one stands only inches from immortal beauty: a single wall is often all that keeps the passer-by from untold treasures, some still undiscovered, some wrongly attributed, others overpainted, mouldering; treasures under restoration, closed to the public, in storage, on loan to exhibitions in America. One sees such a tiny fraction. I hurry by, intoxicated at the thought. I feel the dead ages all about me, and walk smaller and smaller and smaller. The stones echo Florence's old power and glory.

Via della Colonna ends in a narrow tunnel which opens gloriously into the most lovely square in Florence. Perhaps there are few *piazze* in all Tuscany so fine.

The 'tunnel' is an archway over which runs a corridor linking the Ospedale degli Innocenti and the Museo Archeologico. Before it, on the right, there stretches an exquisitely tended garden: gashes of bright viridian and terracotta glimpsed through railings, with prickly succulents in giant pots sporting gay vermilion flower-spears, and quiet tombs guarded by silent white statues. It has all the lushness that the majestic, endless Boboli Gardens lack: they are sprawling and dusty and leg-defeating, and can be cruelly vulnerable to the sun. Here is something more English: secret and small, shaded and jealously kept. The treasured, precious order: the contrast of marble and topiaried box-hedge, the neat arrangements of hibiscus and geranium of the traditional country cottage. Florentines nod and cry '*Che bellezza!*', no doubt preferring, in their hearts, the grandeur and formality of the Boboli. But this is a little paradise: through it and above it visitors pass between inscription and fountain and grassed-over Etruscan tomb, and the gardeners go quietly about their watering and potting. Late one night, in the bright moonlight among the tombs here, a thin cat smiled at me. He smiled as if he *knew* something.

Strange people, these Etruscans, who gave so much to Rome. Do they rest here in peace, I wonder, among the scarlets and greens and bright garden hoses? Do they sleep and forget they have been torn from their proper sepulchres to be exhibited to an alien people? Do they smile at the gropings and guesswork of scholars as they hug to themselves the secret of their language? Each week another necropolis is looted and vandalised; but those almond eyes seem still to mock. The earth of Tuscany teems with Etruscan treasure, and the loudest shout goes up not for another burial chamber uncovered, but for one that is found by scholars before the grave-robbers get there.

After the little, dark passageway, the Piazza della Santissima Annunziata (formerly known by the more manageable title of 'dei Servi') bursts upon the consciousness in a brilliant explosion of light. Balance, elegance, poise. It is a rectangle aligned on a north-east axis to the Duomo: three sides are lined with arcades. On the right is the Annunziata itself, mother church of the Servites, or 'Servi di Maria', founded in 1234. Left, is the Ospedale degli Innocenti (the 'Innocents' are the massacred children of Bethlehem, patrons of the thousands of orphans who were housed here), ennobled by Brunelleschi's superlative portico (begun in 1422), earliest example of the new Renaissance architecture – each space exact in its dimensions, and each of a measurable relation to the whole building. And opposite, modelled on it, is Sangallo's sixteenth-century arcade for the Confraternita dei Servi di Maria.

At the corner of the Via dei Servi, facing the church, is the stately Palazzo Grifoni (now the Budini Gattai), with its three tiers and ornate figures. Ugolino di Iacopo Grifoni was Cosimo I's secretary, a wealthy man whose privately owned man-of-war fought in the Battle of Lepanto in 1571. In 1563 he paid Ammannati 100 ducats to build him this palazzo. The façade on Via dei Servi is of brickwork, making it practically unique in Florence, where plaster or stone is the norm. The sculptural details are attributed by some experts to Giambologna himself.

Roughly in the centre of the Piazza, facing the Duomo, and with his back to the church, is Giambologna's bronze equestrian statue of Grand Duke Ferdinand I (1549–1609), his last work, begun in 1607 when he was in his 80s, and made from a pair of Turkish cannons captured at the Battle of Lepanto (where Cervantes, I recall, lost the use of his left hand). It was finished by his pupil Pietro Tacca, who also executed the two bronze fountains here in the shape of slithering green sea monsters. Browning's curious poem in *terza rima*, 'The Statue and the Bust', fancifully explains the direction of Ferdinando's gaze towards a window in the Palazzo: the Grand Duke, falling in love with a bride of one of the Riccardi, had della Robbia make a bust of his lady, and commissioned 'John of Douway' to set him on horseback in the square where he could adore her likeness for all time. There is no bust, probably was no bride, and the first Riccardi to come to the Palazzo in question arrived in 1800.

Jean de Boulogne was born at Douai in 1529, learned his craft in Flanders, and came to Italy in the mid-sixteenth century; after the death of Michelangelo he was the most celebrated sculptor in Florence. Giambologna, as he came to be called, assisted Ammannati in the making of the more successful parts of the Neptune Fountain in Piazza della Signoria; his *Rape of the Sabines* stands nearby in the Loggia dei Lanzi, a sculpture in the true Mannerist style, composed to be walked round, to be viewed from every angle.

The equestrian statue of Cosimo I (1519–74) in the Piazza della Signoria is also by Giambologna – a noble monument to a remarkable man, perhaps greatest of the later Medici. It was he who moved from the Palazzo Vecchio to the Palazzo Pitti, across the Arno; he was responsible for linking the two strongholds by the corridor designed for him and built in secret by Vasari (in five months, he boasted, but with the loss of five lives, because the work was done so hurriedly). Cosimo was a hard-headed, merciless general, but an intelligent patron of the arts, and a determined political leader. When he assumed power, Florence was weak, bankrupt and dependent on outside help: when he died, he left her among the strongest cities in Italy.

The two great monuments, which have been riding aloft in two celebrated squares for 400 years, are father and son. No earlier Medici had had costly monuments set up to themselves or to their predecessors, and the later statue seems based on the earlier: the attitude of rider and horse is the same, though Cosimo's head turns to the left, and his mount raises front right and nearside left legs – a mirror image, in fact, of Ferdinand. Cosimo is a grim figure, formal, foursquare: he has more in common with the antique Marcus Aurelius of the Roman Capitol than his Renaissance forebears – Donatello's *Gattamelata* in Padua, and Verrocchio's *Colleoni* in Venice. He sits rather forward, and leans a trifle far back for modern style, weightily glued to his saddle. The horse is immensely powerful in the forequarters, his neck arched and controlled with no tautness of reins, all muscle and heart. His mane and tail are shaggy and windswept. All in all, the horse's restrained movement and strength contrast strangely with the rider's stillness and ordered, military manliness. Cosimo appears in total control.

Ferdinando is a later figure in every sense: more human, however imposing, as his horse is more naturalistically equine. It was this Ferdinand who moved the butchers, linen merchants, hosiers, greengrocers and blacksmiths from the Ponte Vecchio and replaced them with the goldsmiths and jewellers who still monopolise the place; he started the building of the Princes' Chapel behind S. Lorenzo, and the Medici family vault, which involved the founding of the *Opificio delle Pietre Dure*, or workshop of craftsmen in semi-precious stones, which is still in existence. (This *intarsia*, or inlay of marble with stones, has become a great Florentine speciality.) Ferdinando also constructed aqueducts, built the Forte di Belvedere, the Villa of Artimino, the Villa Medici in Rome, and brought to Florence the Venus de' Medici – in the nineteenth century the most revered sight in the city – all of which argues energy and taste. On the back of his plinth is a plaque added by Tacca, which shows bees swarming around a queen bee, and bears the legend: MAIESTATE TANTUM, implying that Ferdinando (who, to his credit, renounced a cardinalate before becoming Grand Duke) relied on *auctoritas* rather than *imperium* – a pretty enough tribute to a busy builder and enlightened ruler, but the sort of thing one might expect for any powerful Medici Grand Duke, good or bad. In fact, Ferdinando, who succeeded in 1587, was capable and popular. He threw off his city's dependency on Spain, and built up a strong navy; he encouraged music and science and the arts. Opera can be said to have been invented and first performed at his court. Under his wing Galileo carried out much of his experimental work. After Ferdinando, the Medici story is one of decline and gradual decadence.

Cosimo, then, was the first Medici to be honoured with an equestrian statue, when Ferdinando commissioned Giambologna in 1587. (The sculptor was 58 years old.) To cope with the enormous technical difficulties of casting a monumental horse and rider (the horse was cast in one piece), the Grand Duke built Giambologna a new studio with foundry and furnace attached. This studio is at Borgo Pinti 26, the Palazzo Bellini: a bust of Ferdinando surmounts the door. Here were cast both the equestrian statues, father and son, as well as others, including a copy of Cosimo's charger for Henry IV of France (which, after a picaresque translation, stood on the Pont Neuf until it was removed, and, with nice irony, melted down for cannon during the Revolution); and here Giambologna finally died in 1608.

Today, equestrian statues are no novelty, but one appreciates them better when one learns something of the sheer technical expertise required for their execution. Bronze-casting, though age-old, seems even today an antique operation. The atmosphere of every foundry is the same, a medieval ambience created by the mingled smells of sweat and flux and the urgent heat of the furnace. Pouring-day brings with it a restless nervous energy: pouring demands immense skill and concentration. It can so easily go wrong, and it so often does. We know from Cellini's own words how when he was casting his *Perseus*, and everything was going wrong, he desperately threw his own domestic plate (200 pewter plates, dishes, pots and pans, bowls and salvers) into the molten metal to fill up the mould. His workshop had caught fire, and rain had poured in, cooling the furnace disastrously. Then there was a mighty explosion when the furnace-cover cracked open in the intense heat. The alloy had been burnt to nothing, the molten bronze streamed out. Cellini brought the dead to life again and rescued his *capolavoro* for Cosimo and posterity. But at what personal sacrifice and with what immense effort are such works produced!

The artist can do little but stand and watch and pray. Even if the cast is more nearly perfect than was hoped, there is a mountain of work left to do: the vent holes have to be filled and filed down; then there is the chasing and burnishing, the colouring and polishing. And this operation must be repeated for every single object, small or large. Imagine, then, the excitement Ghiberti's *John the Baptist* (1414–16) generated when it appeared in the niche at Orsanmichele, the first life-size Renaissance statue cast in bronze; and the miracle of a giant horse cast whole!

Viewed from any angle the Piazza is harmonious and lovely. The best view is from Via dei Servi, but every view is sweet, the Foundling Hospital sweetest of all. In the pendentives of the arcade are the famous medallions which Andrea della Robbia added around 1487, twelve roundels of cerulean blue enamelled terracotta, each 3 feet 3 inches in diameter (all but the end-pairs, which are nineteenth-century, are original), each featuring a pure white baby in swaddling bands, arms spread in pathetic, mute appeal. Each, on close inspection, is slightly different. These are 'those divine babies whom no cheap reproduction can ever stale', which Forster's Lucy Honeychurch so enthused over, 'their strong white arms extended against circlets of heaven'.

The Hospital, now the 'Istituto degli Innocenti', still continues the charitable work it began in the 1420s. Originally boys, when old enough, were sent to become apprentices to shipmasters in Livorno. Today many are adopted, and abandoned infants ('*gittatelli*', or 'castaways', was the fifteenth-century term) are happily less common. In the left corner of the arcade, under the portico, is a small barred window, where once unwanted children were left on a wheel, the '*rota*', which was used until as late as 1875.

These charitable institutions are affecting places: their motive quite obliterates the feverish, hard-nosed commercialism and venal attitudes of the burghers of today – these men of flint, who Dante said 'came down of old from Fiesole and still have stone in their souls' ('*e tiene ancor del monte e del macigno*'). Rock-like they may have been, and some remain, but charity was never far from their thoughts. In 1330 no less than 12 per cent of the entire population lived on charity. The Compagnia dei Buonuomini di S. Martino, the Arciconfraternita della Misericordia, the Compagnia di S. Maria del Bigallo are just three examples. The Ospedale di S. Giovanni di Dio was a hospital founded in 1380 by the Vespucci family; and S. Maria Nuova, of such humble beginnings when Folco Portinari founded it in 1286, is now vast and modern and superbly equipped.

The Ospedale degli Innocenti has a proud history. Between 1395 and 1485, of 7,534 children registered in the books of this hospital and that of San Gallo, with which it was then affiliated, 1,096 had mothers who were slaves. Dates of arrivals were kept meticulously, with the names of mothers where known, and the records make pathetic reading.

Inside, as one might well imagine, the walls are saturated with history and festooned with precious art. The slender Ionic columns of the Chiostro delle Donne (the cloister reserved for women working in the Ospedale) leads right off the main cloister, the Chiostro degli Uomini; and here a series of plays and concerts were presented in 1987 in connection with the 40th Estate Fiesolana, a little raised stage having been erected at the west end. There was rain and the constant threat of rain, but it is impossible to convey the enchantment of the setting: remote, intimate, timeless. One felt privileged to be sitting in such a place. In a sense, the acting and music was irrelevant accompaniment. I felt I could not feel *enough*.

The church, S. Maria, consecrated in 1451 by the sainted Antoninus, Bishop of Fiesole, was completely rebuilt in the eighteenth century, but the della Robbia *Annunciation* in the lunette over the side door more than compensates. Mary kneels reading, her right hand held across her breast in humility. Her book rests on a stand supported by a Classical plinth. A wonderfully winsome angel, hair curled and tousled, also kneels, his right hand pointing, his left hand holding a bunch of lilies: his wings just fit the curve of the lunette. He is caught at the moment of speaking, eyebrows raised, lips slightly parted. Between the angel and Mary stands an ornate vase containing more lilies, their slim leaves bright green, their blooms purest white. The dove flies above Mary, and, at the crown of the lunette, a bearded God the Father hovers, looking down on the Virgin, his hands parted, palms upward. He and a platoon of five sweet *putti* are swathed in clouds. In an exquisite semicircular frieze, thirteen more divine, chubby cherub-heads float, each different, each haloed and cushioned on angel wings, their background a cunning deeper blue against the sky-blue background of the Annunciation-scene. One can see the various sections in which the scene was assembled: the drapery, especially that of the angel, is breathtakingly fluid; the hands a marvel of delicacy. This composition, based on Leonardo's *Annunciation* in the Uffizi, dates the work somewhere around 1470.

Upstairs in the gallery overlooking the cloister and in a long room beyond is a collection of pictures and detached frescoes. But the best here is Luca della Robbia's pure white *Madonna of the Innocents*, 2 feet 8 inches high, ravishing in its eloquent simplicity. Mary supports the naked Christ Child in the crook of her arm, her expression humble and resigned, already tinged with suffering and helplessness. The lovely child unfurls a banner reading EGO SVM LVX MVNDI, while Mary points with the index finger of her right hand to an inscription on the blue base: *Quia respexit Dominus humilitatem ancillae suae*, the second verse of the *Magnificat*. The simplicity of this work is outstanding; the later and flamboyantly polychromatic works of Giovanni, however superb in technique, can be garish and overdone. Luca is my hero, and Andrea comes next.

In the same room is Domenico Ghirlandaio's gloriously bright *Adoration of the Magi*, the colours yesterday-fresh, with splendid portrait heads in miraculous, incredible flesh-tones. (The predella, by another hand, can safely be ignored.) This work once stood on the High Altar of the convent church below: here at the end of the long, narrow gallery it is framed by an elegant arch and its brilliant reds and blues draw all eyes towards it, as if it were a gateway to somewhere wonderful. In the foreground, a pair of foundlings kneel in conventional, but moving humility; in the background is a *Massacre of the Innocents*: the children's mothers, in the desperate flight, are caught between a river and the executioners. The river, fading into the distance, divides the serene landscape typical of this artist and much early Tuscan painting: a lovely mountain crest is seen against a sky of transparent blue.

I greatly admire Ghirlandaio. Berenson dismissed him contemptuously as a mere 'illustrator', and his verdict has been endorsed by most writers, with the not altogether reassuring exception of John Addington Symonds, who wrote that Ghirlandaio possessed 'the keenest intuitions, the deepest thought, the strongest passion, the subtlest fancy, the loftiest imagination' and judged him superior even to Mantegna! (How words acquire a momentum of their own and run away with truth!) Today, Ghirlandaio is considered essentially prosaic as a painter, and more important for his historical interest, his scenes and portraits of contemporary Florence. Even in his own day he was thought rather old-fashioned. But he has real virtues, and his works are an abiding pleasure. Berenson was more than once wide of the mark; Lord Clark was disastrously mistaken on at least one famous occasion; and time has shown that Ruskin frothed at the mouth over quite the *wrong* things. One must not be intimidated by reputations nor duped by fashions. At the very least, Ghirlandaio was a master craftsman.

I stand with my back to Ferdinando and look towards the Annunziata, the wide *antiporto* (completed, as the inscription proclaims, at the expense of the Pucci) sheltering the broad main door and two smaller side doors; above and beyond the atrium, the classical tympanum, and beyond that the tiled dome covering the apsidal rotunda. I am always content here.

Why are arcades so satisfying? Why is the rhythmic rise and fall of arches so soothing to the human spirit? It springs, no doubt, from our natural longing for order and proportion. Nature is never regular for long: forest trees grow where they please. So the artist must make his sky to suit his landscape. And here is man's improvement on nature: tree-columns placed at orderly intervals, with the upward arching of their branches reduced to a stylised perfection. Cloisters seem always quiet and remote

Duke Ferdinand

and conducive to reflection, like the 'lonely woods' of Lully's song, a 'haunt of peace' where, even in the heart of a teeming city, civilised man can be alone with himself and from where he can 'go forth strengthened and renewed'.

The sky is cloudless, deep cobalt above, and pale, transparent sapphire where it rests on roof and hilltop. All at once a hot day in 1966 comes back – a day when I had cause to be grateful to the hospitals of Florence.

My wife and I were staying in Via Pietro Giordani, which runs east of Piazza d'Azeglio, in the apartment of an old family friend. It was the month of August, on such a day as this. We had trundled our ten-month-old son with his floppy white sun hat and four tombstone teeth along exactly the road I have walked today, into the coolness of the Annunziata – a pleasant morning's airing.

Then, as I waited on the veranda for lunch, I became aware of a strange sobbing noise. I found my wife in the kitchen at a strange angle to the floor, her eyes closed tightly, in a state of shock. She had all but severed the top of her left index finger. Luckily the baby was fast asleep. But blood was everywhere and, ominously, my wife was beginning to shiver. I rushed to the floor below and rang the Cordiès' doorbell. Soon, too, I discovered that Carlo was a Professor of French Literature at the Sorbonne, and we conversed rapidly. A taxi was called: it would arrive in seconds. Meanwhile the solicitous Signora Cordiè tried to sterilise the wound by squirting alcohol on it. As she thanked her, my wife collapsed. Half carrying her, I got her to the lift, begging our friends to keep an eye on the baby. Then, as we reached the steps of the front door, her eyes rolled up and she fainted a second time. I recall the exact sequence.

She was wearing a flimsy summer dress. As she fell, I drew my arms round her tightly, and she slithered, or rather her body slithered, limply but gracefully into a fluid heap on the pavement. I was left clutching her dress. A taxi screamed to a halt and somehow I bundled her into the back seat, her finger, grotesquely bandaged, pointing heavenwards rather like Giambologna's *Mercury*. By the time I had closed the door of the taxi we were hurtling along in third gear. We went like agents of destiny, shooting through red lights, round hairpin bends, along narrow cobbled alleys, flying over crossroads, with only a token adjustment of the throttle. Our driver knew his job.

This alarming ride, fortunately not witnessed by my wife, took only a few minutes. All at once we were drawing up at the far corner of a venerable building, frescoed and grand; the façade of what was plainly a church, in its centre, was scarcely reassuring. A brilliant illuminated sign read PRONTO SOCCORSO. The taxi driver hooted impatiently for attention. Then, when my wife was out of the car and leaning against me, he suddenly disappeared. (I was subsequently notified of the fare: 400 lire, the price of a large Campari in those far-off days. Fresh eggs were 24p per dozen, and butter had climbed to the acrophobic height of 36p per lb.)

Looking back, this was probably the point at which my wife ought to have staged another collapse. But she remained standing, a dead weight against me: my shirt had been white when I put it on; now I looked like one of Garibaldi's freedom fighters. Through her dishevelled hair I watched four men advance towards us with a stretcher. They were all in black from head to toe, with strange antique caps covering their ears. One, I recall, was a poorly shaven bluebeard, a portrait straight from the National Gallery. At their waists they wore heavy rosaries. I remember praying my wife would not see them, but, as she came round a second time, I felt her stir, then stiffen: then she fainted again. On the stretcher she looked ghostly pale, a frightful contrast to the black gowns of the medieval porters.

Later I was to find the Brothers of the Misericordia a common enough sight in the city, and once, turning a corner near the Badia, I witnessed a whole platoon of them, this time wearing tall, pointed hoods with slits for the eyes, and with streaming torches in their hands, as they swayed along an alleyway carrying one of their Brothers to his final rest. Here was the full ceremonial, and I stood numb and still as it passed. And now, on this first occasion, their sudden epiphany, air of anonymity and fatal urgency, seemed hardly calculated to revive the spirits.

The interior of the Ospedale was a model of modernity, sparkling and crisp and clean. Solicitous staff ushered us through spotless, shining corridors into the side-room of a theatre. After a few minutes I thought I heard singing. It *was* singing. Someone nearby was giving a very decent rendering of '*La Donna è mobile*'; the voice was tuneful and manly, and, in the difficult cadenza, commendably accurate. In walked a cheery surgeon, his mask hanging loose below his chin, still singing Verdi between mouthfuls of chicken, which he gnawed from a drumstick. In a second, he sized up the situation. His eyes twinkled. He finished a last bite of chicken, threw the drumstick over his shoulder – bullseye – into a pan, washed, put his patient on a couch, unwrapped the bandage, flung the gauze away, examined the cut, and finally smiled dismissively. It might have been a heat-rash.

'*Vivrà!*' he said. '*Vivrà!*' She'll live.

Several stitches and anti-tetanus injections later, she did live. Back at the apartment, our son was still beatifically asleep and the spaghetti could have been plaited for ship's cable.

One week later we all returned to the Ospedale to have the stitches removed and to pay for the treatment. No one was remotely interested in taking our money. Administrative staff (delicious, coal-haired nurses called Emma and Gisella with tight uniforms and dazzling teeth) seemed touched at our gratitude, cooed at the English *bimbo*, and, when pressed, estimated the charges at 1,000 lire, then about 55 pence. When I could find no one to give the money to, I put it in a poor box.

It was a good year to get the feel of Florence in 1966: in every sense the year was momentous. Ever since, I have experienced a thrill of recognition as I come across an old haunt, or recover long-forgotten tracks in the quarter I first knew. Exactly twenty years on, on the very same day and within an hour of my first visit, I found myself standing outside Folco Portinari's hospital. A mere coincidence, of course, but why do these coincidences happen so uncomfortably often?

The S. Ambrogio market; the flea-market; a small wine shop in Via de' Macci; a *rosticceria*, perhaps, in the same alley, with a familiar face; and birds singing from cages in the same ancient windows ... all these are the stuff of my earliest experience of the city, its smells, colours, noises, tastes, the pulse of its bustling life.

Our apartment was full of precious antiques, an environment which caused anxious moments for a young couple with an energetic, inquisitive child. Inevitably there were mishaps. An antique bedside table was overturned, a brass handle snapped. So I found my way about the artisans of Oltrarno and learnt a small, specialist vocabulary of words for brazing and soldering (the work cost me 8p). When a fragile old bedspread was soiled, I had to make the rounds of the dry cleaners and, in the process, was initiated into the arcane science of fabric-cleaning. A sweet middle-aged lady took such pains to explain the operations to me: the coverlet was too old, too delicate, she would have to fade the whole piece. It was a risk. It was up to the Signore. She would do her best.

Then (it was naturally a Sunday, the day before the Feast of the Assumption) *en route* to the Certosa del Galluzzo, the dynamo of my aged Austin decided to die: a red light glared brightly at me from the dashboard, and Five Star Insurance, so reassuring in England, meant less than nothing in *Ferragosto*. The Automobile Club gave complicated directions to the only *Elettrauto* open in Florence – somewhere north of the city, deep in the suburbs.

It was to be a long trek, but finally I found it and a pleasant young mechanic waited for the engine to cool. There was no question of replacement: in those days dynamos were dismantled and repaired. By 9.40 p.m. the job was done. (It would last until I got home again, I was told: it lasted in fact until I sold the car some 5 or 6 years later.) It had taken several hours: the charge was 6,000 lire, then £3.43. I had only 3,000 lire on me, so drove the young mechanic back to the apartment, paid him in sterling, and returned him to his garage.

And so one's armoury of Italian is built up. By now I could get by in cars, babies, markets, laundries, metalworks, wine and museums. Twenty years later, I know more: words like inflation, divorce, ulcer, credit card; I know about spectacles and detached retinas, AIDS and Fine Art, but doubt I am either happier or wiser. As the brightly lit, carefree snapshots show, they were golden days. The faces were unlined, skin smooth and tight against the bone, and smiles spontaneous. How wonderfully, blindly confident those young profiles were! With what unquestioning faith they trusted themselves to the future! Who were they, I wonder? By what mysterious process did they become what they are today?

Those strange, black-hooded men were representatives of the Arciconfraternita della Misericordia, Brothers of Mercy, the best known charitable institution in Florence and one of the oldest such institutions in the world.

It was founded in the days of Dante, and arose out of the Black Death, which (according to Boccaccio) carried away nearly 100,000 Florentines in the second quarter of the fourteenth century. Against the bubonic plague the doctors were helpless: whole families were annihilated; there were ghastly mass-interments. The few who (unlike the seven ladies and three young men of the *Decameron*) stayed in the city and survived had to act as porters, transport the sick to hospital, organise burials of the dead. From these grew the kernel of the Brotherhood.

The headquarters of the Misericordia has always been in the Piazza del Duomo, in the shadow of the great *campanile*. Originally in the Bigallo, across the way, in the sixteenth century it was transferred to the corner of Via Calzaiuoli, where it is today, in the very heart of the city.

The Brotherhood exists to give spiritual and material help to all who need it. The Brothers (and Sisters – there are more women than men) are volunteers drawn from every social class: they are unpaid, and give their services anonymously. All that is required of them by way of qualification is that they are Catholics, of decent reputation, and over the age of 16.

Today, the characteristic black capes, with hoods or balaclava-type hats covering the ears and part of the face, have gone: these were adopted during the plague of 1630, and were originally red. In other respects, too, organisation has been modernised: dispensaries and rest-homes are run with great efficiency; blood-donoring is organised; emergencies of every sort are met by professionals and lay staff. There are dialysis centres, health advice clinics, a First Aid Station. The Brothers collect and transport to hospital any victim of an accident within the area of their jurisdiction, they collect corpses and take them to mortuaries, assist the bedridden, provide night attendance for the sick, and carry out medical examinations at their headquarters, where a team of doctors is always at hand. All a Brother gets for his work is the ritual 'God give you merit for it'. Financed entirely from private donations, the Misericordia has to be run on a tight budget. But the noble work of charity goes on, the Brotherhood is thriving.

When I called on the Archivist, a bundle of restless energy called Don Foresto Niccolai, I had to wait a long time outside his door while a lady in obvious distress was given counsel. Then Don Foresto had to hurry away to officiate at Mass in the Duomo. He is a wiry, dynamic man, totally dedicated to the Brotherhood and its ideals: he loaded me with vast tomes, inches thick. 'You read Italian? *Bravo! Allora* ...,' he gives me a harassed smile. 'It's all there!'

In 1987 the Brotherhood numbered more than 20,000, counting Heads of the Watch (priests and laymen), 1,645 on active daily call, 'paper-tearers' (Novices), sisters, medical specialists, etc. Everything is abuzz with life: the whole headquarters, apart from a marvellously restful oratory (with a magnificent della Robbia altarpiece, and a marble *St Sebastian* by Benedetto da Maiano) exudes an air of friendly but businesslike urgency. Black housecoats have replaced medieval gowns: doctors in white coats sit coiled like springs waiting for the next emergency. I read a list of the *provveditori* of the Misericordia since the 1570s, and names like Rucellai, Gherardini, Corsini, and Guicciardini are prominent. There are pictures, too, of the Brothers at work: one, of the 1348 plague, in which 'Giotto's' campanile is certainly leaning, and the Duomo, without its nineteenth-century multicoloured icing, looks very fine. Another shows the operations of the Misericordia during a cholera epidemic as recently as 1855.

The Compagnia di S. Maria del Bigallo (its charming little Gothic *loggia* was erected at just the time Orcagna was working on the gorgeous Orsanmichele tabernacle), on the opposite corner of Via Calzaiuoli (Hosiers Street), was originally founded in 1244 by St Peter Martyr for the suppression of heresy, but subsequently concerned itself with the welfare of prisoners and the care of orphans and foundlings. (Infants were left in the *loggia*, and the Society assigned them to foster mothers.) The Museo inside, which possesses many precious works of art commissioned by the Misericordia and Bigallo, is currently closed to the public. But after centuries the work still goes on: most recently, a sort of reception centre has been set up inside the ancient loggia, where lost tourists and unhoused students can receive immediate advice from a team of cheerful polyglot helpers.

But the sun is high. Soon the Annunziata will be closed, and there are treasures inside too rare to miss.

I step over the ancient flags past the blind beggar and the toothless *nonna* with her votive candles. The *atrium* beyond was one of my first sights of Florence and it is one of the city's glories. First loves, last loves.

The *atrium* was the entrance hall to a great Roman house, an inner court open to the sky: this one is a small, colonnaded rectangle built in the mid-fifteenth century from designs by Michelozzo based on those for the courtyard of the Palazzo Medici, which was covered in the nineteenth century with a sensible ceiling of glass. (The effect, for an Englishman, is nostalgic: I am always reminded of bowls of cherries, croquet, and the gentle, earthy exhalations of exotic plants.) There are never more than a couple of sightseers here, and today, though Mass begins at midday and a trickle of locals hurries to the church entrance, I am on my own. The priest's versicles, magnified via a microphone, and the congregation's straggling responses, are already swirling round the *atrium*.

The walls glow with rich colours. This is the Chiostrino dei Voti ('Votive Cloister'), so called because faithful pilgrims had life-size images of themselves made and hung them here: originally these hung from the rafters inside the church, but by the seventeenth century they overflowed – there were as many as 600 *ex votos* here. A curious sight it must have been, like a ghostly mass-execution, and the practice has been long discontinued.

The frescoes on these walls (all but one of which were painted in the second decade of the sixteenth century) are important. They have been detached, restored and returned to their places with great care, and among them are undoubted masterpieces. Since the flood of 1966 and the restoration that followed, tourists are in some respects better off than their predecessors. A recent, thorough, cleaning has uncovered high on the north side of the Chiostrino a *trompe l'oeil* picture of a man and a vase of lilies peeping from a little window – a charming *jeu d'esprit*, and a healthy reminder that these artists were, after all, humans.

Decoration of this cloister began soon after its completion. Baldovinetti's *Nativity* is earliest – an enchanting, atmospheric work done in the early 1460s, though now the colours are faded (the artist mixed them wrongly), giving the shepherd and Baby and fluttering angels and much of Mary and the adoring ass an eerie phantom-like quality. But the ivy-clad stable is refreshingly realistic, and nothing can detract from the beauty of the background: a plain with meandering river, dotted about with the sort of trees one glimpses in the long nurseries flanking the Florence-Pisa auto-route, and bounded by heaving mountains. The carefully lopped tree framing the stable and the fruit trained to climb on an adjacent wall could only be Tuscan.

It was Cosimo Rosselli (painter of the S. Ambrogio fresco) who was commissioned to paint the first of the S. Filippo series, the *Vocation and Investiture* in which God appears aloft in a strange, canopied chariot drawn by what appears to be a lion and a lamb. Del Sarto did the other five.

Andrea d'Agnolo di Francesco was born in 1486 in the parish of S. Maria Novella: he is known as 'del Sarto' evidently because his father was a tailor. He is 'the faultless painter' of Browning's dramatic poem. ('Ah, but a man's stretch should exceed his grasp / Or what's a heaven for?') Vasari and Michelangelo considered that he had exceptional genius; but today he is less admired than he deserves. Vasari's biography exists in two versions (1550 and 1568), the second being a corrected edition. But in both del Sarto's lovely wife Lucrezia (whom Vasari must have known: he claims, after all, to have worked in the Master's *bottega*) comes off badly. We are told she exercised such a potent fascination in Andrea, had him so completely in her thrall, that he neglected his talent and remained poor. After 1513 she is recognisably present in nearly all del Sarto's paintings. She was, says Vasari, 'impressed upon his soul', and 'he never depicted a woman's face anywhere without taking it from her.' 'But had you,' Browning makes him say, '– oh, with the same perfect brow, / And perfect eyes, and more than perfect mouth, / And the low voice my soul hears, as a bird / The fowler's pipe, and follows to the snare – / Had you, with these the same, but brought a mind!'

The *Scenes from the Life of San Filippo Benizzi* (a thirteenth-century Servite friar who rose to become head of the order in 1267), commissioned by the Servites of the Annuniziata, are now in a poor state of preservation, but show del Sarto experimenting in the early stages of his maturity (1509–10). There is a naturalness, a mixture of the solemn and sacred and every-day, which is surely quite new. In the *Curing of the Possessed Woman*, the four figures watching from the lofty gallery are a characteristic, personal touch, as is the light and tranquil countryside seen through the central archway, with its delightful wispy tree and silvery river. The *Resurrection of a Child at the Saint's Deathbed* is amusingly called by the Florentines

'*I Morticini*' ('The Two Little Dead Boys'), because the child, dressed in a white shift, is depicted both dead and risen! This is the fresco restored very early by Passignano (died 1636). While work was being carried out on the façade of the church, the face of an old man (in the group on the far left) had fallen to the floor of the cloister and crumbled into fragments. The Duke sent his best painters to repair the loss, but none of them dared tinker with the work of so great a master. Passignano persevered, however, and piece by piece glued the fragments together so that the repair was almost invisible.

Fra Mariano, sacristan of the Annunziata, had predicted that del Sarto would make his name with these frescoes, and famous he became indeed, so that he was pestered with a hundred commissions. But he kept his links with the Servites (he is buried here, to the left of the great triumphal arch of the sanctuary beneath a statue of St Peter) and accepted, with a raised fee, an invitation to paint two more frescoes. In 1511 he worked on the *Voyage of the Magi*, to the right of the entrance door, connecting it in theme with Baldovinetti's *Nativity* on the other side of the door. Records show that he received his final payment for this picture in December 1511, and the *Magi* marks a significant turning-point in his career. It may be that he travelled to Rome with his young pupils, Pontormo and Rosso, then teenagers, and there saw things which inspired him to try a new style. Certain it is that del Sarto knew what Raphael and Michelangelo were up to around this time.

In the *San Filippo* series the compositions are constructed round a central axis, and the distribution of the figures is rigidly balanced. But in the *Magi* there is no 'centre': the procession, complete with camels and a towering giraffe, winds from the distant right towards the façade on the left, and, if del Sarto had painted a *Coronation of Herod* in the lunette over the door, as he intended, it would have seemed to be progressing there, and on again to the *Nativity*. (The giraffe is interesting. A giraffe had come to Florence in 1487, when Andrea was one year old, as a diplomatic gift, and immediately became a celebrity. It lived for many years – long enough, in any case, to find its way into paintings by Franciabigio and Piero di Cosimo as well as del Sarto. Nothing like it had ever been seen before.) This is an extraordinary and a challenging painting, and its atmosphere is novel: it is human and anecdotal. There is also a certain detachment which allows a feeling of ambiguity to affect the scene, and it was this that signalled the undermining of solid Renaissance composition, and the beginnings of the movement called Mannerism. Del Sarto was one of the pioneers of the Mannerist *avant garde* in Tuscany, and it is in this that his greatest importance lies. I wonder endlessly about the 'supernumeraries' – the distracted, beautifully realised figures in the fore-ground. The group of three at the extreme right (in clothes that contrast starkly with the richly-costumed Magi) are (left to right) del Sarto himself; his friend, the sculptor Sansovino; and Ajolle, a musician at the Annunziata. But who is the character on the left seen in profile, as he looks, almost smugly, over his left shoulder?

The *Birth of the Virgin*, next to the *Magi* on the right wall, is justly reckoned one of the artist's masterpieces. It is signed and dated 1514. The room is high-ceilinged, elaborate, elegantly classical; the bed has an enormous canopy, on which little angels frolic irreverently; the womenfolk busy themselves happily over the child's ablutions; they wash her in front of the fire, and tend the pensive Ann. There is a peace and serenity about proceedings, and the slightly ironic mood of the *Magi* is continued with the solitary figure of Joachim, slumped in meditation on a settle, the old girl peering from behind a curtain, and the challenging glances of the maids who look out of the picture (the girl on the extreme right of the bed, holding a trencher, is surely *provocative*). These outwardly turned faces, linking the spectator with the events depicted, are a trump card in the artist's hands, and they can be startling and haunting.

Here the great *quattrocento* tradition of Ghirlandaio and Filippino Lippi is quite transformed: we have grand architecture cheek-by-jowl with dom-estic events; the figures move about with apparent indifference to the sacredness of the moment. Colours are bright and warm, and the choice of mauves and purples, against yellow ochres, viridian and muted reds, points forward to the palettes of the arch-Mannerists.

In this picture, too, one recognises the typical 'del Sarto' women: these are drawn from Lucrezia, his wife, or are at least variations on her. Those widely separated eyebrows, often seen in his Madonnas, with an inverted triangle between them; the bridgeless nose, and the slightly protruding upper lip, are characteristic. The story is told (by Baldinucci, a century later) that when Jacopo da Empoli was copying this picture in 1570, Lucrezia, now an old lady (her husband had died forty years before), stopped on her way to Mass and pointed out her likeness to him. Again, there is no central focal point: two separate groups, harmonious in them-selves, cluster round child and mother, and the balance is achieved by rhythms and tones rather than a rigid symmetry.

As I stand here, seeing and remembering more, I realise suddenly that Mass is being said in English. I am drawn into the dark interior, and at once my attention is claimed by the famous tabernacle. It is immediately left, aflame with candles; a hundred *ex votos* glitter around the miraculous

Annunciation at its heart, and rows of silver sanctuary lamps and chandeliers gleam and wink in the darkness.

This shrine is perhaps the most revered and elaborate in all Florence: it is instinct with mystery, crowded with extravagant ornament of the kind associated with the Counter Reformation. The painting itself forms the backcloth to the altar, and is a fourteenth-century copy of a much older work, itself much repainted. Legend tells of a thirteenth-century monk called Bartholomew, who was painting an *Annunciation* on the wall. Despairing of ever being able to produce a face perfect enough for the Virgin, he fell asleep and woke to find the work completed. Naturally angelic intervention was inferred. The Virgin has subsequently been repainted more than once, and rather poorly, but the legend persists, and medallions and lockets by the score attest the powers of the painting. The intervention was certainly angelic in one sense: the shrine became famous, and the church a busy centre of pilgrimage. The tabernacle is by Michelozzo (1396–1472), who happened to be the brother of the prior. Its canopy, however, is seventeenth-century, and to my mind a miscalculation of taste. On the floor, an inscription boasts proudly that 'the marble alone cost 4,000 florins'.

Everything is adrip with costly embellishment; the pavement is inlaid with porphyry and serpentine; a heavy bronze grille protects the miraculous painting; rich gilt and marble and bronze cry aloud the baroque reaction to austerity and restraint at its giddy apogee. Once I thought this the most enthralling church in Florence: every step reveals more lavish gifts of the Medici Grand Dukes. But I am no longer happy among the glitter and confident exuberance.

Mass is reaching its climax. After the Consecration, a handsome Irish priest leads the congregation (a few lay, a flutter of women religious) in singing unfamiliar words to the tune 'The King of Love my shepherd is'. (In Prato once I heard the sad Somerset folksong 'O Waly, Waly' sung unaccompanied during the Distribution, and Benjamin Britten's plangent setting seemed a strange memory of life in a far distant world. A musical priest of my acquaintance assures me he heard, in exactly similar circumstances, a good rendering of 'The Foggy, Foggy Dew' in a Roman church.) The service ends with a splendid '*Ave*' led by the Irishman, and to this the nuns warble a pretty, tuneful descant. The priest has a fine baritone voice, and he enjoys his singing. As he vanishes with the silverware, the nuns are left to their gentle soprano, and the singing finally dies away.

While the people disperse, I wander among the chapels, aghast at the mad baroquery of the Feroni Chapel (by Foggini, 1690–3), where del Castagno's *Vision of Julian* on the altar was rediscovered as recently as the nineteenth century: next door is the same artist's horrifying *St Jerome with two Holy Women and the Trinity* (St Jerome is haggard and toothless, with a bony, unattractive chest bared to the midriff. The crucified Christ is shown above in ambitious, and not very successful, foreshortening. The artist's attempt – a *pentimento* or 'second thought' – to disguise the awkwardness with an *a secco* overpainting of seraphim has peeled away to reveal exactly what he had attempted to conceal!) Of the plethora of distinguished art here, the Perugino *Assumption* in the fourth chapel right, and Bernardo Rossellino's monument to Orlando de' Medici in the last aisle chapel draw me the most. At the end of the aisle is the glorious, early sixteenth-century organ, now superbly restored, and I long to hear it thunder and set the vaults of the rotunda shuddering. The High Altar, with an elaborate silver ciborium, is High Baroque; the frontal is again by Foggini.

I determine to penetrate the semi-circular tribune to see Giambologna's crucifix and tomb, and pass through a narrow passageway in the left transept. But Confession is in progress. I hear hushed tones, a broken, stuttering murmur, and the priest interrupting poignantly every few seconds with '*Mio figlio! ... O mio figlio!*' So I withdraw. The church is about its business, and there will be other opportunities.

Out in the Chiostrino again, a man and a woman appear at my elbow and ask, in foreigners' Italian, if I would 'explain' the picture to them. I begin in Italian (no reaction), continue in German, falter, and go on in French. Finally, to their relief, I begin again in English. But the Franciabigio was a blind: what they really want to know is where the 'Giottos' are.

So I tell them, and return to the frescoes.

Franciabigio's *Marriage of the Virgin* was painted in competition with Andrea's *Birth of the Virgin* in 1513. This painting is mutilated, because the artist flew into a rage when he found that the Servites had dared unveil the fresco before he had granted permission. He took a hammer and smashed the *intonaco*, and would have done more damage had the friars not heard him and restrained him. As it is, almost all the Virgin's face is missing. (The man behind Joseph, poised in the act of striking him, is giving him 'a reminder', comments Vasari, 'a modern custom at marriages'. The curious seated figure in the right foreground is apparently 'breaking his rod which did not flower'. According to legend, each of Mary's suitors was to bring an almond stick, and the owner of the stick which budded overnight was to be regarded as God's choice.) Out of respect for Franciabigio, no other artist would make good the damage, so the disfiguring mutilations remain.

Jacopo Pontormo (1494–1556) is next. His *Visitation* (1516), a lovely composition based on del Sarto's *Birth of the Virgin*, stands out even in this distinguished company. It is youthful Pontormo (he was 21), graceful and cunning: a pyramidal central grouping (whose apex is the Virgin's head) is fitted into a semicircular group, full of movement, which mirrors the curve of the classical colonnade behind. Upon the architrave, between cherubim, sits God the Father. The familiar soft palette is in evidence: pale pinks, greens, red-browns; and a brilliant white moves through the centre of the fresco, confidently and tellingly balanced. A delightful, naked boy, whose relevance escapes me (but whose beauty does not), sits on the steps absently examining his thigh; and there are the now familiar faces staring at the spectator. A woman, too, seated on the steps, centre left, with a dazzling white headscarf, is disturbingly lovely. Against the classical architecture, the costumes (decidedly 'biblical' rather than uncompromisingly contemporary, like del Sarto's, or a mixture, like Franciabigio's) contrive somehow to seem utterly right.

A kindly, long-suffering friar, his smiling face unruffled, is loudly closing doors. He is old now, and bent, and knows me from many years. I pretend not to hear him.

The remaining fresco, last in the series, an *Assumption* with choirs of smiling angels encircling Mary, is the work of another of del Sarto's followers, Rosso Fiorentino (1494–1540), a friend and almost exact contemporary of Pontormo. It is his first dated painting (1517), and in fact represents a second attempt, the first finished work having been rejected by the friars some three years before. The talented Rosso was to go on to better things. This is the least happy production of the series, and a good note on which to step out again into the world. There is so much here at the Annunziata, so much kept behind locked doors, out of reach of the casual sightseer! At least I shall carry with me the Baldovinetti landscape, the del Sarto *Magi*, and the Pontormo *Visitation* – enough to feed on until I find a *trattoria*.

But instead I go back to my room and sleep a tortured sleep. I had been reading the 23rd Canto, Forese Donati's tirade against the 'brazen women of Florence', and before that, the Canto dealing with sloth, with *accidie*, and the fourth of the seven terraces of Purgatory, where Dante found great crowds of penitent spirits stirred to energetic action by *buon volere* (right will) and *giusto amor* (proper love). These are the spirits of Laodiceans, the lukewarm, half-hearted souls who have failed in life through negligence, through procrastination, through lack of love. And their cry, translated, seemed to me pure Gerard Manley Hopkins, and haunted me:

Make haste, lest time for little love
be lost, that zeal for well-doing
may make grace green again.

For these poor souls (I realised) cannot pray: they must wait for the gift of grace, and the waiting racks them.

And when my eyes open again, the air is noticeably cooler, and the sunlight slanting, and I am ravenous.

'Paoli', in Via dei Tavolini, almost in the shadow of Orsanmichele, is an old favourite of mine. The waiters wear black ties and white jackets, and the setting is unique. The building was once a chapel: one sits under large, slow fans in romantic lighting, the ceiling is vaulted and the walls frescoed (the name Annigoni is whispered – 'when he was a poor student, you understand'). 'Paoli's' *antipasti* are a triumph; and I have had a *saltim-bocca* and a *costoletta Bolognese* there which were the 8th and 9th wonders of the world.

Tonight an old friend greets me, a portly, moustachioed waiter who for some reason always hails me as '*professore*'. I prepare for a Lucullan repast. The choice here is bewildering. Bepe is on top form: his attention is personal, his recommendations made *ad hominem* as if based on a life-time's intimate acquaintance, and his acceptance of my final choice comes like an accolade. He compliments me on my Italian: I compliment him on the food. This seems an entirely satisfactory arrangement. That beatific sense of the sweetness of life envelops me as I watch the white jackets swimming about the place, engulfed in flames, or brandishing pepper mills a foot long: the new incense is brandy-impregnated, the sanctuary candelabra have been transmogrified into portable wine-coolers; the acolytes flutter among the congregation, stylishly helping them to food and wine, advising, and explaining their mysteries with a superb economy of gesture. Our tables are spread and running over: together we grovel in worship at the altar of earthly pleasure. And, at the next table, as the crown of the feast, is a lovely Swedish girl to look at, her features cool and clean and aristocratic, arresting in the candlelight.

As a lone diner, I know I am the curse of restaurateurs. In order to avoid the temptation of staring at fellow diners, I carry a small volume about with me. Tonight I am determined to finish with *Purgatory*. A nutty white wine is working its way about my resolve, but I climb through lust, pass through fire, find Beatrice in the car at last, and with Dante feel the shock and loss of Virgil's sudden effacement. Somehow, with another mouthful of *osso buco*, the nettle of remorse stings not quite so badly. (I catch the Swedish girl's eye: she has remarkable bones, and she is tanned the colour of honey.) But it does sting. *Purgatory* ends in a message of hope, but as I drink the chill waters of Euone (Vernaccia) and fork the last luscious gobbet of meat into my mouth, I am in the third circle of *Inferno* again with the tormented glutton Ciacco, rained on, pelted by sleet, beaten down until the sounding of the Angel's trumpet. (The blonde, deserted momentarily by her friend, can avoid my eyes now only if she moves her chair. It is a straight choice between loss of face and conversation with a stranger, and we are soon talking. She has a marvellously low, musical voice.)

Perhaps half a bottle would have been enough. Does a *pasta* course on top of *antipasti* automatically damn one as a glutton? Who is the beautiful woman on the steps in Pontormo's *Visitation*? Whose are the lovely, staring faces? (The girl friend has come back, but the fine-boned blonde seems to be smiling with her eyes.) Well, I had no lunch, and tourism is hard work. At least the third act of Dante's *Comedy* promises to be less harrowing.

If I work hard at it I might well be into *Paradise* by the small hours of tomorrow.

CHAPTER

V

Villino Stibbert · Palazzo Davanzati: the Museo della Casa Fiorentina
Antica · trattoria 'dell' Agnolo' · the Annunziata again:
Fr Lamberto · Cappella di S. Luca · the Servites and
Montesenario · Perugino's Crucifixion *in S. Maria Maddalena dei*
Pazzi · Firenze notte

 But heaven is where I cannot be. Paradise this morning seems somewhere else, outside of Florence. Via the Cenacolo di Foligno (shut again), I head for the station, a half-formed plan in my head to see something new.

I have never ventured out to the Villino Stibbert. A bus sits waiting, and I hop on it: the trip is fated. A large, very old and dirty Franciscan, with a straggling white beard, takes his place in front of me as the bus shudders into motion.

Frederick Stibbert (1838–1906) was a colourful character. Scottish son of an Italian mother, he fought with Garibaldi, made himself a millionaire, and became a compulsive collector of, among other things, armour and weapons, paintings and porcelain, furniture and tapestries. His villa is the result of a nineteenth-century amalgamation of two fourteenth- and fifteenth-century villas. The collection is eccentric, wide-ranging, and displayed with unusual flair. At his death, Stibbert left it to Britain; Britain renounced it in favour of the Comune of Florence; and ever since it has remained intact, despite the thefts which are the inevitable outcome of opening a house to the public.

From Via Vittorio Emanuele I walk up the Via Federico Stibbert, a pleasant incline with a feel of great salubrity to it: we are in smart suburbs, where the city is merely a distant hum, carefully trained blossoms peep over high, exclusive walls, and the air is noticeably cleaner. The villa stands in its own quiet, shaded park : it is state-run, public, and therefore littered. Mothers push prams about; old folk sit and read their papers in unaccustomed peace. At the entrance a large notice is erected with its enigmatic imperative translated into five different languages: COMPLY WITH FORBIDDEN ADMITTANCES! The mystery is immediately compounded by another: WATCH CHILDREN AND BOYS! Guided tours are hourly, on the hour, and I wait blinking in the sunlight.

Soon a young couple of Italian holidaymakers arrive, and then our guide, an unattractive, bored, middle-aged housewife with aching feet. At a pace which permits no loitering she leads us through the 64 rooms of the museum. Questions are parried or answered with a grudging lack of enthusiasm. The paintings are generally unlabelled and badly lit. Yet this is an experience I relish. Here is a glimpse into the mind of an extraordinary man, into the nineteenth-century passion for recreating historical atmosphere. I ignore the hostile guide and lag behind the two Italians, stopping as I please, and apologising each time with greater fluency as I am rounded up and scolded.

Stibbert was obsessed with weapons, ancient and modern, western and oriental. Against heavily flocked wallpaper, and on inlaid floors, or below bucolic friezes, the most bewildering variety of objects is displayed. I stagger from room to room, up and down stairs, look over a balcony at a beautiful, intimate ballroom, or wander in a daze through a vast, grim hall round a squadron of sixteenth-century mounted cavalrymen. Every room is crammed with richness, beauty and interest; the exhibits number around 110,000. In a dining room a fine little spinette with an Orfeo scene painted beneath its lid begs to be touched into life; swords, daggers, arquebuses of every age and size stand in endless cabinets shouting murder and mutilation; all the instruments of death are here, giving the place the eerie ambience of a Madame Tussaud's – a feeling heightened by the mounted cavalcade in the lofty Great Hall. The life-size horses are made of *cartapesta*, and were moulded by Stibbert himself on the bodies of dying horses. In other rooms saddles and bows and quivers are on show, and a thousand fancy helmets: spears, kimonos, pikes, clubs, all bought over the years from antique dealers. Lacquered cabinets, Samurai swords, ceremonial breastplates, and headpieces ranging from the picturesque to the macabre and terrifying (a rearing cobra; a swooping eagle; a dragon; vast, red, rearing antlers); long, supple, deadly bows; face-armour complete with whisker-guards; Turkish scimitars, coats of mail, helmets with wicked spikes, wondrously figured flintlocks, shields, daggers inlaid with turquoise, amber and bloodstones.

A shy Tiepolo is passed without comment. There are works, if one can find them, by Crivelli, Giordano, Allori, Bassano, Luini, Moroni, Neri di Bicci, and frescoes by Ademollo (Milanese, 1764–1849), the artist who painted the faded *Last Supper* in S. Ambrogio. A fine painting of the Wooden Horse of Troy intrigues me in passing; and another (unlabelled) depicting a smiling young lady who offers a pert nipple to a pathetic old man: this is Pero feeding her father Cimon in prison, surely – a scene popular in the seventeenth and eighteenth centuries, and usually referred to as 'Roman Charity'. I am also taken by a splendid portrait (by Chelon, 1793) of a grey horse, a favourite mount of General Stibbert, in the grounds of Portswood House, Southampton.

There are splendid statues, wonderfully fashioned Flemish tapestries, fine coloured terracotta bas reliefs; a whole room of crosses, chalices, crucifixes, copes and vestments in gold and crimson; chasubles in emerald velvet and scarlet and ochre; ikons; seventeenth-century costumes of incredible intricacy, all intact behind glass; riding boots, spurs, livery in satin and silk; slippers and belts, long gloves, leather stretchers, shoehorns, patterned stockings, ladies' purses with gold leaf fine as cigarette paper; fans and lamps and harness and tack; petticoats and patterns and lorgnettes and reticules; painted cupboards and desks, gorgeous décolleté ball gowns; richly embroidered silk waistcoats; seals and morses and miniatures; combs, scissors, hair adornments; table-runners of every rainbow colour; curtains with patterns of peacocks and deer and parrots and rabbits in gold silk on a background of heavenly ultramarine; and miraculous silk firescreens worked with gold and silver wire.

The master bedroom is very grand. A curved wooden bed, like a crescent moon on legs, has elegant curtains falling into an ogival arch, all gathered above into a grand coronet. A large mirror, six feet by four, is at hand; and a spinette coloured *eau de Nil* and gold with floral decorations, and pear and ebony keys. The walls are frescoed, rather unsuitably, with scenes of gladiatorial combat: one shows a naked Christian, Androcles-like, facing a particularly ferocious lion.

The grounds, with their avenue of stately limes, are a splendid retreat. Ilexes, bays, oleanders, strawberry trees, cedars abound, and one comes upon sudden, secret arbours. Everywhere there are terracotta urns, patient stone lions on mossy plinths, and ugly orange bins bearing the legend FIRENZE PULITA (these are empty). People are picnicking beneath slim pillars and antique capitals. There is a silent yellow lily pond, its banks piled high with pine cones nine inches long, in which a rocky islet rises, overgrown and unreachable, with a luxuriant fig tree laden with fruit, and in its shade bright goldfish lurk like rows of orange submarines;

from its centre, a fir climbs to the sky, and its roots reach far below the lake and the confines of the island. There are bamboos and poplars, umbrella pines, a large-leaved oak with small acorns. The air is heavy with the perfume and music of summer. Blue butterflies flit and settle, ducks quack happily. A tiny Egyptian temple, with bell capitals painted bright blue and orange, is guarded by lions and sphinxes and shaded by dusty acacias. There are grottoes and dried-up fountains and a leaning megalith, brick showing through the flaking plaster.

The park is a romantic and sequestered place, ideal for a tryst, and with that faint hint of decay which is so appealing. It requires an effort of will to leave it and plunge again into the cauldron of the city. Dehydrated and glum, I drink a cold beer in a bar where I am served by a glittery-eyed homosexual wearing a bright nylon wig.

Stibbert's Villa once belonged to the Davanzati, whose town house in Via Porta Rossa, a tall elegant palazzo with four storeys and a loggia, is another world apart. Today it is a museum of Florentine life in the fourteenth and fifteenth centuries, the Museo della Casa Fiorentina Antica. Since the suicide of the last of the Davanzati, the palazzo has changed hands several times and its antiques have been variously dispersed. The museum was originally the idea of Elia Volpi; in 1924 a New York antique dealer bought it from him, but in 1951 it was finally acquired by the state. It is now one of the best kept and most impressively run museums in the city; stepping through the main portal, I always think, is like stepping through a wardrobe door into Narnia.

Elia Volpi had had an interesting career before he came to own Palazzo Davanzati. He came from Città di Castello, a poor and ambitious young man, and began by copying paintings in the Florentine museums. Then, as he became known in the world of *antiquari* by frequenting auctions and meeting dealers, he inevitably attracted the attention of the collector Stefano Bardini, who offered him a job. Soon he had learned all he wanted to know, and longed to move on and be his own man. Much to Bardini's anger he quit Florence. He returned soon enough, with a beard and the title of professor, and his rivalry with his former master was fierce and protracted. Volpi was talented and determined: his methods of restoration in Palazzo Davanzati were, to say the least, unorthodox, but the results generally looked right, even if, according to strict propriety, they lacked authenticity. The expense finally broke him, however, and he was forced to sell some of his furniture. On the proceeds he tried to make the museum work again, but by 1924 he had finally to sell up and leave.

The entrance *cortile* is a formidable stronghold, its windows caged off from the outside world by massive wrought-iron grilles; yet there are

Villa Stibbert

frescoes (one of a fine hunting scene) to relieve the gloom, and one can see ports through which goods were brought into the palazzo direct from the streets at the back and sides. One is grateful for anything reducing these grim fortresses to the domestic and everyday: the painstaking lace-work samplers; the tiny lavatories upstairs at the end of the living and sitting rooms, with their pixie-hat covers and floral patterned walls; the pulley system in the wall hatches, like hotel laundry lifts, for drawing water from the well; a high-heeled lady's shoe found in Boccaccio's house; the long bamboo-like guttering that snakes down the inside of the court-yard, with the careful overflows directed into the *impluvium* of the *atrium* (the central court was originally uncovered: now there is a sliding sun-roof); and the homely and not very convenient kitchen on the third floor, its tangled vista of TV aerials, towers and rooftops over the domes of S. Frediano and S. Spirito; the complex rôtisserie (*girarrosto*) device in the fireplace; the spinning and weaving apparatus; the clumsy butter-churns; the poles on brackets outside the window for washing; the giant pulley-operated fire bellows. One seizes on anything for comfort, and longs (over the clang of a hundred iron bolts driven home) to hear the chatter of serving-girls. Even in the sitting room on the first floor there are four trap-doors against the contingency of unwelcome visitors.

There is still a breath of the old life within these walls: not all the medieval ghosts have been exorcised by the Comune. The *graffiti* (draw-ings, diagrams, references to contemporary events) are a constant surprise and delight. And the majolica, faience, hangings, sculptures and paintings are arranged with a nice discretion. The Palazzo Davanzati stops short of being a museum: it rather gives the impression of a richly ornamented private house. This is what a Florentine nobleman's home might have looked like in the middle ages. There are 'important' exhibits here (a bust by Antonio Rossellino, for example; a Granacci panel from the *Joseph* series for the Palazzo Borgherini), but one remembers best the ceilings painted with parakeets and flowers, the vast fireplaces, and touches of domesticity: the stout double bed, its intricately embroidered bedcover telling the story of Tristan; a lovely seventeenth-century cradle, of walnut, richly carved; handwarmers in the shape of boots; exquisite *cassoni* for linen. The second-floor bedroom too has a lovely frieze illustrating a medi-eval French romance (the Camera della Castellana di Vergi), a four-poster, a della Robbia tabernacle, and the small wooden *manichino da processione* – a girl in a blue dress in the niche of the north wall, which would have been dressed in the appropriate saint's clothes, and carried in procession on the saint's feast-day.

The collection is not all of a piece, but excellent listing of its contents, helpful and friendly custodians, and a video lecture theatre (plus loos with studded 'medieval' doors and twentieth-century hand-drying machine) make each visit a new pleasure. It may not have been too uncomfortable in its day: there is a surprising amount of light; it has its own water supply. One wonders only about the sanitation. The particular odour of tanners' and dryers' workshops must have been disagreeable, to say the least: tanners cured hides with horse urine. The livestock around the streets, too, would have added a certain tanginess to the atmosphere. People commonly relieved themselves in the street, and householders emptied slops and refuse from upper windows into the alleys. The locals still jettison every kind of filth into the Arno, which, every now and then, wreaks its revenge.

Smells and dirt are a part of Florence, now as then: the inveterate tourist acquires a suspicion of sparkling cleanliness. There is a veneer proper to extreme age, and an odour proper to antiquity. The best soup comes from the oldest pot.

I prefer to think of the lovely Ghirlandaio ladies who inhabited the Palazzo in the fourteenth and fifteenth centuries, of all their flowery finery and rich colours, the wonderfully brocaded dresses stored in those *cassoni*, kept fragrant with pomanders and sachets of herbs and florets, and the strange upstairs-downstairs existence of the servants. What stories these walls could tell! (One *graffito* actually refers to the Pazzi Conspiracy; others comment scathingly on the Tax Assessors of the *Catasto*, who in the *cinquecento* had their offices on the ground floor here.) The walls of Florence have been scribbled on by all and sundry. They have everything: scurrilous abuse, mathematical equations, shopping lists, notes of dramatic political events, and even sketches by the greatest of great artists.

I am in the mood for pasta, but the heat is prickling, and I head back towards Piazza d'Azeglio for a shower. Outside I spot BOBO, surely, Lisa's rusting Fiat – the bloom on its old metal ripe, a rear light recently smashed; the aerial either stolen or dismantled; honest, foursquare, BOBO seems immortal. There is not much left to fall off now, but she takes one-in-three hills at a canter, and can rub shoulders with all comers; she has been hooked under every kind of bumper, leant against by every kind of moped, sat on by a million tourists, booked by a thousand policemen, stolen by teenage layabouts, and made love in by students. After two heart transplants, even if her bodywork is past its first freshness, BOBO is mechanically as good as new.

But the Fiat is bad news: a council of women!

In the dark I grope for mail, and find a fortnight-old postcard from England. The antique lift climbs uncertainly, smelling of last night's cigarette smoke and coffee beans. At each new level I hear voices raised; either the families are quarrelling, or watching TV, or both at once; they are at lunch and therefore *in famiglia*; there will be conflict. Ambrosial smells of tomatoes and garlic and oil impregnate the stairwell.

I turn the long key, and click open the front door. Female voices. In the tiny kitchen the two Florentines sit smoking and talking at each other. There is an atmosphere of vitriol and conspiracy. An assassination has been in progress, an assassination of Man. *All* men: Lapo, Fiammetta's current partner, Ivo, Giorgio, Giulio, Marcello; they are all peegs.

They sit drinking a glass of water. Fiammetta has removed the strange water-purifier from her cold water tap. (Apparently it gives you cancer.) Now pure, horribly chlorinated Arno water shoots out, non-carcinogenic filth out of which only yesterday a well known singer ('*cantante lirico*') was fished by canoeists.

'You want to swim?' Lisa suggests. Fiammetta observes my reaction critically, as, dragon-like, she lets smoke pour from her nostrils.

'I still have some things to see at the Annunziata.'

'Why didn't you see them yesterday?' (Lisa *knows* I have been to the Annunziata!)

'There wasn't time.'

I pour myself some white wine from the refrigerator.

'How can you dreenk that,' Fiammetta cries, 'in the middle of the day?'

'I'm hot.'

'Best is hot tea,' Lisa chips in. 'You want some hot tea?'

'No, thank you.'

'Why don't you go to the Duomo?' Lisa is trying to be helpful.

'There are things I must see at the Annunziata.'

Fiammetta persists: 'You want to see a *mostra*?'

This year there is a large exhibition in the Palazzo Medici entitled '*ORO di KIEV*', the Gold of Kiev; in Forte Belvedere there is '*Pop Art America Europa*'; a third on '*Arte Protoceltica a Salisburgo*' somewhere; and another, in the Palazzo Vecchio (of all places) on '*Henry Moore, Sculture e Incisioni 1972–84*'. Not my year.

'Come with me,' Lisa chirps, 'to the Annunziata.'

'The Annunziata is closed.'

'At three o'clock.'

'It is closed.'

'Three thirty, in the Piazza.'

Fiammetta has shopping to do. Lisa seems set on meeting me in a scalding piazza to wait an hour and a half for a church to open.

After a shower and change of clothes life feels different. The little market in Piazza Ghiberti is closing down; outside the covered building there is a wilderness of discarded rotten fruit and limp greenery, plastic bags, newspaper, and shattered wooden boxes; their vast bottoms in the air, women stoop and with gnarled hands pick out the best: *cuor di bue* tomatoes, tiny plum tomatoes, overripe peaches and scarlet apples, greengages, squashed plums, squishy water melons, bunches of drooping herbs, wilting lettuce leaves and the odd clump of chicory. Their bags are soon bulging and the eternal pigeons can strut and peck at their leisure. Inside, among the hams and salamis and unnamable offal, a few late shoppers still linger. At the centre of the market a dapper, moustachioed little man and his jolly wife serve hot meals: *bollito misto, lasagne, baccalà alla Livornese* (salt cod in a tomato sauce), *bocconcini* (rolled veal with cheese). The choice is small and the prices amazingly low; there is no ceremony. The little man has eight seats for his customers, and a counter, and the atmosphere is that of a cheery canteen. The patrons are artisans, in every state of undress. Just across the way is a smart modern bar where, unobserved by Lisa and Fiammetta, I can indulge the English vice, so I drink a beer and watch the milling life of the market. Here are the other faces, coarse and ill formed, that make up the real world, baggy and loose-lined, scarred and lived-in – a shocking antidote to the sublime afflatus of del Sarto. But there are also open, friendly looks, and conspiratorial smiles; there is generosity and a sense of fun, quick, good humoured exchanges of greeting and anecdote. I watch the fishmonger and his wife hose down their stall, stuff surplus squid into polythene bags, pack the last dogfish away.

Just round the corner in Via dell' Agnolo (no. 21r) is a popular *trattoria* run by a harassed, short Neapolitan. Its exterior is scruffy and, in this déclassé purlieu of town, there is always a circle of doubtful characters hanging outside, the overspill from a tiny *vinaio* opposite, where, with the halt and the blind and the plain rowdy, I often enjoy a glass of wine poured by the giant, bearded proprietor while waiting for the tables to clear.

It is an education to observe the *pizze* being made in 'dell' Agnolo'. Wine stands waiting on every table in two-litre bottles, and the customer is charged for what he drinks. How many contented hours I have spent here watching, and chewing over the day! Today I am seated in an inner room overlooking the kitchens, and drink happily for some time before I am given the long, fishy menu.

On impulse, because the name is so pretty, I ask for the *Spaghetti Posillipo*.

An argument boils over in the kitchen as the chef prepares it: the owner's temper is even shorter than he is. Two ageing beldames at the next table fan themselves with one hand as they attack *pizze* a foot in circumference. I am joined, after chivalrous enquiries, by a young unshaven southerner; his skin is old leather, and he has a long scar down his left cheek. My spaghetti comes on an oval trencher, swimming in *vongole* (baby clams), garlic and parsley, and until I taste it it seems more than I can manage. Who is the strikingly lovely woman who whispers her order as if she has lost her voice? She gestures in a strange dumb-language. It is evident that she has an arrangement with the owner. He nods, *subito, subito*; and pours *acqua minerale* with a stylish twisting movement, his elbow impossibly high, so that the liquid pearls into the glass from all of three feet away. At another table, a young woman, with heavy breasts almost wholly exposed by a cut-away vest, smokes and talks in a deep baritone to an effeminate boy. The place has character.

Outside, clouds of pale yellow fringed with grey float against a ground of uniform turquoise. Happily I stumble along the gutter of Via de' Macci, louche thoroughfare, and once, if no longer quite so obviously, the haunt of the low life of the S. Croce quarter. It used to be Via Malborghetto ('Street of Ill Repute'), and in this neighbourhood prostitutes and re-storers, fishmongers and grocers vied for their trade. There was once a Franciscan nunnery at the southern end of the street, and it was these nuns, the nuns of S. Francesco dei Macci, who commissioned del Sarto's most famous work, the oddly named and enigmatic *Madonna of the Harpies*, which today is kept in the Uffizi. What the nuns asked for, and stipulated in a contract of 14 May 1515, was a *Virgin and Child* crowned by two angels and flanked by St John the Evangelist and St Bonaventure. What they got (the painting is dated 1517) was a *Virgin of the Assumption* and two cherubs between SS. John the Evangelist and Francis. The picture was instantly recognised in Florence and elsewhere as a masterpiece, and close on a hundred years later Ferdinando I acquired it for the Medici Collection in Palazzo Pitti. In exchange he gave the nuns a copy, and had Foggini, High Priest of Baroquery, rebuild and redecorate their church. As to whether the Grand Duke or the nuns got the better of the bargain, art lovers will have their own opinions.

Lisa is waiting in the piazza, and, with a glance at the horse-borne Ferdinando (who seems sorry at his Harpy-snatching), I join her by one of Tacca's slithery fountains. She is wearing emerald green silk, and cuts a slim and very youthful figure with her tight curls. I have been accorded one of her best pairs of drop earrings made of tiny pearls in grape-clusters. (Her brother is a jeweller on Ponte Vecchio, and she has an eye for the best.) She wears, on her dainty fingers, four or five gold rings, one an intricately engraved signet. The day is now uncomfortably warm; clouds blanket the sky and rain may be imminent. Lisa leans against the railing and pretends to sleep. I pretend to wake her.

'Three-thirty.' The doors of the Annunziata are shut tight. 'How are we going to get in?' I try to disguise the triumph in my voice.

'Come on.' She jumps to her feet and advances on the frowning portal.

'It's shut.'

'*Momento.*'

Not a stone stirs; the piazza is deserted, the church sleeps; somewhere a bell tolls. I watch cynically as Lisa raps smartly on the woodwork. Nowhere on earth looks as tightly closed as Florentine churches. Imagine my incredulity when, almost at once, a slim door creaks open, and the head of a young monk peers round it. It is smiling.

'*Eccoci.*'

'Lamberto!'

'Lisa!'

I witness a warm, unecclesiastical embrace and listen to prolonged greetings. Lisa will interpret: after introducing me to the pleasant young priest, she tells me that Fr Lamberto speaks and writes English fluently, but does not *care* for the language. He will conduct the tour in Italian. There is something disturbingly human about Lamberto, who rummages beneath his worn black habit for a cigarette before re-entering the church.

'Lamberto is an old friend of the family,' Lisa tells me. 'A sort of relative.'

I see Fr Lamberto draw deeply on his cigarette, then finally stub it out beneath his sandal. As we walk down the aisle under the richly coffered ceiling, he gives a running commentary. It is soon clear that he is no ordinary friar: Lamberto is a scholar. But he wears his learning lightly, and is pleased when I show interest.

The nave has five chapels on either side: the transepts are very shallow; then, at the far end is Michelozzo's tribune, circular, radiating its nine chapels like the rounded petals of a flower. The Annunziata, basically a fifteenth-century building on the site of the thirteenth-century oratory, was substantially rebuilt in the seventeenth and eighteenth centuries: the result is an opulent mixture, predominantly baroque.

For the first time, I am able to wander freely through the tribune. The east chapel is the showpiece, the chapel of the Madonna del Soccorso, where Giambologna lies in his sombre tomb: the dark bronze crucifix on the altar is by him, as are the series of bronze bas-reliefs telling the Passion story. The rest, except for the lovely fourteenth-century panel on the altar, are by his pupils, the frescoes and pictures by various contemporaries, including Poccetti and Passignano. In the chapel next on the left there is a very accomplished *Resurrection* by Agnolo Bronzino, the Mannerist painter whose leaning was in such a very different direction from his master, Pontormo. Perhaps his most brilliant productions were portraits; but the allegorical and enigmatic *Venus, Cupid and Folly and Time* in the National Gallery, London, is a disturbing mixture of refinement and overt eroticism, of hot and ice-cold, which stays long in the mind's eye.

From a huge bunch of old, jingling keys Fr Lamberto selects a surprisingly modern one to open the little nine-sided choir behind the High Altar – a splendid private enclosure of marble, containing two fine eagle-lecterns of gilded bronze which are fifteenth-century English works.

From the tribune, after a short walk via a north transept chapel covered in eighteenth-century *trompe l'oeil* frescoes (and redeemed by the austerity of a terracotta *Baptist* by Michelozzo), we pass into the Renaissance Chiostro dei Morti (the 'Cloister of the Dead'), still lovely with its raised well surrounded with azaleas and bays and pink and vermilion geraniums in sunbaked pots. As we emerge from the church Fr Lamberto lights a cigarette and draws on it eagerly. Plants stand by each slender column here, and on the walls, crowded with memorial tablets, there are colourful (though poorly preserved) frescoes telling the Servite story. A stonemason is hard at work nearby, and for a moment I am dazzled by his skilful mallet, fascinated by the play of strength and judgment.

But Fr Lamberto is pointing to a lunette above the door we have come through. '*Madonna del Sacco*,' he enunciates like a speech therapist. '*Capolavoro di Andrea del Sarto*.' Of course. (By what inscrutable law do people always take such care to tell me what I know already?) Del Sarto's masterpiece.

It is glassed over now, though I remember when it was not. The 'sack' which gave the picture its name is one on which St Joseph is leaning. 'The story is', wrote John Evelyn in the 1640s, 'that this painter in a time of dirth borrow'd a sack of Corne of the Religious of that Convent, and being demanded to repay it, wrought it out in this Picture.' Del Sarto has depicted the Holy Family pausing for rest on the flight into Egypt; they are arranged on a high step between two pilasters. This was a late work done in the last five years of Andrea's life, a commission made by the Servites in fulfilment of the votive offering of a certain woman, who had left a small legacy to the convent. The composition, accommodated with beautiful naturalness to the lunette, produces an atmosphere of rest and simple domesticity – the simplicity and naturalness that result from a complete mastery of technique. The Virgin has real nobility, and there is a sweet humility in her downcast eyes; Joseph slumps relaxed against the sack, and the Babe wriggles restlessly, as babies will, on his mother's knees, longing to grab Joseph's book and tear pages from it. The heads are exquisitely lovely; the drapery superlative; the colouring soft and miraculously harmonious. The counterpoint of the limbs and bodies of the three figures, their rest and movement, is in itself a study of harmony.

But I am being called away. Fr Lamberto has finished another cigarette, and ushers us through another door along the east side of the Chiostro. A tiny vestibule contains a crucifix of inlaid wood by da Sangallo, and a lunette of *St John the Evangelist* by the della Robbia *bottega*. Here we enter the tiny Chapel of St Luke, or, more correctly, the Cappella della Confraternita di S. Luca.

The Confraternity, founded in 1339, has been based here since the sixteenth century: this is the Chapel of the Artists, and below are the remains of Cellini, Pontormo, Franciabigio, Bronzino, and others. Montorsoli also lies here, the artist who was himself a Servite friar and who bought the chapel with his own money. Here, Lisa tells me emotionally, her parents were married, and I cannot think a more recondite or privileged spot exists anywhere.

The decoration is as rich as one might expect, with grisailles everywhere and ten imposing stucco figures in niches at the far end (by Montorsoli and others); a *jeu d'esprit* on the altar by Vasari (a self-portrait of the artist as St Luke painting the Madonna); and a fresco of the Trinity by Allori (dated 1571) on the right wall which is of more than passing interest, because (Fr Lamberto tells and Lisa relays in her fluent, alarming American) when it was detached after the flood for restoration, under the painted marble of the two pedestals at the bottom of the picture portraits of Pontormo and Bronzino were discovered. These identifications were prompted by the initials of the two artists; unfortunately their heads are now visible only in silhouette. Bronzino died in 1572, in Allori's house, and it was Allori who declaimed Bronzino's eulogy before the Accademia del Disegno; so this is likely to be a tribute by the artist himself to his Master, and his Master's Master. (The portraits recur, interestingly, in Allori's *Last Supper* in the Cenacolo of the Carmine.). The fresco is a tall swirl of rather limp, naked figures: three busy *putti* support a swooning Christ as he is taken down from the cross; three more hover above in stark foreshortening; the Dove flies above the head of a sorrowing and noble God the Father.

The ceiling is covered by Luca Giordano's *Assumption*, and on the entrance wall is *Solomon directing the building of the Temple*, an allegorical work by Santi di Tito (1536–1603), with portraits of himself and Michelangelo.

But the most compelling picture (I was struck by it as soon as I stepped inside) is on the left, a *Madonna and Child with Saints*, an early Pontormo, done when he was about 20 years old, and brought here in 1823 from the demolished church of S. Rafaello (= Rufillo) del Vescovo in the Piazza dell' Olio. The saints are identified as Lucy and Agnes, Zachary and the Archangel Michael. St Agnes, on the extreme left, looks out of the picture directly at the spectator, as she holds aloft a salver containing the two eyes of St Lucy, who sits next to her, gazing sightlessly heavenwards in an ecstasy of martyred suffering. (Some scholars believe it is St Lucy on the left, St Agnes seated.) While the Christ Child petulantly recoils from the attentions of the kneeling Zachary (whose face is all but obliterated), the Madonna turns to gaze intently at St Michael Archangel, who holds in his right hand what appears to be a portable anemometer. Fr Lamberto seems amused by this work. No one knows what the object is, he tells me with a shrug. They are scales, surely, balance-pans. But their precise significance here escapes me.

When this fresco was detached in 1967, an intriguing *sinopia* was discovered of a *Madonna Enthroned with Four Saints*. The names are carefully inscribed below, and, because Pontormo used the cartoon method of transferring his design, he had merely trowelled his *intonaco* over the existing *sinopia*. For some reason it was never overpainted: it stood as it was, an outline-drawing merely, and the haloes were later painted in yellow. St Michael is clad in armour, and here, too, holds scales; there are also two female saints; but the second male saint is named as S. Alessio (S. Alexius). The Madonna and Child are most beautifully drawn, the work of some Florentine master working at the end of the fifteenth century; but, though possibly less than a score of years separate these two paintings, the style seems antique in comparison with Pontormo's nascent Mannerism, which is so energetic and colourful and rhythmic.

A delightful little organ, built in 1702, stands near the entrance door, and, sportingly, Fr Lamberto pumps life into it while I improvise on the tiny keyboard. (There are just 3½ octaves; and below, a range of five pedal notes projects, a sort of token display, with one of the flats missing.) The sound is robust and edgy in the tiny chapel: I feel almost guilty about disturbing the great names beneath. A special Mass is said for them each St Luke's Day, and I should like to see all the City dignitaries in their finery forgather here to pay their respects. The Annunziata was badly hit by the flood. Until then, however, it had not been known that the artists were buried in their own robes. Now that we know, these are all lost for ever, lost and gone.

When we emerge again in the cloister, rain is falling in heavy drops. Fr Lamberto lights another cigarette and enjoys a private joke with Lisa as I walk round the frescoes.

The Servite Order was established in 1233, when seven Florentine noblemen retired to become hermits on the hilltop of Montesenario in the Mugello. The place is high on a hill, with fine views, the air is bracing, and the hillside is riddled with caves and grottoes where the Seven Founders (canonised as late as 1888) lived and prayed in solitude. From this community there developed an order of mendicant friars. Their first leader was S. Buonfiglio Monaldo; and one of the outstanding Brothers was St Alexis Falconieri, a Lay Brother, whose modesty would never allow him to take Holy Orders. He died finally, aged 110, in 1310.

One day Lisa and I drove to Montesenario from Pratolino. Here on their airy hilltop, among acres of heaving broom, the monks seemed happy and friendly and at peace. I had rarely seen such peace and contentment, and I remarked on it. 'Yes,' Lisa snapped. 'Of course they are at *peace* with the world. They are not *in* it!' And I thought: there is the Tuscan.

Surrounded by hydrangeas, hibiscus and blood-red begonias on the terrace of Hotel gli Scoiattoli (squirrels abound here), we waited for the monastery church to open, ate a *panino* with *prosciutto crudo*, and relaxed in idyllic pine-shade. Lisa admired especially some pink geraniums. 'The red ones are so *common*,' she explained scornfully. I asserted myself, drank a glass of beer, and took a photograph which turned out unusually well.

I have it by me now. Lisa is wearing green. A luxuriant laurel hedge frames her smile; the Florentine 'good eye' is narrowed and twinkling, laughter lines fanning like beams from a baroque sun-splash. The 'evil tongue' is silent.

After lunch we climbed the hill again to the little church and found it open. It was baroque; but behind the High Altar was the old Chiesetta, and there in the Chapel of the Apparition is a polychromatic terracotta by Lottini (sixteenth century) of quite surpassing loveliness: a *Pietà*, with Ann assisting a swooning Mary; the Magdalene, distraught, bareheaded, supporting the prone Christ's feet; and a handsome, curly black-haired young John tenderly bearing the weight of the Master's lolling head. The silence here is audible: everything is still and pine-scented; even the handful of tourists catch the mood and whisper. A ghastly gift shop sells clumsy baby Jesuses (some crudely modern, some crude imitations of antiques), soap, Aztec Indian work, eggtimers and fretwork cuckoo clocks, kitchen utensils and gimcrack rosaries made of anything from coffee beans to tiger's eyes – a scene to set the teeth on edge; and yet, among the rubbish, I spotted a showcase full of objects discovered during a recent restoration, and among them were two marble heads of *putti* I could have eaten.

The Annunziata was built in 1250 as the Servite Oratory. Today there are only eleven Brothers to walk the fifteenth-century cloisters, study in the magnificent library, officiate at the services, and pursue their life of prayer. A superb wooden crucifix hangs in the fourteenth-century cloisters; in an enchanting little thirteenth-century cloister a lovely Montorsoli bas relief hangs. All around are microphones, amplifiers, electronic typewriters: the new wrestling with the medieval, the tensions producing the continuum of Italian life.

There is a hush of holiness in the Annunziata which can make S. Maria Novella, S. Croce or the Duomo seem barbarous by comparison. Yet so much has vanished, so much has been stolen, looted in war. The great library, once possessing more than 30,000 volumes, rare books and *incunabula*, is now dispersed. A great deal was lost when the convent was suppressed in the last century. Then, when the monks returned, much was ruined again. 'The monks had zeal,' Fr Lamberto smiles, 'but little taste.'

Sadly, he shows me a bronze eagle-lectern; the claws were of solid gold. 'I was in the church myself when they were taken,' he tells me hopelessly. Only eighteen months ago a statue of Faith which stood on another lectern was removed. Just the other week, a precious, heavy candlestick, chained in position on its altar, was sawn free and stolen. The thieves work in teams: they are very clever. One engages the priest in conversation, the other busies himself elsewhere. They know what they are looking for. From time to time the stolen works turn up in shops and fairs. Around the little marble choir in the tribune tourists have scribbled names with black felt-tip pens. Fr Lamberto gives a final sigh, and we walk back through the church. He points out the tondi high up around the nave. 'See,' he nods. 'All the frescoes have been restored. The state gives us money. But look!' he indicates two or three still black with grime. 'Those are painted on canvas.' He spreads his hands. 'No frescoes, no money!'

There is one more revelation before we leave. Passing the miraculous *Annunciation* in the tabernacle, he opens the little Medici Oratory, just to the right, and for the first time I stand wondering inside. Lisa exclaims at the steps of silver and semi-precious stone, the intricate inlay-work on the altar; but I have eyes only for the door of the tabernacle, the glowing panel of del Sarto's *Redeemer*. There is exceptional poetry in this work, and, standing where it does, exactly where it was intended to stand, it has an intensity which is hypnotic. Christ folds his arms across his breast (we see the top third of his body only, presented at an angle, and emerging

115

from dark shadow). He is lightly bearded, with long hair, and wears a square-necked rose-pink robe with gold border. Faintly touched in behind the head is an ornate, lobed, gold halo. Through a masterly, controlled progression of tones, Christ seems to loom out of the darkness.

I turn away finally to find Fr Lamberto staggering towards me with two colossal, glossy tomes on the art treasures of SS. Annunziata – one, a *catalogue raisonné* of all the works in the convent, is his own compilation, a work of love and painstaking scholarship. As I thank him profusely, he is reaching under his habit for yet another cigarette. The rain is now spectacularly heavy, and we stand in the portico watching the piazza washed clean. We say our goodbyes to Fr Lamberto, shabby, cheerful and thoroughly at ease in his world of cloisters and fine art, prayer and tobacco. With a final cheery wave he vanishes into the darkness again.

Already little urgent runnels are gurgling about the steps of the Ospedale; thunder crackles in the distant hills, and the skies are angry and determined.

'I'll get a taxi,' I suggest.

'We'll walk.'

'Is there a bus?'

'What's the matter?' Lisa seems suddenly cross. 'Frightened of a bit of rain?'

'But your dress!'

'It'll dry.' Cryptically she adds, 'No way.'

'My books!' I sense I am being difficult. From nowhere Lisa produces a plastic bag. It is 6.30 p.m. The rain falls in furious sheets; ankle-deep puddles have appeared everywhere. I am wearing a teeshirt and summer slacks; Lisa is in the flimsiest silk. In no time we have to shelter under an overhanging roof while the gutters overflow onto the shining cars in violent, pissing streams. Lisa's silk clings to her: but she clings to her colossal dignity. *Bella figura*. Daintily she picks her way round a pond and tiptoes over slithery cobbles until we reach the parting of the ways.

'Come to dinner.'

'Well...'

'Eight o'clock. *Ciao*!'

She is gone, victorious, indomitable, and sodden. The downpour continues, but on my own the going seems easier, and in a few minutes I am at the foot of Borgo Pinti. At the corner I take shelter again and look idly in a shop window. There used to be a *trattoria* here, a cheerful place where I spent many happy mealtimes, and the waiter served nourishing pasta in steaming bowls with a cigarette secreted in his palm. Now an incongruous Chinese restaurant has sprung up in its place. Across the road is the large, ugly Post Office, where queues are as long, and the service as awful, as in England. On reflection, I always felt at home in this quarter of the city.

I wander on up the street, and with an incredulous thrill see a hole in the great black door of no. 5! Can it really be true – S. Maria Maddalena dei Pazzi *open*? The fact that it should not be (or should be, but never is) at this hour does not occur to me: I leap inside before the door can close. From the narrow, gloomy road, I emerge into a large *cortile*. (This, I discover, was designed by a real local, Giuliano da Sangallo, who lived at no. 68.) After the funnelled din of the street, there is a sudden pall of peace, the calm of the convent again.

Not a tourist in sight, and the church interior is lovely. It was originally a Benedictine foundation, built in the thirteenth century, but several times added to, particularly in the *quattrocento*, and finally redecorated completely in the later seventeenth, when it was dedicated to the mystic Maria Maddalena, a Carmelite nun of the Pazzi family (1566–1607, canonised in 1669).

It is the chapter house I must see. I recall the notice, rather in the form of a 'Monopoly' instruction, telling the visitor to '*rivolgersi a Via dei Pilastri 54*'. No. 54 was inhabited by grimly efficient Carabinieri. I talked through plate glass, then waited patiently for clearance. Finally the *Capitano* arrived, whose plan to make me understand consisted of talking louder and faster. No, I must return with identification. Not Tuesday, not Saturday. 'The church is closed; but in certain cases, scholars ... you understand. ...' The following Wednesday, I found a new guard and a new captain. There was a slight *contretemps* as I offered him my passport: I had wedged a £20 note in it for safe-keeping and, as it slipped gently to the floor like a tired butterfly, the *Capitano* eyed first me (knowingly), then his Sergeant (conspiratorially). It was an uncomfortable moment, but somehow I seemed to have established my *bona fides*. I was shown the little church and choir, and very charming it was. There was no talk of a chiostro, nor signs of a famous fresco. And the church was eighteenth-century, surely, High Baroque.

'There are so many churches,' the young carabiniere explained. 'So many called S. Maria.' He shrugged gormlessly. I retrieved my passport and £20 note and left, evincing a strangled '*Grazie*'. After all, it was the wrong church! What I had been shown was S. Maria dei Candeli, by the extravagant Foggini.

I make for the crypt, and, via the crypt, through a long, winding, dramatically lit passageway to the old Capitolo, where Perugino's *Crucifixion*, one of the great hidden treasures of Florence, covers almost the whole of one wall.

The flood reached to within one foot of the painting, but since 1966 all is in sparkling condition. The fresco, finished on 20 April 1496, is a triptych, and, with the exception of a few cracks in the left-hand scene, it is quite miraculously preserved. Each scene is made, by fictive architecture, to fit neatly between the pilasters that support the arches of the vaulting, and the square pilasters framing each scene, by enforced perspective, lend greater depth to a composition that already carries the eye deep into the lovely landscape of trees and hills and blurred, distant towns.

This is one of the artist's undoubted masterpieces. Vasari wrote that Perugino was not a religious man, and Berenson dubbed Perugino a 'villain' and an 'atheist'. But God chooses the strangest souls to be vessels of grace, and the serenity of these figures and their harmony with the landscape behind, the attitudes of the Maries and the saints, seem to me evidence of reverence and deep devotion. I find it hard to accept that the artist who painted these lovely figures was the venal tradesman Vasari thought him.

There is a chair to sit on – luxury rare as the fresco itself! A sweet old lady has conducted me here: now she sits upstairs and watches me on a closed-circuit television. The air, its humidity carefully controlled, is cold as a morgue.

The colours glow as if they were mixed last week. On the left are St Bernard and the Madonna; in the centre, the crucified Christ and Mary Magdalen ('No! No!' Lisa corrected me once. 'She would not have a halo!'); to the right, SS. John the Evangelist and Benedict. The six figures, thrust forward by the deep space beyond them, are all in different attitudes, the outside pair kneeling to point the climax of the cross.

The face of the Magdalen who kneels at the right of the cross is of particularly superlative quality. Somehow, like that other brilliant *Magdalen* in the Pitti (a study in remorse, painted in sombre colours), this could never be a Madonna. Despite her humble and repentant attitude, her hands delicately joined in prayer, the eyes are too *knowing*: despite the rosebud lips, her face speaks of wordly experience. The painter has painted the unseen. Contrast the Virgin, her simplicity and purity, as she alone of all the figures gazes, not at her son on the cross, but out of the painting at the onlooker. Christ's body in death is beautiful, his expression beatific, restful. There is no concentration on anguish here: the torment is over, and the world's redemption has begun. St John, a youthful, long-haired figure, spreads his arms in adoration and wonder; St Bernard, in white, kneels in humble prayer on the far left. Balancing him, St Benedict, in a blue cloak, crosses his arms on his breast and gazes in rapt devotion.

The sweet open countryside, realised in pale greens and fresh ochres, fades to distant blue hills; a silver river snakes to the foot of a mountain;

the vast tract of heaven, beginning the palest turquoise at the horizon and climbing to a swathe of greyish clouds, serves to link all three sections at their upper extremities. The whole wall is filled with a typically Umbrian landscape – a view from the artist's birthplace, maybe, or from the hill of Assisi, with its graceful trees ('larches and olives', one critic names them, but I am unconvinced: they are just beautiful *trees*) and long, sweeping hills. And, seen close to, the background is delightfully impressionistic; you can count the slashes of green paint on the hill framing St Benedict's face, and the trees that flank it are shorthand scribbles, the merest suggestions, but utterly convincing.

Berenson played down Perugino's 'stereotyped' figures, and one modern authority criticises the 'vacuously pious' expression on the faces of the mourners here; another remarks on the 'gentle piety of the figures' becoming 'more impressive the longer one contemplates the scene'. *Quot homines tot sententiae*. There is room for many sorts of painters in creation, and there are many kinds of greatness, on whose order of importance perhaps no two scholars would ever agree. Great art humanises us, it reconciles us with life. As I gaze at this triptych in the cool chapter house of S. Maria Maddalena, I know I am in the presence of greatness.

Outside, the rain has vanished and the sky is tranquil again. The streets hum with busy humanity. The Florentine girls are out wearing almost nothing: nut-brown, cow-eyed like the figures on Etruscan sarcophagi, they bounce past on scooters with their lovers, legs splayed gloriously, glossy, carefully tangled manes streaming behind them. Or they tiptoe on stilts down narrow alleys, naked under long thin cotton shirts pulled in at the waist with broad leather belts. They move with brazen magnificent arrogance, aware, provocative, gorgon-headed; this year large sunglasses are in vogue; they perch on aquiline noses, shield slanting siren eyes.

On my way to Lisa and Lapo, I stop at the Bar 'Magnini' in Via Carducci. The owner, a giant with a pimpling nose who carries his years lightly, and wears his swimming shorts with panache, is Ardico Magnini, a famous soccer player of long ago who won more than thirty caps for his country. Ardico was a striker, strong and fast and full of heart. Those were the days. . . . One word of enquiry sets him reminiscing. He rattles off on his long fingers the famous names he played against: Swift, Finney, Lofthouse, Mortenson. . . . Such *players*! It is hard to know his age, but, he informs me, he never played on a single winning side against *Inghilterra*! England? They were too fast, too good! Ah, it was long ago. . . .

Lapo has had a bad day at the hospital and is warming to a combative evening. The atmosphere crackles as he calls for wine. Lisa reminds him that he must not have it. He wants wine, wine for his guest! Lisa mutters to herself and shrugs.

Dinner begins with *uccelletti*, a series of tiny birds impaled on skewers. There is a great silence.

'What sort of bird', I venture, 'are they?'

'*Uccelletti*!' Lisa snaps, crunching bones audibly. '*Little* birds! *I* don't know!'

They taste, rather honestly, of tiny dead birds. But their taste is forgotten as soon as delicious *porcini* (*cèpes*, fleshy, meaty, brown mushrooms of a most delicate flavour: *boleti*) are brought on, drenched in olive oil and wild savory (*nepitella*); and *peperoncini dolci*, long sweet peppers, lightly deep fried, the food of the gods. The chilled white wine is slightly *pétillant*, deceptively gentle on the palate.

We move onto the balcony, and I watch Lisa ignite a towering fire of pine cones and cook a monumental *bistecca*. The flames, lit with such panache, leap twelve feet high and scorch the geraniums on the terrace above. The scene, with little bats circling madly in the twilight, is like some pagan sacrifice, but the steak is perfection, with a tang of herb and pine. Salad follows, crisp and fresh and clean; then grapes, apples, peaches, apricots, greengages and plump green figs. As I peel a peach a gecko watches me, motionless on the wall.

Without a sign or a word Lapo removes himself to sit in front of the television. I hear him switching repeatedly from '*Poliziotti alle Hawaii*' to '*La Famiglia Smith*' and back again.

When I trudge back finally to Piazza d'Azeglio, on the Old Bridge police are gesturing angrily at miscreants and shrugging as they are ignored. Negroes and orientals with strange, shining eyes dance to the music of terracotta pipes; half-castes sell trinkets spread on woven ground-sheets; at the north end, where the pagan statue of Mars stood for so long, a tree-like Abyssinian blows a cool alto saxophone. Hippies bang tambourines and prance at passers-by. Yanks quack; querulous, nasal French go by in tight familial knots; Japanese twitter, their black plastic-cased cameras slung round their necks, fine, black hair ramrod-straight. A few artists still sit at their easels under the open sky in the *piazzale* of the Uffizi: most of their work is awful, but the tourists want pictures of the Ponte Vecchio and *case coloniche* and pines, views of the Duomo and the David, and business is always brisk. The artists sit and smoke: one, a young girl, breast-feeds a tiny moss-headed baby. The portrait painters are most in demand, all of them claiming to have been pupils of Annigoni. Charcoal and Conté crayon are popular: silhouette-cutters can produce prodigious likenesses in only a few minutes. One painter displays two large portraits, one marked *RITRATTO* (portrait) the other *CARICATURA*, as if one might confuse them. So, within a hundred yards of del Sarto and Rembrandt, of Lippi, Botticelli, Masaccio, Giotto and Michelangelo, the rankest amateur plies his trade and makes a better living. In old times, the Sassetti and Tornabuoni could buy their immortality, and today one observes the power of their wealth in S. Trìnita and S. Maria Novella: there they stay for all time, unless the Arno rises again and takes them from us, or a Polish dentist or British soccer fan obliterates them with hammer, pocket-knife or spraygun. Who knows but what some frightful 'act of God' may destroy the real art one day, and these ephemeral chocolate-box doodles, framed in gilt and displayed in air-conditioned parlours in San Diego or Berlin or Basle may actually outlive them.

Nearby a classical string trio plays Mozart *con brio*. Not ten feet away, an insouciant lout screams hoarsely to a taped accompaniment, blooping offensively to an insistent Afro-rhythm. Outside Orsanmichele a madrigal group sings Gibbons and Weelkes; among their audience dolls and bracelets and masks and belts and silver and topaz earrings are touted by pitch-black boys, who are periodically moved on, and return within the hour.

'*Quanto?*'

'*Diecimila.*'

'*Quanto?*'

'*Ten towsson.*'

'*Va benny.*'

'Have a nice day.'

All Florence floats on a tide of Eurocheques, traveller's cheques, plastic credit cards. Florence is the home of banking, that ugly non-profession which used to be called by a less deceptive, less ceremonious name.

When Dante went down to Hell he found it full of Florentines. The place was choked with them: sodomites, panders, hypocrites, thieves, personators, alchemists, simonists and barrators; and, at the descent to Malebolge, even in the *Inferno*, the usurers, tormented by flames and scalding earth, eyes bursting with pain, still keep their precious pouches round their necks.

CHAPTER VI

The market of S. Ambrogio · S. Marco: church, Museo *and* convent · *Fra Angelico · Ghirlandaio's* Ultima Cena · *Savonarola and the Humanists · Chiostro dello Scalzo: del Sarto again · Mercato Centrale · S. Barnaba · 'La Maremmana'*

 Above the hum of morning life floating up from the piazza, gallant birds chirrup to one another in the planes. Through the leaves early sun is refracted into a thousand shades of green and gold. Before the cicadas have their way, while everything is still fresh and pullulating, I have a mind to join the locals and see the sights of S. Ambrogio.

Before eight the city is bright-eyed and clean. The bars waft coffee over the pavements, and early tobacco smoke mingles with the fragrance of pastries. Behind the rush screens of nearby scaffolding, coffee-skinned workmen, in hats made of folded newspaper, gesticulate violently to each other. Outside the florist's shop, a field of vermilion and scarlet and juicy greens assaults the eye; the blooms are drenched with water and, where they drip onto the thirsty stones, the spots dry as one watches. Signor Magnini, working the pumps of his Espresso machine with one hand, eats a sandwich held in a small paper napkin in the other. The pretty girl in the delicatessen, her hair piled up today to reveal a pale, slender neck, spoons olives onto a sloping tray, the green oil slipping down in slow glutinous waves. Just as I pass she looks up, and with eyes like large blackberries she smiles.

The market explodes with life. From it come squat dames in black, padding along with bulging plastic bags from which bread and wet bunches of herbs protrude. The stallholders, their vans and trucks parked round the square, have been here since sun-up, and some are already breaking for beer or coffee in the little bar. It has been said that the god who created the hills round Florence was an artist: it was the same god who inspired the markets. The sheer exuberance of colour, the daring juxtapositions, the master-touch of brilliant scarlet to relieve the green monotone; the shining plenty, all that forest and farm and greenhouse and vineyard and sea and river can produce, all the best bounty of the earth trundled in during the dark hours to sparkle and tempt, all arranged with flair and economy in long shining rows, in dizzy pyramids, or piled in lavish higgledy-piggledy profusion.

Around the covered area the vegetable market booms: on the north side cut flowers, pot plants, seeds, seedlings, wickerwork, trinkets, shoes, toys; on the west and south sides, every variety of vegetable I can name: giant *cor di bue* tomatoes (*pomodori*), scarlet, orange or yellow green – the overripe ones are for cooking, while the crisp, pale orange or yellow-green tomato is for salads (two or three slices with oil and vinegar and basil are one of the summer's best reasons for going south). Plum tomatoes, cheap and prolific, make a superlative sauce for pasta. Radishes (*rafani, radici*) tied in fat bunches, squat, turnip-shaped; long, slender fingers of red and white; short in-between sized radishes, they are all on parade like guardsmen; taut, glossy aubergines (*melanzane*), deep purple bombs the colour of deadly nightshade; peppers (*peperoni*), yellow, red and green; cucumbers (*cetrioli*) ribbed or knobbly or smooth as a sausage; courgettes (*zucchini*) begging to be sliced and deep fried, or eaten in cool, herby salads drowned in oil; and their flowers, gaudy orange or green, an exquisite delicacy when lightly deep-fried (*fiori fritti*).

Squashes (*cucurbite*), and impossibly shaped gourds (*zucche*) like calabashes, truncheons, pumpkins, pale ghostly green, aureole yellow or flame-orange are jumbled together and sold to eat, or as conversation pieces, maybe – or perhaps to ward off the evil eye. Some of them are certainly '*fascinati*' – a Latin word properly used of a snake mesmerising its victim, hence the 'evil eye'. Latin *fascinum* is a 'spell': the word comes ultimately from Greek *baskanion*, the *membrum virile*, or an apotropaeic, phallic charm hung round the necks of children. These charms are still quite a common sight in the marketplaces of Italy; they can be lockets or key-rings, and the youngsters use them with as little awareness of their true significance as we English have of the etymology of 'treacle'.

There are all sorts of onions (*cipolle*): purple, ordinary, spring onions (*cipolline, cipolle porraie*), they come in great strings, or with the outer brown layers peeled away; earthy new potatoes (*patate*) are carefully presented with fibrous earth still clinging; cabbages (*cavoli*), red and white; lettuces (*lattughe*), cos and density, and endives (*indivie*); succulent, trimmed fennel (*finocchio*, also slang for 'homosexual', and not to be shouted across a crowded stall); the famous white beans of Tuscany (*fagioli*), in pods or ready shelled (*sgranati*), and an epicure's delight either boiled, with oil, or '*all'uccelletto*', cooked in garlic, sage leaves and tomato sauce; 'French beans' (*fagiolini*), short and plump, or one foot long and stringy; broad beans (*fave*); button mushrooms (*funghi*) and *porcini*, costly and sought after for their subtle flavour; beetroot (*barbabietole*), carrots (*carote*) scrubbed and uniform, without a single blemish; pimentoes (*pimenti*); globe artichokes (*carciofi*) peeled back to display white hearts in a sea of muddy green.

One does not see ready-made salads so often here as in Rome, but all the ingredients can be had from one medium-sized stall, and the herbs to go with them: rosemary (*rosmarino*), chives (*cipolline*), lordly basil (*basilico*), *menta* (various sorts of mint) and *nepitella* (a wild savory that grows everywhere in the countryside), thyme (*timo*), sage (*salvia*, wonderful with calves' liver), garlic (*aglio*), parsley (*prezzemolo*), marjoram (*maggiorana*) cultivated or wild (*acciughero*), origano (*oregano*) cultivated or wild (*santoreggia*), juniper (*ginepro*). No one bothers to buy *alloro* (bay): it can be pulled from every other tree in town, and stale bay leaves are a pale shadow of stolen fresh ones. Bunched and rubber-banded, washed and costing almost nothing, these herbs are essential for the authentic Italian flavour. Radishes and lettuces and chicory (*radicchio*) and spinach (*spinaci*) are easily recognisable; but shoulder to shoulder in a variety of subtle greens and russets are salad-leaves not all of which appear to have English equivalents: *ricciolino smerlato, acetosa, carciofina* or *spugnina bianca, foglie di quercia* ('oak leaf' lettuce), and the ubiquitous *ruchetta*. This last is 'rocket', a delicate red-brown leaf well known in fourteenth-century English vegetable gardens, subsequently neglected for centuries, and currently undergoing something of a revival among modish cooks. Rocket adds life to green salads, a suspicion of agreeable bitterness in the bland green jumbles of summer. To the Mediterranean chef, salad is not a wilting, bitter lettuce-leaf, a quartered squashy tomato, and two transparent slices of cucumber: it can involve up to seven or eight different greens – cabbage, lettuce, heart of cos, curly endive, fennel, chicory, rocket and water cress (*crescione d'acqua*). The flavour of rocket varies a great deal: the toughest of the stalks and coarser leaves must be picked off, and the rest needs careful washing as it can be gritty. But then, in cheap abundance, it is an attractive and versatile ingredient for all salads, the sort of small but subtle addition which lends distinction and makes a meal memorable.

In summer fruit is varied and plentiful: lemons (*limoni*) can be small and tight or the size of grapefruits; apples (*mele*) of all kinds are on show, from small yellow to giant, waxy crimson (the enormous Snow White variety that shine like magenta mirrors are of disappointing flavour); bananas (*banane*), pears (*pere*), all of uniform size and shape and displayed against mauve tissue in rough, white, slatted boxes; greengages (*susine verdi*, or *claudie*), apricots (*albicocche*), peaches (*pesche: pesce* means fish) in bewildering profusion, small, unripe, bruised ripe, and some as big as small footballs; nectarines (*noci*) bursting with sweetness; plums (*prugne*); great water melons (*poponi*) halved and quartered, like pink-hearted medicine balls; yellow 'honeydew' melons (*meloni*) as sweet as syrup; white, black and musty red grapes (*uva*), blackberries (*more*) wild, and cultivated the size of strawberries, each drupel sheer perfection, and piled high like an Aladdin's cave of coal-coloured pearls; oranges (*arance*), white, red, and black cherries (*ciliegie*) and plump green-purple figs (*fichi*).

Inside, the *pizzicherie* spread their cheese and hams; *salame toscano* (piquant), *prosciutto crudo* (sweet), *finocchiona* (fennel-flavoured), *cinghiale* (sausage of wild boar); bread, butter, eggs (sold individually) and wines; oils and grains; and anchovies scooped from huge, tin preserving-drums, or swimming on oily trays. Italian cheeses are perhaps an acquired taste: they are also expensive. Parmesan (*Parmigiano*), made with cow's milk, originated in Parma, home of so many delicacies, and the best types are said to be *Reggiano* and *Lodigiano*. Fresh and moist, with salt crystals to crunch, it is a king of cheeses: after a few days, it goes rock hard and is fit only for grating, but as such is indispensable. *Pecorino* is made with ewe's milk, and Italians tell you that the aromatic herbs cropped by the sheep who give this milk on the slopes of the Apennines can be tasted in the cheese. (My palate must be a coarse one.) There are various types of *pecorino*: today I can spot *Romano*, a strongly flavoured variety, and *Sardo* (Sardinian), which is mild. *Mozzarella* is a white, soft cheese ideally made with buffalo's milk: it comes usually from Rome and the south, where buffalo herds are quite common. The famous *Gorgonzola* is made near Milan; the pear-shaped, yellow cheese is *Provolone*, from Campania, with a strongly individual taste; *Stracchino* is a very soft, fresh variety from Lombardy, in the north; *Groviera* is a rather poor imitation (like the name) of Gruyère. The other popular types, *Dolce Latte* and *Bel Paese*, are familiar in supermarkets or even village stores in England. *Ricotta*, of course, is not cheese, but coagulated milk and whey: Italians like to eat this strange, dry, almost tasteless mixture of leftovers with sugar, or fresh fruit. Lisa often produces a dip made with cocoa powder. But it is commonly (and better) used in cooking: *crespolini* stuffed with *ricotta* and spinach are a sensation.

125

And there is pasta in every shape: *rigatoni* (tubes), *fusilli* (twists), *penne* (also tubes, but the word means 'feathers' and is used on account of the slanting, quill-pen shape of the cut ends), *lumachine* (snails), *conchiglie* (shells), *stelline* (stars), *farfalline* (little butterflies), *capelli d'angelo* (angel's hair), *ditali* (thimbles), *quadretti* (squares), *semi di melone* (melon seeds), *perline* (little pearls) – and so on, as well as the less fanciful varieties available in all supermarkets: *ravioli, tortellini, spaghetti, maccheroni, tagliatelle, cannelloni, fettuccine, lasagne*. Fresh pasta is ineffably superior, it needs no saying, to anything in a packet.

There are two or three butchers in competition. Veal and chicken come undisguised in every shape and form; calves hang from hooks, flayed, with lovely deer-eyes staring dolefully; yellow chickens are sold with their necks twisted beneath their wings. Beef (*manzo*) and pork (*maiale*) are here, too, in various cuts familiar and unfamiliar, but chicken and veal are most popular. Meat is dear, and even offal expensive by English standards. Liver (*fegato*) of different hues and textures seems to stretch for acres over the white tiling (*fegatini di pollo* can be ambrosial); tongue, sausages (*salse*), *ris de veau*, brains (*cervelli*, wonderful in lightly fried fritters), tripe (*trippa fiorentina* is the only way I will eat it, sliced fine, with tomatoes, marjoram and other seasoning), hearts (*cuori*), and, for pets, lungs (*polmoni*); and a strange white haggis-like pudding, six inches long, four inches wide, whose label has slipped, face down onto the slimy slab. I return later and see it has been put back in position: *TESTICOLI*.

The sole fishmonger (just beyond the snack bar, which today is serving *bollito misto* again – islets of meat swimming in a sea of fat – and *peperonata*, casseroled peppers) displays his wares honestly in two halves: frozen and fresh. It is an education merely to stand and look. S. Ambrogio is not the largest market in the world and only the second largest in Florence, but the range of fish, crustaceans and molluscs is impressive: dog fish (*palombo*), red mullet (*triglia*), grey mullet (*cefalo*), hake (*nasello*), whiting (*merlango*), sea bream (*dentice*), angler fish (*rospo*), Dover sole (*sogliola Dover*); sea bass (*spigola Atlantide*), grayling (*ombrina*), trout (*trota*), mackerel (*sgombro*), cod (*merluzzo*), plaice (*pianuzza*), sardines (*sardine*); there are squid (*calamari*), cuttlefish (*seppie* – the colour sepia is derived from their ink), slithery octopuses (*polipi*), mussels (*cozze*), baby clams (*vongole*), prawns (*gamberi*), giant prawns (*gamberoni*) and 'Dublin Bay' prawns (*scampi*).

Among the *frutti di mare* are creatures I cannot put a name to, and many have local names or colloquial nicknames that do not find their way into the dictionaries. Many of them can be sampled at 'La Maremmana', a superlative *trattoria* in Via dei Macci, which offers, as one of its attractions, a fixed-price *antipasto misto di mare*. One fills one's bowl from a table crammed with different dishes – mussels, squid, anchovies, prawns like small lobsters, slices of octopus, cuttlefish, whitebait, and all the other piscine delights. Marine studies, conducted in such places, are pure pleasure : research is a constant delight. One's vocabulary increases, one's wallet thins only slightly; and if, at the end of another session, the precise translation of *'cicale'* still eludes one, it never seems to matter quite so much.

Wasps are in evidence, too, in marauding squadrons, hovering heavily, landing on everything sweet and brightly coloured. They are a long-bodied variety, the length of a finger-joint, with stings like hypodermics. Rough brown hands wipe them away with the carelessness of long coexistence. These dark folk that converge on the city in the dark hours seem to spring from the earth, as old as the rocks and water; they issue from frescoed walls and dusty necropolis as indomitable, as immortal as the rabbits of the English countryside, throwbacks to a forgotten world so old that city dwellers seem by comparison the merest modern intruders.

The old and the new jostle perpetually. I pick up yesterday's *La Nazione* and read an article on Madonna – the only Madonna, that is, who finds herself regularly in the news in Italy: a popular singer from Detroit who likes to appear on stage in her underwear. This young person's grand-parents came from the old village of Pacentro under Monte Amaro in the wild, snow-capped central Apennines (a provenance she shares, if nothing else, with the film star Alan Ladd, whose real name was De Lisio). Apparently she is to tour Italy – but which cities, the newspaper asks, will she favour with her visitations? Will Florence be one of the chosen few? Will the City of Flowers be granted a vision of the corsetted, peroxide Madonna?

From Piazza d'Azeglio it is hardly worth boarding the bus to S. Marco, but I have bought a block of tickets. (These are sold at any bar or tobacco-nist displaying the ATAF sign. Licensed *Tabacchi* are also, charmingly, required to sell stamps (*francobolli*), candles (*candele*), and salt (*sale*), so covering simultaneously many dark contingencies.) I have bought my block of tickets because I am British. Florentines, it is well known, regard the buses as a free taxi-service, and daily, despite constant threats of incon-venient fines, run a calculated risk of exposure. Bus conductors would stop this fare-evasion at a stroke, of course, but the buses are manned solely by drivers, whose job is merely to drive and chat to passengers.

I alight in the Piazza San Marco, central point of the University and the Academy of Art, and still in summer as lively as a beehive. An eigh-teenth-century loggia on the south-eastern corner, the Loggia dell'

Ospedale di San Matteo, always catches the eye, ravishing with its della Robbia lunettes despite the graffiti. The Accademia, where Michelangelo's *David* and *Prisoners* can be seen, is just nearby: its entrance is in Via Ricasoli. But I head for S. Marco, the Dominican church and convent on the north side of the square, across the central garden, where a couple of tramps, watched by perky strutting pigeons, are performing their morning ablutions.

The church itself, founded in 1299, was rebuilt in the fifteenth and sixteenth century, and now has a run-of-the-mill Baroque façade. Inside are the tombs of those two great Renaissance Humanists, Pico della Mirandola and Poliziano, who died in the same year, 1494.

The poet Politian (his real name was Angiolo Ambrogini, but he was called after his birthplace, *Mons Politianus*, i.e. Montepulciano) studied Classics at Florence, was tutor to Piero, Lorenzo the Magnificent's son, and later filled the chair of Classical Eloquence in the Florentine *Studio*. (His portrait can be seen in the Ghirlandaio fresco-cycle in the Sassetti Chapel at S. Trìnita.) His brilliance brought scholars from all over Europe. Today he is perhaps best known for his love lyrics (those singing the charms of Simonetta Vespucci, the beauty who may (or may not) have been Botticelli's inspiration for Venus in his *Primavera*); and for marrying the grandeur of classical poetry to vernacular, Florentine poetry. His pastoral laments strike me as pure Theocritus or Virgil ('*La bella ninfa è sorda al mio lamento / e 'l suon di nostra fistula non cura*'), and his drinking songs seem plucked straight from the Greek anthology ('*sicché, fanciulle, mentre è più fiorita, / coglian la bella rosa del giardino*'). His '*carpe diem*' philosophy comes from Horace, and passes via him to Ronsard ('*cueillez dès aujourd'hui les roses de la vie*'), Herrick ('Gather ye rosebuds while ye may') and countless others. In the space of a single day, Poliziano composed *Orfeo*, a pastoral ballad-play written for the carnival, which is reckoned to be the first ever *libretto*. Pico was a Platonist and Aristotelian whose attempts to reconcile philosophy with the dogma of Mother Church brought him papal condemnation and exile, and imprisonment in France. (He was one of the neo-Platonist Academy that gathered around Marsilio Ficino at Careggi and the Badia at Fiesole, where Lorenzo had his library.) Pico was eventually forgiven by Alexander VI, out of regard for the Medici family, and finally returned to Florence where he reverted to Christianity and decided to become a Dominican friar.

The tombs of these two celebrated men are on the wall before the fourth altar on the left: a place of pilgrimage for all scholars who suffer under the New Barbarism. Beyond this altar, in a projecting arm, is the chapel of S. Antonino (1389–1459) designed by Giambologna, whose hand is evident everywhere here – in the bronze S. Antonino in the sacristy, for example, and the S. Zenobio (Zenobius (d. AD 407 or 424) was first Bishop of Florence, and is one of the city's patron saints) of the triumphal arch.

Antonino Pierozzi was the founder of the monastery of S. Marco (1436), when Eugenius IV allowed the Dominicans of Fiesole to take over a ruined convent, a daughter house of the Fiesolan priory. He was a Dominican reformer, and later Archbishop and Protector of Florence, a mighty figure of perfect integrity and boundless charity. Under his leadership, and with the financial support of Cosimo, Michelozzo rebuilt the convent, Fra Angelico beautified it with his paintings, and S. Marco became a centre of Renaissance Humanism. S. Antonino's incorrupt body (it is pretty well corrupt today, but not unrecognisably human) lies under the altar here.

As I contemplate the wasted remains of the saint, the organ bursts into life, and the joy of music courses through me and lifts me almost into a faint of joy. I mount on bright wings and listen at heaven's window. The vaults are irradiated with sound. Someone is practising, that is all, and the reeds are out of tune. But the sudden, unexpected thrill lifts me high above the organ casement and its silvery ranks, and I float around the apse among gilt cherubs and languid golden angels.

The organ alternately crashes and thunders, and with gentle, breathy figures and tiny, piping piccolos floods the nave with arabesques of sound. I wander around with only a quarter of my mind left for sightseeing. The Fra Bartolommeo *Madonna and Saints*, the striking eighth-century mosaic of the *Madonna in Prayer* from Constantinople, the *Annunciation* fresco over the altar on the entrance wall, the grand Giottesque crucifix over the door, the venerated wooden figure ('*Ecce homo*') in its niche – all these pass me by in a blur. I hear angel trumpets in my ears and only Fra Angelico can satisfy me now.

Next to the church is the narrow entrance to the Museo. As for many years the convent was Fra Angelico's home, so now it is the home of many of his greatest masterpieces. It is a perfect setting, because for many of these works, it was the setting intended for them. Gradually other works were housed here, paintings from S. Trìnita and S. Maria Novella, for example; but this is where the blessed Angelico prayed and painted, and the feeling is, generally speaking, indisputably *right*. It is impossible for me, as I consider the visionary, glowing landscapes and rapt expressions, not to be moved – not by technique or cunning perspective, nor Giottesque directness, nor the solid Masaccio-inspired figures, nor the intensity of the brilliant blues and pinks; but by the motive spirit behind these paintings, their inspiration. Through their vision, I learn more about the faith and mysteries of the Church. They are material for meditation – precisely the end for which they were created.

Guido di Pietro was born at Vicchio in the Mugello around 1400, and took his vows around 1418–20: by 1423, he was already a friar and known as 'Fra Giovanni'. (The sobriquet 'Angelico' was perhaps in the first instance merely eulogistic.) He joined the Priory of S. Domenico at the foot of the long, winding hill to Fiesole, and became a friend of S. Antonino. His first datable work is the *Madonna* he painted for the *Linaiuoli* (the Cloth Guild) in 1433. This tabernacle, in its lovely arched frame, and set in marble by Ghiberti, is here in the Museum. The style is partly Gothic (the Child is a perfectly formed, tiny adult), but this work also demonstrates the artist's awareness of the revolutionary new style of Masaccio – an awareness that was to develop later. Angelico's style, as can be seen at a glance, was profoundly influenced by his religious convictions, and the touching story is told by Vasari that he would never take up his brushes without a prayer, and would never retouch his pictures. 'That was how God wanted them,' he would say. Fra Giovanni was a saintly and deeply spiritual man.

'The convent', wrote Fra Lapaccini, Prior of S. Marco in 1444 and from 1448 to 1453, 'always seems to smile upon all who enter.' That is still true today. As I enter the lovely Chiostro di S. Antonino and sit for a while on the low wall, the garden *does* smile on me: but it is always fresh, always radiant, always welcoming. Beyond is another cloister, that of S. Domenico, but it is tightly locked against an intrusive public. How often I press my nose against the barred glass window of the guest wing, or peer wistfully down from the great library! Its secrecy and quiet make it doubly desirable, like the orchard beyond the high garden wall of one's childhood, with the unreachable, rosy apples.

The Ospizio dei Pellegrini (Pilgrims' Hospice), immediately right of the entrance, is full of glorious works by Fra Angelico: stepping over the threshold here is like entering Paradise to the sound of angel musicians. Immediately the *Deposition* from S. Trìnita stands out (*c.* 1435–40), with its intricate harmony of rose and blue, its mysterious, dreamy background of turreted city, looming castle-topped hills, neat, stylised trees (including a date palm), and sky with squadrons of gold-winged angels cut off at the waist by wispy streams of cloud. Each of the mourners is a masterpiece in its own right; and the black-hooded figure immediately behind the body of Christ is none other than Michelozzo, the painter's friend, and architect of S. Marco.

Nearby is another *Deposition*, with Italian faces among the crowd; in the background an Italianate city spreads, with luscious greenery reminding me of Hockney's backdrops for the 1978 Glyndebourne *Magic Flute*. I note from the brief entry I made in a journal after my first visit the prominence of five words: *redemption, order, piety, devotion* and *awe*. The Church paid for much of this, rich merchants the rest. But sincerity is not bought. Fra Angelico was a man of God inspired. By painting these holy happenings he teaches us about the meaning of life on earth.

I love the series of panels (from a cupboard belonging to the Annunziata) telling stories from the life of Christ. Here is the most exquisite brushwork in miniature. The *Flight from Egypt* is especially appealing: Mary is a tall, long-legged blond, rosy-cheeked, in a blue cloak, perching elegantly side-saddle on a donkey (who steps out purposefully, ears well back). Clutching a doll-like Babe wrapped in a scarlet shawl, she eyes the southern distance and the future with calm, but not without apprehension. Joseph strides along beside her through the hilly terrain, black-capped and black-stock-inged, in a robe of brilliant saffron-gold hitched at the waist, with his walking stick and water-bottle. Trees like lollipops recede into the distance, with foliage touched into sparkling life with gold.

There is a similar attention to fine detail in the tabernacle from S. Maria Novella (*Coronation of the Virgin*), where the heads are no more than half an inch high. How I would love to see the brushes the master used for this fine work, how he applied his colours to produce such a patina! An altarpiece (*Madonna Enthroned*, with Cosmas and Damian, the patron saints of the Medici, kneeling below) painted for the church of S. Marco has a *predella* that always intrigues me: one of its scenes depicts a primitive, jolly attempt at a leg-transplant. SS. Cosmas and Damian, according to legend, were twins who practised medicine without charging fees. Some scholars have attempted to deny their historical existence, claiming they are nothing more than a Christian version of the Dioscuri, Castor and Pollux, the Gemini, twin sons of Zeus. But there is evidence that they did exist, and they are still invoked as co-patrons of the medical profession. What 'the holy, moneyless ones' would have made of the prosperous, relatively leisured practitioners of today is hard to say.

There is also the *Madonna delle Stelle*, a ravishing little tabernacle with angels playing harps over the frame, and saints pictured beneath. And in the celebrated *Last Judgment* (*c.* 1430) from S. Maria Nuova, Angelico shows the superiority of his creative imagination in Paradise to his dim and saintly idea of Hell. I should love to have met this holy friar.

A perfect little courtyard, dripping greenery, leads to the *Foresteria* (guest quarters). In S. Vincenzo Ferrer's cell there are splendid detached frescoes, and an outstandingly beautiful *Madonna and Child* by Luca della Robbia. Three feet high, she has yellow hair tied by a head-band, and eyebrows outlined in blue; her cloak is blue with green lining; she wears a red-brown tunic, high-girdled. The Child, clutching a fruit to his little breast, smiles most beguilingly. I look at the mother's fingers, so long and elegant and perfect, as they cradle the babe, her left hand, with delicate modesty, covering his genitals. She sits, in simple serenity, on a pedestal of pale mauve. Coming upon such beauty without warning is alarming. I itch to reach out and touch and hold, I war with a wild impulse to lift her bodily. Kenneth Clark fell to his knees before Piero della Francesca's Urbino Diptych. Dorothy Wordsworth screamed at her first sight of the Alps. Among the early Italian paintings I find myself alternately weeping and smiling, and if the initial aesthetic shock has faded long ago, constant attention reaps new rewards. If our attention wanders (as it must: we have our hours of expansion and contraction) we must wait for it to revive. The semaphore of art is hardly to be learned at a trot.

I pass back along the side of St Dominic's Cloister and, in the small refectory, collapse onto a hard wooden chair to look for a few minutes at Domenico Ghirlandaio's *Last Supper*, which covers the far wall. The setting is cunningly illusionistic: the artist has adapted the vaulting of the refectory as part of the loggia in which Jesus and the disciples sit, behind a long table, at supper (the 'upper room'). A mosaic floor with slanting diaper-pattern assists the pictorial sense of depth. Through open arches one glimpses delightful fruit trees: lemons and oranges, a date palm, cypresses, and swooping birds of various colours; a peacock perches on a window ledge and trails a glorious rainbow tail – all happy signs of an earthly paradise, and symbols of Christian significance. The long table is covered in a fine linen cloth embroidered at each end with an ornate border; on it an assortment of bowls, decanters and fruit are delicately touched in. The effect (quite deliberately created by the background) is one of idyllic calm, an effect corroborated by a small, rather underfed cat who sits in the foreground and stares at the spectator, as cats will.

The composition and iconography of the *Ultima Cena* in Florence are an interesting barometer of style and taste. This fresco was painted some time after 1480, and is a close variant of one in the Cenacolo of Ognissanti. In both, Christ and the Disciples are seated behind (more authentically, of course, they should be reclining at) a long table, with Judas Iscariot isolated on *this* side – an arrangement which goes back to Castagno (*c.* 1450) and Taddeo Gaddi (fourteenth century). In this version, all the disciples sit bolt upright, except for 'the disciple Jesus loved', who reclines in his Master's bosom. Judas alone has no halo.

The tourists arrive in garish colours: first a gloomy French couple, he slim and athletic and handsome; she mountainous, heavy chested. She watches as her son takes a series of running leaps at the wall, jumping higher each time and leaving plimsoll prints as he tries to reach the fresco itself. *'Doucement!'* she whispers. Slack American jaws come in; withered, faded matrons with tight hair and mottled wrists. Their spouses waddle behind them in shorts, hating the heat, Italian incompetence, lousy hotels, poor sanitation: *Americanus contra mundum.* The doorway is filled with suicidal-looking Germans. A serene Indian couple – rare sight – float in, an oasis of stillness and peace. The whole world is here, and the temperature rises by the second. Time to move on.

At the top of the stairs is the famous *Annunciation* fresco of Angelico. It is miraculous to come upon it suddenly – one of the greatest joys of Florence, and only a foot away! Mary is a simple blond-haired girl, no *quattrocento* palace-bred princess, sitting on a wooden stool in a lovely loggia; her cloak may be a rich ultramarine, gold-bordered and green-lined, but her robe is the simple white of purity. Her hands, folded across her bosom, imitate those of Gabriel, in a gesture of acceptance and humility. Her face, brown-haloed like the angel's, is a delicate study of apprehension and modesty. The angel is seen in profile, on one knee, and, dressed in flowing pink with a glorious golden motif across his breast, around his cuffs and hem, has wings of consummate loveliness, like those of an exotic butterfly, marked like the marbled endpapers of old books. Behind the angel is a lawn bright with flowers, and above a plain wooden fence is the variegated foliage of luxuriant trees, all ordered, all gay with the annual rebirth of nature. At dawn on 5 November 1966 there was a curtain of driving rain outside: the Piazza was described by one eye witness as 'like a storm-tossed lake'. A violent torrent poured down the Via C. Battisti from the Piazza dell' Annunziata and washed against the doors of the church. Miraculously, the *Annunciation* was untouched.

I look again and see the angel's eyes narrowed slightly, as if he smiles at Mary, and Mary's headband in rose pink answering the lovely pink of her long robe as it falls in perfect folds to the ground.

Behind the Virgin is a door with a tiny barred window – the door, surely, of the sort of cell that lines the corridors of the monastery here. All the cells, forty-four of them, look out onto a giant cedar of Lebanon and the red tiles of the convent roofs, or onto the Duomo and the streets that run away towards it; and each one, otherwise austere and bare, is decorated by a fresco-scene, many of them by the Master himself.

The first cell was certainly decorated by Fra Angelico. I pause in the doorway and peer through it at the lovely contrast: the fresco is each

133

cell's focal-point, its only embellishment, its colour wonderfully concentrating the attention in surroundings of such blank monotony. I pause also because a young couple are inside, their handsome young backs joined closely from shoulder to ankle. Tenderly, in the seclusion of the cell, the youth caresses the girl's arm, then lets his hand drop lightly onto her buttock. They are gazing intently at the fresco, which is entitled *Noli me tangere*.

I pass to the third cell, and another simpler, but equally moving *Annunciation*. Mary kneels on a footstool in abject humility, while the angel, blond like Mary, dressed in glorious rose pink again, and with a golden aureole, stands gazing down at her. His wings this time are more bird-like, with peacock eyes of maroon and dark olive at the feather tips. Behind him, outside a simple vaulted room much like the cells in which the monks spent their lives, and in which Mary's footstool is the sole furniture, St Dominic stands, his hands clasped in prayer; he wears the white habit and black cloak of his Order, and has the gory pate of St Peter Martyr.

In a mist, I move from cell to cell: a *Nativity*, a *Transfiguration*, *The Maries at the Sepulchre*. Life spent largely in solitary confinement is not for many today, but solitariness is not loneliness. The call to a life of prayer and meditation seems to modern man a curious thing, a soft opting-out, perhaps, a sad waste of life. *Tempora mutantur*. In earlier centuries when man walked more closely with God, the urge to remove oneself from the contamination of the city and retire to some lonely spot on a lofty eminence, maybe, somewhere lifted among the clouds and above seething humankind, surrounded by trees and rocks, inaccessible and unviolated, was felt more keenly. Dotted around the dramatic Tuscan countryside were eremites, shaggy John the Baptists dressed in rags, skeletonic, existing on berries and honeydew and who knows what. Elsewhere, as in the case of Montesenario and Vallombrosa, like-minded men grouped together under a common impulse and pooled their spiritual resources, formed a powerhouse of prayer. And so the religious Orders grew up. The Dominicans, at S. Marco and S. Maria Novella in Florence, were above all preachers and teachers and suppressors of heresy. Interestingly, one of St Dominic's last projects was to install nuns at S. Sisto in Rome (he always stressed the importance of women in his Order) and to send thirteen of his Brothers to Oxford. These are the Blackfriars, ensconced in a lovely old building in St Giles, and it was among them all those years ago, that I began to learn the rudiments of Hebrew.

Cell 31 is the cell of S. Antonino himself: a death-mask, a case displaying some of his manuscripts and various other relics of the holy man remain, and a fresco, *Christ's Descent into Limbo*, painted by one of Fra Angelico's assistants. When I look at the little devils cowering in terror here, I often wonder how the Florentines of the early Renaissance regarded these scaly, serpent-tailed, horned beasts – whether they were ever seen as literally accurate by a credulous, fundamentalist flock, or were always considered as a metaphor. The feeling they inspire today is more one of amusement than terror. But the artists made their point: whatever they are not, they are *disagreeable*.

In Cells 32–35 there are more fine frescoes, also probably by the painter of Cell 31. Cell 33, a double cell like 32, is generally regarded as that of the Master himself. If tradition is correct the beatified Angelico had two rather inferior paintings as companions of his solitude: the *Arrest of Jesus* and a (now fragmentary) *Entry into Jerusalem*. But perhaps this prolific Master had not much solitariness to contend with. Vasari expresses his incredulity that any man could produce so much first-class work in a single lifetime.

In Cell 35 there is an interesting *Last Supper* which has become transmogrified into the *First Eucharist*. Eight of the disciples sit behind a bare table; four kneel in the right foreground. In the background are recessed windows showing tiled roofs and other convent windows; through an archway we see a little well, and beyond it a palm tree. All twelve disciples are haloed, and, on the left, a woman (also haloed, and presumably Mary) kneels. Jesus is pictured distributing the Host to a beardless John; in his other hand he holds a large chalice.

Cells 38 and 39, *en suite*, are more commodious. These are the rooms Cosimo occupied when he went into retreat, and which Eugenius IV used in 1443 when he consecrated S. Marco. I climb the six little steps to the lovely *Epiphany* fresco, which has much of the finesse and feeling of Fra Angelico himself, though heavily restored in the nineteenth century. The aumbry beneath presumably held the reserved Sacrament.

At the end of the corridor running east-west are the quarters of the Prior. Room 12 was once a little chapel. In Rooms 13 and 14 St Antonino lived during his incumbency; but the compelling portrait identifies the room's most celebrated, not to say notorious, occupant. The strongly hooked nose, sensuous full lower lip, and prominent cheekbones are arresting enough; but, to add to these physical attributes, we are told he had blazing grey-green eyes. The sinister, pale, black-hooded face is that of Fra Girolamo Savonarola, *éminence grise* of later fifteenth-century Florence, and the chilling profile was done on panel from life by a fellow Dominican at S. Marco, Fra Bartolommeo. The legend reads *Hieronymi Ferrariensis a Deo missi prophetae effigies*: 'Portrait of Jerome of Ferrara, the prophet sent by God' – a haunting face, and, in the light of later events, a haunting comment.

I suppose Savonarola is one of the most dominant and fascinating personalities of the Florentine Renaisssance. Here, in this narrow cell, he lived and composed his vitriolic sermons; here, it could be argued, he started the movement that sparked the whole Reformation. His personality was so potent and magnetic that nothing he touched remained unaffected: the thick walls of his rooms, his coarse robe, the bibles and texts of his sermons here seem impregnated with his memory.

Savonarola came to Florence in the summer of 1489, and was elected Prior of S. Marco in 1490. Now, in the last quarter of the *quattrocento*, a group of poets and scholars had gathered round Lorenzo il Magnifico to form an Academy – famous names like Landino, Marsilio Ficino, Poliziano, and Pico della Mirandola. This was never a formal institution: it was merely a congregation of like-minded intellectuals who read and discussed together the best Classical authors, and who shared a love of Plato. They became known as the 'Platonic Academy', and they were called 'Humanists'. Lorenzo was head of, and host to, their meetings.

The Humanists quarried the Greek philosophers in their search for a new way of life. They were not atheists: they tried to reconcile their Humanism with Christianity, but they pursued reason, and inevitably their Christian orthodoxy was undermined. Not only scholars like Poliziano, but religious, too, became more materialistic, eager collectors of art; and the artists themselves, giving their works a thin religiosity, in reality became more licentious and pagan. Man had become the measure of all things. The saints and apostles were no longer venerated as much as Greek philosophers and Roman poets.

The new mood was one of confident gaiety, of the pursuit of beauty for beauty's sake, even of extravagant pleasure-seeking. Whatever the high-minded aims of the scholars who met with Lorenzo at the lovely villas outside Florence, the result of their convictions was that the temporal ousted the spiritual. Florence was the 'new Athens'. With luxury came effeminacy, as happens, and under Lorenzo there appears to have been a marked increase in homosexuality (which of course had excellent Greek precedents) and prostitution.

Into this world came Savonarola, a mesmeric preacher and dynamic demagogue, determined to reform the laxity of the Church and the immoral laity. In a series of blistering homilies in S. Marco and the Duomo he denounced Humanism and all its works, and predicted the imminent punishment of all those who turned their back on God. With violent gestures and ranting voice, Savonarola called for a return to purity and simplicity: he attacked usury, gambling, fine clothes, cosmetics, and festivals. In these tirades he shows a splendid turn of phrase: 'In the early Church the chalices were made of wood and the prelates of gold, while today the chalices are of gold and the prelates of wood.' Even the Virgin Mary, he said, had been painted everywhere as a harlot.

Under his direction, all 'vanities' were heaped on bonfires in the Piazza della Signoria and burnt: playing-cards, books galore, paintings, wigs, masks, dice, cosmetics, hats, dresses, mirrors, musical instruments – *all* the instruments of pleasure were consigned to the flames: 'The Bonfire of Vanities'. Boys' hair was cropped shorter, organised groups of altar boys raided houses and seized decks of playing-cards. Claiming instructions direct from Heaven, this turbulent priest prophesied the invasion of a foreign army; in a vision he saw a dagger held over the City of the Lily. Swords, flaming arrows and firebrands hailed down; there was war, famine, plague.

As a proselytiser and crusader Savonarola won many adherents. People flocked to join his Order. Pico himself decided to join the Dominicans, but died before he could do so. Ficino, Poliziano and Botticelli heard and believed in the man. Sixty years later, Michelangelo said he could still hear the *frate*'s voice ringing in his ears.

Much that he said was the plain truth. Under a Borgia Pope (Alexander VI, who had six children, one called Cesare) Rome had plumbed the depths. The Church was in disarray, Order squabbling with Order; papal dispensations were regularly forged and a source of fat income; criminals could always buy their freedom. (Cardinal Borgia, charged with this palpable injustice, is alleged to have replied: 'The Lord requires not the death of a sinner, but rather that he may pay and live.') Pope Sixtus IV had made a packet of money out of brothels.

After Lorenzo's death in 1492, his sons Piero and Giovanni and Giuliano proved unequal to the situation. In 1494 the French invaded, an incursion of 31,500 men to which Savonarola alluded in terms that made his audience's hair stand on end. ('Barbers with giant razors' would descend on Italy, he told them, and *chastise* her!) Florence survived by bargaining, and there followed a diffident alliance with Charles VIII. The Medici went into exile, and Florence constituted a Grand Council of 500, drawn from different sections of the citizen body, which was empowered to elect the *Signoria* and to pass laws. Savonarola played an important part in these constitutional changes, and he became supremely powerful. He ordered the whole city to fast three days in the week on bread and water, and two further days on bread and wine; he even removed glorious illuminated missals and precious furniture from S. Marco. It is hard to imagine the atmosphere of remorse and self-chastisement which prevailed. Later Botticelli was actually to abandon the painting of nudes, because Savonarola had condemned it.

A personality like Savonarola's excites violent attachment or violent opposition. He had claimed divine inspiration, preached pro-French sermons, and was a thorn in the flesh of a Pope committed to ridding Italy of invaders. He tried first to buy off Savonarola with a Cardinalate ('Give me *another* sort of red hat,' the inflexible reformer said, 'one red with blood'), then excommunicated him.

For six months Savonarola prayed hard to see the way ahead; then finally, on Christmas Day 1497, he defied the Pope and celebrated Mass in S. Marco. But when the Pope threatened Florence with an interdict, the Florentines begged Savonarola to stop his preaching, and, after one last lambasting of the Church and its corrupt hierarchy from top to bottom, the turbulent priest was silent. With his silence, his star began to wane. There had always been opposition; now there was disaffection among his followers. His personal enemies, no doubt spurred on by the arch enemy in Rome, set about accomplishing his downfall.

The Franciscans had felt especially keen resentment at this self-styled latter-day prophet, and it was one of their number who challenged him to an ordeal by fire. The two monks were to walk through a tunnel of flame, and the one who survived would prove the truth of his word – a final, indisputable test of the Dominican's *bona fides*. All was prepared: a 75-feet-long platform was built in the Piazza della Signoria with a path 3 feet wide, tinder-dry and ready to roar and crackle at the lighting of a faggot. The crowds swarmed to see the show. But the event, after repeated (deliberate) questionings of the rules, and disputes with the presiding magistrate over procedure, was finally cancelled.

Thwarted of its fun, the mob turned against Savonarola; overnight anger turned to violence, and on Palm Sunday 1498 they stormed S. Marco, killing any Brothers who dared defy their clubs and swords. The magistrates had meanwhile ordered Savonarola's arrest on a trumped-up charge of heresy, and he was taken to the Palazzo Vecchio, thrown into a minuscule prison (the *Alberghettino*) and repeatedly put to the torture by rack and *strappado* until he signed a 'confession'. It was a 42-page document.

On 23 May Savonarola was brought out onto the *ringhiera* outside the Palazzo with an iron collar round his neck, and, with two other Dominicans, degraded, stripped of his vestments, his face and hands shaved, and hanged. Then his body was burnt and his ashes thrown into the Arno. Gunpowder was thrown onto the fire so that the good citizens could enjoy their beloved fireworks; and, as arms and legs fell from the corpse, stones were hurled to destroy them utterly, in case people should rummage for relics and souvenirs. The Papal Envoy, the General of the Dominican Order, and 'many canons, priests and monks of Divine Orders' were there, and to judge from the pictures which record the event, it was a colourful scene.

I find the congeries of relics in Savonarola's cell unbelievably poignant: his crucifix and rosary, his chair, his tattered sackcloth of penitence... Here was no heretic nor fraudulent miracle-worker: his aim was to reform, and he made the mistake of telling the truth.

I step again into the brightness of the corridor and make for the library. But Savonarola is everywhere here: a tablet on the entrance-wall marks the exact spot where, on 8 April 1498, he was finally arrested.

The famous library was built by Michelozzo in 1444, and is arguably his masterpiece. It is like an elongated basilica, with two arcades each resting on eleven columns with Ionian capitals; the central aisle has a simple barrel vault, the side aisles are cross-vaulted. Above all, this is an easeful place, elegant, full of light as libraries should be. Most of the important books from the collection have gone to other libraries now, to the Biblioteca Laurenziana in particular; but a selection of the manuscripts still at S. Marco is always on display. These decorated antiphonals, graduals, and psalters with their brilliant miniatures, elaborate initials, and blocked plainsong, belong to a vanished world that can never be recaptured: the painstaking brush and penwork, the precious gold and silver leaf so unerringly and lovingly applied, leave one feeling like a clumsy, clodhopping rustic. Such finesse! My hands on the case look like a peasant farmer's! Many of these treasures were bought for S. Marco by Cosimo himself, and a gorgeously embellished missal, which probably came from the mother convent in Fiesole, is thought to be a work by the young Fra Angelico. Whoever painted it, it is a priceless possession, with its rich, thick leaves of bright gold, and touches of electrifying royal blue and scarlet. The scholars and the artists and the books may have gone: but I seem to feel something of the peace and beauty they once engendered.

In the Piazza the sun is a spur: all the colours have hardened. Perhaps Fra Angelico has dulled them for me. A no. 7 bus, crammed with students and tourists, sets off for Fiesole again, and in the square, by the undistinguished statue, a clutch of school-children picnic where the tramps had been washing themselves.

Just down Via Cavour, which runs roughly north–south past S. Marco, is the Chiostro dello Scalzo. Today it is run by the Comune, open every morning except Monday, and entrance is free: the door even stands open in welcome. But for years one had to shout into a grille outside no. 69 at a deaf concierge, and pray for the door to buzz ajar. (*Si prega di dare la mancia*: tip expected.) I remember on a number of occasions almost giving up. But at the second or third attempt my diffident Italian was usually rewarded.

'*Scusi, posso vedere il chiostro?*'

Inside, silence: outside, an orchestrated cacophony of traffic bedlam: soprano Vespa klaxons, air-brakes hissing, a policeman whistling, and acres of burning metal; from several directions radios play insistently ugly music. An advertisement on a nearby wall catches my eye: NON SARETE MAI SOLI. FIRENZE VI AMA. I ring the bell a second time.

'*Mi scusi. Io sono uno scrittor inglese*' (my second gambit is more ambitious) '*e le sarei molto grato se volesse farmi entrare – .*'

A click, and the door opens slowly to reveal a grey, wizened face. An ancient lady wearing an apron stands before me, her eyes sunken. I begin again, but the grey face retreats; I am being shown in. The door shuts automatically behind me, and I find myself alone in a small, frescoed courtyard: slender columns are arranged in pairs with gracious Corinthian capitals. Here everything conspires to delight, and, alone, I can take my time. The walls are decorated with breathtaking monochrome frescoes by del Sarto. These were done originally for the Confraternita di S. Giovanni Battista, which was nicknamed '*dello Scalzo*' ('*scalzo*' means barefoot, discalced) either because the Crucifers traditionally walked in the Confraternity's Easter procession barefoot, or because the monks generally went around barefoot. The community was suppressed in the eighteenth century.

These scenes, done in *grisaille*, are in tints now sepia, now greyer, touched with brilliant white lead highlights, and bordered with elaborate grotesques and festoons designed by Andrea di Cosimo Feltrini (who had collaborated with Andrea at SS. Annunziata). Here del Sarto executed the grotesques himself; as was the practice, the 'frames' were done first, then the episodes inside them.

The frescoes form a cycle telling the life of the Baptist. I rush first to the *Baptism of Christ* on the right end wall, and fall in love with two angel faces, and know I must take them home. Of course, there are no postcards or guide books: hoping against hope I take a few hand-held camera shots at a speed so slow I can identify all the phases of the shutter mechanism as they operate in order. Clunk, click-click. 'I want these faces,' I scribble in my guide book in a fever of excitement. (And I got them. Against all odds the images were sharp and stood a mighty enlargement. The faces, even in reproduction, are miraculously lovely.) But the whole cloister is peopled with beautiful forms. These scenes were, says Vasari, 'the study and school of many youngsters who today excel in these arts.' Del Sarto was considered the greatest Florentine draughtsman of his day, and this is his monument.

The sequence goes from right to left, interspersed with four allegorical figures: Faith, Hope, Charity and Justice (of whom, fittingly, Charity is greatest – a glorious group less like a wall painting than a sculpture, so solid are the shapes as they emerge from the 'niche' behind them). These paintings represent the first monochrome attempt to combine fictive sculpture with fictive architecture, and their effect is highly dramatic and quite extraordinary. There are records of payments for this series from 1515 until as late as 1526, and this concentration within a small area of so many years of the artist's work offers a unique opportunity to see the development of his style and the evolution of his artistic personality.

To begin with, Andrea was tied to the tradition of the *quattrocento*; but, as he became aware of Michelangelo's originality, his work became more animated, with more harmonious rhythms. It was del Sarto's response to the innovations of Michelangelo and Raphael in Rome that led to his foundation of Tuscan Mannerism. A fairly close chronology can be established: when Andrea disappeared to France (he was not in great demand) and the friars were perhaps despairing of his return, his friend Franciabigio was commissioned to paint *The Baptist's Leavetaking* and *Meeting with Christ*; these were executed in 1518–19. Ironically, the latter is among the clearest and best preserved of the whole cycle, enabling us to see that the young St John will have to change a great deal if he is to look like the John who baptises Christ or preaches in the wilderness. He has a fleshy face; del Sarto's Baptist is gaunt and hollow-eyed. He may not wear a shirt of hair, but he certainly *looks* as if he has lived on wild locusts.

The Baptism of Christ, whose kneeling angels are with me always, is the earliest del Sarto (painted some say in 1507–8, others *c.* 1510), a rather bare composition, worn now, and done in sepia with white highlights. One angel is seen in profile, her robe gathered in ample, flowing folds; the other, with head tilted, is shown almost full face, a vision of beauty.

The *Charity* comes next (*c.* 1513), a wonderfully harmonious group, greyer in tone, but with touches of gold, and Michelangelesque in its plastic, monumental quality. There is a well established tradition that when the sculptor Sansovino returned to Florence in 1511 and worked in the same *bottega* as Andrea, he actually made models for the figures in the Scalzo frescoes; and one can easily believe it.

The *Preaching of the Baptist* (1515), too, has faces and attitudes among the crowd, and the *Baptism of the People* (1517) muscular bodies in Classical postures, which are designed to display anatomies in tension and relaxation, heroic poses and counter-poses, that are strongly reminiscent of Michelangelo. The male nude at the extreme right of the latter could be an *ignudo* from the Sistine Chapel. I recognise Andrea's wife, Lucrezia, her brow and nose unmistakable, in the woman seated at the saint's right leg: it may be that she is there too, in the woman seated on his right side.

In 1517 Andrea completed also *The Taking of the Baptist*, a dramatic, triangular composition with Herod at its apex, and the haloed, half-naked John below to the right. The figures are frozen in mid-action, their limbs and attitudes suggestive of violent drama. A pale, spectral figure trips down steps on the far left, with a sidelong glance (of guilt?) at the proceedings. Who *are* these anonymous spectators, I wonder, that gaze down from galleries, peer through windows and linger on stairways?

After 1517 Andrea did nothing in the Chiostro dello Scalzo for five long years: he was active elsewhere, mainly in the court of King Francis at Fontainebleau, and it was in this period that he painted the great *Madonna of the Harpies*, and a magnificent *Madonna and Child with Angels* (these angels have flown down straight from heaven via the roof of the Sistine Chapel) which hangs in the Wallace Collection.

When he returned to Florence, Franciabigio stood down (Vasari's talk of rivalry is surely tittle-tattle), and the scenes he painted between 1521 and 1526 show a new subtlety and greater dramatic power, as if distancing himself had enriched his creative talents and added to his imaginative vigour. His compositions now are more *heroic*. Salome, chastely covered, is a voluptuous but decorous figure, both when dancing (1522) and at *Herod's Banquet* (1523), where the Baptist's head is brought in. The angel in the *Annunication to Zechariah* (1523) is seen in profile, hair tousled, wings swept back, the line from brow to tip of nose unbroken, a powerful and beautiful creation. In the same year came *Faith*, a lovely girl holding a cross and communion chalice, her drapery exquisite; *Hope*, blind and simply clad, her hands clasped, without ornament; and, ironically, the *Decollation*, in which the executioner displays a splendid physique (rear view) and the haloed and bearded head of the Baptist, imposing in death as in life, evokes interesting and different reactions (neither of triumph, nor even satisfaction) in the faces of Salome and her mother.

The *Visitation* (1524) is cracked and worn, but a fine study in rest and movement; the old man on the left and the young man mounting the steps with a bundle on his shoulder are very Pontormesque. In one of the candelabra to the left, the signature of 'il Poppi', Francesco Morandini

(1544–97), has been discovered, and it is probable that Poppi added some final touches to areas left unfinished by the Master.

Last of all, curiously, was *The Birth of the Baptist* (1526), a scene of domesticity and solemn stillness, in which Zacharias sits placidly at the bedside writing, the midwife tenderly holds the babe, and Elizabeth, her labour over, appears to be rearranging a pillow; and another of those shadowy extras gazes at the spectator, this time a lady in the background who, with pitcher in her hand, is about to fetch some water.

This little, secret cloister has so far been quite unspoilt by coach parties and trippery: it is a jewel, and, as I look now at my snapshots of the sunlight playing on the thin double columns, the grotesque stands out like real pargetting, the Charity group is living sculpture perched in an alcove; and the thought of what line and shading and highlighting can do to a plain wall of white plaster is astounding. Del Sarto died of the plague in 1530, still in young middle age. His reputation was at its apogee at the end of the sixteenth century. Critics have tended to write him off as a clever draughtsman, competent but conventional – a technician rather than a painter of inspiration. Of Florentines, to my mind, he is second only to Michelangelo.

I sign my name in a large Visitors' Book and leave. Hunger lends wings to my feet. Flying along Via Guelfa and turning up Via S. Orsola, with its stalls of cheap clothes and army surplus, I turn my back on the heaving market and, while my knees revive and my head clears, drink several flutes of chilled *bianco spumante* at 'Zanobini'. On the blackboard behind the bar are listed a dozen wines on offer by the glass: 'Zanobini', in Via S. Antonino, a narrow street full of interesting shops (a first-class cutler, for example, and the best *prosciutto* shop in the city), is a glittering oasis composed almost entirely of wine bottles. The son of the owner, recognising me, nods and applies himself to vigorous glass-drying. The red-faced local bibber, holding his *Nazione* and shopping bag, talks to tourists in a mixture of French and platt-deutsch. I slide out greatly refreshed. Bang opposite, leaning against the wall, lobster-coloured in straw hat, Terylene short-sleeved shirt and khaki drill trousers, I see a perfectly pleasant, thoroughly worthy colleague of mine from England. I dart into the teeming Mercato Centrale, among the yellow chickens and pinky meats. It is never more than two steps from angel faces to the raw stuff of reality.

The lower floor of this monstrous edifice, a vast greenhouse put up in sections, is given over to grocers' shops, meats and fish; I wander the alleys noting what is on offer here that cannot be had at S. Ambrogio. For a start, there is *cinghiale*, wild boar: on slabs and hanging from

Central Market

stanchions, in death they assume the appearance almost of cuddly toys. The deadly, curling tusks seem to impart a silly grin, and the coarse black bristles remind me of Japanese dolls, and a curious shaggy carpet upon which I was photographed once as a naked baby.

And I recall a day years ago in Montalcino at a restaurant owned by friends of Lisa. Our host, the restaurateur, a titled, adipose, courtly young man, with manners a hundred years old, appeared in a Jäger hat, plus-fours, gartered stockings, climbing boots, and, strung round his neck on a silver chain, the metal scoop of a *sommelier*. His name is lost in the fog of years, but I remember a rather melancholy, nervous wife with a young, fractious child to nurse; and the house was the sort of out-of-the-way country establishment, centuries old, with old-fashioned standards, first-class kitchens, and exceptional cellar, that John Fothergill ran at Thame. There were heaped logs on a smoky fire, giving the place a sharp, almost bitter taste of the land; domestic animals roamed about; and guns, swords, gleaming hunting paraphernalia hung from every beam: the smells were of wood smoke, damp, leather and gun-oil, the incense of the countryside. The scene was far more familar to an Englishman, I felt, than an Italian. I half looked for fudge, Bristol glass, copper kettles, smoothing irons, scones and trug baskets in a bay window. Our host was *sui generis*, a character who had strayed from the pages of a Walter Scott novel, or Henty, perhaps, or Dumas *père*. With many a nod, heel-click and graceful inclination of the head, he took our order – or rather explained it as he wrote it down, because he had already selected what we were to eat. The idea was a meal of many courses, and all from recipes going back to the time of the Medici. I knew from experience that this meant simple, tasty, nourishing fare. The Tuscans were plain-living people: even today many of their best dishes make much of little: *bruschetta* (or *'fett'unta'*, crisp toast with oil and garlic), *pinzimonio* (fresh raw vegetables with a dip of olive oil, pepper and salt), and *ribollita* (rich vegetable soup from a stock-pot) are basically peasant fare.

And so it proved: perhaps there were eight or nine courses, from *crostini* (toast-fingers, in this case with chicken livers) to a sweet almond biscuit served with *vinsanto*, each a subject for conversation, and each flavoured by the wood smoke from the fire (could it have been fragrant turkey oak?). We drank a ten-year-old Brunello, the local vintage, brownish, strong yet delicate, and still my favourite Italian wine. Lisa took her token sip and launched into an effusive monologue about the superior *acqua naturale* of the region.

One of these many courses (brought in leisurely succession and punctuated by cigarettes and gossip) was *cinghiale*, loin-slices of young boar sautéd in white wine. I complimented our host, and asked him where he got such delicious fresh meat.

He mimed a rifle shot. 'I shot it!' His well bred features registered something approaching hurt. 'For you! This morning!' From the corner of my eye I saw Lisa mirror his offended pride. Were there many wild boars about the hills, I asked him?

Oh yes, many, too many! They hid in the chestnut trees, in the forests, in the deepest part of the woods, and came out at night to feed. You might not see them, but you could smell them, especially the old males. They were very strong, very fierce! With a gracious nod of 'by-your-leave' in Lisa's direction, our host unrolled his sleeve and showed me a long, deep scar, still livid, from his elbow to his upper forearm.

'They starve,' he continued, 'and they go mad. Only last week, not far away, a boar came out of the forest and took a baby from a pram and ate it.'

So much for the cuddliness of the *cinghiale*: at least, on a slab in the Mercato, they can do no more harm. Nearby there are hares (*lepri*), rabbits (*conigli*), quail (*quaglie*), pigeon (*piccioni*), turkey (*tacchini*), guinea-fowl (*faraone*), duck (*anitre*) and pigs' trotters (*zampe; zamponi*, pigs' trotters stuffed with spicy pork sausages and eaten hot, is a favourite Tuscan dish).

The fishmongers, who take up the whole of the far end, are a special haunt of mine: many of the fish here are alive and squirming, slithering and snapping. The crayfish stir sluggishly, but spring into a terrifying surliness if a customer attempts to pick one up. Some claws are already closed with hefty rubber bands. 'VIVI!' shouts a blurred, slimy card, and, as if to prove the point, glass-eyed eels, some thumb-thick, some like small, sinewy submarines, more than six inches across, flicker suddenly into life and disturb the neat silver rows. There are oysters, too, clams large enough to use as ashtrays, and a dozen varieties of squid swimming in their own inky discharge. There is something shark-like, cut in steaks a foot in circumference, *pesce spada*, sword-fish, unmistakably; a few, costly grey-brown turbots (*rombi*); sea trout (*trota salmonata*); lobsters (*aragosse*); a mussel-like shellfish called *arselli*; and *merlini* (marlins), with strange spiky snouts. All these names I note down for reference, deflecting quizzical glances with the best vague English smile I can manage. Then gradually these looks, at first merely curious, become alarmed: brows are contracted, the odd *sotto voce* remark is made; finally, I see glance meeting glance across the alleys and pocket my notebook to hurry upstairs.

The upper floor is for vegetables, flowers and fruit, nuts and seeds, a great jumble of colour under the bright canopy of the greenhouse roof.

A moment's hesitation beside a heap of melons and *chomp*! – a slice appears on the end of a wicked shining blade. Walnuts, polished and perfect, lie in a wrinkled sea; figs, growing purple and tight; ripe apricots and enormous black misty grapes; maize, yellow-green and orange; plums, pears, herbs, salad greens, shelled nuts, sunflower seeds, all in a bewildering kaleidoscope; lettuce, spinach, endive, chicory, chard, peppers...

But too much is enough: 'Zanobini's *vino spumante* has got about my wits. Suddenly at my elbow, as I scribble in my book, I sense company. Even among the milling shoppers I know I am being watched. Nonchalantly as I can, I turn.

Three of the stallholders from below, a butcher, a grocer and a fishmonger are eyeing me, one of them with palpable hostility. I consider my options. I can explain that I am merely attempting to enlarge my vocabulary, or I can leave.

I leave quite swiftly, and, anticipating pursuit, dart left at the top of the staircase into the toilets.

A lady, sitting among buckets and mops at a sort of reception area, acts as concierge. Hearing footsteps advancing, I feign desperation, I walk straight past her. There are two cubicles, both, amazingly, with lockable doors. Both are locked. But while I stand praying, dreading the confrontation, one of them opens, and a cheery porter ushers me in behind him. There are no seats (one crouches as if beginning a slalom run) but nothing matters. Here is asylum. For a moment I am left with my thoughts. Then, from directly outside, like a laser beam, comes the woman's voice.

'*È Romano?*' I hear her call nasally. 'Are you Roman?'

Have the stallholders sent her in to establish my identity? I say nothing. After all, what *can* they have thought of my performance below? A stranger appears and moves methodically from counter to counter, from stall to stall, noting prices and listing merchandise in a little book. Who can he be but the Enemy? An Inspector of Weights and Measures? A Sanitary Inspector? Someone, certainly, from the Comune to check up on trade practices, on customer services! From *Rome* – why not?

'*È Romano?*' The voice achieves an unheard-of nasality. This is no casual enquiry: the owner wants an immediate answer. Will she call the men in? What will they do? My mind races. (Samuel Johnson maintained that the brain was at its most active in a privy, and I am wondering seriously if he was not right.) Now she is rapping on the flimsy woodwork.

Then, suddenly, an explosive flush is heard from next door. The cubicle clicks open and I hear a playful baritone.

'*Eccomi, tesoro! Eccomi!*'

Relief courses through me. I flood with relief. All round there is flooding. The woman has been looking for her husband, after all, and his name is Romano! Romano simply wanted to be left undisturbed.

A large weight rolls from me. In the blessed anonymity of the market, again, I drift along jostled by tourists and lovers, between leather and alabaster and cameo, mohair and silk, ties and headscarves, chess sets and magenta and emerald and olive and brown; turquoise and silver, jewellery, gloves, handbags, suitcases, postcards, trays, pictures of David's genitalia and enlargements of pictures of David's genitalia; melons, ices, coconut-pieces.

In the shade of the looped awnings hung with necklaces and bracelets and bangles, I float on with the tide, my heart still thumping. In the heat my hunger has gone. The octopus-like market has now dwindled to nothing. I find myself outside the little church of S. Barnaba. This is the first time the door has ever been open for me, and I pass gratefully into the gloom. How I wish the fine baroque organ, in its lofty gallery, would burst magically into life in celebration! To judge from the gilt casement, it is in beautiful condition. And the della Robbia lunette at the entrance portal reminds me that Luca and his nephew Andrea had their kiln somewhere near here, in Via Guelfa. On the north wall there are fresco fragments said to be by Spinello Aretino – a poignant choice of artist when one considers this church was erected as a thanksgiving for the Florentine victory, on St Barnabas's Day, 11 June 1289, at Campaldino over the Aretines – a battle in which Dante fought.

No one comes here, and S. Lorenzo could be in the North Pole, so far it seems. Once away from the pulsing heart of the city, the old Florence beats out the little lives of men, in still, mysterious churches, cloistered gardens, and stately private houses with walls of peeling stucco. In a few secluded spots, there is still the feeling of an old world unchanged, of time hanging suspended, like a fly in amber. History is a pattern of timeless moments: in this secluded chapel, in little S. Barnaba, history is now and Florence.

Full of impressions I return to Piazza d'Azeglio. Fiammetta is in a house-coat watching a Grand Prix on the television. As I shower I hear the 'phone ringing repeatedly, and later learn that a young friend of mine, recuperating from a fractured heart, has announced that he will be arriving at the station tomorrow at eight.

My débâcle at the Mercato Centrale and the anticipated arrival of an uninvited teenager are wiped clean from my head when I dine at 'La

Maremmana'. *Tabulae rasae*. I strike up with a portrait painter, an agreeable and knowledgeable American called Walter who has taken a studio for a year in Via Ghibellina.

We share an indecently large *scoglio*, described on the menu as 'for a minimum of three people': the word means 'rock', and the dish, when it comes, is a Sargasso sea of tumbling spaghetti heaped with garlicky shellfish (the effect is that of a rugged, edible island or reef, with a thousand gastronomic eddies breaking the surface). The meal lasts some hours, as we range over Giotto, Masaccio and del Sarto. By now I have heard many things that interest me. Walter has strong views on art, he has the challenging and sceptical attitude of the professional. We speak of our heroes and secret places and finally part under a starlit sky.

Walter was a lonely fellow; he must have been waiting months to unbosom himself to a kindred spirit. We might have become friends, I think, but I lost him through a silly misunderstanding. His other interest was never mine.

CHAPTER

VII

 With an amazingly clear head I contemplate a crowded day: arranging lightning tours of Florence needs courage and a sure hand, it concentrates the mind wonderfully. Young persons are apt to demand explicit answers. In less than an hour my friend will be arriving, and expecting me to know *everything*.

I had considered showing him a few secret things, one or two memorable sights to carry away and treasure up. Then I thought: no, it has to be done. We shall have to see the Duomo and *David*, eat an ice cream at 'Vivoli', and take snaps on the Piazzale Michelangelo. I found myself wallowing in selfish pique.

This morning, Mozart's Wind Serenade in B flat is running through my head. There is a reason for everything, no doubt, and as I shave in a windowless bathroom the size of a broom closet, it comes to me with the glorious *Adagio*. The Serenade had filled my summer evenings of 1985 and 1986, and it conjured back a little jasmine-scented terrace, when my young friend and his sweetheart would sit and watch the night come down, holding hands when the candle on the garden table was lit. I was the merest spectator, and knew a rift would come.

In Via della Colonna I buy a *Nazione* and am soon drinking coffee in the fragrant S. Lorenzo area. In these old streets a blind man might

150

move with the certainty of perfect eyesight, where meat wrestles with cheese, salami with herbs – basil and thyme and tarragon – frying garlic cloves, hot olive oil, freshly ground pepper, coffee, and early-morning tobacco smoke. They are all ambrosial, somehow.

This morning I take a *caffè corretto* (with a dash of *grappa*) and life seems fairer. *La Nazione* has dire news about AIDS: the female mosquito is now the culprit. (It is only the female of the anopheles species who bites, sucks blood, digests it, then returns to lay her eggs.) Last night there was a power-failure in Piazza d'Azeglio (my *fornellino*, a little stove which burns anti-mosquito lozenges, had ceased to function) and I have been eaten alive: fingers, toes, ankles, buttocks, knees. The whining noise woke me a number of times, but the trouble with *zanzare* is that they can dematerialise. My bedroom is the arena of much sleepless stalking, and old wall-trophies stir one to new, more heroic efforts of insecticide. But for all the blots and smudges left as warnings, and for all the thousands of *piastrine* burnt as incense to *Zeus Apomyios*, the same number of females still breach my defences.

Most of the local prostitutes (says *La Nazione*) are now males, and the best looking boys, spotted young by pimps, are despatched south for hormone treatment. Florence has more than her share of *cherubini*. In the Cascine, the long, thin, wooded public gardens to the west of the city, they gather nightly, a host of gorgeous butterflies, and business is brisk. So utterly feminine are these creatures, so alluring, that in order to avoid disappointment the aspiring client is forced to enquire their sex.

Another body has been fished out of the Arno – this time a young man disappointed in the form of the local football side. There is also news of more vandalism in churches and museums, news of prospects of this year's Chianti vintage, and more swipes at Berenson's association with Duveen.

And there is more trouble over Henry Moore's *Guerriero* ('Warrior with Shield'). For thirteen years after Moore's 1972 Exhibition at the Forte Belvedere, the *Guerriero* had been in Florence, but no one could agree on a proper site in which to display it, and it ended up in a minor courtyard of the Palazzo Vecchio which was used as a car park. This angered the sculptor, who demanded the statue back. So back it went, in the summer of 1985, to Much Hadham in Herts, home of the Moore Foundation. Too late the Florentines saw the error of their ways, and their mayor, Massimo Boggiankino, a former administrator of the Paris Opera and La Scala, persuaded the *Banca Toscana* to put up the purchase money. But Moore died in August 1986, and his widow presented the British Institute with the work: this way neither she nor Florence will incur death duties.

'The Warrior' will rest in peace at last – in front of Brunelleschi's Cappella dei Pazzi, a masterpiece of juxtaposition which will distract attention from the one, and show up the other, and which ignores the artist's clearly expressed wish that the bronze should not stand outside. *Mai bene*.

In curious English, but in English, a series entitled 'HOW WHERE AND WHEN' tells Anglophones where to get all-night petrol, hire mopeds, and go for 'movies, music, dinner'. It also disseminates tourist information of a well-meaning and interesting, but often spectacularly unreliable variety, as one quickly finds out.

I pass into Via Nazionale: 'In Via Faenza,' I read, 'n. 42, you find the Cenacolo of Foligno, situated in the Refectory of an ancient Convent: here there is the beautiful *Last Supper* by Perugino. On holidays it is open only in the morning.'

I find the door, which looks as likely to open as a cliff-face, and ring. Eventually a comfortable paunch appears, with several metal teeth. I launch into my Italian lines, smooth with practice. *Chiuso*. The chubby hands gesture eloquently: they hardly move.

'*Ma, le sarei molto grato se volesse farmi entrare – per pochi minuti solamente. Ho fatto più di mille chilometri per vedere questo capolavoro,*' etc.

There is no one here! Everyone is on holiday! The paunch is adamant. *Sì, sì!* The *Ultima Cena* is here: he points maddeningly. Only a few metres away. No, I cannot see it! He is the concierge, yes, but no one can enter, no one.

I make for the station, a blank, unlovely complex of buses and taxis humming with the restless infectious air of human transit. As I negotiate the teeming road, vaulting a barrier, I see a clutch of Jews, black-hatted and black-coated in the heat, with corkscrew curls, black cases and spectacles. If there were ever a race apart, an exclusive, solitary people, non-proselytising, esoteric still, it must be they. The Jewish community in Florence spread east from Livorno. We have census figures from the early days, presumably because here, as elsewhere, they were taxed. The synagogue in Via Farini, near Piazza d'Azeglio, with its bright green cupola, is said to be one of the finest in Europe. It was built in 1874–82 in the Moorish style, and its erection followed the demolition, along with the Mercato Vecchio and many medieval buildings, of the old Ghetto, created in 1571, which ran from the north side of the ugly modern Piazza della Repubblica as far as the Via de' Pecori, which lies on the old east-west grid (like Via Strozzi and Via Porta Rossa and Corso). '*L'Antico Centro della Città / Da Secolare Squallore / A vita nuova restituto / MDCCCXCV*' reads the smug inscription on an enormous neo-Classical archway separating the Banca Nazionale di Lavoro and the Pensione Pendini. '*Vita nuova*' indeed. The result is a disgrace. High on her column Abundanzia-Ceres (early eighteenth century) looks utterly bewildered amid the jumble of garish advertisements, tourists pushing food into their faces, and the clutter of pedestrian, grandiose and boring modern buildings. Here, after all, was the Roman Forum, and the Old Market, the heart and soul of the old city; round it ancient towers, churches, tabernacles, and *loggie* stood in a confused network of narrow streets, each one an improvisation on the last. And near the commercial heart, of course, was the Jewish Ghetto. No doubt, as the centuries passed, repairs and refurbishments were essential, some demolishing and rebuilding necessary: but this levelling, this wholesale razing to the ground was nothing more nor less than a barbarous and philistine deracination of the city's past – a scheme misguided in concept, and in effect drab and unforgivable. I never go there: it has nothing for me, not even the massive and splendidly appointed General Post Office. The employees move as if brain-damaged, and queues wind endlessly like spirals in some microscopic biochemical illustration.

'Ghetto' is quite likely to have been the medieval Venetian word for 'foundry', and it was in the north-west of Venice, on the site of a disused ironworks, that the first 'ghetto' was established in the sixteenth century. Jews were forced to wear a special identifying costume, were taxed almost out of existence, and their settlement, windowless on its outside walls, was patrolled after dark by (Christian) guards who enforced a rigid curfew. No wonder they are exclusive. Once the western state religion was established as Christianity, the wandering Jew had been endlessly, malicously penalised for the sin of his forbears.

I step over the prone bodies of a dozen students comatose in their sleeping bags and emerge in the booming, echoing hall.

And here Andrew stands on the platform (somehow Italian trains arrive punctually: I am a minute or so late), taller than I remember him. And now the sun has bleached his hair and turned his eyelashes to long spikes of gold; he is a young Apollo. He seems to tower above the people as they mill around him, muscular and athletic, a momentary smile of recognition lighting his face. No further displays of emotion are allowed to embarrass us: the ritual handshake is endured and quickly over: eyes are deflected and a neutral conversation is embarked on without delay.

We make for S. Maria Novella, directly across the sea of traffic, beyond the soft drinks and bracelets and cheapjack clothing, and take it in turns to carry his pack. I draw a series of deep breaths before launching into the guided tour. Where to begin? I try to see the façade with his eyes.

No good talking about exceptional features until he is familiar with what is normal. So I say, brilliantly: 'Isn't it beautiful?'

Because it simply *is*: proud Gothic; white marble, inlaid with squares and bands of grey-green. The large, high oculus-window mirrored by two green inlaid circles, one on either side, and one above in the tympanum of the pediment. Harmony and balance. The arches of the *avelli* (arcaded recesses for tombs) are mirrored above, in tall, arched blind windows and in the arch of the main portal. The four green marble columns supporting the architrave are in turn mirrored by the banded pilasters in the upper façade; and the banding is carried round the old cemetery and along the eastern side of the church, above the long series of tombs where the noble Florentine families buried their dead. (Ghirlandaio himself is in one.) And the loveliest touch of all is the two 'scrolls', or volutes, connecting the lower aisle roofs with the nave roof, and preventing the bald effect of a rectangle sitting high on a lower, longer rectangle. This feature was to become a fixed part of Renaissance and Baroque façades.

The lower half is fourteenth-century: the upper façade is by Leon Battista Alberti, and the date of its completion, 1470, is recorded in the frieze below the pediment. It was a commission of Giovanni Rucellai (*Oricellarius* in Latin), son of a celebrated Florentine family and a leading intellectual of Renaissance Florence as well as a fabulously wealthy businessman. (His family name comes from *oricello*, a rare, sought-after red dye for which the city was internationally famous – a purple red got from a lichen imported from Majorca, as prized, it seems, as the *purpura* or 'purple' from Tyre that Roman matrons and emperors so esteemed, which came from the *murex*: this was, as Pliny tells us, the colour of clotted blood; *purpureus* is anything from red through violet to purple, and connected with Greek *pur*, 'fire'.) The Rucellai have their family chapel in the eastern transept, opposite the Strozzi Chapel. The same Giovanni Rucellai had also used Alberti for the extraordinary (and extraordinarily inaccessible) Cappella di S. Sepolcro in Via della Spada just near the family Palazzo in Via Vigna Nuova, which was almost certainly designed by Alberti; this contains a marble, inlaid model of the Sanctuary of the Holy Sepulchre. In more than twenty years I have found the door open only once.

I have to be brutal. We sweep past Beata Villani's tomb, past the Masaccio *Trinity*, and up the long high nave (nothing homely or simple about this: the Dominicans were out to impress). An old man performs elaborate genuflexions and crosses himself head, lips and breast first one way, then in reverse order, before the Madonna of the Rosary – a statue of rebarbative modernity but credited by the Florentines with miraculous powers, as the wall, aglitter with trophies like Liverpool United Clubhouse, attests.

The three tall sanctuary windows, predominantly yellow, but with touches of blue, emerald, purple, brown and scarlet, draw us through the banded arches and over the marble floor like moths to a flame. One side of the sanctuary is covered with tarpaulin and scaffolding, but the other is clear; it shines brilliantly with illumination from a slot machine, and, at the head of the shallow cross of the church, there are so many painted figures it is like coming upon a gaudily dressed crowd. This fresco is the work of my friend Ghirlandaio.

Originally Orcagna had painted the Cappella Maggiore, in 1348. Then in 1485 the Tornabuoni had it repainted, probably using the original design. Tornabuoni paid 1100 florins, and Domenico Ghirlandaio, with the help of his brother Davide, his brother-in-law and pupils, perhaps one of whom was Michelangelo, painted, on the right wall *Scenes from the Life of the Baptist* (the Tornabuoni patron saint), and on the left, *Scenes from the Life of the Virgin*. On the altar wall, there is a *Coronation*, and lower down, the two donors piously kneeling: Giovanni and his wife Francesca (Pitti). It took five years and is surely his masterwork.

Today we can see the Virgin's life and not the Baptist's (next year, no doubt, the Baptist's and not the Virgin's), and among the tiered scenes there are portraits of many fifteenth-century Florentines, of the artists themselves, and of members of the Tornabuoni family, among whom, in the *Birth of the Virgin*, are the ladies in all their finery, in gold-edged pink, and chalk blue; and, in a glorious gold-embroidered gown, a girl with red-gold hair which falls to below her waist. In the *Visitation* a background includes towers and campanili and the contrast of marble and brick so typical of Florence, against gentle wooded hills and heaving mountains. And, as one looks today over a similar view at Piazzale Michelangelo, three men here in maroon hose and caps gaze idly over a terrace at the city spread out below.

Opposite, in the charming *Birth of the Baptist*, a midwife suckles the infant, while Lucrezia Tornabuoni, with braided hair, wearing a heavenly pale pink, sleeveless mantle patterned with gold stars, stands serenely by looking (none too cheerfully, but with great poise) into the twentieth century; and a lovely servant girl, in a whirl of movement, carries fruit on a tray on her head, and wine in flasks. Elsewhere (not visible today) there are more portraits, of the illustrious Marsilio Ficino, Poliziano, Christoforo Landino and others. How I should love to collect them all! To compile a '*prosopografia fiorentina del quattrocento*'. The volume would be bulky, but a delightful companion. Increasingly I like to fit faces to names.

As the trippers file past I steer Andrew towards Benedetto's lovely tomb of Filippo Strozzi in the next chapel, and point out the lunette of exquisite flying angels, and the tenderest of Virgins in her flowery tondo. Here, tradition has it, Boccaccio's seven young ladies and three gallants met on that famous morning in 1348 and planned their escape to the country. (The *Decameron* is not particular on the point, but here I like to think it was.)

I lead the way to the sacristy, and, beneath the Giottesque crucifix, show Andrew one of the best collections of postcards in the city. While he pores over them, I turn to refresh myself at the lovely della Robbian lavabo to the left of the door. '*Ablue fonte prius te quam pia sacra ministres,*' it warns; '*Non licet impura tangere sacra manu.*' And the scene above the wash basin is in the freshest of fresh blues and greens.

Next we make for the Strozzi Chapel in the west transept, entirely frescoed by Nardo di Cione (*c*. 1357). This is always a remarkable sight. The three walls are like illustrations to Dante's *Divine Comedy*: on the right wall, the *Inferno*; on the left, *Paradise*; on the altar wall, the *Last Judgment*. I put a coin in the machine and watch as the seconds tick electronically away. But what a jewel! Best is the end wall, and there, in his familiar floppy hat, third from right, second row from the top, is Dante himself. The donor Strozzi and his wife appear here, too – happily, in Paradise, where they are led to the land promised to all rich donors. Here the haloed saints, clutching their various symbols, rise in rank above happy kings and monks and other saved souls, and a white-robed angel helps the pious to their feet in welcome. On the other side, the damned fret, gnash their teeth and tear their beards in anguish; as they rise through trap doors a little devil stabs them like a picador.

On the right wall, faded and almost impressionistic now, is the Inferno, a spiral of the multifarious circles and *bolgie* of Dante's Hell, where alchemists and imposters, hypocrites and gossips, live out their various punishments. (In case we miss the point, they are carefully labelled: 'Here are those who. . . .') Some are roasted in their coffins, some attacked by centaurs, some undergo impossible Sisyphean labours; others, seen in gaunt black landscapes, with tree stumps rattling bony fingers at them, are assailed by Harpies.

As we move back down the aisle, a priest whose face I know takes a teenage girl into the confessional. All around are the irritations of tourism, sudden pops of flashguns, the Babel of foreign voices, some hushed and inhibited, others quacking and grating and intrusive. The priest sits, dons his stole, shuts the gate and pulls to a swing-door which hides his upper half. A few minutes later the girl emerges; she walks slowly and deliberately and I see her later looking very thoughtful. A shuffling old man takes her place and the same words pass again: the guides shout, the cameras snap, and the Church continues its work of salvation.

In the bustling piazza, I leave Andrew with a guide book and a great emerald *granita di menta*. We arrange to meet again in half an hour.

The Cloisters are fresh and inviting, and the Spanish Chapel is almost empty. Here another wave of colour breaks over the eye. The frescoes, dated in the 1360s, are by Andrea da Firenze (=di Bonaiuto), and they cover all four walls and the cross vaulting as well. Here is a thoroughly Dominican view of life and faith: on the entrance wall is the *Life of St Peter Martyr*; in the vault is the *Resurrection, Ascension*, the *Navicella* (the allegorical Ship of Faith), and the *Pentecost*; on the altar wall (the sanctuary is recessed, and a lovely Daddi polyptych with gilded cusps stands on the altar) a massive *Crucifixion* scene above, and below, left, Christ walks with the cross to Calvary surrounded by soldiers and townsfolk against the background of a turreted city. The Crucifixion, set against a lowering black sky and flights of angels, is a busy composition, with gorgeously caparisoned horses, lances piercing the gloom at various angles, and a crowd of multicoloured bystanders. While devils attack the tortured bodies of the two thieves, Christ is shown at rest, attended by all the squadrons of Heaven. Below, he descends into Limbo, carrying the white oriflamme with its blood-red cross; as he stands, key in hand, crushing a black, scaly, bat-like demon, and other highly coloured devils gaze in awe and terror from niches among the rocks, the haloed faithful greet him.

On the left wall is the *Triumph of the Catholic Church*: St Thomas Aquinas, enthroned, reveals all human knowledge. At his feet sit defeated heretics: Arius (who denied the divinity of Christ), Averroes (an Arabian Aristotelian), and Sabellius (a Unitarian); on either side of his throne are the ten greatest teachers of the Old and New Testament. Below, in fourteen muse-like personifications, the Sciences and Liberal Arts are represented, and at their feet are portraits of the most famous teachers and exemplars of each. The second from right is Rhetoric, in the person of a very womanly Cicero – the least masculine, in fact, of all the portraits here. The iconography is interesting: on what, for example, did the painter base his Euclid and Zeno?

On the right wall is the *Church Militant*, the Church in its active role, and the black and white *Domini canes*, the 'Hounds of the Lord', are everywhere, both as tub-thumping monks refuting heretics, and as fierce, terrier-like creatures rounding up the sheep and guarding them, and tearing apart wolf-heretics. All human life is here; the Duomo itself (in not its final form), the Church and its works, and the portraits of many Florentine worthies: Cimabue, Giotto, Petrarch, Boccaccio, Dante and others. (The donor, Guidalotti, is shown kneeling at confession.) To the right of the

Duomo sit four allegorical figures: two girls, one fondling a pet, one playing a viola, and two men: one with a sporting hawk, the other gloomily plunged in thought. These are said to be the embodiments of Vice: music, hunting, lapdogs (?), and *accidie*, or self-pity (?).

Below them are without a doubt the most attractive figures on this vast wall: divincly slender girls, one of whom beats a large tasselled tambourine, while the others hold hands in a circle and dance, three with radiant Titian hair moving with lissom grace in line upon a flowery meadow; others slope off to thickets, or climb trees and gorge themselves on forbidden fruit. A youth accompanies them on bagpipes. Those to whom the priest gives absolution are shown the way to rose-pink (not pearly) gates, and awaited by all the happy hosts of Heaven. Above them Christ sits in majesty on a throne surrounded by choirs of angels, and flanked by the symbols of the Four Evangelists.

But the allegorical figures worry me. Is the pensive man in grey angry, or brooding bitterly on something? I wish I knew exactly what was in the artist's mind. In desperation, as I leave, I ask a jolly custodian. He is no Kenneth Clark, but he does his level best.

'According to the *Direttore*,' he confirms, 'they are Four Vices. But me, I do not agree. I think they are just four ordinary people. They are waiting for confession.' He spreads his hands. Easy.

Perhaps we all look too deeply.

The restrained, grey *pietra serena*, and plain white walls of the interior contrast strangely with the rough, unfinished brick façade of Brunelleschi's S. Lorenzo. Outside, the market seethes; the unwashed sit on the noble steps and play loud music on their transistor radios, or sleep, propped against each other like playing-cards, their shorts and teeshirts sticking to them in the heat. Inside, all is cool and quiet. Yesterday's chianti bottles and pizza-wrappers litter the forecourt: in the church there is order and scrupulous decorum.

I have given up all hope of dragging my guest around everything. After a brief look at the dignified columns marching away in ordered progression towards the sanctuary, and the splendid gilt of the panelled ceiling, he opts to visit the Medici tombs. The entrance is outside, at the back of the church, so he leaves me to guard his pack and wander the church on my own.

The Chapel of the Princes, mausoleum of the Medici Grand Dukes, is an octagonal building covered with marbles of various colours, and *pietre dure*. The work took craftsmen more than a century, and the result to my eyes is costly and elaborate beyond the limit of good taste. The

San Lorenzo

trouble is that one has to pass through it to reach the new sacristy, a sombre, ghostly mixture of the grey *pietra serena* and white of the church interior (though here the white is marble). This is the creation of Michelangelo. I feel no twinge of pity for the death of these grandees. But in such cold and solemn surroundings, so palely lit, it is difficult not to think sombre thoughts. One is moved here as one is moved by any passing funeral: not out of pity for the dead, but for humanity at large.

The superlative allegorical representations of *Dawn, Dusk, Day* and *Night*, sprawling on the volutes of sarcophagi beneath idealised statues of Lorenzo, Duke of Urbino, and Giuliano, Duke of Nemours (both died young, the former half-mad), show, if anything ever did, how the genius of art can mitigate the ugly fact of death. The face of *Dawn*, in particular, with her frowning brows and limbs struggling from sleep, lips parted, thighs separating in the very moment of raising herself, is of unforgettable nobility and perfection: sensuous, languid, melancholy and warm from sleep. She was the first female nude the artist created. Now we know that Michelangelo considered the female body inferior to the male (only one life-drawing by him of a woman is extant), and his female subjects are always based on studies of men. What he has done here is to adapt masculine torsos and forms, and this is why the thoraxes and abdomens of *Day* and *Night* are so extraordinarily muscular and unfeminine, and why the breasts, the dominant focal point of female beauty from antiquity, seem almost afterthoughts. Neither *Dawn* nor *Night*, for all their noble expressiveness, approaches a modern concept of feminine beauty. Yet, for an artist with a predilection for the male anatomy, these two female figures must be significant. Perhaps an exact interpretation of the allegory is impossible, because the work is incomplete: more tombs and figures were planned, but still unattempted when the sculptor left Florence in 1530 after the fall of the Republic, and the return of the Medici.

So my young friend goes one way, I another: he leaves me with his pack and wanders off to be dazzled by porphyry and travertine. Guiltily I pass Rosso's fine *Marriage of the Virgin*, in the second chapel right, where traditionally young couples have their engagement rings blessed: it is appallingly lit, and time presses.

But who can ignore Donatello? His last commission was a series of bronze reliefs for the Gospel and Epistle pulpits here, which were subsequently raised on pillars. The scenes on the earlier, left-hand pulpit (1465) are of events after the Passion; on the right-hand pulpit, there are scenes of the Passion itself. Though pupils worked on their completion, the pulpits are unfinished. Perhaps the old Donatello, who died aged 80, was simply unequal to the physical labour of chasing and polishing. The surface, at any rate, shows the working of assistants, and two of the scenes on each pulpit are seventeenth-century imitations in bronzed wood.

But there is such poignancy in unfinished things! Florence abounds in these reminders of lapsed inclination, of the mutability of human fortunes, of political instability, of niggardly Popes, and the artist's constant struggle to finance the creativity with which he adorns his age. Flitting from one commission and city to another in the course of a troubled existence, Michelangelo left so many of his works unfinished. The celebrated Captives ('*Prigionieri*') seem to be striving to wrench themselves free of their marble blocks in the Academy. But whether the '*non-finito*' effect was in fact calculated, or is merely a result of the marbles being abandoned at an early stage of their creation, is still a matter of keen scholarly debate. The effect is undeniably powerful: only the artist's intention is unclear. Something tells me that in these matters of high aesthetics, the unromantic explanation is often the right one.

I scrutinise the panels and ask myself what I see today that is the signature of genius. What have I failed to notice before?

The scenes are in sequence: the *Agony in the Garden, Christ before Pilate, Crucifixion, Deposition and Entombment, The Maries at the Sepulchre, Resurrection, Christ in Limbo, Christ appearing to the Apostles* and *Pentecost*. (The gruesome *Martyrdom of St Lawrence*, who was roasted alive on a grid, is an intrusion.) Immediately noticeable is the detailed modelling of the figures, and their scale, which varies from scene to scene. It seems Donatello worked in close-up increasingly as the story progressed. In the *Deposition*, for example, the nearer thief is cut off at the knees; the further at his shoulders. Remarkable.

And what of the iconography? In the *Resurrection*, the Christ who rises from the tomb is of a strange sort never encountered before: here he wears his winding-sheet, or shroud, his eyes still slitted from sleep in the grave. In the *Limbo* scene, too, Christ's figure is grim and bowed, as the shaggy figures of waiting souls fall on him and mob him. This is quite novel; it was plainly Donatello's private vision, neither based on a precedent, nor imitated later. And the tension of contrasts is so tellingly exploited: the smoothness of flesh against the roughness of drapery or tangles of hair; the movement of flowing folds exaggerated by a background of geometric, chiselled shapes; the Classical frieze above in light relief, against the crowded scenes below, divided by projecting buttresses which give an illusion of great depth. (Donatello was a master of relief work; the scenes on which his pupils rather than he worked here have altogether flatter surfaces.) The *Maries at the Sepulchre* implies, in the space of centimetres, a deep and cavernous recess: we see the roof, loggiaed front, sides and back of the sepulchre. The foreshortening of arms here is remarkable (though the angel's extended right arm seems overlong), the whole concept audacious. The flowing robes of the angel with his back to us appear to capture the precise moment of the momentous announcement.

Today, these wonderful pulpits, apparently used only during Holy Week, are free-standing ornaments; but originally they were meant to rest against the piers of the crossing. The supporting pillars belong to the sixteenth century, but the present, floating position of the pulpits was settled in the seventeeth century. No one knows what was in Donatello's original design for them: perhaps something as daring and defiant as the panels themselves. Genius seems careless of convention.

At the end of the right aisle is another example of quite breathtaking workmanship – a tabernacle by Desiderio da Settignano. This stood at the Altar of the Sacrament when it was installed in 1461. Most lovely *putti* gaze in adoration above, where a naked Christ Child stands over a chalice in the act of bendiction. Either side of the central tabernacle, low down, are two slender and elegant angels, standing winsomely with tilted hips, and carrying candles. Their profiles are exquisite. The tabernacle itself is a marvel of *trompe l'oeil* relief-work: the door to the cupboard where the Blessed Sacrament is kept is the end wall of a long barrel-vaulted room (the effect of distance is enhanced by the slope of the vault and the steep rake of the pavement); and from each side wall emerges a series of angels dancing ecstatically, tiny in comparison with the flanking angels, and themselves assisting the illusion of depth.

Below the tabernacle the artist has sculpted a relief of a *Lamentation over the Dead Christ*, so that above we see the Babe triumphant, below suffering, and the lovely lyrical innocence of the Child and the two angels contrasts piquantly with the scene beneath. Desiderio died aged about 35 in 1464, and this work has been singled out as the greatest decorative achievement of the century. The perfection of its details and the harmony of the whole composition simply defy description. Before I move away finally, I notice the extraordinary bravura with which Desiderio, scorning the limits of the possible, made not pilasters, but two, apparently round (no, *palpably* round) fluted pillars to support the cornice of the fictive hall. Pilasters were not difficult enough, it seems: so rarely is beauty achieved by the broad, well trodden path.

I look in wonder at the Child and the Chalice, and a weight is suddenly lifted from my shoulders. I turn to find my young friend taking his pack again.

'Amazing!' he grins.

I glance at my watch and lead him away. There is time only for a glimpse of the Donatello medallions in the old sacristy, but he must see them, and after their restoration they are finer and brighter than ever: they are seen in a new glory.

The sacristy is dedicated to St John the Evangelist, and in the coloured stucco roundels in the pendentives of the cupola Donatello modelled in relief four scenes (1434–7) from the life of the saint: the *Raising of Drusiana, Vision on Patmos, Martyrdom* and *Ascension*. In the lunettes are medallions of the Four Evangelists. These are somehow disturbing works, revolutionary, daring flights of genius.

The restoration has made the most sophisticated use of chemicals to remove the layers of dust and smoke, and to arrest the permeation of moisture. A pretty frieze of cherub-heads, for example, had in parts been all but obliterated. Infra-red and ultra-violet photography, too, has been of inestimable value in gauging the original colours and patterns. We are now able to see Donatello's craftsmanship in a detail denied to tourists for centuries. The change is sensational – so sensational, in fact, that it has sparked mixed reactions.

We now know that Donatello worked on scaffolding *in situ* using simple tools, and very often his hands, or a stick. He worked with incredible speed, with the stucco in strips, like ribbons of pasta, creating an unusually expressive effect, which is accessible enough to twentieth-century eyes, but was unpopular in the fifteenth and sixteenth centuries, and indeed was considered unsatisfactory by Brunelleschi – and possibly the artist himself, because parts are left unfinished.

There was an inherent difficulty, of course, in fixing pendentive *tondi* on concave surfaces: here nails (the traditional support for vault reliefs) were driven into the wall more or less deeply according to the degree of projection of the plaster in relief. On the flat wall surfaces fewer nails were needed, and there a framework of wood or reeds or tow was probably embedded in the wall. This fact has helped a reconstruction of the areas where the stucco is damaged.

For his background and scenery, Donatello used a very fine, reddish-pink material, a mortar of lime and sand and ground brick (*cocciopesto*) which he laid on and marked with strong strokes of a spatula and with stylus-lines. For the figures he used white plaster (lime and sand, simple *intonaco*), and these he made project strongly. It is also interesting that lower down, the projection in each tondo is greater than higher up, which has the effect of stretching the circles almost into ovals. On areas he left in red stucco, shadows are made by a darker red in relief; the figures are left in white, and polychrome used only for certain special effects. Finally, the skies were done with a coat of aconite *a secco*, so that the clouds (white stucco) shine through as a sweet, chalky blue.

At some stage these reliefs were brightened with white lead and then a layer of rich gold. Between the white lead and the relief no dirt has been found; so, whether part of Donatello's plan or not, the overpainting was done soon after their execution. Perhaps these were 'corrections' or 'improvements' by the Master himself: one cannot say with certainty.

The cloister is brilliant and still as we climb to the library, the famous Biblioteca Laurenziana; at the top of the stairs a charming *Annunciation* fresco greets us, unremarked by guide books, ignored by tourists: another free gift.

The staircase to the Biblioteca – Michelangelo's work – is simply vision-ary, with sweeping, curved treads ending in flowing rams' horns, all in grey *pietra serena*, like a waterfall: the centre spills outwards like a flood, a cascade issuing from the elevated library doors and swirling down in cataracts. One longs to sweep up the central flights, to make a grand 'ascent': but the main access is roped off, and mere tourists must approach the library by a series of horizontals on the left side; we are allowed to press our feet on only the final five stairs of the central section. The whole lofty vestibule, and its richly carved ceiling, was designed as a dramatic foil to the celebrated library, to its almost oppressive calm, to the serried rows of restful reading desks. In the reading room, the walls continue the Brunelleschian motif of grey and white, but the floor between the desks is richly inlaid, with swags and friezes in light red and dull yellow, and the ceiling is (most unusually) raftered and of intricately carved, chestnut-coloured wood. Michelangelo designed the benches and lecterns here, too. At the direction of a cross girl we sign the Visitors' Book, and drift along the aisle on a spongy runner deciphering the titles of the volumes formerly kept on the desks, which are listed at the end of each row. This is one of the greatest scholarly collections in all Italy, and here, at one time or another, all the great men have come.

Here is all the fabulous wealth of the Medici, invaluable manuscripts, priceless *incunabula* and first editions, a collection founded by Cosimo and housed at S. Marco, then carried off to Rome by the Medici Pope Leo X, and subsequently restored as a gift by Clement VI (the other Medici Pope, who was responsible for commissioning Michelangelo to design this library). It is an enthralling place for a book lover. In the days of Lorenzo, Florence was one of the foremost cultural centres of the world: among the Humanists it boasted some of the greatest minds of the Renaissance, and the library both reflects their cultivated tastes

and shows the fruits of their labours. There is usually an exhibition in
the rooms off the main hall: ancient maps, maybe, classical texts, or (this
year) 'Man, Beasts and Countries in the Laurentian Miniatures'. It is
difficult to do more than skim the surface of this great treasure-house.
One just looks and looks, and takes in what one can.

Outside again, we walk round the upper floor of the cloisters, and,
among the greenery of a sweet, neglected garden, we hear the dull clatter
of typewriters, and, through a line of shuttered windows see scholars
at work with ultraviolet lights, magnifying screens and chattering word-
processors. The former cells are locked and fitted with alarms: candles
have given place to fiercely efficient strip-lighting.

Back in Borgo S. Lorenzo, we shoulder our way through a moving
wall of trippers. At the kerbside wall-eyed negroes sit selling trinkets.
One unfortunate youth with shrivelled arms and twisted legs does a pitiful
frog-hop towards us, with both hands extended, showing black rows of
stumpy teeth and fiery gums: he is unshaven, yet closely cropped, and
I have seen him somewhere before – on a fresco, perhaps, in some hellish
Limbo or *Inferno*. Was it among the cripples in Orcagna's fragmentary
Last Judgment in the museo of S. Croce?

'There.' What *else* does one say?

The Piazza del Duomo bursts upon us, a colossal juxtaposition of
coloured marbles: the plain and lovely banded marble of the octagonal
Baptistry, austere and full of quiet dignity; and the refined and slender *campanile*, with its storeys of multiplying arched windows, matching
the colours of the cathedral, yet somehow lighter, its greens less heavy,
muted, used in less concentration. It *soars* – though it might have soared
to more effect if Giotto's original design had been carried through. (He
meant it to end in a spire with crockets rather than a projecting cornice.)
The original plan for the windows, too, was different. By the time of
Giotto's death, only the base was built and his successors thought they
knew better.

The multicoloured Duomo, pink marble from the Maremma, grey-green
from Prato, and white from Carrara, is a dazzling mass of saints in niches,
oculi, pinnacles, crockets, buttresses, lunettes, all crowned with the great,
pointed, octagonal cupola. The greatest and highest cupola of its day,
it is still visible from miles away in the surrounding countryside. The
effect of all this is dwarfing, frustrating: there is no one angle, in fact,
from which it can be seen whole. One needs a helicopter and fish-eye
lens. But the lovely terracotta tiling of the dome, its series of fenestrations,

like so many murder-holes, trailing black stains where rainwater has spewed over the years; and its eight strong white ribs, leading the eye to a most elegant lantern, seem to draw the scheme together and superimpose a sense of purpose and distinction.

The Duomo dominates, and the Piazza is a road running round it. Much of the city lives and works in its gigantic shadow. Inevitably, one's first reaction is to take several paces back.

'Amazing!' breathes my young friend, in awe. His whole face seems lit by the marble.

The façade, though its details are no doubt splendid, strikes me as fussy and overdone. It was designed and put up in the late nineteenth century, and photographs of the west end as it was before (after the original, unfinished façade was pulled down in the sixteenth century to make way for something grander) show a dignified, blank frontage, not unlike that of S. Lorenzo. No doubt Queen Victoria, who was present with other luminaries of her day at the unveiling, thought the effect very tasteful. (I fear that this and the façade of S. Croce were financed either partly or wholly by well meaning English residents.) The bronze doors, which stand in brightly gilded recesses under gaudy lunettes, are even later.

By contrast, the Baptistry smiles contentedly; its famous doors of gilded bronze are in a class apart. From the eastern door, the door which faces the Duomo, the so called 'Gate of Paradise', Ghiberti's lifework and masterpiece, a portrait-head of the artist and his friends look down in smug security. Pigeons, popcorn, postcards. Crowds stream in and out of the side doors of the Duomo and rest weary legs on the steps; guides carry placards bearing the names of tour-groups, hotels, curious townships in mid-west America. Photographers ply their trade; miles of celluloid are used up as the obliging little monkey is passed from hand to hand. The longer I spend here, the more I crave the noble simplicity of the Baptistry and dislike the excess of the west end of the Duomo.

Quickly I lead the way inside, point out the inlaid pavement, the mullioned windows, and the terrifying mosaic in the cupola. This place can have a peculiar effect on people. Perhaps the old ghosts still linger in this most ancient and revered of buildings. (All Florence came here to be baptised. Here in 1265 Dante was christened; and later broke the font accidentally while trying to rescue an infant from drowning.) I have seen people go pale, shiver, and run for the sunshine almost immediately. But my friend, with the confidence of youth, seems made of sterner stuff.

Until the archbishop's throne was moved from S. Lorenzo to S. Reparata (the church which preceded S. Maria del Fiore, the present Duomo) this was the old cathedral of Florence, and the lower granite columns, with their gilded Corinthian capitals, are Roman. In the cupola a grim, huge Christ sits in judgment: below, the pavement is a vast medley of zodiacal and geometric motifs – that disturbing juxtaposition of contrasts one finds in all the oldest religious buildings, and a reminder that the pagan and Christian existed alongside each other, and the new faith, as it developed, adapted and assimilated to itself for its own purposes the symbols and superstitions of earlier history.

Astrology, of course, was a subject of perennial fascination: the mural in the cupola of the Old Sacristy of S. Lorenzo is a celestial hemisphere referring, it is thought, to the Council of Florence, a meeting of the eastern and western churches in Florence in 1439, when the crucial *filioque* clause in the Creed was debated – the so-called 'double procession' of the Holy Spirit. (The theory that Gozzoli's fresco in the chapel of Palazzo Medici refers to this same Council, exploded first by Gombrich, is still perpetuated in otherwise reputable guide books.) The Neptune Fountain in Piazza della Signoria is covered in astrological symbolism alluding to the achievements and ambitions of Grand Duke Cosimo, who rides serenely nearby. And one could spend a whole lifetime attempting to unravel the references to astrology in Dante's *Commedia*.

Looking up at the stark, colourful mosaic, I can well believe in the influence, if not the hand, of a Venetian artist. This Christ, with his preternaturally large feet, is a fraction less awesome than the Byzantine figure in the calotte of S. Miniato, but below, to his right, are some of the most gruesome and grotesque scenes imaginable, a Dantesque nightmare of all the cruellest torments of Hell. (The newly baptised would mercifully have seen merely a gorgeous jumble of golds and blues and greens, like a shoal of fish, or a jeweller's tray.) Dante's lines spring immediately to mind:

> *Da ogni bocca dirompea co' denti*
> *un peccatore, a guisa di maciulla,*
> *si che tre ne facea così dolenti.*

> (Inferno XXXIV 55–7)

('In each mouth he (Satan) crushed / a sinner with his teeth as with a heckle / and so he kept three of them in pain.') There they all are, naked and terrified, and a horned devil seizes them with his six arms, and stuffs them into his hideous maw, like a giant lizard crunching a locust: one body threshes with his legs in agony, his head inside the monster's jaws; others in terror await their turn. There is no escape, and ingestion is preceded by excoriation:

A quel dinanzi il mordere era nulla
verso 'l graffiar, che tal volta la schiena
rimanea della pelle tutta brulla.

('To the one in front the biting was nothing / to the clawing, for sometimes
the back / was left all stripped of skin.')

We are standing now by the tomb of John XXIII (Baldassare Coscia
had been elected Pope in 1410, but was deposed in 1415, after the Council
of Constance healed the great schism in the Church, and made to yield
to Martin V). This magnificent work is inserted between two of the Roman
columns near the Altar Chapel. I am pointing out the superb drapery
over the gilded, recumbent 'antipope' (the bronze effigy is probably by
Donatello, the rest by his pupil Michelozzo), when suddenly there is
an explosion of abuse, a flurry of movement, and two gypsy women are
arrested.

These are fine straight-backed women, of handsome figure, and with
their dull, dusty burnous and bare feet they seem almost Arabian. Only
lined faces and poor teeth betray their history of hardship; otherwise
they are regal beings. They come straight from the sands of Africa ('They
are from the north,' Lisa insists), and they stand out among the frenzied
trippers like unwashed goddesses. I cannot understand the language they
use to each other, but to the policemen they use their beggars' Italian,
and it issues in whining, constricted mendicant tones from somewhere
high in their noses.

Two policemen are on the scene and voices are soon echoing round
the dome: the policemen are cynical and calm; a fat Italian woman screams
and waves flabby arms; the *zingare* stand their ground, eyes averted, one
shaking her arms free petulantly as the policeman tries to take hold of
her. At her brown breast a baby sucks in blissful oblivion. An elf-child
belonging to the other woman, who also carries a sleeping child, watches
events with wide eyes. She has seen it all before. The whole scenario
has the feel of the penultimate night of a seaside repertory company's
summer run. The lines are strolled through: there is no real animus in
the exchange: as a finale, the gypsies are bundled into a waiting car and
driven away.

The demonstration over, youth chooses to climb the cupola of the
Duomo; it is his turn for the pack, but I hang on to it as we penetrate
the gloomy interior. After the crowded, fussy ornament of the façade,
the nave seems empty as a hangar, its ceiling so high it can hardly be

glimpsed in the half light. The lovely pavement, too, is lost. A few chairs are grouped near the choir; otherwise there are only the colossal grey clustered pilasters, like primeval trees, and the soaring cross vaults. The sanctuary, for once, faces east: it forms one of three apses, each with five chapels, which radiate from the central point of the crossing – a position occupied by the octagonal choir, directly beneath the great dome. Between the north and south apses are the two sacristies.

We pass the Dante picture, with its familiar Florentine roofscape, and my friend leaves me for the long ascent. There are 463 steps, but he is young and eager. He will climb between the two skins of Brunelleschi's cupola, up and over the curve as it becomes more and more pronounced, until he emerges in a brilliant apocalypse of light on the balcony of the lantern.

There are only a couple of nasty moments during the ascent. On the top one feels quite secure. The worst is past when the level below the dome is reached, and one looks down (one must) at the sanctuary and Chapels of the Tribune and sees a dizzy vista of the receding nave. (As compensation, there are good views of the stained glass in the seven roundels, and of the frescoes, if they are not masked by matting and scaffold.) The dome is 45.52 metres in diameter, 91 metres in height. It took fourteen years in the making, and the exact technique Brunelleschi employed is still argued over. No one in his day thought it could be done: no one today can work out how it was done.

But done it was, layer by layer, and without the aid of a central supporting frame. The inner shell is almost twice as thick as the outer; the eight marble ribs are locked together by chains of iron and lateral courses of stone, and they need to be: the total weight of the dome is estimated at 25,000 tons. Brunelleschi's pulleys and winches and ropes and other tackle can be seen on a landing of the cupola, and in the Museo. At the crossing, one feels ant-like and vulnerable, but on the stairs following the curve of the cupola, at least, enclosed and safe.

The air becomes rank and stifling as one ascends. Continuous diversion is provided by the volumes of graffiti: for many have trod this path before, not only the Etruscan in S. Ambrogio who sells water melons, and the waiter in 'dell'Agnolo', but princes and popes and poets, condottieri, lovers and statesmen. The *BARI METALFANS* have puffed their way to the rooftop of Florence; and an enterprising *puttana*, who left an immortal visiting-card: *Per liete ore chiama 0118282; chi chiama da Roma deve mettere il prefisso 055.* More ancient scribblers, too, have left their mark: 280 steps up, there are the signatures of several of the Lanzichenecchi, the *Landsknechte*, oafish Swiss Lancers in Duke Cosimo I's pay who gave their name

169

to the Loggia dei Lanzi in the Piazza della Signoria. Like any soldiers serving abroad, they saw the sights and made their little bid for immortality.

Andrew will see the maze of rooftops and towers, and the other ant-folk on Giotto's campanile opposite; the shape of S. Miniato on the distant hill (if the sky is kind, it will shimmer into incandescence); the secret rooftop terraces; a glimpse of the white Neptune Fountain in the square outside Palazzo Vecchio; Galileo's Observatory in Arcetri; the green mushrooms of the Cascine; the neat geometry of the Boboli Gardens, its theatre just discernible; the planes of Piazza d'Azeglio; the lovely dome of S. Lorenzo, hemmed in, but not spoilt by the railway station; and the rectangular modernity of the Mercato Centrale. At this height, the colours of the city are rust-red, a million shades of terracotta, and the dun of stately stone. There is a broad seascape of television aerials and a network of scaffolding, yet from here the modern is somehow drowned by the ancient, or else mingles without obtruding itself. Monte Oliveto, Bellosguardo, pleasant eminences to the south-west, each with its distinctive buildings; Piazzale Michelangelo, aglitter with coach and car; Forte Belvedere, foursquare on its lofty eminence; the menacing Torre del Gallo; the slender folly in the Torrigiani Gardens, with its pretty spiral staircase; the façades of S. Croce and S. Maria Novella, like so much marble icing over the plain stone and brick of the rest. Then little Fiesole lies north-east, and round it the lovely scattered villas it gathers to itself; and north the heaving Apennines like sleeping cattle, the foothills and distant cordilleras of the Garfagnana.

But standing at the door of the New Sacristy, I have no sense of the weather outside. The magnificent bronze doors are, surprisingly, Luca della Robbia's, as is the *Resurrection* lunette over the door (these constitute his only work in bronze, and his earliest major work in enamelled terracotta, both landmarks), a glorious composition of white, raised figures prominent against the inimitable blue background: while the soldiers lie sleeping, Christ hovers above his tomb in benediction, and angels flutter either side to adore him. Inside, there are inlaid cupboards of quite exquisite workmanship crowned by a frieze of adorable *putti* holding a chain of garlanded flowers that continues, in ravishing loops, all round the wall.

Here (the association is too strong to resist) Lorenzo fled for sanctuary on that fateful day in 1478, when the Pazzi (a rival family of bankers), backed by Pope Sixtus IV, tried to overthrow the Medici. It was during Mass. Giuliano they stabbed to death: nineteen wounds were counted on his corpse. Then, at the moment of the Elevation, they went for Lorenzo, who was standing on the south side of the choir. A priest called

Maffei, who was in the conspiracy, laid a hand on his shoulder, intending to stab him as he turned; but Lorenzo acted with lightning speed. He drew his sword, wound his cloak about his left arm, and was only grazed in the neck by his assailant's dagger. While stalwart friends stopped others of the Pazzi from joining the attack (one was killed outright for his loyalty with a stab to the stomach), he rushed here, into the New Sacristy, north of the choir, where Poliziano and others quickly bolted Luca's stout bronze door. At first, while the conspirators slipped away, there was panic and numbness, then followed an orgy of revenge. About 100 suspects were executed. Botticelli was paid forty golden florins to paint the ringleaders on the walls of the Palazzo Vecchio and the Bargello. Lorenzo himself composed their epitaphs. The Pazzi coat of arms was destroyed, their property confiscated. Jacopo Pazzi's body was actually disinterred from its resting-place by some youths, dragged by the neck through the streets, and thrown into the Arno. Some of the conspirators were tortured, mutilated (their noses and ears were lopped off) and hanged. Others were decapitated.

It all happened suddenly, here, among the gum-chewing and bikini-tops, on 26 April 1478. The guides thread their way past. Move along please, folks. Thirty seconds a masterpiece. We gotta deadline.

Outside, the Piazza is a cauldron. I turn to the north side of the cathedral and the Porta della Mandorla, named after the oval glory, an almond-shaped *Assumption* Nanni di Banco sculpted on the gable over the mosaic lunette, still lovely despite the heavy grime of traffic pollution. (I imagine the joy of cleaning it, of uncovering the original beauty of the figures, as the artist intended them to be seen when he left them, unfinished, in 1421!) Elsewhere, in the *Four Saints* standing in their niche outside Orsanmichele, for example, Nanni is severely Classical in style. Here, he leans more towards the Gothic, with billowing drapery and a light, lyrical feeling in the postures of the angel musicians who surround the *mandorla*. Four angels support the oval; three more form the apex of the composition, one blowing on a recorder, another on a flared pipe like a *tibia*, and the topmost, gaily striding out, and with a heavenly smile lighting his face, is playing bagpipes. Nanni died young; one wonders, had he lived, how far his talents might have carried him in rivalry with Donatello.

Today, at last, I have found the celebrated 'Hercules' commented on in the guide book; no wonder I have missed him so often before! He lurks in the door jamb, enveloped in leafy scrollwork: there is also a (less celebrated, but equally fine) rear view of a female nude.

I look for a postcard of the famous door, but postcards here are poor fare: most are of the Uffizi and Pitti, views of the Ponte Vecchio lit

171

by night fireworks, and David's groin. The Duomo and Baptistry are on an island surrounded by a drifting tide of Fiats and Vespas, and I am beginning to lose heart when my young friend rejoins me, a bloom of sweat on his cheeks. I know he is about to tell me the view from the cupola was amazing.

'Tremendous,' he says. 'Really tremendous.' He waves his camera. Another terrible decision has now to be made.

'How hungry are you?' It is midday, and he must have been up for at least six hours.

'I'm fine, thanks.'

He is hungry, but well mannered. The Museo dell' Opera del Duomo will have to wait for his next visit. (I shall get him to tickle the *porcellino*'s snout at the Straw Market.) Next time he will probably bring his bride. They can find the Michelangelo *Pietà* and compare the *cantorie* of Luca and Donatello together. A taste is all I can hope to give.

But I regret those two *cantorie*. I prefer Luca's: the lovely children beating tambourines and banging drums and cymbals, blowing pipes and strange, elongated trumpets, playing harp and lute, dancing in a circle, singing their hearts out to Psalm 150. This singing-loft was designed to go over the door of the new sacristy, but was removed in 1686 for the wedding of Ferdinando de' Medici and Violante Beatrice of Bavaria, and languished in the storage room of the Duomo until 1883. During this time various bits of the structure were lost, including two angels holding gilt bronze candles; these found their way into the Musée Jacquemart-André in Paris, and have, no doubt, an interesting tale to tell.

While Luca divides his works into scenes, one occupying each panel, Donatello's *putti* flow wildly across his cantoria behind a row of *colonnettes*, orgiastic in their abandon: an original concept enclosed within lovely classical friezes against the coloured inlay of the background (which reminds me, irreverently, of a horrid underpassage on the front at Hastings, where some local visionary has seen fit to cement broken bottles into the walls). But the faces of his *putti* are not so pleasing.

Also in the Museo dell' Opera is Donatello's *Magdalen*, sculpted in wood for the Baptistry – a tormented, expressionist figure, gap-toothed and skeletonic, and quite unforgettable. This statue, which had for centuries been regarded as monochrome, was badly affected by the flood of 1966: restoration has revealed that the flesh was painted to look like flesh, and the hair and tattered robe were gilded.

And the *Pietà*, how can one pass that by? Michelangelo's swan song, intended probably for his own tomb, stands now on a landing half-way up the staircase. The hooded, sorrowing Nicodemus, who, with his rugged features and broken nose forms the apex of this unusual group, is said by Vasari to be a self-portrait of the artist. Mary is barely sketched in the brown-coloured stone; Jesus collapses in a sensational, lifeless zigzag. The feeling of weight (something Michelangelo handles so brilliantly) is palpable, almost oppressive.

The story goes that Michelangelo, despairing of this group, smashed the left arm and left leg of Christ (the leg is still missing). After his death, a young Florentine artist of whom he was fond, Tiberio Calcagni, added the Magdalen – an intrusion unfortunate both for Calcagni's reputation and for all lovers of art. (She is a stiff figure, hopelessly out of proportion to the rest, and strikes a dreadfully incongruous note.) The work must be judged without her, and, by an effort of will, I can always make her vanish. What is left is touched all over with greatness, and a far, far cry from the serene young *Pietà* in St Peter's.

Why the great man mutilated his work is not known: Vasari mentions the possibility that the marble was too hard and full of emery, and 'the chisel kept striking sparks from it'. But it is surely more likely that the perfectionist felt he had made a wrong move, and being of a fiery temperament, never content with anything he produced, he struck out in a violence of passion. There are few finished statues by the Master made in his maturity. Those he did finish were produced when he was still young – a troubling reflection for those of us still lost in the middle of our own particular woods. I suppose there is only one thing old men finish better than young men.

CHAPTER

VIII

Orsanmichele · Piazza della Signoria · 'Nella' and Liberation Day · 'Da Benvenuto' · Il Calcio · S. Croce: tombs of Bruni and Marsuppini · Cappella dei Pazzi: the Museo · Piazzale Michelangelo · S. Miniato: S. Giovanni Gualberto and Vallombrosa · 'Toto'

We head south down Via dei Calzaioli. Soon the shopkeepers will be emerging with hooked poles and clawing down their shutters for the big sleep. In the busy centre of the city midday is a series of shivers and squeaks and bangs and shudders.

The churches, too, have their hours of sleep, but Orsanmichele is luckily open. We dart into the blackness just in time to glimpse Orcagna's magnificent tabernacle; Daddi's *Madonna* on the altar, in its exquisitely carved frame; the lovely, intricate Gothic tracery of the windows (now tragically bricked up); the mighty, square, frescoed pilasters; and, in the last seconds of coin-operated effulgence, the glorious blues of the painted vaulting. Then we are rounded up and bundled out. My young friend is at last showing signs of bewilderment and fatigue. But at least he will have pictures to feed on.

'Orsanmichele' is, according to some, a corruption of *Horreum* (= granary) *Sancti Michaelis*, to others of *S. Michele ad hortum* (the *hortus* was a vegetable garden that surrounded the small oratory). An oratory of S. Michele stood here as early as the end of the eighth century; in 1290, Arnolfo di Cambio, architect of the Duomo, built an open loggia of brick and wood to serve as a grain market. A miracle-working painting of the Madonna hung from one of the pilasters here, and the whole area of Orsanmichele was treated

174

with great veneration and awe. No gambling was allowed in the vicinity, nor any noise: and punishment for violation of these rules was either a fine, 'baptism', a particularly unpleasant form of dunking in the Arno, or a month in the *Stinche*. (The *Stinche* was the old debtors' prison in Via Ghibellina, demolished in 1833, situated on the very spot where the Teatro Verdi now stands.) Then in 1304, the market burnt down and subsequently the present, tall, rectangular building was constructed in *pietra forte*, combining the features of market and church. Above the two-aisled church are two roomy floors designed as granaries (now accessible only via an overhead passageway from the Palazzo dell'Arte della Lana) – this to meet the needs of a greatly increased population and the all-too-likely contingency in those days of a siege. It is the most original and individual church in Florence, and one of the most delightful.

But the exterior of the church is of even more importance than the darkly numinous interior. This was decorated by the various guilds (*arti*) of the city, and each was assigned its niche to fill with statuary. A lovely della Robbia medal marks the pier allotted to each *arte*. Naturally all these guilds, greater and lesser, vied with each other to commission the finest works from the best artists, and the result is an exhibition of some of the greatest talents of the Florentine Renaissance.

The first contribution was of stone, a *St Stephen*; but most of the commissions were executed in the first half of the fifteenth century and, once the wealthy Calimala asked Ghiberti to make a life-size John the Baptist in bronze (a scale unheard of then, and as costly as it was risky), a new fashion was set, and all the guilds wanted their own saints of bronze. (The Calimala imported wool, silk, brocades, etc., and the Via Calimala, the north–south axis of the old Roman city, is a corruption of *calle mayor*, or *cardo maior*, 'main street', rather than from Greek *kalos mallos*, 'fine wool', as earlier writers thought.) So Ghiberti's *Baptist* (on the east side, in Via dei Calzaiuoli) represents an important technical advance: it was the first bronze Renaissance statue cast successfully in one piece (except for the second toe of the left foot!). But in style it is pure international Gothic, with drapery looping from limb to limb elegantly, but unrelated to the body beneath, and severely stylised hair and beard. Nanni di Banco's *Four Saints* (on the north side, in Via Orsan-michele), completed a year earlier than the *Baptist* (1414–16) was begun, carries much more weight and conviction: these four figures have *gravitas*, a sense of solemnity; in inspiration they are utterly Roman. (This is the niche of the *Maestri di Pietra e di Legname*; the bas-relief below seeming to depict the drilling of a young boy's umbilicus is in fact a sculptor at work on a statue.)

Donatello's *St Mark* (on the south side, in Via dei Lamberti) was begun when he was only 25, in 1411. This, too, is inspired by Roman statuary, but what an idiosyncratic transformation the young sculptor has worked, and what a happy augury! With this statue Donatello solved the technical problem of the standing figure viewed from below: the torso and neck are slightly elongated (my young friend nods sagely), the latter disguised by an abundant beard; the drapery covering the weight-bearing leg is strongly distinguished from the free leg: we can locate the exact spot where the knee bends. The figure has conviction and weight.

'What's the cushion for?' Suddenly Andrew comes to life, and, startled as I am, I can actually answer his question. Vasari, for one, believed the cushion was a deliberate ploy to emphasise the solidity and weight of the figure (the saint's feet seem actually to be squashing the soft material), and surely he was right. Ghiberti's *St Matthew* (on the west side, in Via dell'Arte della Lana), done for – who else? – the bankers in 1419, shows several developments in style. The figure is slightly turned, not so static and frontal; the folds of the drapery hang vertically down the weight-bearing leg, which is the central axis of the figure, and there is generally more suggestion of movement. The face, too, is less exaggerated, more natural. Ghiberti was not slow to grasp the drift of contemporary style.

The marvellous *St George* of Donatello (north, in Via Orsanmichele) is a copy: the original stands in glory in its own niche in the Bargello, proud, youthful and defiant, every inch a hero. This was Donatello's reply to Ghiberti's *Baptist*, and it is vastly superior in terms of psychology: the frown contracting the young soldier's brows, the subtle positioning of his arms, the four-square stance – all these are Donatello's commentary on the *character* of his subject. The thrust of his body seems to say: *Nemo me impune lacessit*.

The niche occupied by Verrocchio's *Incredulity of St Thomas* (on the east side, in Via dei Calzaiuoli) had first been filled by the *Parte Guelfa* with Donatello's gilded bronze statue of their patron St Louis of Toulouse, now housed in the Museum of S. Croce. The *Parte Guelfa* were subsequently forced by the Medici to give up their niche to the *Mercanzia*, who removed all traces of their coat of arms, and asked Verrocchio (an approved Medici artist) to produce the group we now see. It took him from 1467 to 1480, virtually his entire career in Florence, and the problem he faced was no easy one: he had to fit into a niche designed for a single figure the two figures of Christ and St Thomas. His solution was to reduce the size of his two figures and leave only Christ in the niche itself: St Thomas, finished possibly ten years later than Christ, stands lower, with both feet below the floor of the niche, his body leaning upwards – a movement accentuated by his hand, as it reaches out to touch Christ's wound, and the drapery of his and Christ's mantles. Again, the anatomies are clearly seen beneath the garments, and the weight-distribution is markedly more realistic than Ghiberti's Gothic *Baptist*.

We move round again. The *St Luke* (in Via dei Calzaiuoli) is by Giambologna (1601), and it replaced a stone *St Luke* by Niccolò Lamberti done around 1405, which now stands in the *cortile* of the Bargello. Poor Lamberti had lost his commission for a *St Mark* from the guild of the linen drapers to Donatello, then his position as Master Sculptor at the Duomo, so in 1415 he left to try his luck in Venice. That year marks the ascendancy of the new 'Renaissance' style. Lamberti's *St Luke*, done only about seven years before Donatello's *St Mark* tells this story more vividly than words. With his blank expression, swaying hips, and impalpable frame, St Mark languishes under a colonnade in the National Museum. The tourists pass him by with scarcely a glance as they make for the stairs leading to Giambolgna, Donatello and the della Robbia.

As we move away, I snatch a backward look at the seated *Madonna della Rosa* (south side), a variously attributed fourteenth-century work: long-necked she is, from the old world left behind by the new artists, but none the less beautiful, and full of regal sadness as her child plays insouciantly with the flowers she holds. She sits in a glorious tabernacle of 1399, and somehow she symbolises, with eloquent poignancy, the inexorable shift of time at Orsanmichele.

A few steps away, the spacious Piazza della Signoria, disfigured temporarily by scaffolding and excavations, is still grandly affecting, its statuary brilliant against the golden stone of the Signoria. Thin horses, still in the shafts of their carriages, munch contentedly at nosebags, thin cheek-bones working busily while their owners smoke cigarettes and wait patiently for the next fare. The horses, mostly chestnuts, are dangerously slim, but their coats are glossy, and they seem well cared for. I came across their stables once, as I wandered around Oltrarno: it was near Piazza Tasso, behind the wall of the Torrigiani Gardens, a remote, secret place, I thought, full of tangy horse smells, never dreamt of by the passing tourist.

Palazzo Vecchio climbs to heaven and dominates the Piazza with its honey-coloured crenellations, and all the proud coats of arms of the Comune and the city wards painted beneath its soffits. I see my friend following the upward, asymmetric sweep of its tower, which grows out of the gallery of the façade, then spouts a gallery of its own. There hangs the famous bell, I tell him (called with typical sarcasm *La Vacca*, 'the cow'), which has played such a critical part in the turbulent history of Florence.

There is time only to point out the *David* (a copy, like the one in Piazzale Michelangelo; the original was moved last century to the Academy); Marzocco (the heraldic lion of Florence: a name derived from *Martocus*, diminutive of Mars, the old patron of Florence); Cellini's *Perseus*, behind screens and metal tubing; Giambologna's *Rape of the Sabines*, and his equestrian statue of Cosimo I. Time only to sit for a few moments on the Neptune Fountain under what the locals know as '*Il Biancone*' (a feeble effort by Ammannati saved by the contrast of the bronze figures beneath), and wait for a breeze to waft heavenly spray in our faces. To think Cellini might have carved this marble! Well, he did not. And Donatello's famous *Judith and Holofernes* used to stand nearby on the *ringhiera* (the raised platform skirting the west front of the Palazzo, where public speakers 'harangued' the people); but when I last saw it, the work was lying on its back under spotlights and magnifying glasses in a studio inside the Palazzo: my first view of a monumental bronze from beneath. The base had been removed, so what I peered into was a hollow Holofernes. *Judith*, no doubt regarded today as a symbol of liberated woman, was first cast as a fountain for the Medici and seen as a symbol of tyranny overcome. Changing times meant that the symbolism was reinterpreted, and in 1504, when the virile *David* reached its position on the *ringhiera*, *Judith* was removed as an unsuitable companion-piece. In 1919 she returned again. The real *David* left in 1873: *Judith* will no doubt make another come-back.

We sit and pore over the scene, and I try hard to look through the eyes of a newcomer. But here there are too many associations, too many ghosts waiting behind every corner-stone and statue. There is the constant torment of recall. Florence (if the Duomo is her Heart, then here is her Mind and Brain) is saturated with histories other than her own. Hers and mine have become almost one. At some time or other everyone comes here, to this square. I wonder idly how many photographs taken here over the past twenty years have included me (and with whom) as a merely passive bystander: on how many shelves I sit, an unwilling extra in the crowd-scene.

Motionless, I remember.

On 11 August, a year or two back, Carabinieri and Vigili Urbani were gathering in some sort of ceremonial parade in the Piazza dell' Unità. There was a great seriousness in the air: something important was afoot. Then, on posters sporting the hammer and sickle I read the words: '11 August 1944 – the Liberation of Florence! Today we must get rid of capitalism and bourgeois government!' Of course, Liberation Day, the day the Allies marched into a battered Florence, and the Ponte Vecchio was the only bridge still standing over the Arno! No one knows why the Germans did such terrible, wilful damage. Nor does anyone know why such a feeble effort was made to reconstruct the old buildings after the war. Philistinism played its part in both operations, no doubt.

On the evening of 11 August I dined at 'Nella' in Via delle Terme, a dark medieval street running parallel with the river from Por S. Maria to S. Trìnita, named after the baths built once by the Romans in the vicinity.

I dined well. Ivo, the proprietor, an old friend, and Bruno his faithful factotum, were a year older, like me, but as friendly and hospitable as ever. Both were bronzed from seaside holidays when I stepped past the old lantern and through the familiar doorway. Ivo is tall, thin of face and wiry, in perpetual motion. (His melon-slicing is an education, done with a knife sharp as glass, and so quick that I always fear for his finger tips. Off comes the ham in uniform sheets of paper thinness; and the melon, pared almost to the rind, seems to fall obligingly in neat, perfect segments as he touches it. Ivo's precision is sculptural.) Bruno was beginning to put on weight; his handsome, curly hair had become snow-coloured; maybe he had lost another tooth. Luciana, Ivo's wife, could occasionally be sighted through the blinds among the pots and pans of her kitchen, pretty and inclined to plumpness. Then sometimes she would emerge, pink-cheeked, to say hallo, and stay to chat a while.

It was late. After the jolliness of 'Nella' I felt like walking off the effects of the meal. (I had had *fegato alla salvia*, I recall, a speciality of Luciana's.) So, in my wandering, I emerged here, in the Piazza, where – I can never forget the sight – the Palazzo was torchlit, all its battlements ablaze and smoking in the blue-black of night! I looked around me at the eager faces, so dramatically lit, eyes glinting in the flames, sending back points of flame, the hard Tuscan set of mouth and jaw.

> *Ho visto il tuo palazzo palpitare*
> *Di mille fiamme in una sera calda*
> *O Firenze, il magnifico palazzo.*
> *Già la folla à riempito la gran piazza*
> *E vocia verso il suo palazzo vecchio*
> *E beve la sua anima maliarda.*

> I saw your palace throb
> with a thousand flames on a warm evening,
> O Florence, your magnificent palace.
> Already the crowd has filled the great piazza
> and calls towards its old palace
> and drinks its bewitching soul.

Dino Campana was right: in remembrances, in celebrations, the 'crude blood' still seethes in Florence beneath the surface ('*L'aspero sangue sotto a te ribolla*'). I was giddy with the sight: in every embrasure, on every merlon, a brand flung its orange hair into the sky, almost blotting out the stars; and this, I remember telling myself, is how the Signoria should *always* be seen, grim and defiant and formidably strong – terrifying, even, when one remembers all it stood for, all the unnameable, unthinkable things its dark interior, the 'iron marrow of Florence', had witnessed.

A stage had been erected; tricolours of red, white and green were draped about its base, and flapped occasionally with the same wind that waved the torches. To celebrate Independence Day an orchestra had been assembled, and it attacked Verdi and Rossini *con brio*. The brass played well, the reeds less well, and the result was the sort of edgy sound so typical of continental bands, but for me fraught with high adventure. I was engulfed by a crowd in holiday mood, rival buskers, ice cream sellers, pickpockets and tight family clusters, toddlers raised high on papa's shoulders or clasping *nonna*'s wrinkled hand; and lovers swaying to the music everywhere. As loudly as the rest I sang '*Va, pensiero*', Verdi's marvellous chorus from *Nabucco*, and applauded the children who, at the end of each piece, ran on in their red and white costumes, waved their banners, then, with their little arms folded, stood obediently still through the next number. A pretty commère announced the programme first in English, then in Italian, smiling into her words winningly, and flirting with the happy crowd.

After thirty minutes of 'Italian Classics', I was surprised to hear announced a selection of 'the most important twentieth-century English music'. Now this was unexpected: the girl's English, carefully rehearsed, had been a nice gesture to the thousands of English-speaking tourists in the city, a recognition of the special relationship that has existed with the British since the earliest days, when Cotswold wool was imported (and despite Edward III's repudiation of his colossal debts in 1339, which ruined the great banking families, and plunged the whole of Florence into a black economic depression). But now, before a local gathering of ordinary citizens on a summer's evening, a selection of 'the most important twentieth-century English music'? How would they receive it, I wondered. Elgar, I knew, did not travel; would we have Vaughan Williams, perhaps, Walton, Delius, Holst, Howells, Parry – or Tippett, maybe? How wonderful to hear, in the brilliance of a Tuscan night, *Variations on a Theme of Thomas Tallis*! But what, I began to ask myself, would those reeds do to *Greensleeves* or *The Lark Ascending* – things so quintessentially English, and smelling of home – green fields, and blue remembered hills, the coloured counties?

With tingling anticipation I waited as the conductor, with an important whir of arms and final slicing movement of his white-gloved hands achieved an almost simultaneous first *tutti*. Very soon I left. But as I reached Piazza d'Azeglio, the sounds were still pulsating in my head. Not Elgar, nor Vaughan Williams, nor Walton, nor Tippett, but the Beatles – and not the sweet, reflective melodies, but a whole series of ear-jarring, thumping, cave-men rhythms. And round the stones of the ancient city it thudded and echoed like a hammer on an anvil. Quickly I undressed and got into bed, consoling myself with the thought that anything *really* English might have been even more out of place.

His eyes go deep and bright when I mention food. We move into the open *cortile* of the Palazzo, ablaze with late ornament, and watch the pseudo-Verrocchio *putto* on the fountain, lovely even as a copy, being captured on a dozen films. Then, as we pass the grand staircase with serious thoughts of food, there is shouting: we hear voices, male and female, and something about them is familiar. As if pulled by a wire we stop in our tracks.

The Vigili Urbani have their office here. A blue and white police car is parked outside the door from where the din is coming. Inside, a woman is screaming. Then a policeman emerges, smoking a cigarette, arguing heatedly with an invisible colleague. He has a bushy moustache and hairy wrists and shouts something over his shoulder. Now a child is crying and a woman whining in a high-pitched wail. I hear a loud slap, another scream.

Flicking his cigarette exasperatedly onto the stone floor, the policeman turns on his heels and goes back inside. For a second there is calm, then a busy motet strikes up (bass, baritone, two sopranos); this is followed by an all-male ground bass with an obbligato of shrieking females.

'Why did you bring them *here*?'

'Where *should* I bring them?'

'Take them somewhere else.'

'Where? Tell me *where*.'

'The baby stinks. They all stink. Get them out!'

And so on. One of the combatants, a harassed lieutenant, comes out still wearing a massive shrug. The two intrepid policemen who made the arrest, having delivered the gypsies, leave in their car at high speed to make further arrests. Their comrades drift out one by one, smoke cigarettes and chat to girl tourists.

The gypsies win: in five minutes they are walking straight-backed into the sunlight again, babies sucking contentedly at their breasts, swinging with the movements of their bodies. The *bimba* totters along holding her mother's hand, high above her head. They will eat a peach and return to sit on the pavement and beg. If they have really stolen a purse or a roll of bank notes, perhaps they will stop for the day and come back tomorrow evening.

I watch their backs as they move unhurriedly away: one day I dream of drawing a gypsy. There is something about their detachment, their feigned professional misery, which intrigues me. What do these strange creatures look like when they smile, when they enjoy food, when they make love? One sees them only with contorted faces, wrinkled brows, anguished lips and narrowed eyes, mumbling their litany of beggardom. But their little *bimbi* look like any other children, with their coal-black elf-locks and dirty knees. When does the one turn into the other? Where are their men? Where do they live? Who *are* they?

Behind another straight back we take Via dei Neri and make for 'Da Benvenuto'. This back is one that particularly interests Andrew: it belongs to an exotic young creature wearing a brilliant white cotton dress, long and elegant, slashed to the waist at the back, and scarlet sling-back sandals with four-inch heels. Her flesh is a deep coffee, darker even than her hair, which has highlights bleached by the sun and reaches below her shoulder-blades in a cascade of glorious waves. A scarlet handbag of soft leather matches her shoes, and on her hair a scarlet butterfly seems to have alighted. There is a white bow in the small of her back, too, where the brown V ends. Ah yes, and her legs are long and very slender; but she is out of reach, ten paces ahead of us, picking her way over the pavement, and does not stop to look in a shop window. She is going somewhere, moving with a free easy swing of the hips into the light.

'Da Benvenuto', at the corner of Via dei Neri and Via Mosca, is one of the liveliest and most attractive eating places in the area. It has all the hallmarks of *trattoria* distinction: sparkling cleanliness, a large clientèle of regulars, local and foreign, swift and professional service, and a varied, reasonably priced menu. Except for a table I have never been disappointed.

Today we share one with English-speaking residents: they are Australians in the fashion trade, a smart, well preserved mother; freckled, green-eyed daughter with sandy hair; and a scrofulous teenage son on holiday from his minor English public school.

Visibly relaxed by our withdrawal from culture and the bottle of cool, green wine we have already accounted for, Andrew orders *penne alle melanzane* (short pasta with aubergine sauce) and *lombatina alla salvia* (loin chop in sage) to follow, with white beans in oil. I decide to be more adventurous, and go for a selection of Tuscan salami, followed by *seppie* (cuttlefish) with spinach, and *fagioli all' uccelletto*, which is different everywhere in Tuscany, but always delicious. A good bottle of *gallo nero* comes along and there follows a silence long and profound. Around us, sad pictures of the flood in 1966 look down on the bright table tops. The green-eyed girl, when I look up momentarily, seems to be scrutinising my friend and soon finds an excuse to introduce herself. Mother graciously picks on someone nearer her age and chats pleasantly while her teenage son, neckless and built like a middleweight, feeds himself greedily and sulks. He is bent on rowing in the Olympics, he announces.

He is reading art and ancient history. Perhaps he will be, if nothing else, a great oarsman.

'Well,' I ask my guest finally, after our companions have left and I order some cheese. 'What do you think?'

He looks non-plussed.

'What do you think?'

'The food, you mean?'

'Everything.' The food, the girl, the city.

The poor boy is blushing, caught in a kaleidoscope of impressions, in the old prison of words; he is saturated with new experiences. I have dragged him over a cultural obstacle-course, and there is more to come. His open face radiates a desire to please.

'How's Sally, by the way?' I drop the name of his great passion as casually as I can. 'I forgot to ask.'

'Fine,' he says, a fraction too blithely, 'as far as I know.' He looks intently at the table. 'We'll always be friends.'

'Of course.'

Then in a second, we're laughing. The long parade of statues and churches may already be lost, buried temporarily, to resurface again when he least expects it. But once again the good wine and food of Tuscany has worked its magic.

When we have found our legs we move on to the end of the road and turn up the busy Via de' Benci.

Piazza S. Croce, past its meridional baking now, is dotted with daring blues and reds: an improvised football match is in progress. The plastic ball kisses and skids over the hot stones, and pigeons, bold and lazy, flutter and hop and settle again. The ugly black Dante statue on the church steps frowns disapprovingly on the happy children, yet this elegant square was the site of tourneys and spectacles centuries before he came along, before the black and white neo-Gothic wedding cake was superimposed on the old church. On St John's Day, 24 June, the Baptist's patronal festival, *Il Calcio* was traditionally played, or fought out, here, and some years it can still be seen in the Piazza. I tell Andrew: he is a goalkeeper, already in his first year playing for the University.

It is a football of a sort: costumed, ferocious and bloody, a battle between the four quarters of the city: San Giovanni, the Greens; Santa Croce, the Blues; S. Maria Novella, the Reds, and S. Spirito, the Whites. The object is to get the ball into your opponents' net (a kind of medieval tent guarded by four goalkeepers), and any means is considered fair: there is kicking, eye-gouging, and karate; in fact it is rather similar to rugby union. The prize is a white heifer.

In its present form, which dates from the fourteenth century, each side fields 27 players and a standard-bearer, and with the Major General Sergeant, who sees fair play from a white charger, and drummers and halberdiers, oxen drivers, arquebusiers and hangers-on (those prerequisites of all Italian occasions), 530 bodies in all take part. There are three games in St John's Week – two semi-finals and the final – and the casualty-rate is high. Despite the presence of six 'Signalmen', a 'Reference Judge', and a 'Commissary Judge', just recently one unfortunate had an ear bitten off. Concussions, of course, are commonplace. Over the last thirty years the Whites of S. Spirito have been the team to beat. Rival teams desperately import 'foreigners' as 'secret weapons'. According to the famous designer, Marchese Emilio Pucci, who is deeply involved with the running of the game, it came originally from Roman legionaries, who used it for exercise and training. There is still great enthusiasm for the tradition, as well as a small anti-bloodsport lobby that believes the continuation of *Il Calcio* tarnishes the image of a 'City of Culture'. But ritualised thuggery dies hard, and it would be a shame to draw Marzocco's claws. This, after all, is a game, like English bowls, that is sanctified by historical tradition. In 1530, when the city had been under close siege for six months by Emperor Charles V, the Florentines staged a special version of *Il Calcio* to assure the besieging troops that their morale was still high.

Through the dark rectangle of the door streams the human maelstrom. *MAI SARETE SOLI IN FIRENZE!* 'The church,' says one guide book, in a monumental understatement, 'is much visited by tourist groups.'

A special, rather dapperly clad *major-domo* is employed by the monks to maintain decorum: he talks constantly to himself and seems quite demented. Perhaps the trippers have unhinged him. Past his uniformed figure the bikini tops and shorts, the bikini bottoms and tee shirts flood into the echoing basilica, and in large eddies drift to their various pools round polyglot guides, who shout their babel commentaries in insouciant professional rivalry. Of all Florentine churches, this is the *chiesa turistica*. The monks are quiet and friendly and blandly patient among the cameras and bubble gum. Their brown-habited calm moves me as they glide about their church and suffer the twentieth century.

Michelangelo, Dante, Galileo, Macchiavelli, the Florentine great all crowd here – Rossini, Ugo Foscolo, too, and Alfieri: but the memorials are a dim shadow of their greatness. Vasari's tomb for the divine Michelangelo strikes me rather as a monument to poor taste. The vandal Vasari left his finger-prints all over S. Croce, but this must rank as his most garish and ill-judged contribution. And his work has been continued: where once the walls were literally covered with frescoes, there are now only national monuments, tedious and uninspired. Of far more interest and beauty is Antonio Rossellino's *Madonna del Latte*, a *mandorla* in deep relief surrounded by the heads of putti on folded wings, which is set in a pillar just inside the church on the right, over the tomb of one of Lorenzo's friends killed in the Pazzi Conspiracy. This was probably Antonio's last work (he died in 1479, the year after the Pazzi affair), and, set against a simulated draped shroud of marble, is on the solemn side. But it has class.

I draw my companion to the tomb of Leonardo Bruni on the south side, a masterpiece of Bernardo Rossellino (1446–7), then, opposite, to Desiderio's monument to Carlo Marsuppini, commissioned during the next decade, and plainly inspired by the Bruni tomb. These are two of the most wonderfully elegant tombs in Florence, a city crammed with superlative monumental sculpture, and, fittingly, they commemorate two great Humanists, scholars and Chancellors of the Republic.

The Bruni tomb, enclosed by fluted pilasters and set in an arched recess, where Bruni's effigy reclines on a sarcophagus, is austere, tranquil, idealised; the Mary in the tondo of the lunette is solemn, the flanking angels sorrowing, dignified. Desiderio's monument to Marsuppini, on the other hand, is more relaxed, a softer commentary on the harshness of death: even the spring of the arch is less severe. Laughing angel-children, holding chains of flowers that fall in riotous festoons half the length of the monument, stand above on pilasters either side of the lunette; either side of the pilasters below are two *putti* turned inwards, each with a shield, each innocently inviting the spectator to moderate his grief. In the roundel of the lunette, Mary and her Child are almost playful, and the lower *putti* are anything but downhearted. These are two of the most ravishing creations of the *quattrocento*, worn to translucence by adoring hands, and, despite the gloom, somehow amenable even to amateur photography. In the face of death they *smile*.

But the tall, coloured lancets, white, yellow-gold and blue-green-pink, are pulling Andrew to the sanctuary (as they are meant to: Franciscans concentrated all attention in their churches on the east end). He will wander among the Giottos, and wonder at Gaddi's mammoth *Legend of the Cross*, where flashguns provide almost continuous illumination.

Rather hidden away on the wall next to the Bruni tomb is a distinguished Donatello *Annunciation* dating from the 1430s. Until recently, I never properly appreciated it: perhaps the sheer originality of the work confounded me; certainly, I heartily disliked the gilding, which seemed to me quite out of character. The relief is so deep that, enclosed as they are in a proscenium-arch, the kneeling angel and the startled Virgin (who has just risen from her chair

185

and is about to leave) seem like puppets in a toy theatre. The faces are idealised and 'classical', but the scene is composed with Donatello's typical psychological insight. The tabernacle is of limestone (*macigno*) and the *putti* of terracotta. Imagine my relief when I learnt that the gilding was carried out in the nineteenth century! What pleasure I should take in removing it personally, millimetre by millimetre!

I rejoin Andrew in the frescoed sacristy. By now the intricate inlay of the cupboards and the curlicues of the splendid grille enclosing the chapel are making the eyes swim; we stagger blindly through a large *libreria*, and (always a surprise) into a leather factory, which is full of craftsmen at work, cutting and moulding, staining, tooling with gold. There is the heady, raw fragrance of hide and polish, and the rich and wonderful colours that characterise Florentine leather: deep emerald, glossy maroon, chestnut and ebony. Every stage of manufacture is on display here, and, only a few steps from the sacristy, plastic cards are brandished and cheques scribbled, as anything from handbag, spectacle case and bookmark to full-length coat and sets of matching suitcases change hands.

The Cappella dei Pazzi and Museo are adjacent, but admission is by a door (*si paga*) to the right of the church façade. So we move out again, past tantalising views of a geranium-covered courtyard, and into the hum of the vast nave.

Through the gateway, the view of the famous chapel (the monks' chapter house, as well as the intended funeral chapel of the Pazzi) is immediately striking: to the left there is an arcade, its graceful curves rising from slender, elegant pilasters; immensely green lawns and white, pink, and blue-pink oleanders line the wall beneath it; and among slim cypresses the white of marble flashes; a gravelled path threads the lawns and leads the eye to the triumphal archway flanked on either side by three tall Corinthian columns. Above the frieze is an attic; and on that is a roofed loggia, above which the conical fish-scaled roof and lantern of the central cupola, with its series of little *oculi*, can be seen.

This is one of Brunelleschi's most perfect creations, a marvellous harmony of the grey *pietra serena* and white plaster with which he loved to stress the articulation of his buildings. There is balance and serenity, the symmetry of immutable order, and a peace and stillness which always surprises – as does the smallness of the chapel. Yet some 4,000 souls are said to have squeezed into it to hear a reading of the regulations of Pius V for the establishment of the Inquisition in Florence.

With the deep, central cupola and the series of vaults to channel every sound, the acoustics are quite extraordinary, and I always long to hear singing here. In this setting, Luca della Robbia's roundels of the Apostles, in white and blue, are additions of the most perfect taste. Outside, Luca covered the

Cappella dei Pazzi

barrel vaulting of the portico with a glorious panelling of squares and rosettes in all his loveliest colours; the frieze of cherubs is by Desiderio. The Pazzi had nothing but the best.

Brunelleschi's second cloister is another marvel of hushed calm. No trippers congregate here. ('There's nothing to see!' I hear one call to a following group. 'Nothing.') A solitary girl sprawls full length on the central lawn reading a book, her long, blonde hair spilling over bronzed shoulders onto the grass. Here to whisper is to shout: any sound would be a violation.

The museum proper consists of six rooms spread along the first cloister. Andrew, I see, is destroyed, so we all but saunter through.

But there are things he must see: in the *Cenacolo*, for instance, Taddeo Gaddi's epic frescoes on the end wall; and Cimabue's enormous crucifix, which lost so much of its paint in 1966, the whole composition known now only from photographs and memories; and Donatello's *St Louis of Toulouse* done for the *Parte Guelfa*, displaced from its niche at Orsanmichele in the fifteenth century, and, in 1860, from a niche on the façade of S. Croce.

Various fresco fragments detached from the right side of the church, and discovered behind the sixteenth-century altars, are also on display, including Orcagna's ghastly *Triumph of Death*, part of an important and monumental *Last Judgment*. The crippled beggars are given a haunting inscription, an early *fumetto*, as it were, which can be completed as follows: 'Since prosperity has left us, / Death, the medicine of all pains, / Come now to give us our Last Supper.' And above them is the stark reminder: 'Neither learning, riches, high birth nor bravery count for anything against the blows of death. Nor can any argument avail. So beware, reader, and stand always ready so that you are not taken in mortal sin.' In one of these fragments is a fascinating view of the Baptistry and Duomo.

The gilded *St Louis* stands heavily, and larger than life, in his scalloped niche, weighed down by cope and mitre; to my eyes he cuts a ponderous and somewhat awkward figure. But he looks exactly what he was (a Franciscan saint who died young, aged 23) and what the *Parte Guelfa* wanted (i.e. costly). The appearance of this statue has suffered alteration since the fifteenth century: the crozier was originally sunk into the floor of the niche at Orsanmichele (and would look better if it were lower here); and there is evidence that the back of the figure was reduced when it was placed in a shallower recess at S. Croce. But it is undeniably impressive, and, bearing in mind the difficulties of the fire-gilding process, which meant that it had to be cast and assembled in pieces, it is also a major technical triumph.

But Gaddi's 34-feet-high *Tree of the Cross*, which covers the whole of the high end wall is of paramount interest: complex, so carefully worked out, and, despite everything, so splendidly preserved. It occupies approximately

120 square metres. Based on St Bonaventure's *Lignum Vitae*, an allegory of the Crucifixion, this massive fresco was detached in a single piece to save it from the ravages of damp.

The *Last Supper* at its base (*c.* 1330–40) represents the earliest version of the theme in Florence, and the first to show the iconography that was to become familiar: the eleven haloed disciples sitting with Jesus on the far side of the table, St John sleeping on Jesus's lap, and a dark-haired Judas, unhaloed and isolated on a stool this side of the table, dipping his hand into the dish with his Master, in the very act of betraying him. Some of the heads are mutilated, but half a dozen are exceedingly fine; each of the disciples is skilfully individualised, and the perspective of the table is striking: its surface seems to jut out at right angles from the wall into the refectory. The way the figures of the disciples overlap the bands that square the *Tree* and separate it from the flanking scenes (*St Francis receives the Stigmata, A story of St Louis, St Benedict in the Wilderness* and *Jesus anointed by Mary Magdalen*) makes them seem to be sitting one stage nearer the viewer: it is exactly as if they sat supping below a vast, frescoed refectory wall.

I would stay to decipher the inscription on the branches of the mystic tree, but Andrew is wilting. I would also try to identify the disciples in order, but the hands of my watch have flown round the dial, and I shall have to return on my own.

'*Vivoli*' is easy to miss, but to the tired pilgrim all roads lead to the Via Isola delle Stinche: one of the tiniest streets, with one of the longest names, in all Florence, but home of incomparably the best *gelateria*.

The place is packed: scattered in the environs on every kerb, and leaning against every spare inch of wall, are happy customers; there is the relative hush of contentment, broken only by the warbling of caged finches from upper windows, and housewives barking at each other across the narrow street. They stand, they lean, they sit. The forecourt of S. Simone seems merely a convenient parking-lot for haversacks. One pays at the *cassa* and chooses: *strega, nocciola, pesca, limone, melone, pistacchio, moca, ciliegia, fragola, menta,* all the colours of the rainbow in long trays beaded with condensation wait to be scooped into one's cardboard tub. My young friend emerges finally with a strange, garish mixture, and surfaces occasionally, as each new explosion of flavour takes him by surprise.

The experience is refreshing. Step by step, as I steer him towards the Lungarno, he seems to become more resolute. Finally with a sigh he finishes his multicoloured *gelato*.

With immaculate timing a no. 13 bus rattles to a halt, and very soon we are across the Arno and beginning the long, winding ascent of Viale dei Colli to the Piazzale Michelangelo, threading tufted pines and villas just beginning to open their eyes again, and with each twist a more lovely view of the city spreads to the right below. We climb on and on. Suddenly, too soon, the needles of the pines seem to become transparent, light pours between the fingers and grows in intensity until each pool of light has joined with the next, and the bus, with a final heave, makes the Piazzale in an apocalyptic, blinding flash. Cars and coaches choke the parking-lots; around the promenade a row of market stalls sell ices, films, souvenirs, rubbish. A bronze version of Michelangelo's *David*, surrounded below by *Night, Day, Dawn and Evening*, looks out from a marble pedestal black with graffiti over the terraced rooftops of Florence. As we step off the bus I can almost feel the irises of my eyes contract: but this is the time of day to see the city. The long rectangular balustrade is cooling, and we gaze out across the river at domes and towers and into looming mountains.

Andrew has been bewildered by the long procession of spectacles; but views he understands. I point out the landmarks one by one. To our left, the walls of the medieval city plunging precipitously from the Forte, buttressed and covered in creepers, dotted with adventitious flowers; a valley of leaning olives; then above, the yellow and white and peach and terracotta of a hundred villas, each guarded by a cypress and wearing its own individual face: smug, smiling, haughty, querulous; the rooftops of Oltrarno, higgledy-piggledy, still age-old and unspoilt despite the odd lift-shaft and television mast. Lines of washing loop from window to window, and between the tiles a sudden intrusion of palm-spikes, or pine-puff, betrays a private garden.

And the eye follows the Lungarno, Ponte S. Niccolò, Ponte alle Grazie, past the Old Bridge and Ponte S. Trìnita, Ponte alla Carraia, and Ponte Amerigo Vespucci, and rests on Baccio d'Agnolo's lovely campanile at S. Spirito, and the orange fish-scale tiles of its cupola; cypress-covered Monte Oliveto, and further west the distinctive, tight dome of S. Frediano – an exquisite exercise in composition and perspective, as the Arno diminishes to a silver thread, and the bridges spanning it merge almost into one, and the Cascine and distant suburbs become a misty plane and fade into pale foothills, and the low ranges of Monte Albano smudge the far horizon. The whole city is unfolded before us, seen here from unfamiliar angles: the grand southern flanks of S. Croce, the Biblioteca Nazionale, the Badia, and the Bargello, the upper story of Orsanmichele, with its warm stone and delicate cornices; from here the cupola of S. Lorenzo's Chapel of the Princes seems almost joined to the Baptistry, and the *campanili* of the Badia and the Duomo are directly aligned. Above everything else, hugely assertive, squats Brunelleschi's cupola, its ribs like the piping on a schoolboy's cap, two deep eyes trained watchfully on the false *David*.

190

And there to the north east is Fiesole, the bell tower and its cathedral clearly visible in a sudden dip; left, the wide valley of the Mugnone, and right, on high, the castellations of Vincigliata, and, nestling below, Settignano, home of sculptors.

I watch a young ice-cream vendor proposition a statuesque, self-possessed German girl. When he refuses payment for her *gelato*, she shrugs, moves away along the terrace. Subtly, he abandons his stall and pursues, never quite obtruding himself so as to become a nuisance, but never actually leaving her side. She leans finally against the balustrade and licks her ice while the curly-haired Romeo cajoles her. Andrew draws my attention to some canoeists, like a tiny centipede, skimming downstream, putting in sudden spurts and creaming the placid surface, then resting, their oarmarks left like morse in the river, a blueprint of their rhythms. Then, when I turn again, the German girl is speaking to the youth, and, by the time we walk away, I see the white of her teeth in a first smile. I, too, have to smile. It has taken between ten and twelve minutes, an object lesson in gentle persistence.

'The last leg!' I promise. But now Andrew has no thought of last legs: he takes the steps to S. Salvatore at a trot, and strides on until we face the steep flight beneath S. Miniato.

Together we mount them, one by one, and suddenly the glorious marble façade of the Romanesque basilica leaps upon us, its inlaid rectangles and rhombi and wheels of white and grey-green marble, its columns reaching so gracefully up to the blind arches of the lower storey.

Its impact is unique, the effulgence, to my mind, unearthly. And in the upper storey, the mosaic of *Christ with Mary and St Minias* above the tabernacle window, its gold brilliant against the sober elegance of the marble, gleams like a vision. There is nowhere remotely like S. Miniato here on its green hill south of the city; it is a blaze of burning white, transcendentally bright. To its right is the brick façade of the Bishop's Palace, summer residence of the ecclesiastical dignitaries of Florence; left, the battlements and tower on which Michelangelo's cannons once roared in defence of the city, and where now, in neat rows, the dead lie beneath pious plain slabs, twinkling lamps, and the flutter of a thousand angel wings. The view over the city is a nonpareil, framed by exquisite fanning cedars, peeping between heaving oaks, a happy dreamscape of pinks and whites and the dun of stubborn towers. No vista is more grand or more sobering: the works of man and the works of nature vie with each other, yet coexist in imperturbable harmony. At night, when the stars are thick and the necklaces of light wind over the prone figure of the city, one hardly knows where to look. I have found it hard, like Elizabeth Barrett Browning, to 'make a choice of beauty'. *Hoi polloi* are contented with the Piazzale, but five minutes more would lead them up to heaven. This is one of the sacred places of the earth: hardly a leaf or stone could be moved without destroying its perfection.

We enter the eleventh-century basilica. Mass begins at 6.00 p.m., and I want Andrew to hear the Olivetan Benedictines at their plainsong.

Here, what one notices immediately is not the pilasters and columns and antique capitals, nor the intricate *intarsia* of the pavement, but the unusual raised choir above the crypt, the glow of blue and gold in the mosaic calotte, and the dazzling, gemlike *Cappella del Crocifisso* at the end of the nave beneath. It was in this tabernacle that the Benedictines kept a celebrated crucifix which, on Good Friday 1018, bowed its head to Giovanni Gualberto dei Visdomini in a gesture of approval when the young 18-year-old forgave his brother Ugo's murderer.

Giovanni Gualberto was born around AD 1000; his father was Lord of Petroio in Val di Pesa, and his family were patrons of the Bishopric of Florence. But within the family there were fierce divisions, and Giovanni's brother was one day murdered. On Good Friday in 1018, as Giovanni rode into the city, he suddenly came face to face with his brother's murderer, alone. It was, according to legend, just before he got to S. Miniato, at a bend on the steep ascent, that he met him, a god-sent chance to even scores.

But the murderer begged him for mercy, throwing out his hands in the gesture of Christ on the Cross, and, on that day of all days, Giovanni found himself unable to strike him down. He forgave the man, asked his pardon, and went into the monastery church to pray before the Crucifix. It was then that the crucified Christ bowed his head, as if to commend this act of mercy, this spontaneous sacrifice.

The young man, deeply affected by this experience, stayed on with the Benedictines and renounced the world and his former existence. After some years he might have become Abbot, but he preferred to strike out on his own, first to S. Romualdo and his monks at Camaldoli high in the Casentino (St Romuald was another fugitive from S. Miniato: he is said to have fled the world when his father killed a relative in a quarrel: these were violent days), then to the slopes of the Pratomagno, north of the main Apennines, a glorious region of forests and streams. There he built his own community and, with two others, began the Vallombrosan Order, following an adaptation of the Rule of St Benedict.

But Giovanni was no mute and passive mystic: he was a passionate reformer and a lifelong persecutor of simony in the Church, masterminding operations from his Vallombrosan retreat and actually arming his monks against the bishop's forces in bitter and bloody confrontations. Though Abbot of Vallombrosa and founder of many associate houses in Tuscany and Umbria, this militant monk-hero never became a priest, nor advanced further than the minor orders.

Today, Vallombrosa ('Shady Valley') is a popular holiday resort, airy and cool and bright, its hills thick with firs and little shrines and chapels recalling the early activities of the new Order. The hills are clad in mixed woodland, but spruce and pine abound, and mile upon mile of sapling beeches; there is a delightful solitude here, and abundant shade, and at the roadside I remember gathering handfuls of wild strawberries under slanting beams of sunlight; there were raspberries, too, warm in the sun and sweet as syrup. The air here can be heady as champagne, and in autumn the leaves must fall knee-deep. In *Paradise Lost* (I. 302 ff.) Milton resonantly describes the legions of the Devil as 'angel forms, who lay entranc'd / Thick as autumnal leaves that strew the brooks / In Vallombrosa, where th'Etrurian shades / High over-arch'd embow'r', and one guide book after another regurgitates the story that these lines were prompted by the poet's stay here in 1638 during his Italian tour. The truth is that he had been reading his Ariosto, and Vallombrosa, with its fine symmetry of vowels, simply *sounded* right. Indeed, I am reliably informed, there is no more than an even chance that Milton's famous meeting with Galileo at Arcetri ever took place. Experts are unromantic souls.

The monastic community, suppressed in the nineteenth century, but since reinstated, still lingers on, and in the village jolly, worldly monks sell herbs and prayer books and soap and postcards and honey and liqueurs and plastic rosaries. The tourists sit and take the air, and there is an atmosphere of happy, pagan holiday. In the seventeenth-century church a young Brother played loudly and joyfully on a modern organ as a wedding was celebrated. And when the fat, handsome bride came out, a milling crowd burst into rapturous applause. Her bouquet, I recall, landed dangerously near me.

I wandered happily among the woods in search of the saint's 'Holy' beech tree, the spot where he loved to pray in solitude, and listened to the sounds of the hills. Here, when the leaves catch the first ghost of a wind, there is a rustling undercurrent, a susurration different from one tree to another, almost as if a million tongues were wagging, like the oak of Zeus at Dodona. And when the trees are angry and rattle their limbs and shake their fingers and moan as they jostle each other in the dark, these hills would frighten the Devil himself.

The famous Crucifix is now in the chapel right of the High Altar in S. Trìnita, a church of the Vallombrosan Order founded by S. Giovanni. The S. Miniato Cappella del Crocifisso is a tabernacle in the form of an aedicule; the barrel vault is decorated by Luca della Robbia in white and blue enamelled terracotta highlighted with touches of gold; on the outside are lovely, overlapping fish-scale 'tiles'. The effect is ravishing. The cupboard designed to house the crucifix was decorated by Agnolo Gaddi (1394–6) with a painting of SS. Miniato and Giovanni Gualberto standing centrally side by side, and, in a series of smaller panels, scenes of the *Annunciation* and *Passion* (one of these, bottom right, is an iconographically unusual *Last Supper*), all rich with gold, blues and reds, so that the dark nave seems illuminated, and the calotte, in all its solemn Byzantine glory, seems almost dull by comparison.

There is just time before Mass to peer through the iron screen in the north wall at another treasure: this is the Chapel of the Cardinal of Portugal, erected in memory of Jacopo di Lusitania, nephew of King Alphonse of Portugal, and Archbishop of Lisbon, who died on a visit to Florence in 1459, aged 25.

Manetti, Brunelleschi's heir, designed this chapel in the shape of a shallow Greek cross, with a mosaic floor and a ceiling of beautiful painted tiles in cubes of yellow, green and purple, producing a strange and delightful honey-comb effect; on this are set five large *tondi* of the *Cardinal Virtues*, with the Holy Ghost, a radiant white dove, at their centre. These *tondi* are in the form of two concentric circles, shield-like shapes, with buff rims and figures against a most delicate gradation of blue fish-scales. The whole ceiling is a wonder, one of Luca's greatest inspirations.

The cardinal's tomb, set in a niche between stone curtains and crowded with *putti* and delightful angels, is a breathtakingly lovely work by Antonio Rossellino. On the tympanum, above the figure of the cardinal (who sleeps, glorious in death, upon a Classical sarcophagus bearing four elegiac verses), is an exquisite garland-enfolded *tondo* of the *Virgin and Child* supported by hovering angels. The base of the sarcophagus, too, is carved with most delicate relief work, and carries a shallow plinth of inlaid *pietre dure*. The left of the two putti who sprawl on the lid of the sarcophagus is not so lighthearted as Desiderio's in S. Croce, but his chubby cheeks and natural pose conjure his face into a near-smile, and the heavy material draped over his shoulder and down his left side provides a marvellous contrast with the plasticity of his flesh.

All in all, this tiny chapel is one of the loveliest sights imaginable; a repository of consummate art – architecture, sculpture and painting. Luca's ceiling and Antonio Rossellino's tomb are among the most splendid manifestations of refinement and taste in all Florence. An old man, toothless and unshaven, smiles and nods and nudges my young friend. He explains, in proud, slurred Tuscan: 'A jewel of jewels!', and Andrew edges to my side, instinctively, thinking he must be begging.

But Mass has begun. We tiptoe to the crypt where ancient pillars loom like the trees of a shaded grove: light comes from behind the altar through thin alabaster of marbled brown, and the little vaults are like overhanging boughs. The celebrant stands with arms akimbo at the altar above the relics of the eponymous, tutelary Minias. Who *was* he – this saint who has caused hagiographers so much trouble?

St Minias, it is generally agreed, was the first martyr of Florence. Nothing much more is certain. In the apse vault he is pictured as a king, and one legend tells the story of an Armenian prince who was serving in the Roman army. Denounced as a Christian, he was taken before the Emperor Decius in his headquarters on a hill outside the city, and thrown to the wild beasts in the amphitheatre. His prayers delivered him from the attentions of a panther, but he was then boiled in a cauldron, hung from gallows, stoned, used for javelin practice, and, as the *coup de grâce*, decapitated. (This is the most colourful account.) On this hill and in the woods around it, in the time, it is said, of Nero, the earliest Christian community lived. It may be that Minias (as different versions have it) was a deacon in this community, and, as his name suggests, of foreign descent.

The saint's relics in S. Miniato are possibly those of an Egyptian, but certainly those of a foreigner. Another version of the mainstream legend talks of the decapitated Minias running head-in-hand towards the *Mons Florentinus*, a place 'thick with olives and laurels' where the Arno bends; and from ancient times a cross, *La Croce al Gorgo (Gorgo = ansa*, a 'loop' or 'bend') marking the exact place of his martyrdom, was venerated by Florentines, and a church, S. Candida, according to Villani, stood on the spot in his day. In the time of Gregory the Great, S. Frediano of Lucca came regularly to worship the saint's relics, and by the time of Charlemagne a basilica had already been erected here.

The tale is lost in time, in the anfractuosities of history and human fancy. Until the saint puts on flesh again and makes all things clear, we are unlikely to know more.

The acoustics of the crypt are exceptional. An old Brother acts as cantor and pulls the handful of monks in choir through the subtle intricacies of plainsong. The hands that clutch his choirbook are visibly arthritic, his mouth-shapes strained and lopsided, and the tone he evinces comes from somewhere unusually high in his head. But he sings out his heart, dictating every little nuance of pause and slur; and, if his Brothers fall behind, he bunches his bony fist and beats time in apoplectic rage until they catch up.

Who was it called plainsong 'the best music of all'? Here, certainly, in the conspiratorial atmosphere of the crypt, any mechanical accompaniment would be unseemly. The Latin liturgy is timeless, the unison hypnotic. The rise and fall of the monks' voices soak the stonework as the ancient rite is performed; and emerging finally from the small dark doorway into the mellow gold of evening on the terrace is like being born again. In my head a hundred horns, trombones and trumpets blast a scarlet-silk glory-chord in D-major; my flesh goes bumpy. I know no other view half so affecting. A slight haze sits on the City of Flowers, and the towers and rooftops spill out below us like a dreamy Aladdin's cave. A precocious slim moon hangs low, and a few small bats flit about in the stillness.

In the apartment at Piazza d'Azeglio, Fiammetta waits for Pino to call; she paces the hallway, smokes cigarettes irritably. I sit and read while Andrew showers; and when I return from my own shower he is curled on the sofa asleep. A postcard has arrived from a friend in Sussex, and, at my desk in the window, I consider the gentle fields and cranky, timbered cottages on a village green; the carefully tended hollyhocks, and rockeries, and the distant yew-framed spire of the church; and I wonder what I am doing here, why I am not climbing the Downs, or clambering through the undergrowth of the still woods at home. Outside, the traffic snarls, and a chorus of hooters send up their gross, unmusical offering. In the park, students settle down for the night with wine and transistors: to while away the hours they will kick beer cans and explode plastic cartons, and all the dogs of Florence will yelp and yap and snarl.

Later, we amble to 'Toto' in Borgo SS. Apostoli. The Old Bridge is now given over to its nocturnal tribes, and the night's exotic cabaret is under way. There is the usual sinister wail of enervating flutes, the sickly tang of modern incense; an insidious mixture of the honest old Roman Bacchanal and weird, oriental abandon. Cellini's bust watches impassively; and under the sturdy arrowed piers, the river laps imperturbably down to the sea.

'Toto' is large and chic: it has the advantage of never closing, and the consequent disadvantage of attracting tourists. But, as it is not one of the cheaper *trattorie*, indeed styles itself as a *ristorante*, a table is usually to be had, and on it a decent Chianti sits waiting.

Service is swift: a trained team of formally clad waiters streams ceaselessly in and out of the kitchens. In the centre of the room is a huge, wheeled wagon displaying *antipasti*, a sprawling jumble of red and yellow peppers, and a hundred salads, as well as shellfish peeled and immaculately presented for the table in delicate flesh-tints. My *tagliatelle*, with mushrooms in cream

196

and ham *ragù*, is so fresh it melts on the tongue. But the speciality of the house is steak – vast cuts of rib, like T-bones, butchered in front of you and individually weighed. Andrew and I sit where we can anticipate the pleasure of this heroic main course by observing the chef in action. He is a pale fellow who slaves away at a giant open grill like the jaws of hell, which from time to time he coaxes to a scalding heat before throwing another slab of beef onto the gridiron.

Knots of tourists drift in and giggle over the long menu, and the waiters dash past exchanging their sarcasm in rapid vernacular. At a table near us, an unmistakably English family sits quarrelling. Mother is smart and must have been pretty; father is loud and assured and well bred. A fleshy daughter with streaky hair and spectacularly large silver hoop earrings (a travesty of her mother's quiet good looks) pouts and sulks across the table, and next to her is a restless, spotty youth. Father speaks to the waiter in a mixture of Spanish and French as if he were a half-wit. The waiter nods with good-natured patience, accepting his dismissal with dignity. Over the sizzle of plate-sized steaks, the chef calls 'BEPE!', and each time he turns a steak to perfection, he calls 'BEPE!' A crucifix hangs on the wall over the Receipt of Custom, an enclosed desk where the owner, cigarette streaming over his cheek and closed right eye, examines each bill and flicks like a croupier through bundles of banknotes. The waiters queue meekly before him, vassals before a portly godfather.

Gulping good wine from Greve, we watch our steaks chopped expertly from a carcass, weighed, spiced (a scattering of pepper and salt and a spoonful of oil is all the *bistecca fiorentina* needs), and grilled with casual expertise. Four eager eyes follow it to the table. The crisp, green salads are generous and have a hint of something interesting. Coriander, perhaps.

'*Buon appetito,*' intones the waiter gratuitously.

Andrew leaves next day for Carrara. His father has rented a villa there and I am pressed to join them.

'I'll be in touch,' he says between mouthfuls of succulent flesh and purple Chianti. 'I've got your number.'

Madame Butterfly is on television when we get back, and Fiammetta has left a note saying that she has gone to the seaside with Pino for a few days, and would I feed the cat? With incredible lack of imagination she calls the cat 'Pussy': I have always called him Pinkerton.

Early next morning I see Andrew off at the station, and wave, in a mixture of relief and sadness, as the train draws away. His blond head fades shimmering into the distant heat and I hear him shout: 'Come and see us!' I nod and wave and hear him call again: 'I'll phone!'

And as I turn back into the bedlam of Florence, in a flash of prescience I know I shall never hear from him again.

CHAPTER

IX

 Even the cries of the market can be music, the sound of rain on awnings, the tones of a hundred different car horns. I tramp back along Via S. Antonino and hear a woman singing high up among the pigeons and television aerials. It is an accomplished coloratura, and I pause to listen. Rossini. I must have music.

To my left a door yawns open : inside is a little oratory I have never noticed before, a hundred candles dancing in a dark room, and through a haze of incense I see blurred figures moving about. Every day another door opens. Now the ham shop fills the narrow street with its salt pungency, and then 'Zanobini' calls, its shelves aglitter with Chianti. A cameo-seller, seeing my interest, takes me to the rear of his stall and shows me his best pieces (not for sale) ; he explains how cameos are made, how long a cutter is trained, where the best craftsmen come from ; he shows me pictures of the various stages of the operation.

A statuesque nymph stands posing for a photograph : she has a bloom on her, the gloss of youth, and an arresting profile as she reaches for a silk scarf. The sun lights her perfectly. She turns her head a fraction towards me and freezes, and I have left my camera at home.

But on the corner of Via S. Reparata and Via 27 Aprile I come upon the former Camaldolese convent of S. Apollonia (martyred in 249 and invoked against toothache); one of its elegant cloisters, with refined Ionic capitals below a sweet loggia, is now used as a car park and plastered with advertisements and graffiti in Greek alluding (one way or another) to the KKE. Despite the gloomy prognostications of guide books, the *Cenacolo* is open on a regular, daily basis. One signs a book, and there are even postcards to be had. It is all extremely civilised.

S. Apollonia is an ancient religious house, founded in *c.* 1339, reshaped in the fifteenth century, suppressed in the nineteenth, and then for years a military stores until it passed recently into the hands of the University. Because of the strict privacy of the Benedictines the *Cenacolo* remained unknown to the world at large, but in 1860, when the nuns were forced to leave and it became public property, visitors were at last allowed in. The *Ultima Cena* was at first thought to be by Uccello.

The Benedictine nuns of S. Apollonia chose to have their refectory decorated by Andrea del Castagno (1423–57). His real name was Andrea di Bertolo di Simone, but he was known as 'Castagno' from his birthplace, Castagno d'Andrea, in the chestnut country of the Falterona. Castagno was perhaps the most influential Florentine painter in the generation after Masaccio's death, and Masaccio's realism is a clear influence in this highly dramatic version of the *Last Supper*.

It was done in around 1450, and dominates the west wall: above it was a *Crucifixion* flanked by a *Resurrection* and *Entombment*, three stories of the Passion painted against a huge, unifying terrain and skilfully arranged around two heavy shuttered windows. Only after the suppression of the convent was this area freed from the covering of plaster which overlay it. In 1953 the upper frescoes were detached for restoration, and the *sinopie*, showing superlative draughtsmanship, were brought to light and exhibited on the opposite wall. The rough plaster and occasional brick showing through contrast deliciously with the dark, strong colours beneath.

I sit alone in the cool lofty room wondering what the great west wall must have looked like when Andrea finally put down his brush. The windows would have lit the frescoes with almost theatrical impact.

The *Last Supper* was an established theme for the end wall of refectories, but this is a world apart from Gaddi's version in S. Croce. Castagno took the fourteenth-century tradition of the long, rectangular table, with Jesus and eleven apostles one side, and Judas isolated on the other, but handled it in a quite revolutionary manner: the background is a multi-coloured marble *loggia*, drawn with elaborate perspective so that the figures (who are named) positively leap out at the eye. The light that plays so precisely on the disciples' heads gives them a startling solidity, and the striped ceiling and foreshortened bench-ends reinforce the illusion of depth and distance. The 'upper room' recedes far into the wall (as Gaddi's projects into the refectory of S. Croce); behind the haloed heads of the seated figures is a series of square marble slabs, each brilliantly convincing, a *tour de force* of streaks and veins and swirls of cloudy marble. The atmosphere engendered by the rich, intense colours and the strongly individual poses of the disciples, is one of restless and fearful anticipation. It is highly charged. A young St John sleeps on Jesus's left; the bolt upright figure of Judas, swarthy with pitch-black hair and beard, separates St Peter and Jesus, and behind all three is a square of marble ablaze with streaks of vermilion and white against a background of ultramarine and grey – an intentionally disturbing square of troubled movement. St Peter is balding; a youthful St Thomas gazes (doubtfully, one supposes) at the mosaic ceiling. St Thaddeus (Jude) and St Matthew are unbearded; Andrew's beard is long and grey; Simon, head in hand, looks confused and worried as St James, his hands outspread, argues some point with him. There is bewilderment and terror: something is about to happen.

The impact of this fresco is immediate, the setting made realistic and the figures palpable by masterly use of light, colour and perspective. Nearby are *sinopie* for Andrea's *St Jerome and the Trinity* in the Annunziata – another strongly individual and powerful work, with violent foreshortenings that are almost too ambitious.

Andrea later moved towards the emotional, psychological style of Donatello: his series of *Famous Men and Women*, now in the first room of the Uffizi, are good examples of his translation of sculpture into painting. These frescoes, which were originally painted for the Villa Pandolfini in the suburb of Legnaia, and spent some time here in S. Apollonia, include the vivid portraits of three famous Florentine men of letters: Boccaccio, Petrarch and Dante.

But there is still no *music*. Eyes searching for a poster, I drift east. And suddenly I know where I should be, and I wear seven-league boots. The Azienda Autonoma di Turismo is in Via Tornabuoni, No. 15. The former Palazzo Viviani (Donato Luigi Viviani was Cosimo III's judge) must be the most elegant Tourist Office in the world. I climb the grand staircase to the first floor and enter a busy room where two women are seated behind a desk piled with brochures. One is bespectacled, and looks efficient and determined: the other is pretty and looks less efficient and determined. The bespectacled one has excellent English, and yes, of *course* there is music! Did I know Poggio a Caiano? Did I like Donizetti? *Allora*: tomorrow night there is an open air *Lucia*; the final concert of the Festival delle Colline. Her hand is reaching for the phone as I ask. Yes, yes, tickets are still available. From the 'Agenzia ARNO'. Was there anything else?

Why not? I ask if she can get me into the Cenacolo di Foligno. She smiles. She will try. I thank her profusely. The fans whir and her dark, lovely companion busies herself tidying leaflets into useless squares. (Soon she, too, is on the telephone. An elderly American couple want to hire bicycles and take them by train to Trieste.) There is a lively exchange with the stolid metal-toothed custodian of the *Cenacolo*. 'Why not?' She waves spidery fingers in gestures eloquent of impatience. *'Perchè no?'* 'But he is a writer, a famous English scholar!' (I had briefly introduced myself, but hardly on those terms.) She meets my eyes and twinkles. 'Who?' She scribbles on a pad. *'Grazie infinite di tutto.'* She makes a face, replaces the phone, and is dialling again, her fingers a blur. The number she has been given is dead. 'They don't *care*!' she cries. 'Nobody *cares*!' This is no news to me, but I am touched by her concern. 'This is typical,' she says. 'Too many people sitting – *hello? Hello?'*

There is a sudden dawning of hope.

'We must call a *dottoressa* at the Palazzo Pitti.'

'I'm very grateful.'

'We can try.'

No one at the Pitti had heard of the *dottoressa*, and we are given a number which is not answered. Next we are put through to the *soprintendente*. My friend is now becoming cross. 'No one knows what is going on!' she hisses at me, one hand covering the mouthpiece. 'No one cares!' We wait for the *soprintendente* to be fetched.

'The *Cenacolo* is closed? *Of course* it is closed!' ('It has been closed for twenty years!' she tells me.) 'Who? *Pa-do-va-ni. Va bene. Grazie.'*

A further call establishes that the *dottoressa* is on holiday, recuperating from an illness, or both. She will return on such-and-such a day. There is nothing more to be done.

'Come back and we will talk to the *dottoressa*. Can you come back? *We have to keep trying.'*

She has been on the telephone for between twenty and thirty minutes, to Via della Ninna, the Uffizi, the Galleria Palatina, and so on, tenacious, indomitable in the face of endless bureaucracy, indolence and sheer bloody-mindedness. I feel very humble.

'We do our best,' she says as I leave. 'Sometimes we win.' She shrugs wearily. 'Sometimes.' So the *Cenacolo* is a possibility; but the prospect of *Lucia* is bright, and the setting will be magnificent. (Lisa is excited: she and Lapo would *adore* to come! Lapo loves his opera! We shall all go together!) Lorenzo's villa at Poggio, on the western outskirts of Florence, the villa Poliziano loved, whose *salone* Pontormo, Franciabigio, del Sarto and Allori covered with frescoes, is a glory in itself: the villa with the grand classical façade, and the strange allegorical frieze in blue and white.

It was at Poggio that Francesco I and Bianca Cappello died, within hours of each other, in 1587. The grounds are heavenly: south of the villa a huge game reserve stretched once, stocked by Lorenzo, of which only the sad ruins of walls and a few foundations remain. Even the Ombrone seems to flow lugubriously through the park in memory of the old, forgotten grandeur.

I am eager to return. Ashkenazy, who gave a concert (I discover) at Poggio in May, would have been my first choice or the Virtuosi di Roma, who played Baroque music in June. But this is high summer, and I am lucky to catch the end of the Festival.

The 'Agenzia ARNO' is in Piazza Ottaviani, a few minutes away, and it is packed. I wait 25 minutes in a concertinaed queue at the head of which a truculent American harridan is attempting to book a pony-trekking vacation in Ireland. When my turn finally comes, I have momentarily fogotten what I came for.

'*Possiamo parlare inglese?*'

'Yes, please.' A pleasant bald man waits patiently for my unreasonable and impossible request. I am temporarily unnerved, because he looks, unusually for an Italian behind a desk, as if he could rise to almost any challenge. He inspires confidence.

'Are there tickets for tomorrow night's *Lucia*?'

'Many.' He spreads his hands. '*Many.*'

'Would you recommend *primi posti*' (I am buying three, I tell myself) 'or *secondi posti*?'

He gives me a puzzled squint. '*Primi posti* are 16,500, *secondi posti* 13,500.'

'Yes, but do you know the layout?'

'Lie out?'

'The seating arrangements. Where we sit.' I continue in Italian. 'Would you recommend *primi* or *secondi posti*?'

'*Secondi.*'

For a few seconds I am silent. But I must ask. 'Why?'

''Is terrible.' (English.)

'What is?' Suddenly I fear he is going to break down and tell me about trouble at home.

'The opera. 'Is terrible.'

'Oh.' I am determined to salvage something after the long wait. 'Are the soloists good? *I solisti*?'

'Not well known. Eef you like opera – *I* like opera – don go. 'Is typical. Run by the state. They don know what to do. The last performance' (now he has wound himself up he is determined to go off) 'I tell you the audience wait so long they threaten to tear the place apart! It din start till 10.30 or 11.00!'

Incredulous, I ask: 'What is the orchestra like?'

'*Ma!*' he searches for the right phrase. 'No good.'

'Perhaps I shouldn't take the tickets.'

''Is an evening in the air! 'Is an experience. Lovely villa, lovely park...'
His eyes mist over as he recalls the beauty of Poggio. 'But the opera is no
good. No time for rehearsals. But at these prices,' he waves a deprecating
hand, 'you can go for sleep!'

I fix his eye. 'But *you* would not *go*.'

''Is a disgrace.' An eyebrow vanishes into where his hair once grew. 'The
state runs it – *capito*? No good! I love opera,' he spreads his large soft hands.
'But... eef you like bad music, eef you are no musical...'

'I'll take three *primi posti*.'

'*Quarantanove e cinquecento*.'

Oh hell! Oh help!

Via Tornabuoni has something for everyone: grand *palazzi* (among them
the Antinori, and the formidable, 'Newgate-like' Strozzi); the most exclusive
clothes shops; the Farmacia Inglese; Seeber and Caldini, among the best
bookshops in the city; smart hotels; the delightful old American Service Bank;
hairdressers; Pucci, Gucci, Cartier, Ferragamo, and until recently, Doneys,
perhaps the most fashionable cafe-restaurant in town, haunt of the Goncourts,
D.H. Lawrence, Ouida, the Sitwells and scores of other celebrities. It has
now disappeared for ever, its polish and flair and all those improbably named
and outrageously priced exotic cocktails.

In Gianni Versace, a lustrous boutique at 13/15 r, one can see the most
tasteful and elegant combination of old and new: the *dernier cri* in fashions
under antique, miraculously restored brick vaulting; and the young creatures
who work there move with silent, perfumed grace among the garments, their
manners and deportment and style exquisite. Each one is straight from the
pages of *Vogue*, every smile shows preternaturally even, white teeth. The place
exudes sophistication.

Via Tornabuoni has everything: there are even a couple of churches. The
road is a long gasp of pleasure and culminates, at the river end, in the Piazza
S. Trìnita, which has some of the loveliest architecture in Florence.

The Palazzo Bartolini-Salimbeni, Baccio d'Agnolo's creation on the corner
of Via Porta Rossa, caused a sensation when its façade, full of sculptures
in niches, and executed in different types of local stone, was uncovered in
1523. And inside, the open *cortile*, which has storeys of open *loggie* and lovely
graffiti decoration, is just as original. In the nineteenth century the palace
became the Hotel du Nord; Emerson, Macaulay, and Herman Melville all

stayed here at one time or another. Since 1961 it has been the French Consulate.

Then, across Via delle Terme, is the Palazzo Buondelmonte, home of one of the most ancient and powerful families of Florence, one of whose sons was S. Giovanni Gualberto. The family died out in the eighteenth century. Here, subsequently, the famous Gabinetto Scientifico-Letterario flourished under the Swiss Gian Pietro Vieusseux, and a large library was formed. Vieusseux himself lived on the second floor, and gathered about him for discussions all the most important figures in the literary, political and artistic worlds of his day: Manzoni, Leopardi, Stendhal, Dumas – they all came to Vieusseux's 'salon' and met Florentine scholars.

Vieusseux died in 1863, and in 1870 his books were moved across the Piazza to the Palazzo Spini. This monumental fortress with its distinctive curving façade (now the home of Ferragamo and the British Institute) was one of the first great houses of Florence, built by Messer Geri degli Spini in 1289. Its four storeys stretch all the way down to the river and the Lungarno once passed under its tower. (In 1823 the tower was pulled down to allow carriages to pass along the riverside.) The vast interior was split, as early as the fourteenth century, between two different branches of the Spini: one side died out, and the new incumbents displayed a more modern taste in decoration, with the result that while the Arno side remained old and simple, the façade facing the Piazza became much more ornate. In 1835 for a few years the whole complex was the 'Hotel Hombert' or the 'Hotel de l'Europe', but in 1846 the Comune di Firenze (until then cramped in the Palazzo di Parte Guelfa at the southern end of Via Pellicceria) moved in, and, when Florence was capital of the newly united Italy (1861–75), the Palazzo housed its mayors. With the capital removed to Rome, and the Comune's removal to the deserted Palazzo Vecchio, the Palazzo Spini-Feroni (the Feroni arrived on the scene in 1786) became headquarters of the Philological Society, and efforts were made to restore the place to its original state. It is still a magnificent, towering reminder of the old Florence. Though today it houses only elegant shops and offices (E.V.Lucas in 1912 remarked huffily: 'It accommodates no longer aristocrats but art dealers and bank clerks'), Poccetti's frescoes and Merlini's elaborate stuccoes for the chapel can still be viewed, and illustrations in Ginori Lisci show some remarkable relief work by Piamontini (1705).

S. Trìnita itself is one of my first and last calls in the city. It was founded in 1092 as the mother church of the Vallombrosan Order, and the inner wall of the façade shows remains of the early Romanesque edifice. The present façade is later sixteenth-century, with intricately carved wooden doors of the seventeenth century.

Santa Trìnita

The interior is Gothic: dark and silent, its austerity comes as a shock after the bright, cosmopolitan Knightsbridge outside. The clerestory is high; the only other light comes from the window over the High Altar, and a few smaller openings in one aisle. One is conscious here of holiness: among the pews there are always people at prayer, and friars hurrying about their business, and their numbers at least equal those of the tourists. There is also much beauty.

The fourth chapel of the right aisle is covered with frescoes by Lorenzo Monaco (*c.* 1423); his *Annunciation* altarpiece is in its own original frame, and the gate of wrought iron is also original. In the fifth chapel of the left aisle there usually stands a lovely wooden Magdalen begun by Desiderio and finished off by Benedetto da Maiano – a bewitching tangle of long hair and tattered rags reminiscent of Donatello's Baptistry *Magdalen*. The face is fine and delicate and full of grief, and the hands are perfection. For a couple of years now this lovely work has been away on loan to various exhibitions.

Then there is Luca della Robbia's wonderful tomb of Benozzo Federighi, Bishop of Fiesole, in the second chapel left of the High Altar. What we see today is only the upper part of the work, which stood originally on a red slab of marble flanked by painted, paired pilasters. The bishop died in 1450, and his tomb was intended for old S. Pancrazio in Via della Spada, where it stayed until the church was finally deconsecrated in 1809 (it became subsequently a tobacco factory, then a *magazzino militare*), when it was removed to the Federighi church of S. Francesco di Paola. In 1896 it came finally here.

The good bishop is recumbent on a sarcophagus, on which two angels support a simple, garlanded inscription. Behind the reclining figure, and under a ceiling of brilliantly foreshortened *putti*, are three marble panels covered in relief work, of the dead Christ, the Virgin and St John. The monument is framed most beautifully with an enamelled terracotta frieze of lilies, pomegranates, pine cones and foliage, set on a rich background of gold – a gorgeous contrast with the pale, dignified, and rather conservative marble. In the top right and left corner are the seven *palle* of the family crest.

There are traces of gilding on this monument: the hair and wings of the angels, the bishop's mitre, chasuble, cushion and winding-cloth, and the haloes of the three panel figures were all originally coloured gold. It is strange to think of the red marble that once supported it: but the gilding would have created a closer bond between frame and monument. In itself the carving is magnificent, but, as the whole work appears today, it is very far from Luca's original design. The fresco fragments here by Giovanni del Ponte are grisly: one is of St Bartholomew being flayed (his emblem is a butcher's knife), another of a saint being decapitated. There seems something dangerously akin to relish in their execution.

In the chapel immediately right of the High Altar hangs the famous nodding crucifix from S. Miniato, the neck restored to rigidity after its lapses in the eleventh century. It is painted on canvas stretched on a wooden frame. Below it are some relics of the numinous local saint. The cross was brought here in 1671 under a canopy, accompanied by senators and all the nobles and religious Orders of Florence in a gorgeous, solemn procession. And here it stayed.

But the greatest treasure of S. Trìnita is the neighbouring Cappella Sassetti. Domenico Ghirlandaio's murals of the *Life of St Francis* and *Prophecies of Christ's Birth* are among my favourite sights of the city. The donors, Francesco Sassetti and his wife, lie in the black sarcophagi set in the walls, and flank the luminous *Adoration* Domenico painted in tempera as the altarpiece. What strikes one most forcibly in this tiny chapel is the marriage of Classical-pagan and Christian. The antique world exerted an enormous and indelible influence on Renaissance art and thought: Christianity was seen as a development out of paganism, and the neo-Platonists represented a serious attempt to find a *rapprochement* between the two worlds, to accommodate the world of Classical ideas within the framework of Christian theology. In the vault are four Sibyls: over the entrance arch is the Sibyl announcing the birth of Christ to the Roman Emperor Augustus; in the spandrils of the arches above the niches of the tombs the dim paintings in grisaille are scenes from the lives of the Roman emperors.

But there is such pride and confidence! In the lunette over the altar, where is the Pope depicted giving St Francis the Rule of his Order but in the Piazza della Signoria! And there are portraits in the right foreground of Lorenzo il Magnifico (he is the black-haired man seen in profile, with a powerful, swooping nose); Sassetti (who ran the Medici bank) and his son; and the white-haired poet and town crier, Antonio Pucci. Opposite stand Sassetti's three older sons. Coming up the stairway are Lorenzo's sons Piero, Giovanni and Giuliano, with their tutors Poliziano (leading), Matteo Franco, and Luigi Pulci (in the rear). These are living, breathing individuals: on the *ringhiera* of the Palazzo Vecchio Marzocco stands in resplendent isolation on his plinth, and between the Palazzo and the Loggia there are glimpses of the towers of Oltrarno.

Again, in the *Raising of the Child* (beneath), the scene takes place in the piazza outside the church, and Ghirlandaio gives us an unforgettable impression of the old Ponte S. Trìnita as it was before it collapsed in the flood of 1557; of Palazzo Spini, and the original Romanesque façade of the church, as well as more, fascinating portraits, including in the far right corner a self-portrait. (Domenico also painted himself, in the fine *Death of St Francis*, standing behind the bespectacled bishop, 'who', writes Vasari, 'is shown to be merely a painting only because one does not hear him'.) The 'child', revived miraculously after an apparition of St Francis, is generally believed to have been a boy of the Spini family, and he is shown, in simultaneous narration, falling from a window of the Palazzo in the background. There are certainly other portraits here among the spectators, including the ladies of the boy's family, and (according to Vasari) Maso degli Albizzi, M. Agnolo Acciaiuoli and M. Palla Strozzi (all prominent Florentines and victims, in one way or another, of the Medici). These are the trio standing behind, and to the right of, the child's couch.

These groups are composed of the faces and figures at which Domenico excelled: straight-backed ladies, gorgeously attired; handsome youths with flowing curls springing free from their caps; heavily jowled worthies, and earnest divines. They hum with life and realism. There are more portraits, in the *Renunciation* scene and the *Ordeal by Fire before the Sultan*. These are no massed 'faces in a crowd', they are precise and deliberate representations of real *quattrocento* Florentines, and their presence here is a source of great frustration. Who, for example, is the marvellously handsome youth standing behind the Titian-haired girl in the *Raising of the Child?*

The mixture of Classical and Christian is nowhere more evident than in the *Adoration*, painted by the artist in 1485, and richly framed in gilt (a companion-piece to the tondo in the Uffizi, and the glowing 1488 *Adoration* in the Ospedale degli Innocenti). The splendid, gaily-coloured procession which winds its way round the hillside and through the Roman archway towards the 'stable', with its fluted pilasters and classical inscription, produces such a nice contrast with the homely, poorly shaven faces of the shepherds huddled in the right foreground. The manger is a hay-filled sarcophagus (a poignant reminder) complete with swag and a Latin elegiac couplet of doubtful syntax which puzzled me for some time until I discovered that its intriguing reference is the merest make-believe. Suitably completed (one of the shepherds has an obtrusive knee) it reads: 'Fulvius, Pompey's Augur, falling by the sword at Jerusalem, declares that the urn which hides his body will one day yield up a God.' Nonsense.

Mary has a typical Ghirlandaio face, and is rather grand, with her gold-bordered mantle and fine, sheer headscarf. Poor Joseph, a superannuated whitebeard gazing heavenwards, scratches his forehead in bewilderment (as well he might). In the far distance a silver ribbon slides between hills dotted with turrets and trees; and high above the horses and richly costumed lords and ladies and squires, an angel hovers delivering his good news to the shepherds. From behind the 'manger' a particularly sweet ox and ass observe proceedings. The Babe lies on his back on a corner of his mother's full cloak, sporting a bright two-coloured halo; he sucks his thumb happily, while the Virgin, the shepherds and the beasts look on in wonder and adoration. Nearby a goldfinch, symbol of Christ's Passion, perches on a jumble of books among the daisies.

Here is 'decoration' of a particularly elevated kind, surely. The shepherds are most memorable: I mentally photograph these swarthy peasant faces and gnarled capable hands and meet them every day behind market stall and begging bowl and in the humble shops of Oltrarno.

In the piazza outside a crowd is gathering to watch a sleek black Mercedes broken into. A small, wild-haired gipsy mechanic jiggles with a coathanger in the space between door and window while a film star dressed as a policewoman chats to him from the pavement. Nearby, ticking over impatiently, waits a truck with crane and pulley. One last, brutal heave and there is a loud click. The assembly applauds as the costly German door flies open, and, before their clapping has died, the Mercedes is trundled unceremoniously away.

It is no distance to the magnificent Romanesque façade of little SS. Apostoli – only a few paces, yet somehow the roar of the city cannot touch it. It stands sunken in a tiny square: this is the Piazza del Limbo, the traditional burial-ground for unbaptised children.

I have always loved the sombre basilican interior, its stately columns of greenish Prato marble, the painted timber roof. This is a very ancient place (legend has it that Charlemagne himself was founder, Roland and Olivier witnesses, but this seems to be based on a false sixteenth-century inscription over the portal, and the tenth or eleventh centuries seem nearer the mark); it stands above early Christian and Classical graves, and Roman baths; and below the baths is a Roman crematorium. It is sandwiched between the turreted Palazzo Altoviti, and, fronting the Borgo SS. Apostoli, the Palazzo Rosselli del Turco, still inhabited by the Rosselli family (that of the painters Cosimo and Matteo), but built by Baccio d'Agnolo for the Borgherini. (On the occasion of his son Pier Francesco's marriage to Margherita Acciaiuoli in 1515, Salvi Borgherini had the bedroom furniture decorated by Pontormo, del Sarto, Granacci and Bacchiaca, among the greatest artists of the time, and the work became so celebrated that on one notorious occasion the Republic tried to relieve the family of it and give it to Francis I of France. But the Republic had reckoned without Margherita. Her husband was in exile, but she was rock-like. 'It is my marriage bed in honour of which Salvi my father-in-law had all this magnificent and regal decoration done, and I revere it in his memory and out of love for my husband.' If the Republic wanted to give the King of France a gift, they were welcome: they should do it 'by stripping their own houses of their beds and ornaments'. Some of the biblical scenes (*Stories of Joseph*) done by Pontormo and Bacchiaca, panels for *cassoni*, are in the National Gallery in London. Pontormo's work is exceptionally fine, the compositions and figures wonderfully elegant, the colours radiant.) The chapel of the Palazzo Rosselli del Turco shares one wall with the church, and has a little window through which Mass can be heard.

Today the church is open because a wedding is in progress. The bride is in white satin and every pillar is festooned with lilies and glossy greenery. Along the aisle a soft, plush carpet has been unrolled. There is a small gathering of family and friends and the atmosphere is intimate and hushed. A few locals enter, dip their fingers into the stoup, cross themselves and kneel muttering in the hard pews. All the women wear veils of lace. I tiptoe along the left aisle to peep at Giovanni della Robbia's wonderful tabernacle (the *Altare degli Angeli*) above the tomb of Donato Acciaiuoli (1333), and find a Franciscan priest kneeling with his rosary there, his concentration tangible. Nearby is the sepulchral monument of Oddo Altoviti, a work by Benedetto da Rovezzano (*c.* 1507), who was also responsible for the relief of the *Virgin and Child* in the wall of the Palazzo Rosselli outside. (The tomb is a mixture: on the one hand there is a sarcophagus with inscription in the Classical style, on the other a skull and slithering snakes. The individual parts are fine, the whole somehow less than a masterpiece.) The Altoviti had been patrons of this church since the fourteenth century, and the Palazzo of the Acciaiuoli is just along the Borgo.

In the third chapel of the right aisle is an allegorical *Immaculate Conception* by Vasari (1540–1), which, most interestingly, is the first representation of a piece of Catholic dogma not pronounced official until as late as 1854.

Rings have now been exchanged, and the priest is tying his stole around the hands of bride and groom: I tiptoe on.

In a niche to the right of the High Altar are preserved the flints brought by one of the Pazzi from the Holy Sepulchre after the First Crusade, which are used each year for the *Scoppio del Carro*, a ceremony held at noon on Easter Day in the Piazza del Duomo. With a spark struck from these stones a dove-shaped torch is ignited, and flies down a wire from the High Altar of the Cathedral to a cart filled with fireworks which stands outside. (This cart, drawn by oxen with gilded horns and hooves, with gaily coloured pennants nodding, is known, in true Florentine style, as *Il Brindellone*, the 'ragamuffin'.) If the fireworks are lit (the poor pyrotechnist is lynched if they are not) and the dove returns to the Altar, the harvest will be a good one. There is wild cheering; bells clang and boom in a dozen belfries. If a child's eyes are washed at this precise moment, they will never be weak; if, during the holy cacophony, a baby takes his first steps, his legs will never be bowed.

And so on. The holy flints are sometimes exposed, but I have never seen them. Nor have I seen the *Scoppio del Carro*: seats are booked long in advance and cost a king's ransom. The ceremony originally took place after Mass at midnight on Holy Saturday, but has been rescheduled for the convenience of tourists. Harvests have, apparently, not been affected adversely by the alteration.

One year, long ago, I heard the Easter bells when I stayed in a room over Viale Belfiore. And how they ring! My room was perched directly above the shunting-area of the station: trains whistled, grotesquely amplified announcements punctuated the night hours, and in the Viale below the traffic was abandoned and frenetic, a veritable Armageddon. For a moment around 3.30 a.m. there was an eerie silence. Otherwise a cacophony of horns, tortured and screaming tyres, police sirens, radios, violent altercations, all rose on waves of heat and aggression, a constant, deafening roar. The traffic was like a raging beast in its final agony, wrenching and tearing its bloody way through the narrow confines of the city, heaving and shuddering and snarling.

The room was interesting, with two spongy beds, a large breast-shaped glass light, and furniture of a functional variety from the 1920s. The parquet flooring undulated, detaching itself here and there from what had been a herring-bone pattern; everywhere over the wardrobe and bed-heads and chest of drawers, veneer was peeling. For seating, rather eccentrically, there were two deckchairs, one uncomfortable of tubular metal, one upright and confortable but always collapsing. In the centre of the room a handsome old table stood on shaped legs with less than half its walnut surface intact. On the peeling walls were two unframed advertisements for Udine, and three plastic ballerinas were attached in *retiré* position to a mirror on the dressing table. Tassels hung from every key. The place had character, certainly, not wholly bad.

Easter Day was all flowers and bells. I was woken by a startling epiphany: Signora Buti, my landlady, who delivered a sweet posy of freesias and a plate of croissants, and herself seemed covered in ribbons and cellophane. And as I lay in bed all the bells rang out, deep-throated and silver in the morning air: bam bam, din din, some like thunderous gongs, others like tin plates clattered together, or broken cymbals. There was no scheme or consonance, just a long, uninhibited tintinnabulation, from the great, resonant Duomo and S. Maria Novella, to the little parish churches of Oltrarno. For me it was a moment of high elation, and of nostalgia. English church bells always plunge me into dark introversion: I think of them wafted on an air that kills, their jerky scales, the vulgar 'Westminster Chimes' of the sitting-room clock reminiscent of choir practice, compulsory church, and quiet, painful family Sundays. Foreign bells are less melodious: their message is a categorical

212

imperative: *'Come!'* Their boom and clash and din are insistent and uncompromising. *'COME!'* No time to charm the flock to church.

The wagon was lit and the dove ran its Easter course. Everywhere in the noisy City of Flowers there were flowers and happy noises. I bought Lisa anemones, I recall, violet and magenta anemones, with white, startled eyes, and heard the organ boom in S. Croce, where the priest's chasuble was brilliant white, with gold orphreys of dazzling splendour.

Lunch began with boiled eggs; next came kebabs of toast, sausage, and *uccelletti* (heads discarded); next roast potatoes and pork; spinach followed, then Easter bread-cakes. In an attempt to recover, I spent the rest of the day among the dark cypresses and apricot stucco of old villas, first in the hills above Compiobbi, eastwards along the Arno, and then at a friend's delightful house north of Fiesole, in a garden of wistaria, bougainvillaeas and burning forsythia. And as night fell I sat and looked over the jagged treescape towards the belltower of the Cathedral of Fiesole, and the blue blur of Florence beyond, under telephone wires speckled with a thousand returning swifts.

I take the narrow alleyway to the Lungarno and head west for Ognissanti, another quiet place, only minutes south of S. Maria Novella, but for some reason beyond the reach of trippery.

The church, now Baroque in appearance, was founded as early as the thirteenth century by the Umiliati, a Benedictine Order skilled in woolworking, and this area of town became one of the headquarters of the industry. The Arno was close by, for washing, cleaning and dyeing, and the monks soon strengthened the existing bridge for the transport of raw materials across the river to the S. Frediano quarter, where the wool workers lived.

Woolmaking, a costly, lengthy and finicky operation, was the basis of Florence's wealth. It is estimated that at its height no less than a quarter of the total population was engaged in the manufacture of wool and cloth. Florentine cloth was reckoned the best in the world and it was sold everywhere. Consequently, the two clothing guilds, the *Arte della Lana* and the *Calimala* became enormously wealthy and left their fingerprints as patrons all over the city. Many of the little streets are named after the various specialists involved in the woolmaking process: *Tintori* (Dyers), *Cimatori* (Shearers), *Tessitori* (Weavers), *Cardatori* (Carders), etc.

Ognissanti was the church of the famous Vespucci family, who lived nearby, were in the silk trade, and had shared interests with the wool workers of Ognissanti. (The family tomb is in the pavement, marked by a circular plaque.) In the second chapel right is a *Madonna della Misericordia* by Domenico Ghirlandaio, an early work dated around 1473. The Madonna is shown spreading her protecting arms over the Vespucci, and the young face pictured between

213

the kneeling old man in the red cloak and the Virgin is supposed to be a portrait of Amerigo, the discoverer of America. It was the Vespucci who in *c.* 1480 commissioned Sandro Filipepi, known as Botticelli, to paint the famous fresco of *St Augustine* (the Filipepi were friends of the Vespucci in the tanning business: *manus manum lavat*) which now hangs opposite the *St Jerome* of Ghirlandaio above the confessionals half-way down the nave.

The *St Augustine* is well worth close consideration. The scholar-saint, experiencing, we are told, his vision of St Jerome, sits in a study equipped with an astrolabe and other scientific instruments. He is surrounded by books, and behind his head is an intriguing manuscript. In what language is it written? It is gobbledegook – except for a few legible lines of Italian. These read: *'Dov'è Fra Martino? È scappato. E dove è andato? È fuori della Porta a Prato.'* No doubt the painter, while working in the church where he is buried (his modest tomb is in the pavement of the baroque chapel of the right transept), noticed one of the brothers quietly slipping his leash in the evenings, because he has written: 'Where is Fr Martin? On the loose. And where's he gone? Beyond the Porta a Prato (i.e. outside the city)!' Amid such piety the humour here is a blessing. One wonders if Fr Martin suspected that he was to be immortalised in this fashion: sainthood was evidently not to be his portion, but he was granted his own sort of fame, and one is eternally grateful to Botticelli for the interpolation.

A chapel in the north transept contains a great and priceless treasure: the habit worn by St Francis when he received the stigmata at La Verna (the *Umiliati* were replaced in the sixteenth century by Franciscans from S. Salvatore al Monte). And the sacristy is most beautifully decorated, with a giant Giottesque crucifix and splendid detached frescoes by Gaddi father and son (a *Resurrection* by Agnolo, and a superlative *Crucifixion* by his father Taddeo), both set in intricate mosaic surrounds.

But I came to see the Cenacolo. To the left of the church I step into the convent and rouse the portly old friar from his reverie. With resignation he plods off to unlock the refectory on the far side of the pretty cloister and leaves me alone in the coolness. Half a dozen rock-hard, backless chairs are set before the huge *Last Supper* of Ghirlandaio (1480), and thankfully I claim one.

The scene is familiar from S. Marco, and at first the two paintings seem like carbon copies. There is the same illusionistic setting, the same vaulted loggia, with glimpses of a gorgeous garden, fruit trees and swooping birds, the same peacock perching on the window sill, the same long table at which Jesus and the Disciples sit. But this painting is infinitely superior. As the S. Marco version is more elaborate in design, so it is inferior in movement: all the disciples there sit bolt upright; here, while the background is one of paradisiacal calm, the foreground is all excited animation; the details, too, of glasses and fruit on the table, are cut to a suggestive minimum to point the drama of the moment: there is no Latin inscription to distract the attention, no gratuitous, gilded friezes or obtrusive cats. The disciples, huddled together, are captured at the dramatic moment of the traitor's unmasking, each reacting individually to the terrible accusation that hangs in the air: 'Master, is it I?' Judas, isolated (as before in the Gaddi and Castagno frescoes) on this side of the table, is already the object of suspicious looks.

To my mind this is a clear refinement of the nervous, over-vigorous style of Castagno. I spent a whole morning here once with a French lady, an *Académicienne* of impossible chic, all in white, with an outrageously wide-brimmed hat. (Merely to look at her was civilising.) Her conversation was assured, informed, intelligent. In the course of our discussion she dismissed Berenson as contemptuously as he once dismissed Ghirlandaio. It was the nearest I ever came to an *entente*.

Torn between a *Seitensprung* in Fiesole and collapsing at home with Dante, I bump into Lisa in the Flea-market. Some of the stands (*gli stands*) are already shut for the *magnum silentium*, but I am only window shopping. There is the battered head of Jesus we haggled over last year, still unsold. That will teach them. (*'Per carità!'* Lisa exploded, putting it back on the table with a dangerous thump. 'Why is it so expensive?' And I heard the old lady say, very reasonably: 'Because it is old.')

And there is the stallkeeper who sold me the *Madonna* Lisa had forbidden me to buy. 'Old, but not antique,' he told me truthfully. *'Gesso!'* Lisa sneered, tapping the statuette with her fingernails. 'Not even old! And look at the *colours*!' I crept back the next day and bought it and have lived happily ever after: to me it is a thing of beauty. But the armless, wooden seventeenth-century St Antony has gone, with its doll-like head and chipped nose. I could have housed him happily, but he was far too dear. Where are the cloisonné enamel ducks? I was prepared this year to afford them, but they too are gone. Bedsteads, brass knockers, daguerrotypes of the Ponte Vecchio, sepia prints of plump Parisian nudes, lampshades, *art nouveau*, cynically forged *etruscheria*, garden statues, battered *cassoni*, gramophones with trumpets, dolls, pyxes, stoups, stamps, crucifixes, lavatory seats, birdbaths, seatless chairs, rings, bangles, umbrellas – the Piazza dei Ciompi has them all: the Mercato delle Pulci, the 'Flea-market', they call it, but there are no fleas on the tradesmen here. The days of real bargains seem to be gone. Vasari's graceful loggia marks the spot, and beneath its shade a youth maybe oils his motorbike, a couple of tired students fall against each other and sleep, and the same bookseller, in the same grimy vest, peddles his wares: picture novels, comics, and pornographic strip cartoons.

'The Madonna!' Lisa announces gleefully. 'She's gone. You remember that ugly Madonna? Someone must have bought her after all!'

'She wasn't bad.'

'You don't remember. She was terrible.'

'I don't know.'

'Those colours!'

'I rather liked them.'

'She was ugly! A peasant Madonna!' Her eyes sparkle with malice. 'A *Madonna Umbra*!'

I let the matter rest, thinking what a mercy it is that, in the normal course of events, Lisa is unlikely to see the Umbrian Madonna, unashamed and beloved, on the chest of drawers in my bedroom.

Lisa has lost an earring and is looking for a singleton to match it. Quickly she picks her way through the stands, giving a running commentary (partly technical, partly *ad hominem*) as she goes. Shopping with Lisa is an essential initiation into the Florentine experience.

On impulse we buy *panini* and *prosciutto* and take the Fiat for an airing. This time I insist on petrol before we leave the city.

'We have plenty!' Lisa insists, without consulting the gauge. Then, her hunch confirmed by a wavering indicator, she adds: 'We have 25 kilometres at least!' This figure can go up by five each time she is challenged.

'Just to be safe,' I say.

Lisa gives a shrug so broad that for a moment her head seems to sink below her shoulders. I must be mad. Have I no courage? The English – who can understand them? I hear her thinking all sorts of hard thoughts.

Out of the city the air thins dramatically, and a glorious thing it is to fly along the Viale Galileo up among the gods, Florence glimpsed in lovely low vistas to the right, and let the wind claw at one's hair. We go a long way round (for petrol: it is my fault), but we go very quickly, and the views across the golf-course at Ugolino are worth any detour. Lisa flirts with the motorway, and for a short space we appear to be on it, travelling in the wrong direction, but then she greets a signpost triumphantly and stays my hand as it hovers over the tattered map book.

'*Eccoci!*'

We lose our way once more, but magically, and without conscious navigational correction, end where we wanted to go. Lisa has only *heard* of S. Caterina all'Antella, but says she knows Bagno a Ripoli (which is quite near). We draw up in the middle of nowhere.

'Ring at the kennels,' says the guide book.

And then we hear dogs, baying and yelping and woofing, and cats screaming like peacocks. Lisa draws up finally outside a greyish building with widely overhanging roof: the oratory, surely. Apart from the mad bedlam of kennel noises, the coutryside here is idyllic. Without them it would be still as death.

A boy of about six, colossally overweight, brandishing a plastic sword, suddenly lunges at my groin from an open doorway, and a little mongrel rushes out to pee over the oratory door. The whole place stinks of dog. An older youth, wearing a teeshirt saying that he works for the Vet Pizzirani, explains in awed, reverential tones that the Doctor is out on call. I walk up the little lane, happily listing the flora and watching bees at work. After ten minutes I hear a car.

'A Fiat 1500 has just come into the forecourt,' Lisa informs the youth, whom she finds watering flowers in the garden. 'Will that be the Doctor?'

'The Doctor?' he echoes, half-shocked, half-amused as he turns the hose on. 'No, no. Dr Pizzirani drives a Mercedes.'

On his arrival, the genial, distrait Vet speaks of the keys as though they were part of an old legend he heard at school, but to which he has never personally subscribed. 'Keys? Keys to the oratory?' If they ever existed, then he doesn't recall where they are. *'Chi lo sa?'*

The dogs howl, the cats howl, and the little oratory forlornly echoes. In the Vet's garden there are some lovely trees with clusters of nuts which will dehisce. I ask him about them. 'They are Paulownia,' he tells me, as if he knows; 'they grow with amazing speed.'

But where is the key?

'Sotto qua!' squeaks the adipose child with the sword suddenly. 'Under here!' Lifting a wooden ramp he holds aloft a massive key. It must be all of six inches long. The Vet nods happily, yes, yes, and vanishes into his garden.

The large door swings ajar with hardly a creak. I have just walked into the *trecento* and stand stock still, my mouth stupidly open. The building is cross-vaulted, with just two bays, and there are frescoes on every inch of wall and ceiling. Even Lisa tiptoes in the stillness. There is only birdsong punctuated by baying and caterwauling, and long thin shafts of sunlight slanting in through high broken windows. All the windows are broken: they let in sun and rain like an old barn. The fine lancet window of the sanctuary is smashed; bars have been fitted to deny access. There are lovely candlesticks, pale green and gold, begging to be taken home and cared for; a *prie-Dieu* leans tiredly against an old altar whose stone of consecration is still intact. Behind it, on the floor, I find part of a ruined reredos, more broken candlesticks. The aumbry doors are in place, and inside is a bell-pull. There is an ancient, cranky confessional: and over eight small pews a thick rime of dust and crumbled *intonaco* which has rained down from the ceiling. I gather a handful of small coloured fragments, but when I get them home they have mostly turned to powder.

When did the last visitors call here? When was the key lifted last from under the ramp? In the dust of the pews I see the imprint of rubber soles and the gloomy fingerprints of damp and decay. When will I come to understand these people? A scene where S. Catherine is on the wheel, on the right side of the sanctuary, is no more than six feet from hail, rain and sleet. What happens when there is a storm?

This oratory was the gift of Alberti (*c.* 1387) on whose large estate it stood, and the artist they commissioned to paint the story of St Catherine was Spinello Aretino, that same painter who did the *St Benedict Cycle* for the sacristy of S. Miniato. He comes somewhere between Giotto and Masaccio. 'His saints, and particularly his Virgins,' Vasari writes enthusiastically, 'breathe an indefinable sanctity and divinity which inspire me with the utmost devotion.' Spinello's palette is distinctive, his use of shading subtle and soft, but it is the *spiritual* quality of his work which is so impressive. He died at an advanced age and is buried, according to Vasari (another Aretine) in the church of S. Agostino at Arezzo: on his tomb is carved a coat of arms he designed himself: it contains, in a nice allusion to his name, a hedgehog.

Here there are nine scenes telling the saint's story: St Catherine is blonde, with lovely, mysterious Giottesque eyes and long, flowing tresses, a disturbingly attractive creation. When she is stripped to the waist for flogging, perhaps convention or a natural reticence inhibited Spinello from painting in her breasts. All we can make out in the blur is an umbilicus: the torso could indeed be male.

This Catherine is, of course, the legendary (possibly fictional) St Catherine of Alexandria, not that remarkable local Catherine of history, the illiterate mystic of Siena. For the simple poor, to come through the doors of this rich little oratory must have been like passing into Heaven. As well as the sad stench of decay the place has a great, moving beauty.

In the autumn of 1907, Edward Hutton found the oratory 'utterly neglected and forsaken', and used as a storehouse for *fiaschi*, but with a splendidly preserved triptych by Agnolo Gaddi still standing on the altar, and the frescoes remarkably intact despite the inroads of creeping damp. Behind the High Altar the outlines of 'a great Madonna' were then quite plain. Dogs and turkeys and chickens congregated inside what had become no more than a curiously pretty barn.

Things have greatly improved, but repairs are still needed and the situation will have to be reviewed regularly if the damp is to be held in check. The restoration has evidently been carried out with loving care, meticulously, yet there is not a pane of glass between Spinello and the Tuscan elements. My tiny fragments are a daily reminder of the risk: and I have seen storms here in summer of terrifying violence – hailstones the size of mothballs bouncing high off rooftiles, smashing window panes; sudden downpours of such fierce intensity that in ten minutes the streets are rivers. And what will the ice and snow do, when winter bites?

The Certosa del Galluzzo (or di Val d'Ema) stands high on a hill just south of Florence off the Via Romana, and I feel from the conformation of the terrain that we are nearing it.

We are making for the alluvial plain west of the city, following the Ema as it bends west to join the Greve – an area unfamiliar to me, and I am torn between basking in agreeable memories and the excitement of new discoveries. But the decision is taken from my hands. As I ask, 'Are we near the Certosa?' I see it, unmistakably, brooding, on the eminence of Montacuto. It covers the summit like some great redoubt, more a castle than a holy place.

Memories as we flash along the autostrada are vivid. My first visit was in 1966: the year *'quand' io senti' di prima l'aere tosco'*. Some years later, I remember the monk who acted as guide taking a great liking to my young daughter, who has long golden hair. He had a dreadful cold, but kept stopping, fired by an overflow of fraternal love, to envelop my bewildered child in his grubby habit and plant kisses on her lips and cheeks and forehead. He was a merry soul, and left an indelible (and inaccurate) impression on my mind of the unique character of the Cistercian Rule. In the Great Gothic Hall I played a two-manual harpsichord which clanged and tinkled with amazing resonance. This Hall, I discovered, was the Palazzo degli Studi. The Certosa's founder, the rich Florentine banker Niccolò Acciaiuoli, who lies with others of his family in the crypt chapel of S. Andrea beneath the Lay Brothers' Choir, had intended the hall as a Centre for Liberal Studies, and I cannot imagine a more magnificent setting. Here, among other important paintings, is the extraordinary Pontormo *Passion Cycle*, painted between 1522 and 1525, when the artist took refuge in the monastery during a time of plague: five large lunette frescoes, removed here from the Great Cloister, which are surely among the greatest masterpieces of Mannerism. They are so unusual that I return to them year after year.

Jacopo Carrucci, called Pontormo (1494–1556), a pupil of del Sarto, was a deeply religious painter whose mature work is revolutionary and disturbing. His work for the Medici at Poggio a Caiano had been full of warm light and gaiety: here we have delicate, ghostly colours, and compositions of a type never seen before. The paintings are in a sad state, but even so their

219

deep feeling and the extreme expressiveness of the faces and postures are remarkable.

The *Resurrection*, showing Christ triumphant over the battered armies of the SPQR, has such a strange modernity to it that I am always put in a mind of Stanley Spencer. The movement in the *Meeting with Veronica*; strong tensions produced by the *repoussoir* figures in the *Prayer in the Garden* and the *Deposition*; and the contrasting gestures of *Christ before Pilate* make these pictures an unsettling aesthetic experience. There is no respite or peace. The cycle is *sui generis*.

In other respects, too, Pontormo was different: obsessed, we are told, with his bowels, he lived an eccentric, solitary life, totally dedicated to his art, a neurotic hypochondriac. Vasari expresses his total bewilderment at the man and the style he adopted for these frescoes, and other paintings. But their impact is immediate and their feeling visionary. They stand on their own, and they are strong meat. No wonder Vasari was non-plussed.

Last year I found I had half an hour to waste before the next guided tour. The day was scalding, but a light breeze was blowing over the hilltop, and in the *farmacia* I found some excellent postcards. Then, with three Italians I followed a little monk around the place. He had a soiled, patched habit and talked without drawing breath as we were joined, first by two French homosexuals in shorts, then by two young girls dressed for tennis, and finally by two more, one wearing a long teeshirt with FANTASY daubed in vermilion over the region of her pudenda. We were now nine, and the monk gabbled on in an imperturbable monotone as the French kept lingering and exclaiming, *'Oh regarde! Oh comme c'est beau! Regarde!'* and holding the motley procession up.

The Large Cloister is big enough for a small cricket pitch, and in the pendentives of the arcade are wonderful majolica *tondi* of saints and biblical figures, leaning, in high relief, right out of their frames. There are sixty-six of these, done by Giovanni della Robbia and his assistants, and the use of colour is restrained and telling. Adam and Eve are particularly fine: Adam has a splendid forked beard, with the serpent coiling about him; Eve's head looks in the opposite direction, tempted, all woman, with lovely trailing curls. Over St Bernard's shoulder a horned green and yellow fiend scowls; over S. Apollonia's is a pincered molar. I became fascinated by some of these portraits, though there was no time to linger. St George is pictured in blue and yellow breast-plate and helmet, the vanquished dragon slithering horribly behind. Next to him, St Lucy is a vision of purity in white. The traditional plate displaying her eyes is at her right shoulder. This is so represented that, most unfortunately, it looks like nothing so much as a large, smirking yellow toad.

The Certosa, of course, was a Carthusian foundation. As recently as 1958

Cistercians took their place. At the suppression of 1810 the monastery was robbed of more than 500 works of art and today, though it still has its glories, it is the merest ghost of what it was. But the monks are relatively comfortable: each one has three rooms, a little loggia, his garden plot, and a divine view for consolation.

The Acciaiuoli tombs are wonderful, the noble, recumbent figure of the cardinal looking as if he might any moment breathe again and speak in prayer. And the intarsia of the sixteenth-century choir stalls is of amazing intricacy. I remember, too, our little Cistercian, at the tour's end, asking with cupped hands for money and striking the ingratiating pose of the mendicant, his eyes averted – then denying me a second look at the Pontormo frescoes, which were only a matter of feet away. And the Frenchmen oohing and cooing in the *farmacia*, where the monk dispensed vivid yellow and green Mannerist liqueurs, honey, lavender and pink rosaries, and totted up bills with the last word in bleeping electronic tills.

Before the car came here, before pylons strode down the olive-spotted hillsides, it must have been paradise. The busy *strada* streams east-to-west in the middle distance, and between it and the Certosa Hotel lies a series of low, flat factories, not quite hidden by trees. On one side of the hill my eye was taken by a camp-site with tents of yellow and blue and orange and green below the slim campanile of a church. It occurred to me, as I floated down to earth, that the last time I felt the prickle of mystery was in S. Caterina all'Antella, and before that in the crypt of S. Miniato.

Even in 1907 Edward Hutton found the Certosa a 'spoiled, artificial place'. (He passes over the *Passion Cycle* without mention and names as perhaps the finest picture Albertinelli's *Crucifixion* at the altar of the Capitolo.) The place, he wrote, was 'little better than a noisy museum... Florence today can find neither pleasure nor delight in these houses of learning and silence. The Badia of Florence has no monks, the Badia at Fiesole is a school [since 1972, it has been the home of the European University Institute], the Certosa di Val d'Ema a national monument.' In 1912 E. V. Lucas complained of paying half a lira to enter the cloisters of S. Maria Novella, and castigated museum custodians as 'jaded figures of apathy' who 'clear their throats as no gentleman should'. These days the tourist has to be made of sterner stuff. Nothing, I suppose, is what it once was, nothing exactly as we like to remember it. No lovely ladies in Via delle Belle Donne, no lovers in the Via dell'Amorino, and precious little straw in the Straw Market.

We are already in the western plain, the alluvial suburbs. And we are lost again. Outside a huge Gucci factory we ask an old lady where the Badia a Settimo is. She shakes her head. Yes, she has heard the name, but...

Eventually we see a lovely old church with a *piazzetta* and fine portico, and find a cloister with lofty palms, a persimmon, and a stately well. This is S. Giuliano, an early eighth-century building with later modifications. It is locked. Friendly neighbours emerge and wonder loudly where the Father can be, and point us towards the Abbey. I am drawn to this ancient *pieve* and must return: the land around seems fertile and lovingly tended, and the people are kindly souls.

The Badia di S. Salvatore a Settimo probably got its name from being the seventh monastery built by Ugo, Margrave of Tuscany, who was warned in a vision while hunting that he must repent his sinful life or face damnation. As a result, Ugo sold all his estates in Germany and built seven monasteries: the first was the Badia of Florence, the seventh the Badia here.

To begin with, Cluniac Benedictines possessed it, and S. Giovanni Gualberto himself, the Vallombrosan, and now Abbot of S. Salvi, was called in 1068 to reform the Order. He ruled until his death five years later, fighting to the last the corruptions and malpractices of the Church; and here, on 12 February 1068, a celebrated Ordeal by Fire was undergone in front of the Badia, to which thousands of the city folk flocked.

The Bishop of Florence was one Pietro Mazzabarba, who had gained the See through the intervention of the Emperor, and the Florentines urged the old abbot to allow God to show who had right on his side. S. Giovanni chose Don Pietro Aldobrandino to undergo the ordeal, and two towering fires were built here in this very piazza – with the narrowest of paths between them. Don Pietro made his communion; then, wearing alb, stole and maniple, and holding a cross in his hands, he said his prayers, gave his Brothers the kiss of Peace, and plunged into the inferno.

Not only did he pass through the fires unscathed (and so was canonised as S. Pietro Igneo), but, finding he had dropped his maniple, insisted on going back to retrieve it. This, on the face of it, reckless tempting of Providence was no doubt merely an egregious example of what theologians term a 'work of supererogation'. It worked. The citizens were entertained to a miracle; Bishop Mazzabarba got his come-uppance; and the intrepid monk ensured his own immortality.

In the thirteenth century, the Badia was given by Pope Gregory IX to Cistercians and they lived here continuously until 1782. The grand buildings are ruinous: stout fortifications were added in the fourteenth century after Hawkwood's depredations; four giant towers soared high above the surrounding plain, but Cosimo's *Lanzichenecchi* (those marauding *tedeschi* of the sixteenth century who carved their names on the stone of Brunelleschi's cupola) loutishly ruined whatever they could not steal or destroy. Wars, and successive inundations of the Arno have made of the place a sad graveyard.

Bones lie on bones, walls on walls, an architectural necropolis, layer on layer: over the centuries of depredation and flood and collapse, the original space and proportions of the place have been forgotten. In 1844 a flood wrought especial havoc: 1966 was even worse. Restorations have been extensive, but here restoration is a way of life. No monks live in the abbey now, and the church itself is vast for the few parishioners who still use it. A skyscraping crane looms above everything else, high above the gateway, even above the tottering campanile, a sort of symbol of man's ancient struggle with time and dilapidation. It is acid yellow and modern and looks horridly permanent.

At long last we rouse someone. He is charming and well informed and seems glad of company. I take him to be a rather superior custodian until I hear Lisa call him 'Padre'. He wears no dog-collar, but has that sharp eye and worldliness one comes to expect in Italian clergymen. Lisa keeps up a stream of chatter, now querulous, now fittingly condolent, now frivolous and ending in raised voices, raised eyebrows and laughter.

He talks of floods and footings and mud and miracles. Outside, with sudden fury, a storm breaks; after half a minute's lull rain thunders on the roof like war drums. The Father shrugs philosophically: 'Look.' He points to a lovely, open timber roof painted with zodiacal signs; it has a decorated walkway with a railing, charmingly off-centre. It also has holes through which the furious rain drops in visible, audible streams.

Successive floods have meant that the arches have had continually to be heightened and the floor raised: the whole church was originally three metres lower. In the Cappella delle Reliquie (left of the High Altar) a mark records the recent flood level at 1½ metres. There are superb frescoes by Giovanni da San Giovanni depicting various martyrdoms, including (on the right wall) that of S. Quintino, who was impaled on spits. Many precious relics of all the apostles are preserved here but especially of S. Quintino, whose bones were one day wafted across the Arno and discovered by the monks of the abbey, who set them in a magnificently worked silver and gold case, a reliquary as priceless as it is lovely. But there is so much beauty in this sad, empty place! Around the choir runs an exquisite della Robbian frieze of *putti* alternating with the *Agnus Dei* (a lamb holding the Resurrection Banner), a gift, appropriately, of the *Arte della Lana*. Perhaps finest of all is the aumbry in the Chapel of Relics, which is variously attributed: guide books name Desiderio da Settignano or Giovanni da Sangallo: the priest assures me confidently that Guiliano da Maiano was the artist. The four attendant angels over the door, too, are so beautiful they quicken the pulse.

The windows are alabaster; the High Altar is in *pietre dure*; and all the altars are covered with most precious frontals. Here and there, I see, the *bottega* of Ghirlandaio has made its contribution, though the best of the paintings have now gone to galleries. But the overriding ambience is of glory past and the dampness of decay. The monks of the Badia, when they were not praying hard, must have learned to be engineers in the hardest school of all.

Even sadder are the monastery buildings we are left to wander, grand cloisters (off which a succession of warped doors open stickily), a *capitolo*, and a rambling, overgrown garden. But someone lives on this large floating estate: I find a bright new car tucked into another cloister, a caravan in yet another.

The great Sala dei Conversi, immemorially old with its oil presses, buried pillars and antique capitals, has a yacht mast where the High Altar should be; near it are brightly coloured deck chairs, packing cases, a pair of skis. Rain drops through holes in its roof, the arches crumble, and there are walls where no walls should be. The Arno continues to seep into the fabric; the monks have left, and the modern *Lanzichenecchi* are doing their worst. In January of 1987 four bronze angels were stolen from the High Altar of the church while the priest said Mass. In the little forecourt, *malvoni* (mallows) bloom mauve and white. The *campanile* cries out for repair; the crane broods like a giant, its ugly yellow an affront to the weathered stone. The Badia survives, a mixture of wealth and decay, motorbikes and old capitals, skis and stoups. Who knows but what, in a hundred years, St Quentin's bones, in their glittering precious ossuary, will be waterborne a second time?

'I liked the priest,' I remark, as we find the car again.

'He is a cousin of mine,' Lisa tells me. 'A sort of cousin.' She holds the keys out to me, lays the passenger-seat horizontal, and falls instantly asleep.

Now comes my chance to negotiate the western approach to Oltrarno all alone. With the sun behind me I head east, trying to keep the river in sight on my left. Then, with scarcely a moment's hesitation on the way, I recognise Monte Oliveto, and find myself in the S. Frediano area. In a few seconds I am shooting up the narrow one-way street (the wrong way) and reversing down the alley, all exactly as Lisa has taught me, and I actually find parking-space in Costa S. Giorgio! I turn proudly to my passenger, who sits staring at her watch.

'*Lapo!* I have to pick Lapo up! Why did you take so long?'

Tomorrow is *Lucia*-day, and one mad scene is enough. But I know just the place for a foretaste. If I miss the Maggio Musicale every year, and if I never get to the festivals in Siena or Lucca or Castagno d'Andrea, there is one place to go in the home of Lully and Cherubini, Christofori (inventor of the piano) and Peri (composer of the first opera), where musical entertainment is assured.

I go to '*Il Fagiano*', an atmospheric rendezvous in Via dei Neri, where patrons are treated to live music while they watch their lobster and prawns grilled over a long, thin charcoal fire.

224

Everything is done with panache and flair. On a hot night it is as well to book a table some distance from the flames – but near enough to watch the antics of the chef, a handsome old greybeard who prepares your crustacean with that timeless mixture of skill, apparent boredom and immaculate, split-second timing that marks the real professional.

I recall sitting in terror, one warm evening at Eastertide, as the first 'perform-ance' began. But the songs were harmless enough, and some of the ballads even catchy. Relieved, I saw the first singers off (the *crespolini*, I remember, were exceptional), and soon I was beginning to feel that sense of *ben essere*, that *douceur de vivre*, that is so much part of this beloved country.

At this stage in the evening the proprietor, hovering behind his wall of flame like a stage Mephistopheles, may himself begin to sing and, despite his broken, old man's voice, you can tell he has sung well in his time, that his light baritone has been trained. Here is no amateur humming among the pots and pipkins, but a singer. 'Yes, yes,' he explains modestly when you press him. 'Time was ... But now ...' The all-expressive shrug. Then you notice the milky eye, the pallor of the baker and furnace worker, and you order your fish and receive the *'Benissimo!'* that signifies approval, benedic-tion, a conspirational connoisseurship. You have chosen well!

The next singer enters late. It is now past 10.00, the restaurant is packed, and this one *cannot* be a pop star. He is bull-necked, short, like a retired fighter; his chest is the trunk of an old oak, his hands wristless bunches of bananas. He is dressed in a dinner jacket, and what hair he has left is licked back. No longer in the flush of youth, but not exactly old, he blinks and nods acknowledgement of the locals' applause. Who is this man? His pianist dumps some promising looking scores at the piano-side.

Is this the ubiquitous, strangled Italian tenor? (*Rosenkavalier ... Capriccio ...* such awful pictures conjure themselves! Will it be *'Santa Lucia', 'Funiculì Funiculà'* perhaps?) No question now of bolting the squid, or swallowing the swordfish : you are stuck. No use calling for the bill, either : the proprietor, nonchalantly shelling a crayfish, is already smiling a warm greeting.

And he sings like an angel. He sings Verdi and Puccini and Mascagni and Donizetti, and in the *Rigoletto* aria (encored twice) he actually, for a moment, *becomes* a lecherous Duke. The breath control, those heart-stopping decrescen-does – all so much more than you ever dared dream of! He positively slaughters the cadenzas; he caresses the grace-notes; his trills and sudden, wicked *rubati* make you gasp. He is a little *maestro!*

'Ah yes!' the owner nods sadly, 'he was the best in Florence, he sang everywhere ... But his voice – ' he gestures, 'is not *big*. Here it is beautiful, yes, but in *La Scala*, you understand ...' he spreads his hands and drops his voice : 'too *small*.' He shakes his head sadly. 'Too small.'

It is past one o'clock before the tenor is allowed to leave. But now the happy diners are calling the proprietor's name, and after several perfunctory waves of refusal, he takes the floor, a reluctant old war horse dragged into battle one last time, all eloquent gesture and sad apology. But, even if the voice is gone, he knows how to put an aria across; there is dignity in his performance, too, a real feeling for words; and his acting more than compensates. He bows magnificently, his lined face acknowledging that he is only the shadow of what he was; he shrugs as if to say, 'There. You see? You made me sing. I could sing once. *How* I could sing!' And, as you say a last goodnight, you see in his milky eyes and sad, handsome smile the memories of many a late night, and every kind of triumph.

CHAPTER

X

Oltrarno: Museo Bardini · *Fondazione Horne* · *S. Felicita:*
Pontormo · *Casa Guidi* · *San Felice* · *La Specola* · *Hare*
Krishna · *Palazzo Guadagni* · *S. Spirito* · Lucia di Lammermoor *at*
Poggio a Caiano

Last night, on lobster and an ocean of innocuous-tasting white wine, I literally danced my way home. Yet this morning's light is friendly, and I wake from a death-like sleep with a mood of nostalgia on me.

My happiest days were those in Oltrarno, south of the river, high up among the rooftiles in Via della Chiesa, behind the Carmine. My balcony overlooked the Giardino Torrigiani, and beyond the sea of TV aerials and giant magnolias, the eye swam to the turreted Villa dell' Ombrellino on Bellosguardo, among cypresses and bushy pines, and to Galileo's Observatory in Arcetri. Perhaps it was the little belfry of San Felice I could see between the gables; tiles of every shade of brown and red, and plaster of ochre and off-white and lichen-orange; washing on lines running from every projection to the next in a bewildering zig-zag, squares of pink and mauve and white floating in motionless air; drainpipes bifurcating, snaking, suddenly swerving; gas-vents popping up everywhere like a strange harvest of hatted worms; chimneypots, cowls, rooftop gardens; windows rectangular, oval, ogival, arched, green-shuttered; terraces, pergolas, window boxes, bird cages, and radio and television aerials jutting from every square foot, none quite perpendicular, and some on masts higher than telegraph poles. From my desk I looked out over plane trees onto the Carmine, its octagonal cupola prominent against distant hills; heaving ilexes and acres of

227

baking stucco and tile stretched away to the Duomo and S. Lorenzo; and this side of the river, Baccio d'Agnolo's slender bell-tower dominated the skyline.

Here was a place dear to me in all its moods. I lived, quite literally, under the eaves, *'molles ubi reddunt ova columbae'*, and in such perfect ease and peace that the temptation was to stay home and dream. A good library was at my disposal, and most of Brahms: it was difficult to make myself descend the five flights of stairs and walk on earth again. Some days it proved too much, and I sat on the balcony and simply watched the world change its colours: the sharp gold of sunrise, the yellow, frantic blur of midday, when all the villas close their eyes, and the pure gold of evening, when the variegated trees of the Torrigiani Gardens take on a deeper richer green, and all the shuttered eyes of the villas re-open. Some evenings the sky at the horizon had a patina of silver leaf; and when the sun went down it left hills of blinding gold and a long pale strip of sky a miraculous turquoise, and over the horizon a knobbly cloud-world of enchanted trees and mountains. Then the pigeons would give way to bats – bats with long wings and incredible agility etching themselves against a sunset that turned suddenly, in streaks, to fiery crimson. Then constantly Newman's words came back to me: 'I say of the Angels – every breath of air and ray of light, every beautiful prospect is, as it were, the skirts of their garments, the waving robes of those whose faces see God.'

Oltrarno calls, and all roads lead there. Today the younger tourists are abroad in force, all going somewhere, full of happy purpose and confident stride. I shall avoid them, and, while my steps are fresh and eager and my eyes wide open, head for the Museo Bardini.

The nineteenth-century building at the south end of Piazza dei Mozzi which houses the famous collection can look intimidating from the outside, but the interior is cool, and the rooms are as full of lovely things as they are empty of people. It is above all a *civilised* environment.

In the 1870s Stefano Bardini was one of the world's leading art dealers, and, like most dealers, he amassed a valuable collection by methods which did not always excite universal approbation. Through him Berlin gained many priceless and important Renaissance sculptures; and it was he who personally detached the Botticelli frescoes from the Tornabuoni Villa near Careggi and sold them to the Louvre. But he made partial amends for his piracy when in 1923 he bequeathed his *palazzo* and its contents to the Comune. And a bewildering mass of treasures it is: sculptures, paintings, furniture, ceramics, tapestries, arms, sarcophagi, fireplaces, coats of arms, staircases, and doorways. The frames of the windows of the first floor are bits of demolished altars from the church of S. Lorenzo in Pistoia. Bardini was an Autolycus, with a good eye and a hard nose.

Today a wretched 'Still Life' exhibition tries to assert itself, but the competition is too severe. In any case, I always rush the ground floor to spend longer upstairs. But the marble *Carità* (an archaic woman with two babes at her breast) by Tino di Camaino (*c.* 1285–1338) demands to be seen; and Sansovino's bust of *John the Baptist*, too, is fine. There is good classical sculpture here; a divine della Robbian altarpiece, and a lovely *angelo reggicandelabro* in yellow, blue, mauve, green and white from the same *bottega*. Giovanni della Robbia's matching angels, 4 feet 6 inches high (white, on green stands) are really exquisite, the eyebrows and eyes touched in with a most delicious blue. There is a splendid holy water stoup supported by *putti*; a sixteenth-century ivory crucifix; a fifteenth-century Sienese gilded bas-relief of the *Madonna and Child* of exceptional delicacy and grace; and a Donatellesque bas-relief, again of the *Madonna and Child*, which was scooped up by Bardini when the city centre was demolished – all these are rare and lovely things.

But the real glory is on the first floor. The problem is whether to rush straight there, or to intensify the pleasure by delaying.

She stands in Room 18, and to my mind she is not only the star attraction of the museum, but one of the most adorable beauties in all Tuscany. *La Senese* is a four-feet-high fifteenth-century Sienese terracotta *Annunziata*, a high-bosomed girl in a glorious, long, flowing flower-patterned dress; her stomach is thrust forward, her back charmingly arched. In her left hand she carries a book: her right hand rests below her bosom, not far from where the Christ Child will grow, in a gesture of humility and acceptance. She has a simple face, her high-arching eyebrows giving her a surprised look. Yet she is trusting at the same time, ingenuous. The hands are slender and miraculously fine. I know of no more refined or virginal or suggestive figure. From every angle she is perfect.

A companion-piece of the same period stands nearby, of St Catherine of Siena. The mystic saint is serene, bright-eyed, full of character (as indeed she was), in every way a person to be reckoned with. A damnable crack runs down the centre of her head, but it cannot impair her loveliness.

And where are the colour reproductions of these jewels? *Non esistono*. A dark and drab, black-and-white postcard can be had at the door for 200 lire. (The *libreria* across the road (No. 6) is closed for much of August.) The only replica I know of stands in a shoe shop near the American Service Bank, in Via della Spada. What wouldn't I give to possess a good, life-size reproduction, to rest my eyes on her every day of my life? But there are none to be had.

Already in Room 19 I am missing her and creep back to steal another final look. I pass through Room 20 in a daze. Here there is a huge crucifix, twice life-size, of overpowering impressiveness; two Donatellesque stucco *Nativities* complete with winsome donkey and cow; a fine pulpit from S. Maria Maddalena dei Pazzi; an inlaid door of the fifteenth century; a pair of sixteenth-century candlesticks, six feet high; choir stalls painted and inlaid; and another splendid wooden *Annunziata* of the fourteenth century. There seems no end to the collection, and there is nothing for it: I must come back with a camera.

Despite heavy losses in 1966, and a staff of zombie-like attendants, the Bardini Museum is a joy. The labelling of exhibits leaves much to be desired, and not everyone will want to spend 18,000 lire on the catalogue; but here one can take one's time, at least, and every year I find new things to love. I would pay the 2,000 lire admission fee to see '*La Senese*' alone.

Inevitably, the Bardini is linked with another private collection a few hundred yards across the Arno. Herbert Percy Horne was born in London in 1864, the son of an architect, and himself became an architect. But he was many other things, too: an accomplished Latinist, an expert on fine bindings, and generally a lover of art and letters. He became editor of the exclusive *Hobby Horse* magazine; host of the Rhymers' Club; and was both poet and designer. Horne was also the friend and literary adviser of the gifted *fin de siècle* poet Ernest Dowson (1867–1900), who contributed some exquisite verses to the *Hobby Horse* and dedicated 'Terre Promise' ('Even now the fragrance of her drooping hair / had brushed my cheek – ') to Horne. Dowson wrote in 1890 that he found Horne 'very erect and slim and aesthetic' – a more attractive memorial than that left by Sir Harold Acton in *Memoirs of an Aesthete*, where he refers to Horne's blood-red lips and double row of teeth.

Horne first visited Florence in 1889, then returned in 1905 to write his *magnum opus*, a monograph on Botticelli. Palazzo Corsi (the work, some say, of da Sangallo, others of Cronaca) was owned until 1489 by the rich Alberti family; then it was surrendered to members of the Corsi family in payment of a debt. After that it passed through various hands until Horne bought it in 1911. He subsequently (1912–14) restored it, and there housed the marvellous collection of paintings, furniture and majolica which he left to the city when he died in 1916. What Horne planned to leave was not a museum, but a palace intact, a memorial to aristocratic life during the Renaissance, as Volpi had done in Palazzo Davanzati, which had caused such a stir when it opened in 1910. Death thwarted him in this ambition, but the result of his labours is still outstandingly fine. The Fondazione Horne (no. 6 Via de' Benci), suffered cruel damage in the flood, like the Bardini, but has made a truly heartening recovery.

The building is three-storeyed, with projecting base socle, and rusticated at the corners, windows and main door; it has rectangular ground floor windows and arched upper windows. The roof has an extensive overhang, shading the upper storey. Immediately inside is a lovely little *cortile*, which has two open galleries, and on the third level a loggia. The whole effect is delicate and charming, and the workmanship is everywhere of the finest. The slender pillars and graceful curves of the arches and the arabesqued *graffiti* of the frieze between ground and first floor are the epitome of refinement and elegance. To my mind Palazzo Corsi is one of the most enchanting buildings in Florence, its charm accessible, no doubt, because it is on a scale small enough to take in. Whoever the architect was, he evidently possessed that truly Italian genius for managing a relatively cramped space with style.

'OPEN MONDAY THROUGH SATURDAY', reads the notice on the wall in Via de' Benci, even when the Fondazione is aggressively shut. In this city one knows when such places are closed: steel portcullises have been let down, and doors are bolted and padlocked into the very stone of the pavement. The eyes are tight shut: the mouth fully closed, like a child pretending to be invisible.

But persistence pays off. The Palazzo is quiet, intimate, deserted. The admission fee is currently 3,000 lire, and for this an immense catalogue is loaned at the entrance. Since the traumas of 1966 there have been removals and transpositions; the numbering is idiosyncratic; and there is much which is simply not listed. But classical music is piped gently through the rooms; three floors are open to the public at present, each full of delight. On the first floor is one of the most civilised *gabinetti* in Italy (entered through a marvellous, slim, arched doorway inlaid with satin wood and cut flush with the wall, like the beginning of a secret passage) which, for beauty of appointment rivals even the *thronos*-room at the head of the spiral staircase in 'Paoli'. The ground floor is confined this year to one small room reached from the charming *cortile*.

Again, there is a bewilderingly varied assortment of treasures, but the *pièce de résistance* is surely the ravishing Giotto *St Stephen*, a half-figure of the proto-martyr, tonsured and in deacon's dalmatic, pictured holding a vermilion Gospel, glowing with gold and silver – a brilliant work, full of pathos, and quite superbly preserved.

In the same room is Beccafumi's *Deucalion and Pyrrha*, and a most delicate Filippino Lippi, *Queen Vashti leaving Babylon*. I am strongly drawn to this panel, which was executed as part of a marriage chest. The subject is plainly homiletic: Queen Vashti of Persia was a proto-feminist who refused to appear at the express command of her husband, King Ahasuerus. For her defiance she was ousted from the throne and replaced by Esther (who was a Jewess

– Hadassar – and knew her place). The seven named eunuchs, Mehuman, Biztha, Harbona, Bigtha and Abagtha, Zethar and Carcas, who were sent to fetch Vashti, presumably represent emasculated mankind in general: men in thrall to Vashti-woman, rendered impotent by her and reduced to running her errands. Well might a bride rest her gaze on such a panel and be warned.

On the ground floor is Beccafumi's lovely *tondo* of the *Holy Family*, set in a glorious contemporary gilded frame; and his *Drunkenness of Noah*, a *tondo* framed by vine leaves and supported by the most delightful frolicking *putti*.

Elsewhere there is a splendid diptych of Daddi, full of breathtaking finesse; a Luca Signorelli *St Catherine on the Wheel*; a Piero di Cosimo *tondo* of *St Jerome*; and a huge, now overdark, *Deposition* left unfinished at his death in 1497 by Gozzoli. Neri di Bicci's *Archangel Raphael, Tobias and St Jerome*, a tempera painting on wood, which is tucked away in a corner as if an afterthought, is worn, but very fine. The *Miracle of St Julian*, once attributed to Masaccio and Masolino, is now thought to be by a follower of Masaccio.

There are statues and *bozzetti* (working models) by Giambologna, Ammannati, and Rustici (1475–1554), and a hundred lovely figures in painted wood and terracotta and stucco, among which a worm-eaten *St Paul* by 'Il Vecchietta' (Lorenzo di Pietro, fifteenth century) is iconographically fascinating. There are cupboards and settles, painted *credenze* and *cassoni* in inlaid walnut (which can vary from a light colour to a dark teak-brown), and cabinets, chairs and showcases. The *intarsia* is everywhere so intricate and splendidly rich that one's head swims. In one corner of a room stands a lovely late sixteenth-century cradle; elswhere are sweeping, glossy tables; rare pieces of majolica; fire-irons; scissors; shears; a rare fifteenth-century woollen carpet; fireplaces; every conceivable collectable item of beauty and refined taste. As if this were not enough, the indefatigable Horne left an important collection of prints and drawings, which used to be displayed on the second floor, but are now housed in the Uffizi.

Bardini has the *Annunziata*, Horne the Giotto. On balance I prefer Horne's collection, which is as rich in furniture as paintings. And each time I leave, it is harder to resist the feeling that I have been born at the wrong time. Horne had the flair of a connoisseur, was prepared to make personal sacrifices, and gathered his treasures on relatively modest means. I dream my way back to the days when all one needed was a good eye and a decent bank balance.

I must make do with the 'Umbrian' Madonna, and be judged by that and my other little pieces. Horne's *Palazzo* is a monument to his good taste. Perhaps he really was, as Lord Clark wrote of him, 'the most distinguished man to be omitted from the *D. N. B.*'.

A stone's throw from the southern end of Ponte Vecchio is S. Felicita, a large, rather nondescript Baroque building today, but once a tiny church on the site of an early Christian cemetery. There were Benedictine nuns here probably as early as the eighth century: certainly a church was consecrated in 1059 (the day after the consecration of the foundation stone of the Baptistry) and this was replaced in the fourteenth century by a Gothic building. In the sixteenth century Vasari incorporated its façade into his Corridoio on its way from the Uffizi to Palazzo Pitti. Then, in the eighteenth century, the place was almost entirely rebuilt.

I can never pass this church without plunging inside for a few moments. In the Cappella Capponi (immediately right through the unexceptionable portal) are two great masterpieces of Pontormo: a fresco of the *Annunciation*, and a monumental *Deposition*, still in its opulent original gilt frame. Pontormo was commissioned to redecorate this chapel by Ludovico Capponi in 1525, and, with his pupil Bronzino, he worked for three years in absolute secrecy. In the ceiling he painted *God the Father* and *Four Patriarchs* (of which only drawings survive, the originals having been destroyed in 1766 during work on the organ); the *Four Evangelists* (*tondi* in the pendentives); the *Annunciation* fresco (west wall); and the great *Deposition* (altarpiece).

The fresco consists of the two figures, angel and Virgin annunciate, one either side of the window, and separated below the window by a fussy tabernacle. The treatment is original and arresting: the angel hovers in mid-air beneath a painted vault bracket, head tilted in rapt, ecstatic gaze, hands clutching the hem of his mantle as if in flight. Mary is caught in the act of climbing some steps: she turns suddenly, and the window light catches her lovely ethereal face as she looks over her shoulder.

Centuries of damp and clumsy repaintings made detachment imperative. In 1967 this was carried out, and the fresco was fixed to a support of polyester resin and fibreglass. The artist's vibrant colours have re-emerged: vermilion, chalk blue, and the soft, sensuous mauve he loved. The figures are warm and voluptuous, beautifully balanced in posture, and the Virgin's face is sensitive and haunting. Her expression betrays many shades of feeling: humility, wonderment, apprehension, acceptance, serenity. Critics talk of a 'proto-Baroque angel', and a 'neo-Botticellian Virgin', but one should not be put off. These are creations of startling loveliness.

The *Deposition*, a composition of strange, bright colours that seem to float in space (the foreground figures have something to stand on: the others are like a flight of angels), is a swirl of movement, a harmonious blend of antithetical gesture, of bright, pastel shades (yellow gold, pale violets, and greeny blues), and pained, expressive, lovely faces. No doubt the colours were chosen deliberately because of the gloominess of the surroundings: they emit a quite disturbing, unreal glow. The dead Christ, convincingly limp and deadweight, his torso twisted, owes something to Michelangelo's *Pietà* in Rome, no doubt, as do the sculptural attitudes of some of the figures. The two youths who support him are ravishing creations, their faces in transports of grief. The one who stands to the left is a typical Pontormesque Apollo: long-legged, long-bodied, immensely tall, but brachycephalic, with a small-featured, oval face, large, expressive eyes, and lips inclined to fullness. Mary, her arms eloquent of love and the abandonment of wild grief, has eyes that are brilliant with weeping. The *Deposition* is an intensely dramatic work, of high emotion and deep spiritual feeling. It stupefied Vasari (who preferred the *Four Evangelists* and spoke of Pontormo's colour-scheme with the bewilderment of utter incomprehension), but 'all Florence marvelled', he wrote. And now, all the world.

In Via Guicciardini the people surge up and down in a human torrent, while a stall in the piazza sells teeshirts and a jumble of consummate rubbish: helium-filled balloons, cowboy jackets, sunglasses. The crowds swirl and seethe and roar like a flood. I fight my way through them in a road choked with Vespas and Fiats, past shop windows crammed with leather, lace, ceramics, *pietre dure*, past Renzo's little bar, the seedsman, a travel bureau, postcards of Venice, night fireworks, and the iris fields near Piazzale Michelangelo, and emerge finally in the grand Piazza de' Pitti. Luca's great pile seems to stretch for miles, colossal and formidable, its endless art collections for another day. The vast acreage of the Boboli Gardens, their dusty walks, shaded grottoes, fountains, theatre and statuary will simply have to wait.

Today I shall finally visit Casa Guidi. It is just there, at the sharp angle with Via Maggio. It has always passed me by. In a treasure house of the Renaissance, I suppose, the nineteenth century attracts few people.

But the Palazzo once belonged to the Ridolfi; then, in the seventeenth century it was bought by a Volterran named Guidi. The Brownings lived on the first floor from 1849 to 1861, and there Robert wrote *Men and Women* (1855), the masterpiece of his middle period, and Elizabeth composed much of her most important work. A plaque outside speaks of her making 'of her verse a ring of gold joining together Italy and England', and that is a noble saying. Casa Guidi now belongs to the Browning Institute, an American Foundation.

A charming American girl ushers me inside. Once cosily and fussily Victorian (a contemporary watercolour exists of the living room), the rooms today are horribly bare. There is an atmosphere of almost claustrophobic sadness about the place. The wall decorations, like those of Minos's throne-room at Knossos, are reconstructed from a few fragments of the original pattern. None of the few sticks of furniture is authentic, but there are photographs, forlorn copies of portraits, and photostats of letters to tell the story. I am on my own walking a chain of empty, hollow, oppressively empty rooms; the misery of association is choking, and the air is dead. There is, to tell the truth, precious little to see here.

As I leave, the girl rambles on about Elizabeth's family estates in Jamaica, Robert's family plantations in the West Indies. Apparently (she says) there was just a suspicion of negro blood in Elizabeth, just possibly in Robert, too.

'So, in a way,' she concludes, with practised but questionable logic, 'they are in fact Americans.'

The Stars and Stripes have I Tatti, they will have La Pietra, and now they want the Brownings.

San Felice, opposite, is one of the Oltrarno's oldest churches, a west-facing Gothic building, though its façade is today in the style of Brunelleschi. It has a colourful history. Originally it was owned by a family, then later taken over by a succession of different monastic Orders. The unusual closed nuns' gallery, which extends to half the church's length, was erected by Dominicans in the sixteenth century.

There have been many changes here. Only fragments of the fifteenth-century mural decoration have survived, and after a serious fire in 1926 there was a major reconstruction. The paintings are poorly lit, and by too many 'followers of' and 'school of' to attract the average tourist. The Neri di Bicci triptych is inaccessible; and the space over the side door where the large Giottesque crucifix hung last year is bare, the cross-shape seared into the wall by dust and age. But I like this place. Everywhere there is a ferment of work in progress. A large polythene sheet hangs from roof to floor where the nuns' gallery ends, and the first three chapels of the left aisle have become temporarily High Altar and side altars.

Legend has it that St Felix, fleeing from the persecution of Decius, hid in a ruin, and a spider obligingly fooled his pursuers by spinning a quick web across the doorway. It is hard to imagine a sudden web appearing in San Felice. Bright flowers stand on every ledge; there is the whiff of polish, and the buzz of hushed conversation. The locals file in, exchange their chatter, say a rosary, and set about their tasks. The parish priest, in mufti, slaps a friend's face hard and pumps his hand. This is a much-loved church, lively and committed: it comes as no surprise to learn that San Felice not long ago made itself a refuge for battered wives.

Just beyond Palazzo Pitti, on the left (at no. 17 Via Romana) is the Zoological Institute of the University, once the sixteenth-century Palazzo Torrigiani.

It is now known as 'The Observatory', *'La Specola'*, because Grand Duke Pietro Leopoldo in 1775 founded here, among other things, an astronomical observatory. Its official name was 'Imperiale Regio Museo di Fisica e Storia Naturale', so one must be grateful.

In this building, in 1814, Sir Humphry Davy with Michael Faraday used 'the great lens of the Grand Duke, a noble instrument belonging to the academy' to experiment on the combustion of the diamond. This lens was a giant magnifying glass, about 12 inches across. Focussing it beneath the strong southern sun, Davy was able to observe several diamonds in combustion, and to establish that diamond is crystallised carbon.

The University's presence is immediately felt: everywhere there are notices, scuffed paintwork, gaggles of students; typewriters clack behind stout doors; shouts echo along shabby corridors. I mount two flights of stairs and find myself in a horrendous anatomical wax works.

These displays are not for weak stomachs. I come face to face with an excoriated goat; and cats, tortoises, chickens, an assortment of fish and human beings with various parts of the viscera displayed for scrutiny, all laid out like so much meat on a slab. There are no mysteries here; but the pubic hair, I notice (and this *is* an observatory), is grey and old and of a uniform, doormat style; all the girls have swollen breasts and lie with one knee slightly bent, like pin-ups on the beach. Even their hands are posed in an attitude of coy sensuality.

A life-sized woman, with heaving bosoms and grey body-hair, lies prone, a slit from her throat plunging down both sides to her groin indicating that she can be opened at will, a medical student's teach-yourself doll. Ovaries, ligaments, lymph-ducts abound, all exhibited with a matter-of-factness made repellant by the reality of the models: these viscera, these organs, seem to come not from cold wax models, but from real, dead beings. There are triplets conceived *ex utero*, foetuses at every stage of development from conception to birth; and, in a curious and rather sinister mixture of whimsy and anatomical precision, rats gnaw and pull at the entrails of a decaying cadaver. These models, made by a man called Susini in the years 1775–1814, are extremely skilful, exact down to the last prominent nipple. They represent years of devoted labour. But, though they are rarely so open as these models, I prefer the insides of churches.

Outside, the sun is high and the air burns. A large, colourful procession is forming in the great courtyard of Palazzo Pitti. Four nuns, two of them coal black, in habits of dazzling white, watch tolerantly as they move off, their alien robes, their oriental, angular movements and caterwauling an out-

236

landish contrast to the massive austerity of the *palazzo*, and the nuns' serenity and calm.

They beat drums, ring bells and chant their enervating, hypnotic chants until the whole city is swamped by the rhythm. Even the traffic seems defeated. A dozen child neophytes walk at their head, and their leader carries in one hand an amplifier, in the other a diminutive son. The men, mostly in white, go first; some are in faded saffron-orange, their heads shaven except for a little bobbed pony-tail. On their noses they all wear a smear of paint. Four men carry a sort of Ark of the Covenant on poles, and two others fan it energetically with ritual, whipping movements.

The women, wearing saris, follow; they move gracefully, clapping in time and joining in the refrain at the appropriate moment. Above all they move elegantly, with strangely smiling faces, their smiles lovely, but fixed and inscrutable, like Buddha's. Some move among the bemused tourists and hand them sweetmeats from a wicker basket: these are pretty little cakes topped with cherries.

The procession winds past perspiring, gawping high-school girls and blinking, amused orientals, over Ponte Vecchio and up Por S. Maria. It will return along the same route. Later, resting on Lisa's balcony, I watch these esoteric figures wind their way back through streets drenched in two millennia of Christian history, and experience a twinge of admiration for their act of witness. I wonder what they believe. They live, Lisa informs me, in a richly endowed colony out at Montespertoli. I have a hunch they are mostly Americans.

The fish float in their thousands just below the surface of the Arno, one long band of fishiness, a shoal so inert they seem dead; but then occasionally they flip over, a long silver plume, half a mile of white fire. On the dry muddy banks the rats scurry, fat and long; knots of little ones run in circles over the rocks and stones and round fallen cornices. They are not so much in evidence as they were, since the river bed was deepened: they survive by scavenging, as the fish multiply and grow fat on filth. I find two little cherry cakes in my hand, and, guiltily remembering the wide, open smile of the pretty girl who pressed them there, I throw them over the balcony.

Oltrarno has character: every street teems with artisans' shops, antiquarians, framemakers, welders, wood-carvers, stucco experts, leather workers; every street and square has its history. The craftsmen were badly hit by the flood, but not like the shopkeepers of the right bank; here the land climbs away from the Arno, and the flood water, following Via de' Guicciardini, reached only just beyond Via della Chiesa.

San Frediano was always centre of the woolmakers. In the fifteenth century the dyers congregated around S. Spirito and there until recently the leather workers had their shops. Pastrymakers, cobblers, florists, jewellers, junksellers flourish, and in Piazza Torquato Tasso, swarthy southerners sporadically appear to flog antiques and relics acquired (who knows how?) from churches and *case coloniche* and rundown villas: candlesticks, crucifixes, chests of drawers, stoups, aumbries, and even the odd, worm-eaten pulpit. In Piazza S. Spirito a little market pops up, mushroom-like, each early morning, selling vegetables, fruit and cheap clothing under gaily coloured awnings.

One can find almost anything here. One year, after glorious breezy sunshine, there was a freak storm. (The climate of August is notoriously fickle.) I was reading in my apartment in Via della Chiesa when, in a second, the sky blackened and hailstones were pounding the rooftiles. Soon after, a vigorous wind got up, and before I could close it, one of the long casement windows had slammed to and shattered: the carpet looked as if it was covered in sugar.

It was a Sunday at the very beginning of August, and on 1 August Florence is squeezed dry like a lemon; all night and all next day 'Campers' creak along every route out of town to Sardinia, Corsica, Elba, laden with provisions, carrier bags, folding tables, packs of mineral water, deckchairs, ice boxes, pets, bicycles, transistors. Restaurants put up their shutters, and the centre is left to banks, souvenir shops and trippers. (In three days, in 1987, there were 60 deaths and 1,935 casualties during the hysterical exodus.) Suddenly one can actually walk alone in the narrow thoroughfares of Oltrarno. 'Ah!' I overheard an elderly Florentine say to his wife in a deserted Via S. Spirito. 'La Firenze *libera*!' And together they drew deep breaths as if the air were perfumed.

At this time of year only a handful of shops stay open, and I needed a piece of glass sized 36 by 140 centimetres. Hopelessly, I detached the entire frame and wandered abroad. Almost immediately, in Borgo Tegolaio, just near the eastern end of Via della Chiesa, I found a *vetraio* working in his shop. Sunday 1 August. It must have been 1982. Yes, of course he would do it. Would I wait?

In ten minutes I was walking back with my window: he had charged me 4,000 lire.

In this colourful, bustling quarter one sees a human kaleidoscope: pigeon catchers, purse-snatchers, nuns, students, transvestites, art historians, gypsies, cheapjacks, knife-sharpeners, Carmelites, sodomites, aesthetes, flâneurs, poseurs, Ruskin-gobbling spinsters, retired blimps, bearded painters, drug peddlers, organ grinders, sculptors, tripe sellers. (Ladies of the night seem thin on the ground: better pickings are to be had across the river, where the money is.) And how often one comes across the visiting academic, pushing baby in a canopied pushchair, and trying to keep up with his wife!

In Piazza S. Spirito, too, the grand rub shoulders with the lowly. On the one hand there is the towering, elegantly loggiaed Palazzo Guadagni, and Brunelleschi's church: on the other, rotten peaches, discarded hypodermics, beer cans, squashed tomatoes, and all the detritus of modern civilisation. The steps of the lofty Augustinian church are black with lovers and students and hippies; on the stone benches tramps and tired tourists lie sleeping; pigeons bathe in the fountain and children splash passers-by. Busy bars and *trattorie* spread their customers over the cobbles; rusting scooters clutter the pavements and clog the kerbside.

In the piazza here I have seen fire-eaters and dark-skinned buskers walk on broken bottles; sometimes there are pop concerts. One night, weaving my way home in the darkness, I found a giant cinema screen erected at the foot of the church steps. It was showing Italy trouncing a stolid *Inghilterra* at football. The goals, slowed to tenth speed in glorious technicolor, were repeated *ad nauseam* to the renewed frenzy of a packed Italian Kop. I slunk through the shadows in shame.

The Guadagni Palace (designed for a silk merchant, Rinieri Dei, who married a Machiavelli) lends dignity and elegance to what is still the prettiest square in Oltrarno. It may be Cronaca's or Baccio d'Agnolo's; the date, anyway, is around 1505. The three clearly-defined storeys topped by an airy fourth-storey loggia, with deeply jutting eaves, are an immensely satisfying arrangement, and exerted a great influence on Florentine architecture. The façade set a style for the town houses of all rich Florentines who wanted somewhere handsome to live, but without exciting the envy of neighbours, or risking the imputation of over-ambition, of *hybris*.

Palazzo Guadagni is a far cry from the grim cube of Palazzo Medici. Its façade, dressed as usual with plaster painted to look like masonry, has a general appearance of refinement and lightness. The rustication is minimal, and the pointed arches of the window-surrounds of the upper storey lead the eye nicely up to the slender columns of the loggia. The wooden doors are splendidly carved with roses.

The Dei family (who have a chapel in S. Spirito for which Rinieri's son Piero commissioned Raphael's *Madonna del Baldacchino*) died out in the late seventeenth century, and the estate was left to the *Buonuomini* of S. Martino, a fraternity whose charitable works are attested in frescoes in the tiny oratory in Via Dante Alighieri. When the *Buonuomini* auctioned the property in 1683, the buyer was the Marchese Donato Guadagni, son of a distinguished and ancient line whose nineteenth-century heirs, the Dufour Berte, still own the palazzo. There were several well known tenants of this palazzo when the first floor was leased by the Marchese Dufour Berte. Urbano Ratazzi, a close friend of Victor Emanuele II, was one. His young wife, the widow of a

Count, wrote a notoriously indiscreet *roman à clef* called *Le Chemin du Paradis* set in 'Bicheville' – plainly Florence, which put many local noses out of joint. 'Bicheville', it occurs to me, is an inspired coinage for the city with 'a good eye and an evil tongue'.

Between 1912 and 1964 this was the headquarters of the German Institute for the History of Art, the famous Kunsthistorisches Institut (now in Via Giuseppe Giusti), which was used by all the greatest art experts of this century. The top floor has for sometime now been a pensione, and there could be no lovelier eyrie from which to observe the teeming life of Oltrarno.

I sit in the square waiting for S. Spirito to re-open. From here the flat, baroque façade, bleached white at the top, and deep ochre where the sun plays with less intensity, appears to rise from the basin of the fountain, and is framed delightfully by trees.

In 1428 Brunelleschi was commissioned to rebuild an Augustinian convent which had stood here since 1250. The façade he planned was never finished. S. Spirito is the last Brunelleschi church (the great man died in 1446, when only the first column had been delivered). What we see now is a late elaboration of what had been left incomplete. When the architect died, his intentions for the south end were unclear: should the arcade be continued across the internal façade? Should there be three or four portals?

Da Sangallo favoured four, and work began in 1487. But this project, too, was abandoned. Today there is one central, and two side, portals. Various designs have been put forward at various times to achieve a richer, more finished look, but happily (to judge from some of the drawings, and what happened elsewhere in Florence) none was adopted. This is probably because no one tasteless enough has appeared with sufficient money.

To the left of the church is the old stone wall of the refectory. Today this lovely Gothic *Cenacolo* houses a small museum given to the city in 1946 by the Neapolitan collector Salvatore Romano. The building has been badly desecrated: the Ammannati cloisters are now a barracks; in the last century the *Cenacolo* was turned into a tram shed, and the large door let into the east wall destroyed what tardy restoration work has revealed as the most monumental *Crucifixion* scene of the *trecento*, and a *Last Supper* by Orcagna and his brother Nardo di Cione (or followers).

The *Last Supper* (*c.* 1360) is vestigial: only two apostles, both on the extreme right of the table, survived the trams; tantalising fragments of others can be seen on the far left, and the fresco is flanked either side by a black-robed Augustinian monk. The *Crucifixion* positively seethes with life, with flights of angels above, and below, knights and saints and womenfolk, a jostling

Santo Spirito

crowd on horse and foot. Even in its present state, the mural is exciting and suggestive, but what must its impact have been when pristine?

The museum itself can be hard to penetrate: advertised opening hours are not unerringly adhered to. But a well informed lady acts as custodian, and she knows the answers to all my questions pat. The two splendid marble sea lions come from the altar of a church in Naples; the lioness's head from Capua; the very early font from Torcello. The worn caryatid and fragment of an adoring angel are by the Sienese Tino di Camaino (c. 1280–1337). Among other interesting pieces are a sixteenth century vestment table (Florentine); a fifteenth-century fountain-surround attributed to Ammannati; a fine fifteenth-century stone portal; and two saints, fragments of a bas-relief from a Paduan screen attributed to Donatello.

Beyond the refectory rises Baccio d'Agnolo's graceful *campanile*, rated by many as the loveliest in Tuscany. Its unusual pyramidal top, and the buttresses and volutes of the upper storeys, have made it a distinctive feature of the skyline of Oltrarno, and a sight I have come to love.

A side door opens suddenly, and through it a black-habited monk peers into the bright afternoon. He eyes my advancing figure with something less than enthusiasm, but without hostility. S. Spirito is one of the largest churches in Florence, and its interior is imposing. The scattering of pews serves only to emphasise the magnitude of the place: the long nave and two aisles, a vast Latin cross of grey *pietra serena* and white plaster – the solemn, restful colour-scheme of S. Lorenzo, and Brunelleschi's hallmark – with light pouring from a clerestory of high, round-arched windows. The grey stone pillars march away like the monumental trees of some silent forest in an unbroken series continued round the nave, round transept and chancel and back again, rising and falling uniformly with harmonious rhythm. The impact of the church is in its inevitable movement towards the crossing: the parts are related perfectly to the whole, and the High Altar, the focal point of everything, is, as it were, the head of Christ hanging on the cross. The long colonnade of thirty-five pillars, each with Corinthian capital, pulvins and imposts, leads the eye away to the one object in the nave, the climax towards which every arch deliberately springs: the High Altar in the crossing.

Between each arch, in exactly similar niches round the whole church, is a succession of semicircular chapels – and Brunelleschi had wanted their curve to be shown on the exterior walls, an exciting innovation not, in the event, carried out. The High Altar, too, seems to me a mistake: it is seventeenth-century, with twisted columns supporting a *baldacchino* under which stands a ciborium in *pietre dure*. Amid such stylish plainness it is altogether too fussy.

If Brunelleschi had written a book instead of designing a church, I suppose one might speak of his 'concinnity'. Here is the pared-down austerity of the old master, of Beethoven in his late quartets, a reversion to basic forms and rejection of unnecessary lines, which in the hands of a genius, produces an unsurpassable beauty. There is tranquillity and an immensely satisfying sense of immutable order : a still, over-arching forest basking in a muted greyish light (Hutton's 'cross of light, a temple of the sun' is typically euphuistic). S. Spirito is the most perfect fifteenth-century church in Florence, and it is for the architecture chiefly that one comes here.

Many of the side chapels have interesting paintings as altarpieces (some removed, some patched up with sticking plasters), but the best have already gone; all the chapels are appallingly lit, and only a few have coin-operated lighting.

The famous painting S. *Monica giving Rules to Augustinian Nuns* (now attributed to Verrocchio, though formerly thought to be by Botticelli) is undoubtedly one of the treasures of S. Spirito, a poorly lit work of high quality in one of the left transept chapels. The architectural details, and a beautiful garden in the background, seem a perfect setting for the gloomily garbed sorority.

In the same transept, in the Cappella Corbinelli, is a marvellous altarpiece elaborately sculpted by the young Sansovino (1492); and in the next chapel left, a *Trinity with SS. Mary Magdalen and Catherine* by the so-called 'Maestro di S. Spirito', whose predella seems to me especially fine. The polyptych of the *Madonna and Child with Four Saints* by Maso di Banco (far right of the east end) is memorable among the earlier work.

The early fifteenth-century *Madonna del Soccorso* in the third chapel of the right transept has been attributed by some to Cosimo Rosselli : a determined Mary protects (with upraised club) two children from the attentions of one of the most miserable and woebegone devils I ever saw. Around his waist a snake coils; he wields a claw-ended implement, is orange, covered with thick hair, bearded, with a plaited tail and scaly belly, and he has lower canine teeth which project almost to the level of his eyes. But these fearsome attributes have got him nowhere : he seems about to burst into tears.

The tomb of Neri Capponi (1458), in the chapel at the further end of the right transept, I visit time and time again. It is attributed to Bernardo Rossellino. Neri Capponi's face, in the disc on the side of the marble sarcophagus, his lined and balding profile, is that of a real *quattrocento* character, and centuries of hands have reached out and caressed him.

The next altar, festooned with votive offerings and dedicated to St Rita, is everything awful in church art, but nearby a fine Filippino Lippi *Madonna and Child with SS. John Baptist and Martin and Catherine of Siena* (*c.* 1490) comes quickly to the rescue. The two donors kneeling in the right and left foreground are presented by the saints to the divine pair, and in the background, between the arches of a loggia, is a charming view of their home, Palazzo Nerli, and S. Frediano. Mary's serenity, the distraction of the two infants (Jesus toys with the wooden cross of the young Baptist), a fine portrait of the worried old Tanai de' Nerli (who was instrumental in Savonarola's downfall), the decorative architectural details and local colour combine to make this a really delightful work.

Of later art, Allori's *Christ and the Adulteress* at the far east end is outstanding. The scene, set in a temple, is full of drama and psychological insight, beautifully composed and richly coloured.

A system of alarms is gradually being installed to protect these works, but a large building is hard to monitor, and electronic security systems are expensive. Perhaps the paintings will all end up in museums: the very best have already gone (the Perugino *Vision of St Bernard* in the right transept is a seventeenth-century copy: the original has emigrated to Berlin). Not long ago an attempt was made to steal the Maso di Banco polyptych; the Lomi *Epiphany* in the neighbouring chapel, too, was interfered with. In August of 1987 the predella of Pier Francesco di Jacopo Foschi's *Immaculate Conception* (sixteenth century), the altarpiece of the first chapel on the right as one enters the church, was badly vandalised. The problem does not go away.

In S. Spirito the chapels are gloomy and one never knows which paintings will be on view. Here and there an altar or altarpiece has been freed from its niche and a sad wall of rough brick is all that remains. The monks have sold their greatest treasures: today they take turns to sell postcards in the sacristy, to police the long body of their church, and keep it from the depredations of thieves and vandals. The body of the Holy Spirit remains: the rest is a glum commentary on modern society. The way we live now.

Predictably, Lapo is in a black mood. He has had a bad day, and from the moment he steps into the apartment he is nursing his wrath to keep it warm. He will not be coming to the opera. A misery and terror coats the walls and furniture. I sit on the terrace trembling and watch the yellow Arno. How can one imagine that this mercurial killjoy, this dire agent of gloom, could ever enjoy an opera? Yet Lapo sings the whole operatic baritone repertoire, he knows the famous libretti by heart. We must leave by 7.30 p.m., Lisa insists. There will be traffic. It is *quite far*. The seats are not numbered and an Italian first-come-first-served arrangement is not for the timid. Lisa will see me through. 6.30 p.m., she decides, would be better; 6.30, then, *and not a minute later*.

I stay quietly on the terrace. At 7.30 p.m. Lisa suddenly appears, and, while waiting for a pizza to cook, writes five applications for her daughter's projected study-course in England. Lapo is opening the wine he is forbidden, darkly determined to remain at home; he draws the cork in silent fury. Plunk. He isn't coming. Gurgle. He stays.

The opera begins at 9.00 p.m., as soon as it begins to get dark. At 8.30 Lisa and I dash for the car, which is, of course, quite empty of petrol. The red light glows like a beacon. Lisa rattles the car into life and asks a question which jolts me from misery into stark horror.

'Which way is Poggio?' She has forgotten. Her mind is a blank. Twice we lose our way. Twice we stop and ask foreigners (who are walking the streets of the suburbs they cannot even name), then in turn an idiot and a drunk, how to get to Poggio. Lisa has become quite silent. I am desperate. We are lost and out of petrol and the opera begins *now*! I watch the minute hand fly to twelve. Out of the corner of her eye Lisa sees me and sets her face hard at the motorway.

'Gas,' she enunciates grimly. 'There's a station on the *autostrada*.'

The *autostrada* is in the diametrically opposite direction to Poggio, and we are speeding along it for quite ten minutes, having waited already at two garages (one of which is shut, but still flying a large OPEN flag; the other sells only propane) before we finally find one open. Perhaps sixty cars line up at the pumps. Lisa stifles an oath and finds a 5,000 lire note for the machine. The note, when our turn comes, is too crumpled. It won't go in. A friendly American changes it for a crisp one, and we exit (well into Act One, in the wood near the Castle, and maybe the huntsmen are already in full cry). Lisa wrenches the gears, pumps the throttle, and hurls BOBO at the *autostrada*. But tonight nothing is simple. It has not occurred to her that, even in Italy, we cannot go back the way we came: streams of cars and trailers are blocking our path and hooting angrily.

'*Porca miseria!*' Lisa shouts, indignant at the stupidity of motorway planners.

'We'll have to go to the next junction,' I say, numbly calm. 'Shan't we?'

In another fifteen minutes we are back where we first entered the *autostrada*, the engine whining and wheezing, the radio aerial tapping out an insane rhythm on the roof, and Lisa muttering to herself disjointed comminations. Once again we are lost. (Is Lucia at this very moment telling her companion the legend of the fountain, singing '*Regnava nel silenzio*', perhaps?) We find a group of men in vests playing cards in the middle of a street somewhere and suddenly Poggio is easy. It is 9.40.

Triumphantly and dangerously Lisa races us to the little town, where there is an atmosphere of happy festival, and parks with suspicious ease by the main gates. The evening is fine and balmy. *Eccoci!*

No, no, the girl at the gate tells me, we are in time. It is only 9.40! The opera has not yet begun. She shoots me a look of tolerant incomprehension.

It is *only 9.40!* I note the price of tickets at the entrance and glumly estimate the 'Agencia ARNO's' mark-up.

The tiered seating, erected plumb in front of the grand, sweeping staircase of the villa, is packed: the façade and its famous frieze are brilliantly spotlighted. Lisa elbows our way to acceptable seats (*secondi posti*) on the far left, and our ears buzz with excited chatter.

For a few hours Lorenzo's elegant villa is a Scottish castle: the scenery is basic but adequate, the lighting fine and atmospheric. The two rival houses, named in the programme as Asthen and Ravenswood, are represented by their banners at opposite ends of the *piano nobile*. Our orchestra, black-tied except for one double bass, comes from Piacenza. Players are still drifting in and greeting each other: a strikingly lovely flautist is besieged by suitors. Finally the plucky conductor takes his bow, waves away a succession of mosquitoes, and points a meaningful baton at the flautist. The chorus is from Rome, a trifle under-rehearsed, occasionally self-conscious, but full of gusto and finally enjoying themselves in their tartan kilts and shawls and sporrans and tam o'shanters. Seen through a haze of *zanzare* attracted by the powerful lights, they are somehow a romantic and nostalgic bunch. After a tentative beginning, a nice sound emerges, too. Lisa 'Tuts' and 'Poohs!' in my right ear, anxious that I should be impressed.

At the last minute our Lucia is indisposed. A pretty, short girl named Masako Degucci takes her place, and from her first entrance steals the evening. Enrico is excellently played by a resonant and fruity baritone called Franco Giovine, who at times, however, has intonation problems. Edgardo Ravenswood is clever and musical (Gianfranco Pastine), but ultimately a rather unattractively nasal tenor. Apart from Lucia and Enrico, acting here consists largely of gesturing towards the audience with one hand, then with the other, and – a trump card reserved for moments of supernatural passion – with both. For high last notes, both hands may even be flung above the horizontal in a gesture of triumphal finality. But who cares? Raimondo Bidebent (sic) struts well; Normanno does his best. Irresistibly I am reminded of Forster's provincial audience in *Where Angels Fear to Tread*. Throughout the *coloratura*, our Lucia, too, is accompanied by sighs; the high notes, if not drowned in shouts of universal joy, are cut short by something very similar. (There is also a great deal of curious overhead clapping.) Tonight, too, the two great sextets are rendered not unworthily: the Italians know all about spectacle, after all, and the standard of the singing is surprisingly high. I sit among happy Americans and Germans drowned in malodorous insect repellant and forget the silly and unsatisfactory plot.

'*Look!*' Lisa whispers loudly at one point; thrusting field glasses at me. 'One of the jewels on Enrico's cap is missing!'

246

I watch a mosquito repeatedly assaulting a second violinist, who can retaliate only just after, or just before, turning a page, so that in the faster sections his hand performs desperate arabesques in the night air. As soon as her part is over, the harpist decamps; all this time, a cellist has, with admirable élan, been managing her score for her. The lovely flautist, low cut, has a flood of black hair which she tosses behind her whenever the tempo becomes demanding, and, as this shows her to best advantage, she does it rather often.

At the side of the performance area, crunching over paths of gravel, little groups of men natter and gesticulate: the smoke from their cigarettes curls in strange blue spirals into the spotlights. They are everywhere, outside every garage, shop, church and cafe in Italy: pot-bellied, in teeshirts, sandals and sunglasses. They are always putting out a cigarette or about to light another, imparting an atmosphere of timeless, aimless, *dolce far niente*. Who *are* they? What are they doing? And why, on occasions like this, will they not do it elsewhere?

In fact, except on stage, there is a relaxed feeling about this entire production. After the second scene-change, the stage hands, who have been taking flash pictures of each other backstage, and illuminating the Tuscan countryside for miles around, their job over, crunch their way over the gravel in droves to chat and smoke and watch Edgardo die. They come not together and as quietly as one decently can, but boldly, telegraphing their arrival, as of god-given right. Behind and below us knots of children snigger and giggle helplessly as Lucia, gripped by insanity, finally slips (very daintily: the costume is a snug fit, and goes back tomorrow) to the earth. Will she rise again to take a bow? Does she dare violate the dramatic illusion? She does, she will, she dares. And she contrives it with aplomb, rising as though only recently dead, acknowledging the frenzied applause as if quite mad, and ashamed of being mad and recently dead.

As the last notes die (the woman in front of me, annoyingly, has been humming all the well known arias, and now stamps her feet on the wooden boards uninhibitedly to beat time to those final, tragic chords), the audience is on its feet cheering and obscuring the view of those still sitting behind them. An ill-rehearsed series of curtain-calls ensues: there are nervous, sidelong glances, unsynchronised bows and curtseys, hand-brandishings and sudden prostrations. Flowers appear. Then the auditorium thins suddenly and the happy audience files out, talking no louder than it had during much of Act 1. More flowers come on; they enter in vast quantities from every direction, before, between, behind, below. The whole cast turns to watch Lucia as she initiates a long, sweeping entry down the grand flight of steps. She enjoys her moment.

'I am satisfied,' Lisa comments at last, as one might after food or sex. 'But the orchestra was terrible – *schifo!*'

'Oh, I've heard far worse,' I tell her truthfully. 'I thought it was rather good.'

'You don't get Callas at Poggio a Caiano,' she grinds on. 'Not for 13,000 lire!'

'Did you ever hear Joan Sutherland?' I ask her innocently. 'Now *there* was a *Lucia!*'

'*Sutherland?*' Not Florentine, not even Italian: *ergo* she does not exist. I must be mistaken. There is a protracted lull in the conversation.

But Lisa has the last laugh.

Back in the city, near the Lungarno, we pass a prostitute dressed in scarlet leather, her face a mask of cosmetics. She is standing at the kerb, waiting for a customer. I see she is young, very striking: even as we shoot past she cuts a startling figure. Both her breasts are exposed under the leather of her jacket; they are plump, rounded, milky. I have rarely seen such an overt pneumatic display. Her skirt, no more than a wide belt, rides thigh-high.

'That girl!' I exclaim to Lisa. 'Did you *see* her?'

'That girl,' says Lisa triumphantly, flying in front of an angry Alfa, 'is a boy. A *cherubino!* He is well known.'

We drive home in silence. My brain is full of questions to which I fear Lisa may have explicit answers. I bite my tongue.

CHAPTER

XI

Albergo Cavour · Dante and Beatrice · S. Margherita de' Cerchi · 'Casa di Dante' · S. Martino del Vescovo · the Badia: Mino da Fiesole: Chiostro degli Aranci: the S. Benedict fresco-cycle · the Bargello: Michelangelo: Donatello: the della Robbia · Fiesole · Via Vecchia Fiesolana · S. Domenico

 *Albergo Cavour*! Why does the merest mention of the name conjure such torrents of piquant nostalgia? Hotel du Lac, Pensione Bandini, the White Hotel . . . each place is charged with its own romantic associations, as if every guest who crossed its threshold, every quarrel, every rendezvous and illicit liaison has left its indelible mark on the furnishings, a gathering film on doorknob and banister, on window casement, on polished dining table, and on every crisply laundered bed.

It was Eastertime, the weather dull and wet. The plane was late, the train was late. I met a dear friend and we fell out. The three rolls of film I took were all blank. The winder of my wristwatch came off in my hand, and I had to wear the watch upside down and gauge the time by deducting six and a half hours. But the fortnight had its compensations. I dined one evening at 'La Posta' in Via Lamberti, across the way from the marbled mansion of the Post Office, ate sword fish and drank a fine, tangy Vernaccia. On returning late to the Cavour, I found I had left my *borsetto* behind: in it were keys, traveller's cheques, credit cards, *lire*, and, for some reason that evening, my passport. Vaguely I recalled propping it against the table leg. The staff of the Cavour were solicitous: immediately the concierge rang 'La Posta': the *borsetto* was discovered; the owner of the restaurant insisted on delivering it personally to my hotel. Reception rang around 1.00 a.m. to report its safe return.

My room overlooked the Badia and I slept among the pigeons that roost in the old *campanile* – or tried to sleep. The Cavour is in Dante's Florence – a complex of narrow, medieval alleys and many-storeyed buildings that almost blot out the sky. Even a whisper in the street is magnified to a shout by the time it reaches the top floor of the hotel; a shout rattles round every wall like a fives ball, and, never dying, emerges at penthouse level exaggerated to a hellish, unearthly howl. The genteel popping of a Vespa is transformed into a nerve-shattering pneumatic drill. Add the shriek of brakes, the scream of tyres, the cacophony of a hundred horns (all in different keys), the odd voluntary from a transistor radio, and an improvised brawl, and the result is something like a Charles Ives symphony. And one cannot switch it off.

Albergo Cavour is on the corner of Via del Proconsolo, a busy thoroughfare which leads south from the eastern end of the Piazza del Duomo, and Via Dante Alighieri. To the newly arrived Englishman, domiciled normally in the more sequestered bywaters of the Home Counties, and used to green hills and gentle rain and to looking up from his terrace if he hears a car approaching, Florence can come as a jolt. He will not wonder for a moment why Tuscany's greatest poet wrote about Hell. It is here. It is all about him. Life is fast and relentless and conducted on a tacit understanding of *sauve qui peut*. Nobody here has any tiresome inhibitions about making din. Day is a constant furore: at night the roar can penetrate even the numbness induced by Chianti, *boules quiesces*, Mogadon. On the eve of his departure, perhaps, the tourist begins to sleep again.

It was from the Cavour I first explored Dante's city, the area within the old walls, the '*cerchia antica*', and today I plan to go back to the little square between the Corso and Via Condotta to see if I can recapture the feeling I once had. Fiammetta is already up and pushing a Hoover around the apartment. I can hear her strange hum above its roar as she moves slowly nearer. The humming is a sinister development: she sounds happy, and she is happy because she is seeing a wealthy Milanese called Maurizio. The best ploy is to get out as soon as possible.

Inevitably, we meet in the hall. The Hoover is silenced, the cigarette removed. She has forgotten to tell me that the Azienda di Turismo 'phoned: she holds out a slip of paper with a name and telephone number. *Dott. Serena Padovani, Palazzo Pitti (Cenacolo di Foligno)*. I thank her profusely, and she is so happy today she unlocks the telephone and invites me to call the *dottoressa* now.

Unbelievably, she is there; and she speaks excellent English! The *Cenacolo* is closed. Yes, the custodian is lazy, but he has strict instructions to admit no one! (My heart sinks.) When do I wish to go there? Very good. The *dottoressa* will contact the custodian and alert him. He or his wife will let me in. No, there are no postcards. I want an illustration? The person to see is *Dott*. Meloni, in Via della Ninna. In a couple of minutes it is settled, and tomorrow, at 09.00, I shall break new ground. The *dottoressa* seems amused at my gratitude. She will 'phone now; of course, *senz'altro*!

With buoyant stride I make the lift, leave Fiammetta pushing her suctionless vacuum cleaner over the white cat hairs, and next look up in Via della Pergola. At no. 59 Cellini cast his celebrated *Perseus*, and there he died. The large building at the bottom end, on the left, is the Teatro della Pergola, a nine-teenth-century construction on the site of a seventeenth-century wooden one. In the seventeenth century the comedies of Ferdinando Tacca (son of the sculptor Pietro, and builder of the wooden theatre) were played here to great acclaim, and court operas were performed in the seventeenth and eighteenth centuries. The Teatro was an elegant place, and the first of its kind, consisting of rows of boxes in a horseshoe shape facing the stage, and with no galleries.

On 14 March 1847, Verdi's *Macbeth* was premiered here in the Carnival, or Lenten Season, a great coup for the shrewd impresario Linari. On the night, Verdi took 25 curtain-calls, and was accompanied by a cheering crowd all the way to his hotel, a mile away.

Since 1900, however, the theatre's reputation has been for the drama. In 1906 Eleonora Duse played here in a production of Ibsen's *Rosmersholm* directed by Gordon Craig.

In the next street, Via S. Egidio, is the Ospedale di S. Maria Nuova, founded in 1287 by Folco Portinari, generally thought to be the father of Dante's 'Beatrice' – Bice Portinari, who became the wife of Simone di Bardi, and died in childbirth, aged 24, in 1290. Via Portinari, opposite the piazza, leads to Via dell' Oriuolo (where another theatre now flourishes), and at no. 24 is the enchanting old Convento dell' Oblate (Convent of the Oblate Nuns), where Sisters of Charity used to live; since 1936, when the nuns moved to Careggi, the convent has housed a Museo Topografico, now called the Museo di Firenze Com'era. There is a fascinating collection of paintings (for the most part abominably labelled, and some labelled entirely in Russian) and maps of the city from the fifteenth century to more recent times. Chief among the exhibits are the famous *Pianta della Catena* (a copy of the 1470 woodcut in Berlin), the first known view of the whole city; and the sixteenth-century Flemish painter Giusto Utens' charming lunettes of the Medici villas. A new and beautiful vaulted *sala* is open this year, packed with interesting engravings, including a lovely view of the Ponte a Rubaconte (now delle Grazie), built in 1236, with houses over each of the piers; of chariot races in the Piazza di S. Maria Novella at the *Festa della Corsa de' Cocchi* (1755);

and of the splendid *Fiera dell' Impruneta* (seventeenth century), a picture bristling with life like a Brueghel.

Between 'Mars and the Baptist' is the old Florence, Dante's Florence: '*l'ovil di San Giovanni*', the 'sheepfold of St John'. Of Dante's life we know only the outlines. According to Boccaccio, a comet appeared in the August sky above Florence exactly nine months before his birth in 1265, and his mother had a prophetic dream of her son's future greatness. But Boccaccio heroised Dante. He was writing eighty years after the great man's death, and, except for entertainment, cannot be relied upon.

While still very young Dante met, fell in love with, and later celebrated a girl called Beatrice. But he married Gemma Donati, to whom he had been betrothed in 1277, and had four children by her. Beatrice's tragically premature death in 1290 prostrated Dante, who immersed himself in philosophy and became active in political life. In October of 1301, while away on an embassy to Pope Boniface VIII, he fell victim to inter-party strife and never returned to his native city. He spent the rest of his life wandering and died finally in Ravenna in 1321. But this exile was a turning-point: it coloured everything he wrote subsequently, and his bitter sense of injustice and the love-hatred he felt for Florence simmered on, or just below, the surface of all his poetry.

Dante's masterpiece is certainly the *Divine Comedy*, a visionary, allegorical epic in which Dante himself journeys through Hell and Purgatory to Paradise: it is a castigation of human weakness and wickedness, and a testament of faith in Divine Justice. The *Comedy* is largely a spiritual autobiography: a journey out of the dark wood of mid-life to a world of everlasting light.

His meeting with the lovely, pure young Beatrice changed Dante's life, and the redeeming and transforming power of love is the theme and motive force of the *Commedia*. Dramatically and permanently he was changed within. Later, Beatrice's smile fired and transfixed him; her mere presence lifted him onto a more elevated plain. For Dante, Beatrice was the truth of God. So a chance meeting, on May Day 1274, was the sparking-point of a masterpiece which has arguably exerted a wider influence than any other great work of western literature.

In every street of the medieval quarter a plaque quotes the Bard, and, beneath his sonorous Tuscan, schoolchildren file insouciantly. And really, his poetry is all that is left: the rest is largely guesswork. Portraits, all based more or less on Boccaccio's prosopography, are dotted about Florence: in the Spanish Chapel; in the Cappella del Podestà of the Bargello (this is the picture discovered in 1840 by the artist and scholar Seymour Stocker Kirkup of which he fortunately made a surreptitious tracing before, next year, a clumsy restoration destroyed its value permanently); and Castagno's portrait from the

Villa Pandolfini, now in the Uffizi. The ugly monument outside S. Croce and the characterless nineteenth-century cenotaph inside are best ignored; as also, surely, is the popular painting by Henry Holiday in the Walker Art Gallery, Liverpool – a colourful, imaginative scene, which shows the eagle-nosed scholar-poet standing at the northern corner of the Ponte S. Trìnita, suffering apparently from heartburn, while three young ladies pass by along the Lungarno. Two of them see him and turn their heads: but Dante has eyes only for the central figure, a grave, pre-Raphaelite creature in yellow, whose eyes are fixed firmly ahead. All four figures seem preternaturally tall for Italians.

The tiny, plain rectangular church in Via S. Margherita may be where Dante married Gemma Donati. It was in the patronage of, among other families, the Donati (whose Torre is nearby), and the Portinari were buried here. It would certainly have been Beatrice's parish church. S. Margherita de' Cerchi, an ancient foundation recorded as early as 1032, is dark and mysterious and bare except for Neri di Bicci's vibrant, golden altarpiece (*Madonna and Four Female Saints*), the flicker of votive candles, and the half-light of severe lancet windows. The '*Chiesa di Dante*', it is called. Over the fourteenth-century portal are the arms of the church's patrons. Inside is the inevitable monument to Beatrice, and a reproduction of the tombstone of the remarkable Monna Tessa, Beatrice's nurse, founder of the Oblates of S. Maria Nuova, and moving spirit behind Folco Portinari's endowment of the hospital of that name.

At the southern corner of this little street, where it meets Via Dante Alighieri, and opposite the medieval Torre della Castagna, is the complex known as 'Casa di Dante'. Dante's house it almost certainly is not but it *is* a house in the Dante area, and in it are displayed maps and documents relevant to the poet's life and times. Ninety-nine per cent of these are photocopies, and much of the information is either tentative, or downright fiction. Generally there is little on offer that is edifying or stimulating, and today I am beset by a bossy, officious, and insistently begging custodian. At least (I tell myself, as I make for fresh air) there are as yet no Dante Pizza Parlours.

Further along the Via Dante Alighieri is another tiny church which claims to be the one in which Dante was married. S. Martino del Vescovo is charming, dingy and minuscule; it was founded originally in 986, but entirely rebuilt in 1479, when it became the headquarters of the Compagnia dei Buonomini (founded in 1442 by the great S. Antonino), yet another charitable institution, this one for the relief of the poor. S. Martino, today a small rectangle, no larger than a fair-sized living room, in the days when it was the parish church of the Alighieri faced in the opposite direction. Remains of its old façade have been found in the little piazza.

Inside are frescoed lunettes of the late fifteenth century (school of Ghirlandaio) as fresh and every bit as immediate as Cellini's autobiography, showing the twelve Buonuomini at their various works of charity: burying the dead, tending the sick, feeding the old, ransoming prisoners, dowering poor girls – a touching testimonial to a side of Florence which still flourishes today. (The Compagnia, like the Misericordia, is a sort of 'secret society' specialising in the performance of good works for the 'reserved poor', i.e. those too proud or ashamed to beg.) In the north wall there was a '*finestra a tromba*', now closed up, through which bread was distributed during the plague of 1522. On the west wall, the present altar wall, are two scenes from the life of the patronal saint: St Martin sharing his cloak with the beggar, and the saint wrapped in glory in Christ's cloak, watched by a heavenly platoon of angels. The Buonuomini frescoes are exciting, authentic *tranches de vie*: the faces, costumes, customs and people of fifteenth-century Florence. Here are the Urim and Thummim of the *quattrocento*! Fascinated, I put 200 lire in a slot, dial INGLESE, and listen to a lengthy monologue in what appears to be gabbled Italian. Then I catch a reference to 'graveduggers' (*sic*) and finally a clearly audible appeal for alms and 'The End. Thank you.' and I realise it has been English after all. None the wiser, I move on to the Madonnas. One is an exquisite painting attributed to Perugino (or Niccolò Soggi, *c.* 1480–*c.* 1552), a distinguished *Madonna and Child with S. Giovannino*; the other is dark and timeless like an icon, a numinous thirteenth-century Byzantine work.

From an adjacent *birreria* wafts the incongruous, dated voice of Pat Boone crooning 'April Love'. An ambulance screams in urgent frustration. Outside the 'Casa di Dante' cameras click and jaws blur in polyglot froth-rant. Either side of the street many-storeyed buildings soar up to the sky. From here, I can make out my hotel room, its shuttered window open wide over the Badia and its bell-tower, the *campanile* that called to Dante and Beatrice, '*tin tin sonando con si dolce nota / che'l ben disposto spirto d'amor turge*' ('chiming with such sweet note that the well-ordered spirit swells with love'). This bell was the pulse of life in the medieval city, and the tower, hexagonal with hexagonal cusp, is strangely dear to me. There was a tenth-century bell-tower here once, and its cylindrical base was used for a new, early fourteenth-century structure, which stood in the Gothic abbey church between the central nave and the north aisle. In 1307 the people smashed half of it down to punish the Benedictines for 'insubordination', but by 1330 it was built up to its full height again. Thereafter it was often struck by lightning and progressively lost bits of its stonework, until in 1794 the windows were walled up and the decorations flattened out. A thorough restoration in 1900, and subsequent cleanings and reinforcements, have made it one of the best loved landmarks of the city.

The Badia

The Badia was the only official abbey within Florence, a rich and famous complex dating from 978, when Willa, wife of Hubert and mother of Hugo (both of them Margraves of Tuscany) founded a church 'dedicated to the Virgin Mary, and a monastery as well, entrusted to the care of an abbot charged with enforcing the Rule of St Benedict.' The monastery was suppressed in 1810 and today the Badia is a parish church. Ugo (died 1001) is buried here, and on 21 December each year is still commemorated as benefactor.

In the years following 1284 the abbey church was rebuilt in the shape of a Latin cross, then completely altered in the seventeenth century. It was around this time that important frescoes by Giotto and his pupils in the Cappella Maggiore were lost. Today only a small fragment (not by the Master) from a scene of *Joachim among the Shepherds* remains. Vasari's particular praise of an *Annunciation* inspired a clumsy attempt at detachment in 1627. Thereafter no references to the fresco are found, so one assumes it was destroyed in the process, as the rest of the frescoes were during the drastic reconstruction of the church.

At the same time, a splendid *Way to Calvary* by Nardo di Cione in the Giochi Bastari chapel (the various attributions since its discovery in 1911 make absorbing reading) was whitewashed over. Only scraps can be seen today: the scene of *Christ Taking Leave of the Maries* ('Of inferior quality,' wrote Offner; 'Their quality is extremely high,' wrote Pogetto) is most complete, and memorable for the elegance of the figures and composition: Christ's face so calm, yet dominant; the soldier's so determined as he threatens the three, strongly contrasted women. The sad fragment above, of a solitary tree, bent as it were in grief as Christ goes to his death, is an eloquent symbol of our loss. Other frescoes, too, have vanished over the centuries. Quite by accident, in November 1967, a year after the flood, a *Transfiguration* by Taddeo Gaddi and its *sinopia* were discovered in a recess in the old refectory, together with a vast *Crucifixion* by Sogliani (1492–1544), which was thought to have been lost. This shows Christ on the cross between S. Scolastica (St Benedict's sister) and the Madonna (left); and (right) SS. John the Evangelist and Benedict (his attributes are a book, a crow and a crosier). In the background is a landscape with a city on the horizon: above, either side of God the Father, are two pairs of angels bearing symbols of the Passion. There is no record ancient or modern of Gaddi's fresco, yet, tantalisingly, we know it must have been visible this century, because sheets of a 1924 newspaper were found under the whitewash against the paint surface. This was an undoubted masterpiece. It was discovered and detached in the nick of time. Drying out took three whole weeks.

What draws me to the Badia today is not Segaloni's seventeenth-century Baroque interior, nor, fine though it is, Gamberai's richly carved coffered

wooden ceiling. Nor is it even the monumental 1558 organ by Onofrio Zeffirini of Cortona, a name as proverbial in its day as Guarneri, Stradivari, Purdey
or Rolls Royce. And this is a noble instrument, worth a pilgrimage on its
own. The casement, all gilt and silver, is framed within a carved and painted
eau-de-Nil wooden structure by Gamberai. It is the only one of Zeffirini's
instruments to survive more or less intact: those of Ognissanti and Sant'Ambrogio have been mindlessly electrified and otherwise destroyed by modifica-
tion; so have the 1571 S. Trìnita and the 1579 S. Croce organs. The great
organ of the Duomo, made in 1567, has been dismantled and currently languishes in damp storage rooms. All this vandalism has taken place, after nearly
four centuries of loving preservation, during the past forty years.

This organ was restored in the years 1978–9. The keyboard extends to
4½ octaves, the pedals to 1½; and the restored, original sound, heard again
first on 21 December 1978 for Margrave Ugo's Commemoration, must now
be one all musical scholars covet for recordings of Gabrieli, Frescobaldi *e tutti
quanti*. What joy to hear its real voice again! But an even greater joy is the
assurance that Italians still care about such things.

And Filippino Lippi's *Vision of St Bernard* (c. 1486), on the left wall immediately as one enters the church is one of his finest achievements. At least two
of the faces of the angels who play around the Virgin are sublime. If, as
tradition has it, the Virgin and angels are modelled on the wife and children
of the donor, he was a lucky man indeed. The painting, from S. Maria alle
Campora at Marignolle, came to the Badia in 1530 for safekeeping at the
time of the siege of Florence; and here it has stayed, a work of brilliant,
vibrant colours, and extraordinary truth of detail. The books of St Jerome
and the parchment on which he writes bear almost limitless magnification:
all the texts which can clearly be read allude to Mary, Mother of Christ.
The attention to realism is exceptional.

These are all rare and fine. But mostly I come to see the carvings of Mino
da Fiesole. There are three pieces of the finest quality here: a marble altarpiece
(the '*dossale Neri*', originally an altar dossal, 1464–9) of the *Virgin and Child
flanked by SS. Leonard and Lawrence*; the tomb of Bernardo Giugni (c. 1468);
and, his greatest masterpiece, the monument to Margrave Ugo (1469–81).

Mino (1429–84) was born near Poppi in the Casentino, and may have
been a pupil of Desiderio da Settignano. He was active in Rome from 1454,
and the influence of Classical forms on him was strong. He is famous for
his tombs, and portrait-busts; his *Piero il Gottoso* (1453) in the Bargello, just
across the street, is the earliest dated portrait bust of the Renaissance, a stiff
work full of character and strongly Roman in feeling.

Mino's best and most characteristic qualities are his delicacy and refinement.
Ruskin wrote of him that 'his chisel seems to cut life and carve breath, the

marble burns beneath it, and becomes transparent with very spirit', and indeed some of his reliefs are luminous, fleshly, seemingly not of stone at all. More recent authorities have criticised his technical abilities and found his style unpalatably sentimental. I find him delicious. I relish him and come back time and time again for more: his faces and hands are among the most lovely anywhere, and at least one recent scholar of distinction has been of the same mind. The differences of opinion among *cognoscenti* afford endless innocent amusement to us dilettanti who have no reputation to protect. I refuse to be a child of my times. If the Mary in the panel between SS. Lawrence and Leonard is 'sentimental', then so be it: I adore her sweetness, her broad fine brow, her utter purity of feature.

Beneath the Badia's grand organ casement and its supports crowded with gilded baroque swirls and curlicues, the great monument to Ugo stands as eloquent testimony to Mino's skill at relief work. The two flying angels who support the plaque on the base, the Madonna and Child in the *tondo* of the lunette, and the figure of Charity, with her lovely, lively children, in the central panel about the recumbent Margrave, are to my eyes superlatively fine. The shield-bearing *putti* at the sides, it is true, are nothing like so good as Desiderio's on the Marsuppini monument in S. Croce. But Desiderio and Bernardo were dead: until Verrocchio and Benedetto da Maiano took over, Mino was the leading sculptor of the day, and he won the commission for the Ugo monument on the strength of his Giugni tomb. It had, in the first instance, been offered to Luca della Robbia, in 1439, but thirty years later went to Mino. And he took his time. (There is a record of the payment of 1777 lire, 14 soldi and 6 denari to the artist as late as 1481.) 'Exquisite,' enthuses one guide; 'a watered down version of Desiderio's Marsuppini tomb,' says another. Vasari, a true second-rater, whose ugly *Assumption* ('among his best works,' claims the guide) looms overhead, thought Mino's chisel-work 'hard and dry': Henry James could think of 'no praise pure enough'.

Through the door to the right of the chapel are steps which lead to the upper storey of the Chiostro degli Aranci, a tranquil cloister constructed in the 1430s and named after the orange tree, or trees, that apparently once grew here (though old documents refer to the cloister as '*del pozzo*', '*della Sagrestia*', '*del Capitolo*', or later '*piccolo*'). On the lower storey are fine tomb-stones of the thirteenth and fourteenth centuries, and the remains of the façade of the old chapter house, its stubby octagonal pillars, coats of arms, and inscriptions. But on the upper level, arranged in anticlockwise succession, is a splendid fresco-cycle of *Scenes from the Life of St Benedict*.

No one comes here: I have never, in all my visits, been anything other than alone, utterly at leisure to examine the paintings and *sinopie* as closely and for as long as I wish; to photograph them, and dream the hours away in the delicious coolness. Today is no exception. I can hear birdsong in the stillness, and as the sun lights the central courtyard, the shadows are short and dagger-sharp.

The frescoes cover the northern and western sides of the portico, and the first bay of its southern side. The scenes they depict were based on the *Second Dialogue* of St Gregory the Great, and their iconography was based on that of Spinello Aretino's *St Benedict Cycle* in the sacristy of S. Miniato. Stylistically the painting shows the influence of Fra Angelico and Filippo Lippi.

Nine of the twelve frescoes are by the same hand, the 'Aranci Master', identified by most writers as the Portuguese Giovanni di Consalvo, whose name crops up in contemporary documents recording reimbursements for colours used in painting the cloister. Further evidence names a Giovanni di Portugallo as one of the followers of Fra Angelico. It is not beyond possibility that Giovanni di Consalvo actually collaborated with Angelico here, and, if this identification is correct, there is also the fact that the abbot, Gomezio, would have been his compatriot. Of the other frescoes, the fourth in the series is an early work of Bronzino (1503–72), and the last two scenes are mediocre efforts by assistants.

The cycle begins at the north-eastern corner, with the young Benedict leaving home, a fine bright lunette, his white horse stepping out proudly at the start of the great saint's career. Benedict was born in *c.* 480 at Nursia in Umbria, and was sent to Rome for his education. But city life was not for him; he fled into the country and, aged about 20, became a hermit near Subiaco. In the second lunette, the young Benedict succeeds by his prayer in rejoining the sieve of his nurse Cyrilla, which had fallen and broken in two on the road to Rome. On the right, the miraculously repaired sieve is displayed above the portal of the church at Enfide near Subiaco.

There are three separate episodes in the third lunette: first (right to left) Benedict, a beardless, beautiful youth, is given his monk's garments; then we see the monk in his desolate cave at Subiaco being given food by the priest who invested him; finally, an angel appears to a priest about to tuck into his Easter dinner and scolds him for forgetting Benedict's hunger. There are accomplished and telling contrasts here between the bright light of the dinner scene, the rich colours and enforced perspective, and the gloomy wilderness outside, all rugged, flinty rock and dark, sombre trees.

The next scene is Bronzino's, painted nearly a century after the rest: an ecstatic Benedict, in order to overcome sexual temptations, throws himself into a bramble bush. (This painting is dark and faded, and hardly of a piece with those surrounding it.) Next is the last lunette of the north wall (occupying only roughly half of the usual area because of an intrusive, but contemporary,

259

doorway), a scene showing Benedict blessing a glassful of wine offered him by the monks of his community. The glass, being full of poison, is instantly shattered. Benedict had left Subiaco at the entreaty of a community of monks (possibly those at Vicovaro) who wanted him as their abbot. Benedict called his rule 'a school of the Lord's service, in which we hope to order nothing harsh or rigorous', but it proved too strict for these monks, and, regretting their choice, they tried to do away with him. The monks depicted here are a curious lot, each represented individually, as they crowd into the cunning perspective of the architectural framework. Surely these are portraits. One figure, in particular, stands out: a smiling, tonsured Brother, immediately behind the two monks confronting the saint; he seems to be beckoning the observer. During restoration, the initials 'I.M.' were found above his head, and experts have taken this as an indication that the smiling monk is in fact a self-portrait of the artist, a member of the Badia community. This would account for him being unnamed in documents: as an ecclesiastic, of course, he would have received no fee. Giovanni di Consalvo's authorship is therefore far from secure.

The sixth lunette shows a scaly devil luring a monk out of chapel (another architectural framework of interesting perspective), and St Benedict (left) belabouring him with his staff to cure his possession. (Benedict was renowned for his acts of exorcism and healing.) Again, the brothers are carefully and interestingly individualised.

Next comes the miracle of St Benedict mending a labourer's scythe (in other versions a woodcutter's axe). The labourer has lost his scythe-blade in the deep waters of a lake while cutting down brambles on the lands of Monte Cassino (this was Benedict's community, which he established in c. 529, and where he died in c. 547), and is explaining his predicament to the heavily bearded abbot (right), who (left) by plunging the shaft into the deepest part of the lake is miraculously able to join the two parts. (This and the *Mending of the Sieve* hardly constitute miracles of the first importance; but theologically speaking, one supposes, a miracle is a miracle.) The large lake, with its pale glassy, turquoise surface, its reeds, birds, eels and fish, has offered the artist an unusual opportunity. In the distance, boats dot the waters and the obligatory walled city, where it climbs the far bank, has a lovely 'fairy tale' quality. The lake 'mirrors' the peace of Benedict and the monks, and the lovely abbey, its rose-pink portico and cusped campanile, its crockets and lancet windows, all speak of the tranquillity and the order of holiness.

The eighth scene shows Brother Maurus sent by St Benedict (right) to rescue Brother Placidus who has fallen into a *torrente* (left) while filling a pitcher with water. (Benedict has seen Placidus's plight in a vision.) Again, the countryside is rugged and dramatic, and contrasted beautifully with the carefully espaliered orange tree behind the kneeling Maurus.

Next comes perhaps the most famous scene: the *Miracle of the Raven*. To the right, a jealous priest, Florentius, offers Benedict poisoned bread; above, from the tree, in a halo of light, a raven looks down on proceedings with custodial interest. But the saint, miraculously aware of the attempt on his life, is shown in the refectory ordering the raven to dispose of it. Once again the monks are carefully individualised as they sit at table. The refectory recedes deeply into the wall, and exactly above the vanishing point sits the saint himself, thrown into prominence by the row of hooded monks and by his gesture as he reaches over the table to point at the raven.

The next two bays feature a scene connected with the building of the monastery at Monte Cassino. The first shows the Devil sitting on a block of stone, sneering at the Brothers' efforts to lift it. Only St Benedict's prayers defeat him. In the second, a novice is crushed to death by a fallen wall; miraculously, St Benedict revives him. The resuscitation-scene is particularly fine, as is Spinello's in S. Miniato, where a devil, scowling from behind the ruined wall, always reminds me of Boris Karloff in a gruesome film version of *Jekyll and Hyde* I once saw.

The eleventh lunette, the last on the west wall, and the scene on the south wall which ends the series, are poorly preserved, and by another hand. The first shows a squire of Totila, sent by the king of the Ostrogoths in his place, to see if the saint could see through his disguise. St Benedict, of course, passes the test with flying colours. In the last fresco, on the south wall, the real king confronts the saint, and asks to receive his blessing. St Benedict hears his confession, absolves him, and rewards him for his deception by predicting his imminent demise.

What happened to prevent the first painter from completing this series will perhaps never be known. I often wonder if he would not have closed, as Spinello did, with the death of the saint. The scholars who see the 'Maestro del Chiostro degli Aranci' and Giovanni di Consalvo as two different persons believe these last two frescoes are by the latter. Those who identify them believe his assistant to be responsible for the two poorer frescoes, and name him as one Macario, a Lay Brother of the community, who studied painting in 1439 at S. Domenico. *Alii alia.* But it would be satisfying to discover the identity of the merry Brother in the 'poisoned glass' scene, and find the owner of the intriguing initials 'I.M.'

After my first excitement at finding the St Benedict cycle, I went one year almost daily to the Badia: a small case displayed Alessandro Guidotti's indispensable little guide, and a selection of postcards, but it was locked, and on inquiry I found that the key had been lost. In the sacristy, a kindly lady

261

discovered 100,000 prints of one (particularly uninteresting) scene, and, until a new key was made, and the case opened, I wandererd around in a cloud of unknowing. Among Florentine churches the Badia is unjustly neglected: all the more reason for the discerning tourist to go, and go again.

My days are running out. Across the road is the massive fortress which was the Palazzo del Podestà, the old seat of Florentine government, the battle-mented Bargello. Here, the grim spectre of history raises its hoary head and rattles its chains, conjuring memories of impalings, immurements and decapitations, torture and executions, starvation, rapine, assassinations, cabals, barbarous pogroms and hideous blood feuds, a thousand thousand wickednesses perpetrated by state and Church, and blood – blood enough to stain the Mediterranean scarlet and float a continent! The Bargello has seen a hundred ways of ghastly death, and today can still be intimidating; but it has been transformed into a house of beauty. This is the Museo Nazionale, an unrivalled collection of Florentine Renaissance sculpture which represents an explosion of creativity equalling, if not surpassing, that of fifteenth-century Athens.

The Bargello is so full of greatness, there are so many examples of man's striving after beauty, and I have only the tail-end of a morning to spare! Here are a score of works that could fairly claim to be called masterpieces, and to any one of which one might devote a lifetime's study. Seen together hugger-mugger, they present a cultural concentration which can easily result in numbness and bewilderment.

Today I shall look at Michelangelo, Donatello, Mino, and the *bottega* of della Robbia. An hour here is five minutes of ordinary time.

In the Sala di Michelangelo the air seems charged with tension: these lovely, dumb figures, twisted every way at the creator's whim; his chisel-marks still visible, conjuring sinews and warm flesh from the most inert, intractable and cold of materials – stone!

The nude is an invention of the Greeks, who idolised male beauty. It is man seen without the cosmetics of clothes, seen in the flesh where all defects are exposed, and nothing can be hidden. It is an affirmation of man's self-confidence: *eripitur persona, manet res*. Michelangelo believed the naked human figure was the noblest theme in art. 'Who', he asked, 'is so barbarous as not to understand that the foot of a man is nobler than his shoe?' The purpose of his art was religious, his means the representation of beauty. The idea that love 'drew the soul upwards' was ultimately Platonic, but Dante and then the neo-Platonist Humanists like Ficino had taken it up, and Lorenzo de' Medici actually defined love as the '*appetito di Bellezza*'. If one climbs the staircases of the Bargello with open eyes and a receptive spirit, the experience is in every way elevating. To sit for a morning in the Sala di Michelangelo is an education in more than the plastic arts.

The *Tondo Pitti*, an unfinished work in low relief, shows a beautiful, solemn Madonna like one of the Sistine Sibyls; she is caught in the moment of looking up from her reading, and her child is all soft, sweet curves as he petulantly leans on her book. (The *Taddei Madonna* in the Royal Academy, which has a young Baptist as well as a similarly petulant Christ Child, is earlier, and also unfinished.) There are wonderful gradations here from rough to polished work, and one can observe perfection emerging in stages from rude rock. The Madonna shines gloriously; the child, his limbs baby-plump, seems clinging and fractious. The juxtaposition of textures is deeply suggestive.

Brutus (the only bust Michelangelo ever sculpted) is stern, unyielding nobility personified: here is a tragic figure, proud and disdainful but at the same time full of pathos. This late work (*c.* 1539–40) was left unfinished by Michelangelo and completed by his pupil Calcagni (the same who, with such disastrous results, repaired and finished the *Pietà* in the Museo del Duomo). The Medici acquired it, and, by adding a Latin elegiac couplet on the *targhetta* beneath, turned what had been intended as a cry for republicanism (Duke Alessandro de' Medici had just been assassinated, and Michelangelo sculpted the bust in Rome among a circle of exiled Florentines) into something quite different, and more to their advantage. The verses read: '*Dum Bruti effigiem sculptor de marmore ducit / in mentem sceleris venit et abstinuit.*' 'While the artist was sculpting this figure from the marble, he remembered the crime, and stopped.'

Bacchus, a young, dissipated, hermaphroditic creature of rounded, fleshy torso, with grape-clusters entwined in his hair, a little satyr at his side, and a drinking cup raised in his right hand, seems to reel and lurch as if drugged with wine. The group exudes a sleek, disturbing air of depravity. This was Michelangelo's first major sculpture, done for the banker Jacopo Galli in 1497, and it stood in his garden among antiquities. Then, in 1572, it was bought by Francesco de' Medici. People itch to touch this sensuous and potent pagan: his feet are transparent; the curve of his belly is taut, pampered flesh.

The best marble, '*statuario bianco*', has an inimitable profundity to it: light can penetrate its surface deeply, then, reflected by the crystals inside, it re-emerges in a warm, soft effulgence, as if the stone were actually alive. This translucence is the 'soul' of sculpture. The cheap stuff is opaque, cold and dead. Marble was always costly, and its quarrying difficult and dangerous: Michelangelo himself came close to death on at least a couple of occasions. The whole business is still chancy and many mistakes are still made. Marble is heavy and eminently fissile. Here is the challenge and the beauty of the medium: one false blow of the chisel, and a work is ruined. But then beauty has always been expensive.

The smaller than lifesize *Apollo* (the '*Apollino*'), an unfinished figure of great beauty, may in fact be a *David*. (The protuberance at the back of the base is possibly a 'head' of Goliath.) According to Vasari it was begun in the middle of 1530 for Baccio Valori. Apollo is in the act of drawing an arrow from his quiver, a *contrapposto* pose which is perfectly harmonious from whichever angle it is viewed. The youth seems melancholy, languorous, weary, yet as well as suffering there is also a spirit of calm, a sort of divine *hesuchia* about him.

In this exalted company the lesser names inevitably pale, though the juxtaposition is appropriate in the sense that Michelangelo lived in an age of intense competition. Those who won the Medicis' patronage prospered: those who failed to usually left Florence in search of work elsewhere. Michelangelo's successors, Tribolo, da Vinci and later Francavilla, represent a gradual, sad diminution of the Master's power: some works are merely accomplished, others merely decorative.

Bandinelli's (1488–1560) gigantic *Adam and Eve* seems stiff and cold, Eve's breasts impossibly elevated. De' Rossi's *Dying Adonis* has a lovely head and swan-like neck, though; and Ammannati's little *Leda and the Swan* (a copy of a painting by Michelangelo which was destroyed) is memorably sensual. The swan, kissing Leda, is poised between her thighs. So, momentously, Helen was conceived. 'A shudder in the loins engenders there / The broken wall, the burning roof and tower / And Agamemnon dead.'

And Giambologna's famous *Mercury* now stands in this ground-floor room, a miracle of airy lightness, borne up on a single toe. Nearby are Cellini's divine *Narcissus* (1547–8), much repaired, in a pleasant grey, Greek marble, done in a violent *contrapposto* dictated, apparently, by fissures in the stone; and the *Apollo and Hyacinth*, also carved from a faulty block (1546). The repairs to Narcissus were necessitated by damage caused during a flood: the statue, standing on a wooden block, was toppled by the water and broke, across the breasts. Cellini tells us he pieced it together again and added a garland of flowers to disguise the crack. The flowers have vanished and the cracks are clearly visible, but the figure is still enchanting. The act of turning reveals the fine musculature of the torso, and the hair is a wild, flowing mane, the profile a model of Classical, epicene beauty.

I move into the *cortile* again to climb to the first floor. Here one grasps dimly the wealth and grandeur and style of the great villas (Castello, Careggi, Pratolino) when all their decorations were *in situ*. I sit for a moment on the little wall. A middle-aged American couple gaze critically at Gemito's excellent Fisherboy, '*Il Pescatore*'. At length the verdict is reached. 'Gee, 1877!' I hear the man exclaim crossly as he consults his guide book. 'It's noo.'

Upstairs is an airy gallery full of Giambologna's turkeys and owls and peacocks, where one can sink onto chairs under the painted ceiling and rest before tackling the Gran Salone, a lofty fourteenth-century hall crammed with glories of marble and bronze and terracotta, all by the greatest names of the *quattrocento*.

There is a hush here, as if tourists are overawed by the scale: everywhere one turns there is genius. And at the far end, set in a shallow niche on the wall, Donatello's *St George* from Orsanmichele draws all eyes to himself, feet wide apart, shield battered but defiant. He frowns in concentration, a proud, beautiful young warrior who threatens any moment to step from his niche: he stands well forward, his left leg before his right, and both arms (he surely held a sword or spear in his right hand) reinforce the impression of movement.

Donatello's two *Davids* are also here: the black, bronze, sensuous figure, hips coyly tilted, somehow more naked for his hat and greaves, is a thing of the rarest beauty. David's hair is long and girlish, his expression that of someone daydreaming; he seems almost to smirk. The crooked left arm and knee, and the soft, silky flesh of his torso, are a titillating contrast to the tightly chiselled locks of hair, the metal greaves, and the severed head of Goliath, on which his left leg rests. This is no warlike David, but a dream-David, a lovely, effeminate youth, based on an Antinous, maybe. (In fact, he may even be a Mercury: scholars are not decided. He stood originally on a column in the courtyard of Palazzo Medici.) There is a story that the perfect limbs were actually cast from a living model.

The marble, clothed *David* is the earliest certain work of the Master, done a good thirty years before the bronze – an elongated figure with legs wide apart, slender, attenuated hands, and an endless neck surmounted by a small head with tightly garlanded hair. This marble was commissioned as a companion-piece to Nanni di Banco's *Isaiah*, to stand on a buttress on the north transept of the Duomo. But the *Isaiah* was removed to the façade, and in 1416 Donatello received 5 florins for adapting the statue for the Palazzo Vecchio.

All round the high walls are tabernacles and statues, lunettes, reliefs of peerless quality, and past them the hordes tramp blindly to photograph *St George*. An Agostino di Duccio bas-relief of the *Virgin and Child with Angels* simply takes the breath away with its delicacy of line, the lovely, flowing tresses and ravishing, angelic profiles; the serenity of the Virgin, her unbelievably slender hands! The della Robbian bust of a young woman, too, is a great love of mine: she is austere and fine, with glorious flaxen hair, her ultramarine cloak, gathered by a daisy brooch, catching the light here through the leaded windows. And Luca's *Madonna della Mela* (*c.* 1460) on the entrance wall, for the beauty of sheer simplicity, would be impossible to better. Elsewhere on this floor are gloriously painted wooden statues, life-size in golds and scarlets, from Pisa and the Marches; crucifixes and majolica; ivories, seals, jewellery and paintings. But there is too much, and I hear the busy beat of time.

The bulk of the della Robbias are upstairs. The *bottega* is copiously represented, so that the gaze slips from Andrea and Luca, from the pure monochrome to blue and white, to three- and four-coloured compositions, and finally to the vast, multicoloured jigsaws of Giovanni that baffle and leave me feeling nauseous with excess. Busts of *St Ursula* and *Bacchus*, she rapt and crowned, he garlanded with grape clusters (a strange juxtaposition sharing a lovely buttercup yellow), are both very fine. A charming, chubby-cheeked boy in white, blue and green, stands aloof and pouting on his pedestal. (This is possibly the young Piero di Lorenzo de'Medici.) But the nearby *tondo* of a girl (*'Ritratto di Ignota'*) is in a class of its own. Until recently her upper lip was chipped: now I see she has been restored to perfection, the disfiguring cold sore has gone. She wears beads – pearls, I always imagine – round her neck and in her hair, which falls in two bunches behind her. With flawless jawline and elegant refinement of feature, she leans on her slender neck so far out of the *tondo* as almost to escape from it. There is something infinitely appealing about the sadness of her eyes, too: her high-arching eyebrows, her averted and lowered gaze, her quiet and reflective modesty. The effect is of utter simplicity: a minimum of colouring has been used, but the modelling is so subtle that a whole character has been caught for all time. This unknown girl is my single favourite work of the della Robbia: I covet her as I covet '*La Senese*' in the Museo Bardini. (No doubt, since Verrocchio's *David* is almost literally within reach, this reflects dimly on both my taste and character.) Whoever she is, I visit her as a pilgrim, I stare at her and she speaks to me. She has become printed on the backs of my eyelids.

In the *Sala di Verrocchio*, as well as his lovely *David* (done for the Careggi Villa; a variation of Donatello's bronze, and almost as sensuous, as he waits hand on hip for applause) are superb works of Mino, reliefs, busts, and tabernacles all executed with brilliant delicacy of touch. The noses, eyelids, lips and fingers, in particular, show exquisite refinement. The rectangular bas-relief of Marcus Aurelius, a deeply Classical work, depicts a beautifully sensitive, youthful profile. Mino is happiest in relief work, low ('*schiacciato*') and deep (*basso rilievo*). His most successful bust here is probably that of Rinaldo della Luna (1461). But in this room there are many Florentine portraits by Verrocchio, Antonio Rossellino, Benedetto da Maiano and others: Francesco Sassetti, whose chapel and portrait are in S. Trìnita; the scholar Matteo Palmieri; Pietro Mellini, a rich merchant; and Giuliano de' Medici, assassinated in the Pazzi Conspiracy. The room is crowded with living creatures, none beautiful or idealised, but human beings of flesh and blood, the men who ruled

Florence and made her famous and wealthy. Look at Matteo Palmieri, his square-jawed, rugged face (made intentionally humorous by what seems to be a very large, red nose). And how grim Pietro is, how lined the wealthy senator Mellini!

The lovely *Lady Holding Flowers* (*Flora*), attributed to Verrocchio (some say it is Leonardo's) is solemn and Roman, but its severity is alleviated by great delicacy in the treatment of the hands, and in the coy suggestion of nipples under the material of the dress. Perhaps this is Lorenzo's mistress Lucrezia Donati. Whoever she is, she is unusually compelling and memorable, and this is certainly partly due to the unexpected elongation (this is the first Renaissance bust complete with arms and hands) : cut off at the usual height, half-way between shoulder and elbow, the portrait would lose immeasurably in impact.

In this same room, I hear the same American explaining to his wife that they are looking at a portrait of Antonio del Poll-ai-o-lo by Giovane Guerriero. A red-faced, bespectacled Briton carrying a plastic bag glowers at Benedetto da Maiano's weathered relief of the *Coronation of Ferdinando of Aragon*. How *can* he screw up his face so at those six divine boy musicians? And who could ever bring himself to part with such treasure (it came here from London in 1900)? If it were mine, war would not wrest it from me. But the reason for these migrations is nearly always the same.

In the heaving street below I contemplate once again the yawning gap between art and life. After such deep draughts of the rarefied air of beauty, I find the city bristles with ugliness, the air positively stifles. Yet *there* is a face that might be lovely, if the brow were broader; and there is a splendid torso, shoulders moulded for a sculptor, deep-chested and tapering – if only the thighs were longer! And crossing the road is a glorious female figure, tall and proudly athletic, with the proportions a painter dreams of! But the face is cheap as a slab of lard.

How can one bridge this gulf between the ideal and the real without experiencing a cold shock of loss and disappointment? Can the artistic temperament ever expect more than frustration, more than passing happiness – the brush of a wing? What sort of life can a perfectionist hope for if he sees people merely as beautiful eyes, or cheekbones, or gastrocnemii or pectorals? The dangers are all too plain. But how could a Menelaus, having possessed his Helen, ever be content with plain, household Kate?

I have to get away. The heat, the crowds, life on the plain. . . . Fiesole has always been a refuge: a twopenny-halfpenny bus ride to an enchanted hilltop that ought to have been the acropolis of Florence, but from which, according to legend, the men came down to found *Fiorentia*, City of Flowers. Traditionally it was Caesar who destroyed *Faesulae* and founded Florence (in 59 BC) on the plain beneath with a mixture of Romans and Fiesolans to guard the crossing of the Arno. Indeed, much of Florence was built of stone from Fiesole.

When was it I shared a freshly made *pizza* (no knives, no napkins) in the theatre there, a *pizza* piled with ham and olives and mushrooms and a scalding square foot of cheese that came apart in long yellow strings? She was my Beatrice, I thought, and Florence lay spread below us that day like a mirage of the promised land. I thought: Can anyone be so lucky? And it *was* a mirage.

Next year, I sat alone in one of the restaurants lining the piazza and watched two lovers at the table opposite. They almost blurred into each other: they could hardly eat. I had an excellent *cotoletta*, a green salad with something bitter in it, and a bottle of chilled Verdicchio. It was a wretched hour. Glassy-eyed I sat and chewed at my food. Theirs was a country Virgil knew, and Dante too; and I had been there once. Their self-absorption was torture.

I planned to distract myself: a visit to the strange congeries of *orientalia* in S. Francesco, perhaps, or the hill-walk to Maiano – anything to break the rhythm of recall. But instead, I perched on the wall overlooking the drab Carabinieri monument and was drawn spellbound to another couple, who flirted and feinted and toyed with each other to the very limits of propriety on the grass below. He was leather-jacketed, close-cropped and curly; she was form one of the *gelaterie* nearby, I think. Their tryst lasted one hour to the minute. At first resisting, but not forbidding, she gradually became slack and, finally, frankly compliant. His restraint and finesse, her planned, disingenuous reluctance, somehow fell short of cynical: I thought them beautiful.

When the klaxon sounded, they broke from their trance in a second and went in different directions without a word of farewell. They seemed like actors in a film: back home they went later to write letters, no doubt, pay bills, cook the evening meal. And I watched night come down and all the scattered stars of night. But no star came down to me.

Today I shall buy a *pizza*, perhaps, enjoy the air, peer over the wall of Villa Mirabello, and amble down the Via Vecchia to S. Domenico. These occasions are always therapeutic: walking is pleasurable, and the laying of ghosts is wholesome. Exercise and exorcise.

There are two splendid works of Mino's to see in the Cathedral of S. Romolo: the tomb of Leonardo Salutati (1465), and a heavenly altar frontal, both in the Cappella Salutati to the right of the lovely raised choir. One of Mino's *putti*, I notice, has been worn to a white dazzle by adoring tourists, but today the gates are closed and photography is thwarted by the ironwork and heavy gloom.

I shall not climb to old S. Alessandro to see the Roman pillars and capitals, and the Mannerist frescoes in the Oratio dell'Assunta, nor even the priest's little garden to the side, so quiet and lovingly tended. There is the prickle of numinousness all about the place: the church was built, I read, on the site of an Etruscan temple. And little S. Francesco will wait for another time. I love the charming little cloister, ablaze with geraniums, the tiny cells where once the monks lived out their lives. Who can ever forget the cell of S. Bernardino, so rude and bare, its trestle table and chair and hard wooden bed, and deeply recessed window lunette? These days, very properly, its door is locked: initials must be carved elsewhere.

The road winds steeply from the summit down to the ledge just beyond Villa Medici. A delicious breeze lifts itself and the vista is strangely clear. Below the retaining wall an orchard slopes away, of olives, apricots, wild cherries, peaches; fennel, thyme, *nepitella* and other aromatic herbs grow in wild profusion. S. Miniato gleams high and far away, and beneath it the glinting strip of the Piazzale. I see the green dome of the Synagogue, the façade of S. Croce; the Duomo, S. Lorenzo, the Mercato Centrale; S. Domenico and the old Badia below; and right, a seething Via Bolognese. And I can just make out the tower of the Bargello. Was I *there*? Am I now *here*?

In the garden of Villa Medici grow tall, stately trees, and the wall presents a stark front to the outside world. Michelozzo built it on the site of a Bardi villa for Cosimo Il Vecchio, founder of the great Medicean dynasty; the Platonic Academy would often meet here under Lorenzo, and from here gallop off to hunt in the Mugello. The villa is a determinedly private place. Landino here wrote his commentaries on Dante; Poliziano composed his *Rusticus*; and the Pazzi, in 1478, originally came here to murder Lorenzo and Giuliano at a party. (As everyone knows, the murder attempt was postponed to the next day: this was because Giuliano had a sudden attack of gout.) The sister-in-law of Robert Walpole, Earl of Orford (Lady Orford, a lady of doubtful reputation but sound taste), bought the villa in the eighteenth century; and Dame Iris Origo spent her childhood here. The place is crowded with memories and associations. The costs of building the foundations, Vasari tells us, were high; but the situation is magnificent, and the views unrivalled.

Opposite, on the rocky soil of the sheer hillside are bright dahlias and bay trees, and lemons trained in large earthenware pots, snapdragons, lilac, mallow shrubs, valerian, acacia saplings, grey-green eucalyptus and lavender and tansy, a confusion of heady scents and summer colours. Just where the lane veers sharply left, at no. 28, is Villa Mirabello, its gate boarded up, and the high, eroded ivy-clad walls that slope to it are covered in vines, old man's beard, and the dusty banks thick with wild garlic and evening primroses.

A slight dip in the circumvallation to the right of the villa itself affords a partial view of the garden. How happy I was here! I lived in a dream: peaches, apricots, plums, figs and greengages fell warm into the hand, and there were persimmon trees (*diosperi*), too, a delightful, unfamiliar sight, which would yield their strange, orange fruit later in the year. In one of the sudden shaded arbours, overlooking acres of grey-silver, gnarled and knotted olives, I would breakfast, in another lunch. The eye was everywhere ravished, the senses reeled. During the day there were giant bamboos to read under; in the evening there were glow-worms, fireflies for light.

And, perched on the hillside as it is, the villa enjoys miraculous views. This was the home of Harold Goad, Director of the British Institute during the difficult years of Fascism, and from his richly-stocked library and high tower-top, the panorama is simply heart-stopping, whether half hidden in the morning mist, or naked, offering all its treasures to a burnished sky. The Badia is directly below; then Florence spreads far as the eye can see from east to west, the hills blue grey in the shimmering distance. And everywhere on the hillside, villas jagged with cypresses, a thousand crenellated high square walls, look grandly down on the suburbs of the city. The vista here is one of unbroken, Olympian beauty.

As I move on down the hill, the road becomes an alley, tiny and thread-like, precipitous and deadly. Wistaria, elder and blue-green firs crowd the crumbling, lichen-crusted walls, and occasionally the lovely lilac-pink of *lagerstroemia* shows itself through a gateway. (This is 'crape myrtle' originally Chinese.) On the entrance to Villa Stefanelli someone has scrawled 'ITALIANS ARE BASE', and from Villa Le Tre Pulzelle smells of hot olive oil, peppers and garlic float to drown even the heady fragrance of wistaria. Next come Villa Nieuwenkamp (Riposo dei Vescovi), and Villa Papiniano, where the splattering of a hidden fountain tantalises, and I glimpse walls bare of stucco, and a sudden pillar with a Roman capital. Then, on the left, a gracious fountain built into the wall by Baccio Bandinelli in 1556 'at his own expense, for public and private use' (so the inscription runs); this was when Cosimo I was in power. Such gestures today are rarer. The lion's mouth vomits no more water, and the noble walls are plastered with adverts and graffiti and scraped and battered by car and scooter. Everywhere the sadness of exclusion assails me: from old, grand villas, each with its own proud history, villas standing in quietly shuttered privacy beyond high walls and prison-like gates; from old gardens matured over long centuries, and radiant statuary lurking between hedges of topiaried box. There is even a claustrophobic feeling to parts of Via Vecchia, down whose lower reaches one scrambles for what seems an eternity without the relief of a single window or unbarred gate, or even the promise of a turning. And, despite the wealth of beauty here, there is inevitably the sadness of glory departed: the scooters howl, the private palace has become a municipal madhouse. The Comune reigns.

In the footsteps of Galileo and Leonardo and Cosimo I tramp finally into the light of S. Domenico, and sit to await the bus. Opposite, a plaque on the wall commemorates two of the convent's greatest names: S. Antonino, later Archbishop of Florence, and Fra Giovanni da Fiesole, called 'Beato Angelico'. The church here provided me recently with one of my proudest moments.

Many years ago, perhaps on my first visit to S. Domenico, I was studying an altarpiece at the east end of the church when I suddenly started, and looked up to see (I *thought* I saw) a figure sitting alone in the dark choir. It was a black-garbed monk, his head shaven to a rime of white stubble, face cadaverous, ascetic, immobile, except for the slight, almost imperceptible twitching of his lips as he told his beads. I saw his eyes were wild; they were points of fire, and they were focussed (no doubt about it) on me. Horrified, I watched him rise: he floated over the pavement towards me, and I ran.

Years later, standing in a side chapel, I turned on some impulse to see the mad monk hovering again. This time he was in white, a ghost in the half light, and, quite unmistakably, he was smiling. Over the floor his steps made no sound at all.

'*Buona sera, Padre,*' I croaked.

He took me gently by the arm, showed me a crucifix by Brunelleschi, then surprised me in the sacristy by asking, '*È padre anche Lei?*' It was a mistake no one had made before, and which no one has made since. 'Are you a priest, too?' I think I half fainted with pleasure.

In the chapter house of the convent is a glorious fresco of the *Crucifixion* by Fra Angelico, and a lovely *Madonna and Child*; and from the *loggia* there are wonderful views of private villas and their gardens, all of them with romantic names and famous connections, while in the convent gardens happy cats fight and sleep and mate among the shrubs and vegetables. S. Domenico has a great and glorious past. Now there is only one Mass a day. The congregation is small. Most tourists drive past to Fiesole. A few stop off, the monks tell me, but only to see 'the Fra Angelico'. This is now the altarpiece of the first chapel of the north aisle, a lovely *Madonna with Angels and Saints*, which originally stood on the High Altar of the church. But it is hardly as the artist intended it. The saints were added later by Rossello di Jacopo Franchi, and the background was repainted by Lorenzo di Credi when a new frame

271

was fitted. The predella paintings are modern copies. The original five panels are in our National Gallery, and they constitute by far the most distinguished hagiographical picture it possesses. It is difficult to imagine what the whole work must have looked like when the saint finally laid aside his brush. By 1610 it had lost its pride of place over the High Altar, suffered additions and other alterations; and, long before 1827, it was acquired by the Prussian Consul at Rome, a man called Valentini. Finally it passed from the consul's nephew to the egregiously named Aeneas Macbean, who sold it to the National Gallery in 1860.

What the saint painted for God, man has overpainted, reframed and finally dismembered. What was intended to glow on the High Altar of a convent in Tuscany is displayed currently, along with a dozen other brightly coloured treasures, all of them plunder, in the stuffy, artificially lit bowels of a northern museum.

Such, I suppose, are the vagaries of fortune.

CHAPTER

XII

Nine a.m., Via Faenza 42. I stand at the door and knock. I ring hard and insistently. What excuse will he have this time, the fat man with the silver teeth?

The Cenacolo di Foligno was once the convent of S. Onofrio, and the *Ultima Cena* on the far wall of the refectory was unknown to the world until 1845, after the suppression of the Convent. S. Onofrio (St Humphrey) was a fourth–fifth-century hermit of the Egyptian desert, who lived naked except for a girdle of prickly vines, and whose reputation for asceticism spread to the most distant parts of Christendom. Onofrio was for some reason the patron saint of the dyers, who once a year staged a horse-race down the Corso de' Tintori in his honour.

The door opens. A woman with a pleasant, worn appearance eyes me warily. The custodian is out. (My heart sinks.) But she had been expecting me. (It revives.) She wipes her hands on her apron, closes the door carefully behind us, and beckons me into the large hall.

It has been worth the struggle. Suddenly, after all these years, I am in the vast refectory, among supine crucifixes, boxes of paints and bottles of varnish, and monumental, soot-black canvases spread on scaffolding, each being restored inch by inch to a brilliant clarity. Via Faenza was at the northern extremity of the 1966 flood, but even here the water reached a height of 1½ metres.

'The restorers', she explains, 'are on holiday. Everyone is on holiday.' She feels she must stay, but clearly wants to go back to her onion-peeling. I cling defiantly to my camera (flash attachment concealed in *borsetto*) and slowly advance to the far wall. After a few moments of silence, I hear her mutter at my back, and she withdraws. I stand knee-deep and shoulder-high in precious things. The hall is full of interrupted work: the tense excitement of restoration hangs suspended in the air. To my right – there, I caress it – a life-size, prone crucifix of superlative quality; the gilded quatrefoil halo, the blood streaming from the Saviour's side, the fine dark hair and beard, the subtle flesh-tones, eyes clenched in death, the loin-cloth and musculature and beautiful undulations of the rib cage all perfection. Giant nails driven through the passive hands stand four inches clear. Where does it belong? Where will it go? It is a masterwork and it lies here, raised on a trestle two feet from the ground and surrounded with brushes and rags and sponges. Shall I come upon it one day and remember this moment? I take half a dozen photographs: I shall never be so near again!

In this light the *Last Supper* (a lunette surrounded by a frieze containing five heads of saints) simply glows, self-evidently sublime. It was at first thought to be the work of Neri di Bicci, then, when an inscription on St Thomas's robe was discovered, of Raphael: but it is now established as a masterpiece of Perugino, dated *c.* 1493–6.

The iconography is that of Andrea del Castagno and Ghirlandaio. The disciples, who are named on the dais below, are seated at the familiar long table with two foreshortened wings; in their centre is Christ, with John asleep in his bosom; and Judas sits alone on a stool this side of the table, turning to stare out of the picture rather shiftily at the observer, and clutching his bag of silver below the table. He is dark-haired, but red-bearded, with a strong, troubled face, and he alone, conventionally, wears no glory. From left to right the disciples are identified as: St James (the Greater), a ravishing, beardless youth of epicene appearance, looking out of the picture frame (this was originally presumed to be a self-portrait of Raphael); St Philip, in profile, with a white beard; St James the Less, red-bearded, looking very like Christ; St Andrew, with a long, grey, divided beard; St Peter, bald, gazing thoughtfully across the table at Judas; then Christ, whose right hand is raised in benediction, and whose left hand rests on the sleeping, beardless John (John has a wonderful face and hair a pre-Raphaelite red). To Christ's left are St Bartholomew, with a red-brown beard, delicately wielding anachronistic knife and fork; St Matthew, knife in hand, and bald, with white beard, a sad, rather refined figure; St Thomas, who concentrates on pouring himself a glass of wine (a youthful character, with long fair hair, he is plainly thinking his own thoughts); and finally SS. Simon and Thaddeus (= Jude) on the extreme right, both young men, one in profile, one three-quarters face.

The geometric design on the floor, and the foreshortened wings of the table pull the eye into the centre of the drama and lend an illusion of depth. Behind the long, gorgeously decorated *bancone* at which the disciples are seated, and beyond a receding series of elaborate classical arcades, a typically radiant landscape, luminous and dreamy, extends; a country of pale greens and blues, and low hills undulating for miles beneath an apocalyptic sky. (This is strongly reminiscent of the *Crucifix* in S. Maria Maddalena dei Pazzi: the landscape and some of the heads are very close in style and coloration.) Through the central arch of the portico, Jesus kneels in solitary prayer, while above him an angel, hovering, offers him the bitter cup; and, behind, three of his followers sleep beneath flimsy, delicate trees. This is one of the hidden treasures of Florence. I balance precariously on a wonky chair and take a dozen pictures in the gloom.

I have been here an hour or more, and, hearing a cough, I turn to find the fat custodian watching me from the doorway. He wants his lunch.

There are other interesting *Last Suppers* in Florence. Franciabigio (1482–1525), who collaborated with del Sarto at the Annunziata and the Chiostro dello Scalzo, painted a fine *Ultima Cena* for the Frati Ingesuati (suppressed in the seventeenth century) of S. Giovanni della Calza at the corner of Via Romana and Via de' Serragli. (The name *'calza'* refers to the white, sock-like hood worn by the Frati.) The church of S. Giovanni was founded in the fourteenth century: today there is a convent of nuns who run an old ladies' home. To gain admission one rings the bell at no. 6 and *insists*. The *Cenacolo* is closed, but the fresco must be seen.

On my first visit, I had to conduct a lengthy, courteous argument with a lady concierge through a medieval grille, until finally, triumphantly, I won the longed-for *'Aspetti'*. ('Wait.') As I waited, I heard the twittering confabulation of dotty old dears float out from the fourteenth-century cloisters to mingle with the traffic din. Then a delightful, smiling, polyglot nun with black incisors escorted me to the refectory and showed me what I had come to see. Franciabigio, she confirmed, yes; but she insisted the fresco was of the *trecento*.

It has been detached, not before time: even so the surface colour is not in the best condition. The fresco covers all of one wall, and the artist has chosen to depict the imagined moment when Jesus says portentously: 'One of you will betray me.' Each saint is named and haloed, his robes highlighted with gold. John sleeps on Christ's left (as in Castagno's version); Judas, sitting as usual this side of the table, is caught in the act of rising from his stool, which topples back as he moves – a nice touch of realism. Behind SS. Philip and Simon, to the right, a deeply recessed window gives onto a typical city street, and two doves perch on the window ledge.

There is a swirl of drapery and a drama of movement (the disciples gesticulate; they lean towards each other, rising, creating carefully balanced tensions) which is strongly reminiscent of Leonardo's famous *Last Supper* (1495–97) in S. Maria delle Grazie, Milan. Now according to Vasari, Franciabigio never left Florence, where he died young, aged 42 or 43: the young artist, we are told, had seen some of Raphael's work, and, realising he was no match, refused to compete with him. It is a typical Vasari-tale, and one on which the external evidence casts doubt. Had Franciabigio seen copies of Leonardo's and Raphael's work, or did he in fact visit Rome? Whatever his inspiration, the device of using antithetical figures at each end, and arranging the rest in a frieze, became popular. Del Sarto's *Last Supper* at San Salvi (begun in 1520); the much repainted version, now attributed to Ridolfo del Ghirlandaio (1543), in S. Maria degli Angeli (a straight and feeble copy with additional figures); and Allori's later Mannerist reworking in the Carmine (1581–2) all adopt the scheme. The power and emotional intensity of the fresco in the Convento della Calza is of a high order, but Franciabigio is no Leonardo or del Sarto, and the drama of his composition is too great for his powers as a painter to sustain. No one could doubt its sincerity, but there is a certain crudeness in the strength of this work.

Having remembered S. Salvi, I must go there. After long years of restoration, it is now re-opened, and has become the del Sarto Museum. From the Cenacolo di Foligno to San Salvi is a very proper walk: the sun is climbing and the streets around S. Lorenzo are beginning to fill. Mentally I map out a route that will dodge the worst of the crushes. It should take no more than forty minutes.

In the flea-market at Piazza dei Ciompi I find the armless *St Anthony* gone, the noseless bust of *The Redeemer* still there (and still much too dear), and a new *St Francis*, half life-size, an Umbrian work carved in dark and worm-eaten walnut whose price I dare not even ask. The paint has flaked and faded, so that the wood is almost bare, and on the saint's head the grain has sprung apart like an axe wound or a grin. But the one who grins most is the proprietor, whose gold-rimmed spectacles glint in the sun as he smokes a fragrant cigar.

At Piazza Alberti all the traffic of the world must meet once every day, and crossing the bridge into Via Lungo L'Affrico by the narrow sidewalk can be unnerving. This quarter, of the gigantic Campo di Marte, the Olympic swimming pool, and the psychiatric hospital, is suburban and ugly, but after the screaming piazza and the teeming bridge (one turns right into Via Speri and right again into the Via di S. Salvi) the Cenacolo seems to sleep in deathly quiet. How many times I have made the pilgrimage in vain! How many times trudged along Via Gioberti over the bridge and down the little street to find the iron gates at no. 16 shut fast, and a blue-shirted custodian horizontal in the lovely garden!

'*Scusi.*'

One eye opens.

'*Mi scusi, mi dispiace disturbarla. Io sono un scrittore inglese e sono qui per scrivere un libro su Firenze. Etc. Etc.*'

'*Chiuso.*' The eye closes again.

'*Ho fatto più di mille chilometri per vedere questo capolavoro, etc.*'

'*Chiuso*' (sleepily).

Would he not open the door just a little so that I could peep in?

'*Le sarei molto grato se volesse gentilmente farmi entrare.*' Just for a *second*?

He has no keys. The restorers have them. They are all away. On holiday. (He rouses himself to mime an 'away on holiday' movement.) *Ferragosto. Chiuso.*

But when can I see the famous fresco?

A motionless shrug. Next year maybe. Or the next? Soon.

So I would make do with old S. Michele next door, bare of most of its old glories, but worth visiting for its pretty cloisters and their charming painted vaulting. The courtyard is neglected these days, but still glossy with bay trees growing as they will.

But Lisa was right. The gate may still be locked, and the same tubby blue-shirt may be lounging in the same striped deckchair, and when I ask, '*Mi scusi. È aperto il Cenacolo?*' he may not bat an eyelid. But the answer, when, after an age of waiting, it comes, is '*Sì*', and there is a sudden click and whirr, and I push the heavy gate back. Another custodian waits inside to relieve me of my money.

And it was worth a much longer wait, a far longer walk.

The *Last Supper* is del Sarto's masterpiece, his largest creation, and it dominates the whole east end of this imposing *Cenacolo* in a huge semicircle – a brilliant composition in terms of colour and movement and psychology. Below, and on either side, are arranged other of del Sarto's works, including fascinating (naked) studies for the figures in the *Ultima Cena*, all of which reveal superb draughtsmanship. The feet and hands, in particular, are masterly.

This was Andrea's last work. A rich Vallombrosan named Ilario Panichi had commissioned him, in June of 1511, to paint a *Last Supper* for the monks of S. Salvi, and Andrea began immediately by painting the underside of the arch in which the lunette is recessed with a curious *tondo* of the Trinity (in effect, a three-faced Jesus set in a halo of glory against a cloud-dappled sky), and, either side, the four patron saints of the Vallombrosan Order: S. Giovanni Gualberto, S. Salvi, S. Benedetto (whose rules the Vallombrosans adopted), and S. Bernardo degli Uberti (first abbot of the convent here). These are done in *tondi* among extremely fine *grotteschi* and, surrounded as they are in space, by the inspired use of colour and clever psychological characterisation, even these seem to come to life.

But thereafter, for various reasons, work was suspended, and the fresco was not finally finished until 1526–7. In all, it took 66 days – an interesting indication of the speed at which a fresco painter worked. It is the greatest *Ultima Cena* in Florence, and one of the most impressive sights of all: a spectacular treatment of immense dramatic intensity and virtuosity which springs upon the eyes and imprints itself indelibly on the imagination. Benedetto Varchi, the historian and friend of Michelangelo, considered it 'one of the most beautiful paintings in the universe'. Vasari enthused wildly, and indeed, it was celebrated in the artist's own day.

Varchi tells the famous story that when Florence was under siege in 1529, and troops were sent to demolish the convent so that its buildings could not shelter the enemy, coming suddenly face to face with del Sarto's fresco, they were dumbstruck, 'as if they had lost the use of their arms and tongues; they stopped their vandalism and refused to continue.'

The fresco is set in a quite deeply recessed lunette, and, by means of perspective, itself creates the impression of recession: we see the familiar long table in the upper room, and, above the back wall, three windows lead the eye out to a *loggia* and the distant sky. So the Vallombrosan monks at their meals would have been on the lower tier of a two-level refectory: the abbot and his community beneath Jesus and his disciples, who seem to sit at supper on a dais above them. High Table and Low Table, as it were.

Jesus and the disciples are seated at a table covered in a white tablecloth: the extreme agitation of the disciples grouped either side of him (each is posed differently, each exhibits a different shade of emotion) contrasts superbly with the tranquillity of Christ. The heads form a beautifully rhythmic wave whose centre of deep calm is Christ. The colours, a gorgeous palette of violent greens and roses and bright yellow ochre, are carefully balanced, and above, through a *loggia*, a sweet sky of pale blue streaked with strata of white and dull crimson provides a perfect resolution of the tense scene unfolding below.

'*In verità, in verità vi dico,*' Christ is saying: 'In truth I tell you, one of you will betray me.' And John, earnest and beautiful (and not, for once, asleep) asks: '*Signore, chi è?*' Judas is the blackbeard immediately (and unusually) to the right of Christ, to whom he is offering the *pane intinto*. Only in Leonardo's, of earlier versions, can this seating arrangement be paralleled: there, Judas is a grim blackbeard seated to the right of Christ, and starts back from him at a sharp angle, his face in shadow, a picture of conscious guilt.

None of the figures is haloed: the painting is a study in psychology, and there is an understatement of emotion here which is very telling. All the disciples are beautifully drawn: rebellious, uncomprehending, fearful, meditative, shocked – they exhibit every shade of emotion.

To grasp something of del Sarto's artistry one need only contrast the fussy, intrusive detail and feeble attitudes of the disciples in Allori's adaptation in the Carmine. The right half of this fresco is a virtual copy, even down to details of posture and colour. The two recumbent cats are purest whimsy (Ghirlandaio's S. Marco version ran to only one), and the wisps of greenery seen through the windows seem almost cynically perfunctory.

In the central arch above the upper room del Sarto has placed two intriguing figures. One is a man, hatted, and wearing an orange jerkin, who leans casually on the stone ledge above Jesus; he glances at a second figure carrying a platter, who turns, as if in conversation with him. Who *are* these people? Are they really no more than servants, two supernumeraries introduced to balance an otherwise bottom-heavy composition, like the fruit trees and birds of Ghirlandaio, and Perugino's 'Agony in the Garden' scene?

Or is it just possible they are portraits?

The shops in Via Gioberti are approaching the siesta. I gaze in the window of 'La Conchiglia', a sparkling and attractive fish restaurant, and decide to treat myself to a visit, when it comes to me with a sudden jolt that tomorrow I shall be gone from here. And tonight I am bidden to my own last supper with Lisa and Lapo. The seconds tick past like little gongs of doom. At home the lawn will be knee-high, lush and rain-fed; perhaps the industrious mole, last summer's visitant, will have returned. If there has been any sun the geraniums and herbs will have died of thirst, the grass will be scorched and dead. On the coconut matting a tide of brown manilla envelopes, all sinisterly fenestrated, will be clamouring for attention. For up to three hours the answerphone will dispense nonsense and frustration. Old flames desperate for romantic reunions will have passed by and dropped fragrant notelets through my letterbox. The pilot light of the boiler will prove unignitable: the car will refuse to start.

Distracted and glum I amble on until the city swallows me. I have half a mind to take a smooth, bouncy coach ride to Viareggio or Forte dei Marmi through oleanders and vines and terraced olives, through a million giant sunflowers, brown, green, gaudy yellow, like little suns, heads averted and drooping, swivelling almost visibly as the coach swishes past. The trip would be worthwhile for the sunflowers alone, and they stretch for miles and miles. A dozen days on the beach, all the same, flash through my head: in the distance the bells ring, but the whole world is *sulla spiaggia*, the sands white

279

and clean against their chocolate bodies. No one swims. Families sit and smoke and play cards and sing. Negroes tout their wares; windsurfers, canoeists, paddleboaters pepper the joyful blue. To north and east the mountains are smudges: pine woods stretch away from behind the coastal strip north and south as far as the foothills. An occasional *'No!'* on a sharply descending note (prohibition), or *'Ah!'* on an ascending note (sudden perception), husky and vulgar, puncture the tranquillity. There is a sense of fun being taken seriously, almost reverently.

But I find myself again in the covered market at S. Ambrogio, sitting at a bar opposite a toothless octogenarian with a white fuzz of stubble for hair. He is eating *bollito misto* with his hands, and rivulets of fat stream from either corner of his mouth; his eyes are slits, his face like a brown prune; I notice the blunt, arthritic fingers, the grimy spatulate nails. He wears a chalk-blue teeshirt and zipless jeans and trainers from which dirty toes protrude. The logo on his teeshirt reads: MOOSE JAW DOWNS 8TH ANNUAL LOG-CHOPPING.

Bocconcini are on the menu today, and the happy little moustachioed chef piles veal and bacon and cheese on my plate: an intoxicating aroma of sage hovers in the air. *Zucchini* with tomato and garlic come next. I eat in a fever because I know that, unless I plan my remaining hours carefully, I shall drift and fritter them away to nothing.

In my pocket there is a single *gettone*. 'You must look me up,' he said when I bumped into him that day at the Savile Club. *Dare* I? I drink a couple of plastic cupfuls of wine. In any case, he is unlikely to be in. He will be at the seaside, surely. Everyone is.

There is the number, clear as day. And after a short exchange with a man-servant, I hear the old, familiar voice again, unfashionably precise, mannered, neither English nor Italian, but unmistakably from another, more elegant age. And, bless him, he remembers me (I mention the name of a mutual acquaintance) and says he will be pleased to see me! The bus stops right outside, he tells me: Via Bolognese 120.

Villa La Pietra, amazingly, is only ten minutes' ride from S. Marco. (I am taken there by a lady bus driver with a flamboyant magenta lily in her hair.) La Pietra stands at the end of a long avenue lined with cypresses and statuary, and the approach is stately and intimidating: lions atop the pillars of the gateway positively glower. An aged, white-jacketed and white-gloved retainer is waiting at the main door and shows me past a fountain into the dark and cool interior. There is a slightly nostalgic whiff of soot. For a minute, I take in the flower-filled table, the signed photographs of English Royalty, the precious pieces of furniture that stand about the room.

But very soon my host enters, stage right, on a stick; a large-boned, vital and imposing figure even in old age. Dressed in a dark suit he is embarrassingly elegant, but his smile is ready and winning; he is effortlessly charming. Sir Harold Acton has style.

We speak of Iris Origo, of other friends, of the Savile (where he remembers Yeats), of tourism and vandalism (after a string of burglaries, La Pietra is now closed to the public), and English life and letters. Sir Harold is eloquent in his admiration of Berenson and vouches for his 'impeccable integrity'. Kenneth Clark is left hanging rather awkwardly in mid-air . . . Sir Harold adores the *Daily Telegraph*, he says. Mainly, we gossip.

Constantly I am struck by his careful enunciation, his great precision with words, the way he lingers on the odd vowel, caresses the odd consonant. The only overtly flamboyant touch now is a large signet ring with a dark green gemstone, which he wears on the fourth finger of his left hand. But is this the living legend who made 'Oxford Bags' the rage; who belonged to the 'Hypocrites' and the 'Railway Club' in their headiest days, and outraged provincial Oxford with his cosmopolitan worldliness? Was this stooping figure the young gallant who kindled so many flames in 'Elgin marble breasts', who revelled in gentle struggles, in showers of burning kisses and ecstasies on the Thames, who set the tables abuzz with his exquisite talk and manners at Fothergill's 'Spread Eagle'?

Sir Harold shows me a particularly good Vasari, and a hundred other lovely rarities collected by his father; then the lovely *limonaio* and the sloping, terraced garden, its immaculate, topiaried box hedges, and moss-encrusted statuary, crumbling now and in places bare to the armature; the flower-filled stone urns and fountains, the stone arches and benches and licheny colonnades and balustrades and dreamy umbrella pines. At its lower extremity I see an entrancing little theatre just made for a masque, a *Comus* maybe, or even a *Tempest* or *Winter's Tale*, on an early summer evening. It hangs poised over Florence, which here spreads out at an unaccustomed angle, immensely photogenic. The air shimmers and foreshortens, so that the city seems offered: it seems so near you feel you can reach out and touch it; one could actually lean and grasp the Duomo! The garden is paradise. Typically 'Italianate', formally laid out, and elegantly symmetrical, it was in fact made by Sir Harold's father from what had been a rather wild *'giardino inglese'*. But the Actons are of Italian stock originally: Sir Harold's relatives are Neapolitan as well as American.

The estate (and those of his other villas, all crammed with antiques) suffered terribly in the war from Fascist looting, German shelling and casual vandalism. The loss almost unhinged Arthur, Sir Harold's father. Not only the fabric of the villa – roofs and window, trees and statuary – had taken a battering from mines and shells, but SS troops had heartlessly smashed furniture and used precious pictures for target-practice. Here the trees and hedges were hacked down for firewood; the two family cars, of course, had been stolen. (At least the Tuscan Primitives were intact.) Many of the garden statues were shattered; some, in a strange aping of the Mutilation of the Hermae, that extraordinary episode in the days leading to the disastrous Sicilian Expedition in 415 BC, had lost their genitals – an amusing and edifying little *jeu d'esprit*.

Sir Harold regards himself merely as the privileged custodian of La Pietra and its treasures. The villa, which belonged first to the Sassetti, then the Capponi, will finally pass, with as much money as he can leave for its upkeep, to New York University. It was offered first to Oxford, who were non-plussed by the whole idea. 'It seemed,' he tells me, 'beyond their experience.' So America acquires, and England loses, yet another treasure.

Despite his glittering days at Oxford, England was never home: Sir Harold was born here. As unpaid British Ambassador, he has known everyone: the whole world has beat its way up that long, cypress-lined avenue. He wears his years well. 'Up here,' he confides, 'life is very *quiet*. There are,' he adds, with the merest suspicion of a twinkle, 'no *temptations*.'

And I remember that tomorrow I shall be 'home' again, and that once the villa is in the hands of a foreign university, like I Tatti, it may become virtually inaccessible. Mentally I photograph the rooms and the garden, fiercely willing them to stay with me. And as I take my leave reluctantly of this kindly, endearing man ('Oh, I write just *reviews* and *prefaces* now, you know; very *boring*, nothing *original*!') I feel a dark foreboding. All the long walk back to the gate, I sense that I may not return.

We had both spoken of our love for S. Miniato, and, with typical thoughtfulness, Sir Harold had rung his friend, the abbot, to ask if he would see me. He had just returned from ecumenical business in England, but my appointment is set for 5.00 p.m., and, after all the earlier restlessness and gloomy misgivings, the day has turned quite unexpectedly to gold. It is as if some benevolent providence has taken over and ordered my final hours for the best.

I am late: not this time having committed the cardinal error of waiting, more and more crossly, for the bus on the wrong side of the road; but having stupidly walked a bridge too far east and found no buses to save me the climb. So I sprint the hill and arrive carnation-coloured.

The *Abate*, a gentle Aretine called Vittorino Aldinucci, opens the door in person and gives me a smile showing two rows of healthy, crooked teeth. All about him is coolness and peace: he moves with a graceful economy of effort that makes me feel hot and clumsy. He smiles often and loves to laugh, but just beneath the surface is *gravitas*, strength, resilience. This little

San Miniato

man in white is the famous ecumenist, a charming, worldly monk, and one of the few Italian saints I know with good English. He has just returned from St Albans, he tells me. Yes, yes, he says, the Revival *will* come. Yes, women priests *are* an obstacle. The *esprit large* shines about him like an aura.

He has been Abbot of S. Miniato now for twenty years, after serving his novitiate at Monte Oliveto, south-east of Siena, and studying at Louvain. The Benedictines pride themselves on their scholarship, their liturgy, and practice of contemplation. Today their rule is not the strictest: the abbot himself seems to set the liberal and ecumenical style of the place. Sanctuary is provided here for all sorts and conditions of Christians, and the monks have strong links with the Protestant Benedictines and Franciscans. Their lovely hall, with its beautifully painted open timber roof, is currently laid out in modern style for conferences. The abbot practically commutes to England.

The monastery was suppressed in the nineteenth century and revived early this century. Today there are only eighteen Brothers at S. Miniato. This is not a rich community, but it is one that survives. Outside, the hordes of tourists buzz and hum, but the ceilings are high and no noise or fret penetrates the Chiostro Monumentale. On the first floor here are frescoes by Uccello in *terra verde*, fragmentary now, and one, much better preserved (of course) by Buontalenti (1531–1608). These, discovered only in 1925, are the *Scenes from the Lives of the Holy Father* mentioned by Vasari, in which the artist threw convention overboard, and painted 'fields blue, cities red, and the buildings in any colours that took his fancy.' So it was a predecessor of this wise and liberal abbot (who lightly touches my elbow and points out here an olive press, there a neat pyramid of cannon balls from the siege of Florence) who, by feeding the great artist a diet almost exclusively of cheese, cheese pies, cheese soups, cheese everything, drove him away with the work still unfinished, terrified he would be used to make glue.

This abbot, like his fellow Aretine Vasari, loves a good story. He was recently in London for a bishop's enthronement, and, catching the Tube at 'Kingcross', he found himself wedged next to a man in suit and clerical collar. A gaunt figure, he was, with large, black-rimmed spectacles. They wished each other good day.

'You are a priest?' the little abbot enquired, guilelessly.

'Yes.' A guarded inclination of the head, a half smile.

'Roman Catholic?'

'Anglican.'

A pause. The abbot continued, 'I know many Anglican priests.'

'Oh yes?'

'Many bishops.'

The humble abbot had plainly engaged his companion's interest.

'Oh? Whom do you know?'

'Archbishop of Canterbury.'

'Really?'

'Oh yes! He is a friend.'

The gaunt stranger raised his eyebrows. 'Do you know . . . the Archbishop of York?'

'Not personally. But I see him at General Synod often. Many times.'

'General Synod?' The stranger was now intrigued. 'May I ask who you are?'

The abbot, no doubt with great humility, introduced himself.

'Do you go to Rome much?'

'Yes, yes, very often! I know . . . *come si chiama?* . . . Canon Root.'

Finally sure, the stranger said, 'Howard Root is a very dear friend of mine! Please give him my love when you see him next.'

'Of course! With pleasure! . . . And whom shall I say – ?'

The stranger smiled and held out his hand. 'John Habgood. Archbishop of York.'

The *Abate* ends his story with a delightful laugh, showing all his crooked teeth. '*Archbishop of York!*' he repeats to himself, 'Archbishop of York!' His eyes are brilliant with amusement. And he says the words with reverence, amazingly, as if the archbishop were one greater than he.

On another of his ecumenical jaunts he travelled to Southwark to see the installation of three bishops. Arriving on the day before the ceremony, he took the precaution of visiting the cathedral to get the feel of the place – only to be refused admission to the choir by a huffy and officious minion. The abbot neither insisted, nor told him who he was: he left. Next day (he tells me) dressed in full fig and walking side by side in glory with the great luminaries of the Anglican church as he processed up the aisle, he found himself struggling (and losing the struggle, he laughs) not to feel pleasure at the embarrassment of the cathedral myrmidons, whose faces, as they recognised the gentle little Italian, went a colour to rival the bishops' cassocks.

There are a few minutes before he has to say Mass, so he takes me on a short tour of the private sections of the monastery, and here I discover interesting and beautiful *sinopie*, detached frescoes, and what is surely a fragment of an *Ultima Cena*. A crypt, parallel with the crypt of the church, is in excellent repair: rows of comfortable modern chairs stand inches from old sherds and statuettes and the clearly visible eighth-century foundations of the original S. Miniato. Near an ancient olive mill is the manger used by the mule who turned the millstone. Outside, I know, is all the sultry, sticky heat of a late Florentine August; but here there is the freshness and sharp chill of timeless stone.

We move up to the chapter house (where the community meets for administrative purposes) and there through large, leaded windows is the most stupendous vista of the city, the best – better even than the view from the terrace, because more elevated. So much perfection of nature and man's making and in such perfect juxtaposition! (It is futile to choose between them: they are married.) I have seen nowhere its equal on earth. Prince Charles, the abbot tells me proudly, stood there entranced on his recent visit; he was spellbound: he looked and looked in silence, and finally asked a long string of questions. One can pick out almost every detail of Florence from here. 'Where is *that*?' he would ask, pointing. 'And that dome? Those trees? That hill?'

'And Princess Diana?' I asked him. 'She was here too?' They had been guests, I believe, at La Pietra.

'Yes, yes. She stood where you are standing now. Just there.' He smiled in answer to the unasked question. 'She didn't say much.'

Slowly, slowly the great windows are pushed to and the heavenly vision is shut out. I feel overwhelmed at the privilege of this sight: a view surely reserved for the gods, for the godly, and for visiting Royalty.

Finally, I am invited to sign the Visitors' Book, and there, not so many leaves from the Queen Mother or the Prince and Princess of Wales, or Sir Harold Acton, or President Mitterand, my own little name will be found. But it is time for Mass. As I shake hands at the door and receive a genial, sketched blessing, all the bells of Florence ring out across the early evening: soup plates, gongs, silvery shivers of sound. The whole city reverberates with bell-music, and my hot irritations and prickly annoyances seem all at once to evaporate. One brief acquaintance with a holy man has put all my frettings in perspective. The bells of stately *campanili*, of tiny S. Niccolò, of magnificent basilicas and tottering steeple din in my eardrums, they peal and deafen with their incessant calling. The sun is on my forehead, and the clatter of bells fills my head. Every bell in the world seems to be calling tonight. I move across the terrace hearing only them.

Mass tonight is a celebration. Gioia and Oreste are a handsome pair: he bearded and balding and natty in a chequered jacket; she glamorous, in a figure-hugging black dress, and clutching an elaborate bouquet of lilies festooned with yards of pink ribbon. They have been married a quarter of a century.

The little crypt, tomb of the dead saint, is packed with gaily dressed locals; there is a flurry of comings and goings, the clatter of high heels, the muttering of loonies, and the stage whispers of dutiful sons to deaf, superannuated mothers. Some stand, some kneel, some sit and converse. During Consecration a tubby monk wearing an off-white habit and pebble glasses moves among the congregation with a capacious wicker basket.

The familiar cantor is in evidence: he steps forward and conducts the congregation for all the plainsong, insisting on the most punctilious phrasing, dotting every *punctum* and *virga*, every *neuma* measured, every tiny *quilisma* observed to a nicety, his impatience at any unscheduled *rubato* or garbled *torculus resupinus* registered immediately on his gnarled old countenance, which is twisted into extraordinary shapes every so often by a mouth whose aperture is far to one side of his face and never quite o-shaped. With knotted hands he flaps his song book, and, to affect a decrescendo or to reach a high note, he screws his hairless face up into what appears to be a grimace of pain.

The celebrant's hands are a wonder of elegance, describing a series of graceful, practised arabesques in the air; his pause at the Elevation just so long, and no longer; and after the Distribution, after the superlatively ordered cleansing of the chalice and the last replacing of the paten, he turns to face the altar in silent adoration, and we sing (a tightly conducted) *Salve Regina*. The Mass is over.

The descent from Olympus for the 'real' world of telegrams and accountants and surcharges can be disconcerting; to step from the cold peace of S. Miniato down to the stifling heat and cacophony of the Arno is like the expulsion from Paradise: there is always that gnawing sense of loss. Yet today, on a low wall facing San Salvatore (Michelangelo's 'pretty little peasant girl'), a girl of distracting loveliness sits with her lover; she has long hair, and the wind tugs it this way and that; she is wearing a simple, black dress, elegantly plain, gold hoop earrings, and lipstick; her feet are bare; she has long legs, slender ankles, nut-brown skin, and at this moment, on this particular evening, I think no one could be more beautiful. The artists of Florence have drawn inspiration from the women, as the women of Florence have drawn inspiration from their art. Flaming, sculpted locks, Botticelli eyes, and Leonardo smiles are not so very rare in the city where beauty has found a home.

And today, the abbot seems to have lent me a measure of his own peace. Buoyantly I stride towards Via de' Bardi, and life seems somehow lighter than before. Nothing matters very much, it has been said; and most things don't matter at all.

Lapo is already home. He sits smoking, watching the television with a freshly showered look: his hair is neatly brushed back; his dapper moustache looks newly groomed. He has added an expensive new pipe to his collection (not to smoke, but to worship), and tonight I can tell from the slump of his body and the way his immaculate surgeon's fingers hold the cigarette, he will be relaxed and congenial.

In the kitchen I scan the local papers while Lisa bustles about. A performance of *Gianni Schicchi* by Puccini Giacomo is advertised; something is going on at Prato where Henry Moore's monstrous 'Square form with split' is on permanent display. There is a concert in Siena, a festival at San Gimignano, an exhibition in Volterra – all too late! 'Why not drive to Barga, in province of Lucca, where it is organised the Barga Opera Festival?' Too late!

For some reason Lisa is distracted.

'No way!' she keeps telling me. 'No way!'

I put the paper aside.

'After a heavy meal,' she says, chopping with fury, 'I get a huge request of blood *here*' (she gestures at her stomach) 'and what follows is brain anorexia. I shiver!'

Poor Lisa. Lapo bellows something at her over the cartoons on the television, and over the sound of her furious chopping Lisa shouts back. I think he calls her *'tesoro'*. Then the doorbell begins to ring. We are to be six.

A sad anaesthetist called Isabella arrives and sits smoking with watery, swollen eyes. When I am introduced, her hand is cold as death, her smile as thin and vaporous as a November sun. She is engrossed in some great sadness, and I feel stupid and intrusive.

There are more new faces: Paolo, a surgeon friend of Lapo, tall for an Italian, and with a noble profile; and his washed-out English wife Brenda, who comes from Brighton, but has gone determinedly native, and regards Tuscany now as a private possession. Her Italian is exaggeratedly fluent, it is triumphantly idiomatic. When he hears I have been party to one of Lapo's detached retinas, Paolo charmingly and quietly engages me in small-talk. He invites me to watch complicated abdominal procedures at his own hospital.

Distracted again, I feel the minutes become hours, and all things at last gathering momentum, as if time were a fugue, and I were coming to a sudden monumental stretto, my legs swept from under me. The end of it all is in view: in a few hours I shall be at Galileo airport, Pisa. BA 529: 1530 hrs.

In the bosom of his family and friends Lapo is expansive; he lavishes his own idiosyncratic brand of *bonhommie* on the attentive company, especially on the two lady guests. The new pipe is handed round for admiration, then many more, each with its own story. The anaesthetist smiles wanly; Fiammetta, back early from Sardinia and coloured a deep brown, draws sulkily on a long slim cigarette, and argues with Lapo in her querulous, husky Florentine. She and her Milanese have parted company, Lisa hisses at me when the coast is momentarily clear. He was a brute: she is on tranquillisers. She is wearing sunglasses, but she also wears the familiar siren look. (Personally, I am quite safe. Like Lapo, Fiammetta is a xenophobe. At regular intervals in the conversation I hear *'inglese'* and *'inglesi'*, and always with the same withering inflection.) She addresses scarcely a word to me, but have I remembered to clear out the cat-tray, and to take rubbish out on Tuesdays and Fridays, and did Lorenzo call? Nor does she speak to the washed-out Brenda.

Brenda thrusts herself, however, with rapid colloquialisms and authentic Tuscan gestures, into the midst of the exchanges, determined to display her resilience and her utter mastery of the tongue. Paolo listens to her adoringly; Lapo makes a host's gallant replies and eyes Fiammetta. Lisa commutes between kitchen and long dining table with a series of delicious courses which briefly punctuate the smoking.

Little skewered birds (again), beaks pathetically wide open as if to utter their *novissima verba*, arrive flavoured with sage leaves and streaky bacon. These are followed by melting, creamy *tagliatelle*; then *peperoncini dolci* (a trencher piled high vanishes as if magicked away) and *piccioni arrosti* (stuffed with nutmeg, cinnamon, thyme, bay, and cooked in white wine) come on, like so many little parcelled bodies after some natural disaster. Lapo and Fiammetta fall on them like locusts. The anaesthetist, pale, but occasionally showing signs that she has been pretty, is forced for a moment to extinguish her cigarette; she tears weakly at a leg, toys with a glistening, stringy wing, then abandons her knife and fork and lights another cigarette.

Now and then Lisa catches my eye, and knowing me, sees right through. Fiammetta wants mineral water, *naturale*; the anaesthetist listlessly mixes mineral water with white wine. Paolo toasts me good-naturedly, and his wife turns from three words of curiously Italianate English to talk in even more rapid Tuscan. Lapo, having a watertight excuse, drinks recklessly. The English *always* drink with their meals!

Then, at the stroke of ten, just as the Old Bridge begins to warm to a roar, the doorbell rings again.

Who is it who so regularly transmutes the base metal of my life into something precious? The doorbell rings, and in one moment my evening is transformed. Up to now it has been ordinary, painful even. Now a young girl of eighteen strides into my life trailing clouds of glory; she monopolises my attention and compels my gaze until I am breathless and giddy. She is Fiorenza, the anaesthetist's daughter. She has called to collect the keys of her mother's car because she is going to a concert in the Cascine. Or somewhere, I don't know. I don't care.

Fiorenza is regal: her back straight as a poplar, her neck long as the Medici *Madonna*'s, and her face has exquisite, sweeping eyebrows that taper almost to a single hair; the cheekbones are chiselled to unusual prominence, and the jawline is utter perfection. Her skin is palest olive. She wears khaki trousers, a white blouse; her hair is tied in bunches, like the della Robbia *'ignota'* in the Bargello; thin wisps curl down over her ears. For jewellery she wears two single pearls in her ears – the supreme confidence of youth. Hands thrust deep in baggy pockets, she stands there, and her dutiful smile shows even, marvellously white teeth. I note the small feet and slim wrists (to my mind the final touch of loveliness), and I see now she is a little shy, anxious to extricate herself, and that in itself is appealing. I can tell Fiorenza has a mind, too, and hopelessly I long to know it.

'Look!' Lisa nudges me, as she joins us at table for coffee. 'Look at those eyes!'

But of course I *am* looking, I am already drowning, trying desperately not to stare. I sink deeper and deeper. I even smoke a cigarette, then make some excuse to sit alone on the balcony and gaze stupidly over the bridge at the thousand lights of the city: the Ponte Vecchio, a mellow honey, and the Duomo and Campanile pale gold beyond, the bead-strings of light towards Fiesole, all the familiar, well loved sights that will soon be taken from me.

And silently, tentatively, shyly, she joins me in the cool of the balcony, speaking in a low musical voice, and apologising repeatedly for her poor English. I can hardly believe it. In the low light she looks ethereal, she seems not to belong to my world at all. She has the looks people paint or sculpt or photograph or write about, amd I find myself wondering how she will age; with those fine bones will she come to even greater beauty?

Odysseus (wily diplomat) compared the Princess Nausicaa to a young palm tree he had once seen in Delos: and there is something of the sapling about Fiorenza, too, something so vital and burgeoning it compels awe with its young urgency. Desperately I look for blemishes. She smokes. We smoke together, up among the gods, and our incense streams away in thin, acrid tapers. For half an hour we sit together, an hour perhaps. She curls elfin legs round her body on the *chaise longue* and meets my eye now with more assurance. (Is she already too knowing for a Madonna?) She tells me of her studies, her home. Her mother, I learn, is from Volterra, and in their apartment near S. Croce, they use antique capitals for ash trays. Invitations hang unspoken in the night air. She wants to speak good English, she says; she wants to study in England.

Then time runs out. Awkward again, she holds out her hand, her black eyes catching the lights of the city, and I am suddenly overwhelmed with gratitude for even this brief meeting. Fiorenza's beauty is printed on my brain. I can never forget her.

I wander back late. All the usual goodbyes and thanks have been said, the duties of host and guest duly discharged. Typically, on the Old Bridge, crossing it one last time, I see quite new things: a little niche with a painted *Virgin and Child* at the south-west corner; an ancient, eroded *elemosyne* opposite.

Then, on the two broken walls either side of the Cellini bust, I find two medieval towers in bas-relief. How many thousand times have I passed and not seen them? How many more new sights await some dark, last evening to surprise and delight?

'Nella' is closed. Ivo and Luciana have sold up, I see; the interior of their homely *trattoria* has been gutted and is currently being fitted out with new, ergonomically approved tables and chairs. I drift east and stop a while to consider the disturbing, modern crucifix in the tabernacle on the corner of Via Ghibellina and Isola delle Stinche. (Who painted it?) Fending off the evil hour, I find 'dell'Agnolo' still heaving, and call in to say more goodbyes: to the swarthy owner (an *amaro*); to my scarred Sicilian protector (two more); and to the big, handsome waiter called 'Mike' (several more, and they are no longer tasting like cough mixture). Mike lives in Sydney, he tells me; he has come back to see his old father. In Australia he already owns a chain of restaurants and plans to expand. I am intrigued to hear a native Florentine say 'Fair dinkum' and 'Sheelah' (which Mike obligingly does), and I note he is now beginning to look, in some subtle way, more antipodean than Italian.

Come back to Florence? Nivver. He finds everything too dear compared with 'beck arm'. Mike is prosperous and happily settled in his *vita nuova*, and with those rugged good looks he must find plenty of friends. Before, we had always conversed in Italian. How typical that I should learn all this tonight!

Will I be back next year, he asks, as chairs are placed upside down on tables, keys are turned in locks, and we shake hands finally? Perhaps, I tell him. Perhaps. Will he?

'Yiss, mate,' Mike says, three fingers held together in salute. 'Scart's honour.'

EPILOGUE

I stand in the Protestant Cemetery. The sky is inky and ominous today, and the thirsty cypresses look up in hope. I have run all the way; this is my last gasp. Briefly, I say my farewells: to the eccentric Landor, who on his 75th birthday claimed he strove with none, and was ready to depart, but annoyed everyone by living on to be 89; who loved young Rose Aylmer, his Beatrice, a girl who died aged 20; to Fanny Hunt, Holman's wife, who died aged 33; to the Claudes and Eustaces and Mary Trevellyns and Miss Ropers, to Lucy Honeychurches and Eleanor Lavishes, to Isla Blagden and Fanny Trollope; and to Arthur Hugh Clough, tortured sceptic, another who died too soon. And finally to Elizabeth Barrett Browning, in her grandiloquent, pillared tomb. It is now known that her father was not the ogre he is commonly believed to have been; that she was perfectly capable of using her weakness in order to manipulate people; but it is impossible not to be moved by her story. Robert buried her here in 1861 and left Italy for good. When shall I return?

When I get back to Piazza d'Azeglio, Fiammetta is out. She now has a part-time job in a florist's shop; her analyst says she must keep busy, meet people. *Tanto meglio*. Lisa, too, was out when I 'phoned her. She will have forgotten. But we said our farewells last night, and, when I told her I didn't know when I'd be back, she said: 'You'll be back. You'll come back next year. You always come back.'

I watch from my window beneath the eaves. The taxi is minutes early and toots imperiously. I turn the key a final six times and post it through the letter box.

Once more I find myself on the plain and practical station wheeling a suitcase through hectic crowds. The Pisa train leaves at 1.00 p.m. People stream from the exits in malodorous waves, each with his case and his money and documents, a wall of perspiring humanity. I let them flood past; I feel them tugging at me, sweeping me back with their tide. These are the new tourists. I have had my time, and Florence is now theirs.

By the information kiosk a long, gangling queue has formed; a hundred rucksacks and teeshirts, beards and beaded chests, wait with plastic water bottles and maps and sunglasses; they sit or lean or collapse and huddle; some even sleep. They have the patience and resignation of the traveller, the resilience of youth. Finally I break through and stand at the platform's edge. There are, of course, no seats to be had. The rain splatters down in great warm drops, and I watch it gather urgency and dance and drum on rail and roof. S. Maria Novella is just there through the rectangle of bruised sky, but somehow it is a thousand miles away. A station is a limbo of drifting humanity, it is everywhere and nowhere. There are cracks of thunder now, and a sudden blinding downpour which drowns the screech of brakes and the scream of sirens and the ground bass of squabbling and greeting. After the heat this rain had to come. And I think I am beginning a cold.

I should like to have been a collector, be taking back with me a della Robbia, a couple of Primitives. But my own treasures have to be memories, photographs and diaries: my second-hand encounters with beauty. After all, one rarely *possesses* the objects of one's veneration: it is enough to see them again and again – the Minos; the del Sartos; the della Robbia girl in the *tondo*; '*La Senese*'; and a thousand sweet Virgins and chubby Jesuses clutching their goldfinches and pomegranates and grapes. These I take with me to the cold north, and they are mine inalienably, for ever.

A train materialises, its doors fly open. I consider the faces that throng the platform. There seem to be several lingering farewells. A knot of young Carabinieri, handsome in freshly laundered khaki, are taking leave of their sweethearts. Twenty tiny children are shepherded in crocodile formation to the front of the train by a harassed schoolteacher. But everywhere I see couples: two is the unit for goodbyes.

Then, in the midst of the mêlée, a moment before departure, I sight a ravishing neck, a taut, angular jaw, and the sight quickens me. (The Greeks were right: a beautiful woman *is* 'a pain to the eyes'.) I wish

I were gone, out of here, away. But if she would move her neck to the left a fraction. . . . Framed between khaki shirts, as if it hears me, the lovely face obeys. The eyebrows, I notice, sweep in a graceful curve that thins and thins until it disappears into her hairline. The spring of the eye-arch is unbelievably fine. But now she has caught my stare, and guiltily I look away.

I seem to know her – why? Our eyes meet through the crowd again. I see now: she has a look of Fiorenza – those cheekbones, yes, the hair in bunches, those coal-black eyes. She pushes to the edge of the platform, she taps on my window with two finger tips, and it *is* Fiorenza, and she is shouting something! The perfect lips mesmerise me. She is calling something!

Porcellino

There is a roar and a clatter of trolleys, and along its whole length the train gives an anticipatory shudder, as if shaking off a long, disgraceful sleep. A final jolt and we are moving.

I rush to the door as the train gathers speed, but I cannot lower the window. All I hear her shout is '... *come back?*' It is a question: I can read her lips. She is waving and smiling and her eyebrows are raised as she shouts: '... *come back?*'

And I am waving and shouting and nodding, '*Yes! Yes!*' until she is a tiny dot, and I am telling myself what Lisa knew, what in my heart I always knew, what never really needed saying.

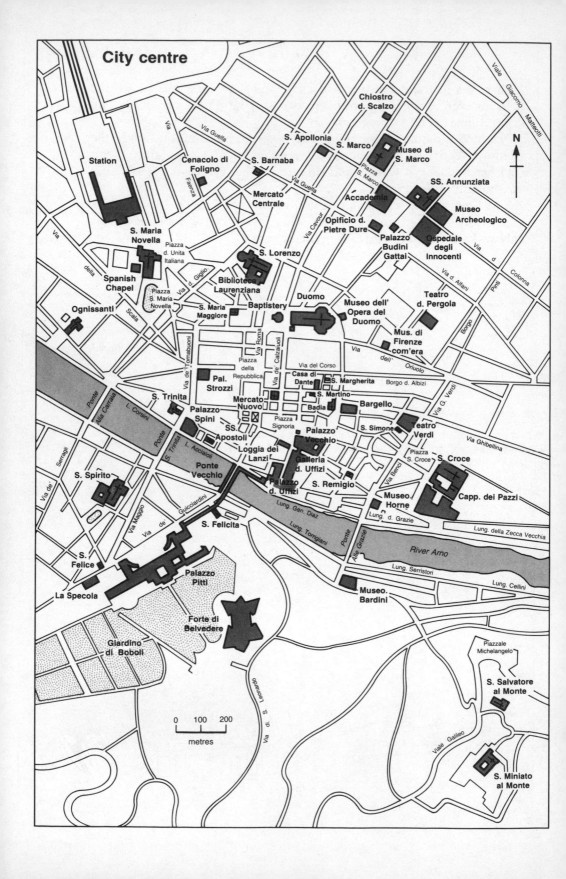

City centre

Station

Cenacolo di Foligno

Chiostro d. Scalzo

S. Apollonia

S. Marco

Museo di S. Marco

S. Barnaba

Piazza S. Marco

SS. Annunziata

Via Guella

Accademia

Museo Archeologico

Mercato Centrale

Opificio d. Pietre Dure

Palazzo Budini Gattai

Ospedale degli Innocenti

S. Maria Novella

Piazza d. Unita Italiana

S. Lorenzo

Via d. Alfani

Spanish Chapel

Piazza S. Maria Novella

Biblioteca Laurenziana

Duomo

Museo dell' Opera del Duomo

Teatro d. Pergola

Ognissanti

S. Maria Maggiore

Baptistery

Mus. di Firenze com'era

Via del Corso

Piazza della Repubblica

Casa di Dante

S. Margherita

Borgo d. Albizi

Pal. Strozzi

S. Martino

S. Trinita

Mercato Nuovo

Badia

Bargello

Palazzo Spini

Piazza Signoria

S. Simone

Teatro Verdi

SS. Apostoli

Palazzo Vecchio

Via Ghibellina

Loggia dei Lanzi

Piazza S. Croce

S. Croce

S. Spirito

Ponte Vecchio

Galleria d. Uffizi

S. Remigio

Capp. dei Pazzi

Palazzo d. Uffizi

Museo Horne

S. Felicita

Lung. Gen. Diaz

Lung. Torrigiani

River Arno

Lung. Serristori

Lung. della Zecca Vecchia

S. Felice

Lung. Cellini

La Specola

Palazzo Pitti

Museo Bardini

Piazzale Michelangelo

Forte di Belvedere

Giardino di Boboli

S. Salvatore al Monte

Viale Galileo

S. Miniato al Monte

N

0   100   200

metres

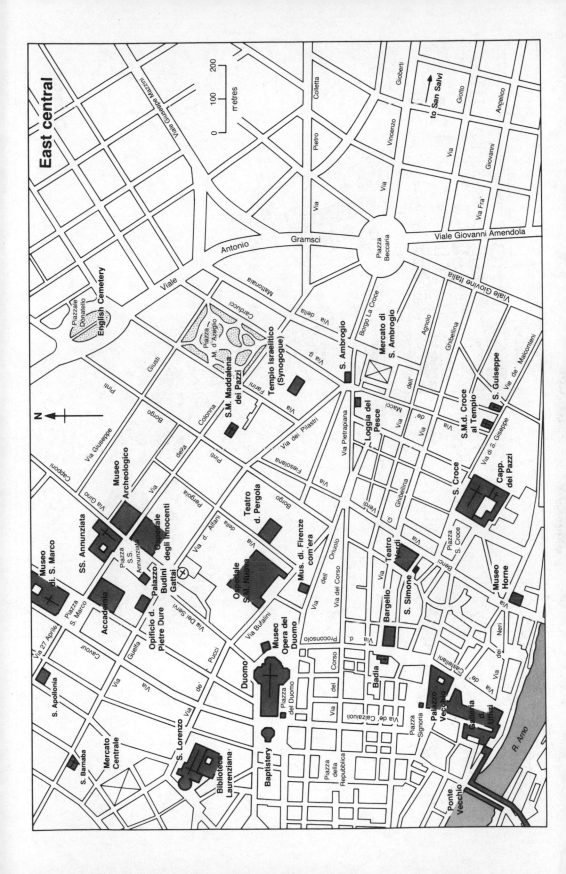

East central

0 100 200
metres

to San Salvi

N

Piazzale Donatello
English Cemetery

Viale Giuseppe Mazzini

Colletta
Pietro
Via
Antonio
Gramsci
Via
Piazza Beccaria
Viale Giovanni Amendola

Gioberti
Giotto
Via
Angelico
Via
Vincenzo
Giovanni
Via Fra'

Viale

Carducci
Piazza M. d'Azeglio
S.M. Maddalena dei Pazzi
Tempio Israelitico (Synagogue)
Mattonaia
Farini
Via g.

Glusti
Colonna
Pinti
Fiesolana
Via del Pilastri
Via Pietrapiana
S. Ambrogio
Borgo La Croce
Mercato di S. Ambrogio
Agnolo
Ghibellina
Via della
Via della

Pinti
Borgo
Via Giuseppe
Museo Archeologico
Via Gino Capponi
della
Perugola
Via d. Alfani
Teatro d. Pergola
Borgo
Via
Via Macci
Loggia del Pesce
Via de'
Via de'
Via de' Malcontenti
S. Guiseppe
S.M.d. Croce al Tempio
Via di S. Giuseppe

Museo di S. Marco
SS. Annunziata
Piazza S.S. Annunziata
Ospedale degli Innocenti
Palazzo Budini Gattai
Via Dei Servi
Ospedale S.M. Nuova
Mus. di Firenze com'era
Verdi
Ghibellina
S. Croce
Capp. dei Pazzi
Via
Piazza S. Croce

Piazza S. Marco
Accademia
Opificio d. Pietre Dure
Via Bufalini
Via dell Oriuolo
Via del Corso
Teatro Verdi
Bargello
S. Simone
Benci
Museo Horne
Via

Via 27 Aprile
S. Apollonia
Cavour
Guelfa
Via de' Pucci
Duomo
Museo Opera del Duomo
Piazza del Duomo
Via dell Corso
Proconsolo
Via d
Badia
Via de' Castellani
Via del Neri

S. Barnaba
Mercato Centrale
Via
S. Lorenzo
Biblioteca Laurenziana
Baptistery
Via de' Calzaiuoli
Piazza della Repubblica
Piazza Signoria
Palazzo Vecchio
Galleria d. Uffizi
Ponte Vecchio
R. Arno

Viale Giovine Italia

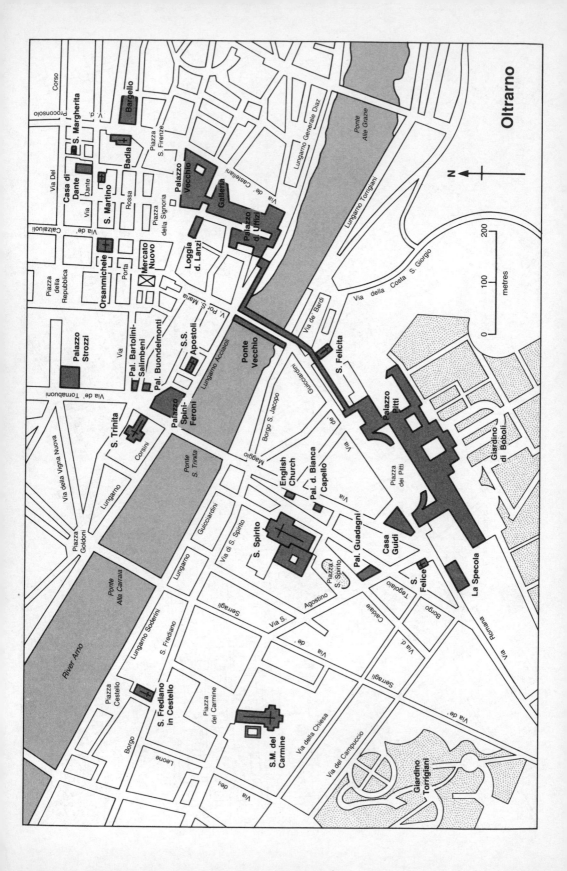

Oltrarno

N

0   100   200

metres

River Arno

Corso
Proconsolo
Via Del
S. Margherita
Bargello
Casa di Dante
Via Dante
S. Martino
Badia
Piazza S. Firenze
Rossa
Piazza della Signoria
Palazzo Vecchio
Galleria
Via de' Castellani
Lungarno Generale Diaz
Ponte Alle Grazie
Lungarno Torrigiani
Piazza della Repubblica
Via de' Calzaiuoli
Orsanmichele
Porta
Mercato Nuovo
Loggia d. Lanzi
Palazzo d. Uffizi
V. Por S. Maria
Ponte Vecchio
Via de' Bardi
Via della Costa S. Giorgio
S. Felicita
Palazzo Strozzi
Via de' Tornabuoni
Via
Pal. Bartolini-Salimbeni
Pal. Buondelmonti
S.S. Apostoli
Lungarno Acciaioli
Palazzo Spini-Feroni
S. Trinita
Corsini
Ponte S. Trinita
Lungarno
Via della Vigna Nuova
Piazza Goldoni
Ponte Alla Carraia
Guicciardini
Borgo S. Jacopo
Maggio
de'
Via
S. Felicita
Guicciardini
Palazzo Pitti
Piazza dei Pitti
Giardino di Boboli
Lungarno
Lungarno Soderini
S. Frediano
Piazza Cestello
S. Frediano in Cestello
Piazza del Carmine
S.M. del Carmine
Via della Chiesa
Borgo
Leone
Via del
Via
Seragli
Via S.
Agostino
Via di S. Spirito
S. Spirito
Piazza S. Spirito
English Church
Pal. d. Bianca Capello
Pal. Guadagni
Casa Guidi
Via
Caldaie
S. Felice
Borgo
Tegolaio
Via d.
La Specola
Via del Campuccio
Giardino Torrigiani
Via de'
Via Romana
Seragli

INDEX

INDEX